SOMERSET CRICKETERS
1971 – 2000

Also Available:

SOMERSET CRICKETERS 1882-1914
SOMERSET CRICKETERS 1919-1939
SOMERSET CRICKETERS 1946-1970

"I love it. I'm awestruck at the amount of research involved, hugely impressed by the presentation, and I relish the vein of dry humour running through it – absolutely perfect."
Ivan Ponting (Author)

"Books as good as this are always going to be few and far between."
Martin Chandler (*Cricket Web*)

"I'm seriously moved by these life stories – they're insightful and written with such warmth and down-to-earth humanity."
John Hook (former Somerset cricketer)

"There are gems to be found on every page."
Roger Heavens (*The Cricket Statistician*)

"Superbly researched and well-written."
Stephen Chalke (Author and publisher)

"Prepare to be surprised and enchanted at every turn of the page."
Vic Marks (Writer, broadcaster and former Somerset and England cricketer)

"Enjoyable and brilliantly researched."
Anthony Gibson (Author and BBC commentator)

"A very good summation of my career including my time at Somerset ... the fairest that I have read."
Greg Chappell (former captain of Australia)

SOMERSET CRICKETERS 1971 – 2000

STEPHEN HILL
With Additional Research by Julian Wyatt

HALSGROVE

First published in Great Britain in 2019

Copyright © Stephen Hill 2019

Every attempt has been made by the author to attribute images correctly but if any errors have been made then they will be rectified in any future editions.

British Library Cataloguing-in-Publication Data
A CIP record for this title is available from the British Library

ISBN 978 0 85704 339 9

HALSGROVE
Halsgrove House,
Ryelands Industrial Estate,
Bagley Road, Wellington, Somerset TA21 9PZ
Tel: 01823 653777   Fax: 01823 216796
email: sales@halsgrove.com

Part of the Halsgrove group of companies
Information on all Halsgrove titles is available at: www.halsgrove.com

Printed and bound by Parksons Graphics, India

Contents

Somerset supporters await the arrival of the conquering heroes in 1979, the year in which the club finally ended its trophy drought

Foreword & Acknowledgements

This is the fourth volume in a series outlining the life of every man who has donned the maroon and black of Somerset in a first-class fixture. The illustrated biographies in this book span the period from 1971 until 2000. The players are listed in chronological order, based on the date of their debut. By the 1970s, limited-overs cricket had become an integral part of the game and would prove the format at which Somerset excelled and for a few heady years were dominant. In idle moments, supporters of the club might wonder how much fuller the trophy cabinet would have become, had one-day cricket gained a foothold earlier in the history of the game. Surely the likes of Herbie Hewett and Sam Woods, of Arthur Wellard and Harold Gimblett, would have brought greater glories to the side. Alas, Somerset CCC have for most of their history had to watch in envy while others shared the spoils.

That, though, was about to change with the arrival at the County Ground in 1971 of Brian Close, a gritty and eccentric Yorkshireman, who took on the task of licking cricket's perennial under-achievers into shape. It would take the best part of a decade to turn things around and Brian had been and gone by the time Somerset landed their first trophies. In the latter part of the 1970s and early 1980s, the county adopted winning ways in one-day cricket, although their performances in the longer form of the game remained a source of entertainment and frustration in equal measure.

It would, of course, be too good to last. In 1986, the county was torn apart by civil war. Somerset's three world beaters – Ian Botham, Viv Richards and Joel Garner – were ousted and the club began a process of rebuilding. Some locally-grown stars emerged, Marcus Trescothick the most evergreen among them. Others, such as Martin Crowe, Jimmy Cook, Sunil Gavaskar, Andy Caddick and Steve Waugh came along and delighted the Somerset crowds. By the end of the millennium, under the leadership of Tasmanian Jamie Cox, the side were finally threatening to win a trophy once more.

The broad thrust of this volume is to continue where the series left off, offering up a pen portrait of each player and – in terms of their cricketing exploits – focussing primarily on their first-class performances. But threaded throughout are references to limited-overs (List A) cricket. Also included are very brief summaries of the four men who played for Somerset only in that form of the game.

Once more we meet an interesting and varied bunch. In its seemingly endless search for excellent cricketers, Somerset has often managed to unearth more than its fair share of one-match wonders and tales of the unexpected. A handful of the men featured in these pages have spent their lives within the game as players and coaches or umpires The vast majority have tales to tell beyond the game, some uplifting and others a salutary lesson in how not to live one's life.

Most of them are still around to tell their story, giving the book a different tenor to its predecessors. The project could not have been completed without the full cooperation of so many former players and I appreciate their support. Hopefully, I have remembered to acknowledge below all of those who contributed. I am grateful to Julian Wyatt – a coach and now hoping also to embark on a writing career – who, as a former player and friend of many of those featured here, introduced me to a number of his erstwhile teammates and conducted a number of interviews on my behalf. David Gurr, too, in his role as Secretary to the Former Players' Association, has been tremendously helpful. Others who have helped are listed below. They include Richard Isbell, who sourced all the autographs, and Benjamin Hill, who painstakingly cleaned up the images. In addition, the many hours spent proofreading by Shaun Mundy were hugely valued, though if any errors have escaped his eagle eyes, then I take the blame for these. I also owe a debt of gratitude to those who have contributed images. In particular, I would like to thank David Wood for access to the superb archive of negatives held by the Somerset Cricket Museum. John Lee and Ivan Ponting have also allowed me access to their wonderful collections. I have made such extensive use of the Somerset Cricket Museum's image archive that photographs from that source are not annotated. In all other instances, I have acknowledged the source, but if I have omitted to credit anyone correctly, then I will happily rectify that in any future edition.

In summary, I appreciate the help of: Jonny Atkinson, Ricky Bartlett, Jeremy Batty, Dave Beal, Paul Bird, Ian Bishop, Ian Blackwell, Nick Boulton, Peter Bowler, Dennis Breakwell, Mike Burns, Neil Burns, Stephen Chalke, Matthew Cleal, Rob Coombs, Andy Cottam, Bob Clapp, Shirley Cooper, Simon Cutler, Mark Davis, Matt Dimond, Brad Donelan, Colin Dredge, Matt Dunn, Simon Ecclestone, Nick Evans, Nigel Felton, Simon Ferguson, Iain Fletcher, Nick Folland, Daren Foster, Trevor Gard, Joel Garner, David Gurr, Richard Harden, Jon Hardy, Mark Harman, Richard Hayward, Vicki Herbert, Benjamin Hill, John Hill, Phil Hill, John Hook, Richard Isbell, Paul Jarvis, Keith Jennings, Steve Jennings, Stephen Jepson, Andrew Jones, Ian Jones, Steffan Jones, Paul Jordan, Greg Kennis, Jason Kerr, John Lee, Theodora Lee-Smith, Roland Lefebvre, Jeremy Lloyds, Malcolm Lobb, Ken MacLeay, Russel McCool, Zak Mahmood, Neil Mallender, Vic Marks, Richard Mosdell, Shaun Mundy, Martin Olive, Richard Ollis, Gary Palmer, Keith Parsons, Andy Payne, Barry Phillips, Adrian Pierson, Ivan Ponting, Nigel Popplewell, Nick Pringle, Darren Proctor, Andrew Radd, Perry Rendell, Craig Rice, Peter Robinson, Neil Russom, Tim Scriven, Philip Slocombe, Roy Sully, Luke Sutton, Nick Taylor, Gareth Townsend, Pete Trego, Marcus Trescothick, Ben Trott, Basil Trump, Gerald Trump, Harvey Trump, Joe Tucker, Murray Turner, Rob Turner, Simon Turner, Paul Unwin, Andre van Troost, Michael Weeks, Giles White, Steve Wilkinson, David Wood and Julian Wyatt.

STEPHEN HILL

1971

"Somerset's seven Championship wins took them to seventh place. Six of those successes were at home; the county had the crowd behind them again."

David Foot

Championship Position: 7 of 17

The arrival of Brian Close at the County Ground was akin to one of those prolonged thunderstorms – welcome and terrifying in equal measure – that clears the air and presages a change in the weather. He came, he saw that the side needed shaking up and he helped them to conquer any inferiority complex. The captaincy was retained for one further season by the veteran off-spinner, Brian Langford, allowing Brian Close to establish a commanding presence at his new cricketing home, leading the batting averages and conjuring five centuries, including one against his native Yorkshire. Somerset stalwarts Roy Virgin and Mervyn Kitchen were both among the runs, offering valuable support. Tom Cartwright was magnificent with the ball, economical and penetrating, with 104 first-class wickets. Behind the scenes, Tom was bringing on a promising crop of youngsters, passing on the benefit of his experience. Where Tom would teach this talented bunch how to play, Brian Close would teach them how to win, though their time had not yet arrived.

Australian leg-spinner Kerry O'Keeffe blazed briefly across the firmament, offering Tom Cartwright valuable support, with seventy-four wickets in his debut season. The third new-join, Hallam Moseley, would prove a popular member of the squad, rendering years of excellent service as an opening bowler, an eye-opening fielder and a shoulder-opening slogger. Overall, it was a season about which the club could feel positive, noteworthy in the main for the arrival of Brian Close.

465
Dennis Brian Close
1 May 1971 v. Leicestershire, Leicester

Brian Close was persuaded to join Somerset by the irrepressible Bill Andrews – sometime player, coach and committee man. Brian was in his forties but was not yet ready to hang up his boots, particularly given that he had a point to prove to Yorkshire, who had decided to dump him unceremoniously after twenty-two years of outstanding service. The club's feeble pretext was that he had been outspoken in his view that one-day cricket was an inferior form of the game. He was a prime example of that slightly hair-raising elision of stubbornness and near-suicidal bravado long associated with Yorkshiremen. He dismissed as a minor inconvenience blows to his body that would have had most men trembling. He appeared to take as much pleasure from winding up pacemen, by refusing to flinch, as from swatting them for one of his trademark slog-sweep sixes. Never was his courage more in evidence than when he stood up to the fearsome onslaught from Wes Hall and Charlie Griffith of the West Indies in 1963, repeatedly taking the ball on his chest, rather than risking a mistimed stroke. Summer, the joke used to run: you know it's arrived when you hear the gentle thud of leather on Brian Close. The photographs of him proudly displaying a torso, marred by a startling polka-dot pattern of cricket ball-sized impressions, told their story. He called his autobiography *I Don't Bruise Easily*. It was a misnomer. His bruises were as livid as the next man's. It was his indifference to pain that set him apart.

Viv Richards – a player firmly of the opinion that, without his captain's input, Somerset's fortunes would never have turned around – relates the tale of the time Gloucestershire's Mike Proctor shaped to cream a rare shorter delivery from Tom Cartwright, whereupon Brian threw himself forward so that the ball hit him square on his pate. He crumpled to the ground before rising groggily to his feet and asking which member of his team had caught the ball after it had ricocheted off his head. No one had. They had all rushed to his side. He berated them. Mike Proctor went on to score a century.

Born in Rawdon, Yorkshire, on 24 February 1931, he was the son of Harry Close, a weaver and a successful league wicket-keeper-batsman, who was married to Esther (née Barrett). It seems scarcely believable, but he was a sickly child, back in hospital within a month of his birth and, in his own account, suffering 'just about every childhood ailment known to the medical profession', including rheumatic fever. Despite his early setbacks, Brian proved both bright and sporty and became a leading light in local and schoolboy cricket, playing his first game for Rawdon CC at the age of eleven and starring for Aireborough Grammar School. He broke into the Yorkshire First XI at the age of eighteen, an event that resolved his personal dilemma over whether he should go to university and set about a career in the medical profession or opt for life as a full-time sportsman. His first season of 1948 was an unqualified success, with the double of 1,000 runs and 100 wickets and a call-up to the England side for the Third Test against New Zealand. At the time of writing, he remains the youngest man to have achieved either feat. It is regarded by most observers as a lost opportunity that he should have gone on to receive only twenty-two Test caps, spread over a twenty-seven year period, a span only topped by Wilfred Rhodes.

Brian Close – fearless on the pitch, he was forthright off it

Having been plucked from his National Service at Catterick, Signalman Close was selected for the 1950-51 tour of Australia against the wishes of Yorkshire coach, Bill Bowes, who deemed him too young to be exposed to the rigours of a tour Down Under. Plagued by injury, Brian endured an unhappy tour that set his international career back.

In the early days, he had combined first-class cricket with a football career. After enjoying some success as a bustling inside-forward at Leeds United, he endured the arrival at Elland Road of Major Buckley, an autocrat of a manager who wore plus-fours and was everywhere accompanied by his terrier, Bryn. Buckley was of the unshakeable opinion that his inside-left should reinvent himself as a left-winger. The pair never quite reconciled their differences and Brian was given a free transfer to Arsenal, where he appeared alongside fellow cricketer, Arthur Milton. His tenure there was short-lived. Yorkshire reneged on an agreement that he would be released for a Reserve Team Cup Final. Arriving just before half-time for the match, he knew that the end was nigh and duly signed for Bradford City, although that adventure ended after only six fixtures when he suffered a major knee injury, after a Port Vale defender clattered into him unexpectedly from behind, with the ball far from view and the referee's gaze elsewhere.

With regard to his cricket, having returned from National Service, he had continued to progress as an all-rounder with his right-arm medium pace bowling and an ungainly but effective approach to batsmanship as a left-hander. There was a setback when he missed most of the 1953 season after a car crash and had to work his way back via the Second XI in the latter part of the season. His erratic behaviour behind the steering wheel would remain a feature for the rest of his career, with a number of his young charges at Somerset finding being seated in the passenger seat of his car an experience even more terrifying than being on the receiving end of one of his tongue-lashings.

Brian was six feet tall but seemed larger, particularly when he stood close to opposing batsmen at forward-short leg. Fearless on the pitch, he was forthright off it, with a lack of deference that often landed him in hot water with the traditionalists. He was made captain of Yorkshire in 1963 and would serve them with distinction, maturing as a player and leading them to the Championship trophy on four occasions. His efforts were rewarded with a welcome back into the England fold in 1963, when he demonstrated his famed courage against the hostile bowling of the West Indies.

The following winter he met his future wife, Vivienne, while holidaying in Bermuda. An air hostess who hailed from Devon, Vivienne is described by Gerald Pawle, writing in *The Cricketer*, as having 'keen intelligence and sense of humour'. She revealed that she had made it clear to her suitor that she had no interest in his advances and was in fact already engaged to an airline pilot, also named Brian. Undeterred, Brain Close made it his mission to wait for Vivienne as she landed back in the UK on one of her BOAC flights, and, sensing a weakening of her resolve, informed her at last: 'If you don't say you'll marry me, you'll never see me again.' She would spend a lifetime watching his progress and they would have a son and daughter. When asked to list his qualities, she cited his courage and loyalty and noted that he was never a worrier. Those who encountered him on the cricket field would have agreed.

Reinstated by the England selectors in 1966, when he was appointed captain and given a brief to toughen up the side, he enjoyed a remarkable period of success, winning six of his seven matches at the helm and drawing one, but again he courted controversy when, back with Yorkshire, he eked out a draw against Warwickshire by slowing down play in an unsportsmanlike manner. He was sacked by England and replaced by Colin Cowdrey. His uneasy relationship with authority rose to the surface again when he was released by Yorkshire at the end of the 1970 season. Determined to ensure financial security, he immediately accepted a job as Liaison Executive for the Bell Fruit Company and this might have marked the end of his playing days, had he not been encouraged by the chairman of the company to continue with county cricket.

Yorkshire's loss was very much Somerset's gain. He relished the idea of joining a county who wanted to build their future around a proven winner, though admittedly some persistence on the part of Bill Andrews was required, mirroring Brian's courtship of Vivienne. Brian would note that:

> *Moving here has been like an elixir for me. I had fallen into a rut of guiding a side and only producing a performance when I had to. This was a new challenge ... When the youngsters are better than me I'll call it a day!*

Step forward Vivian Richards, Ian Botham, et al. Brian was appointed captain from the 1972 season and, aided by the subtler methods of Tom Cartwright, licked the serial under-performers into shape. Not everyone in the hierarchy was delighted by his unflinching and unorthodox ways, but the players responded, by and large, to the slightly terrifying and not entirely sane leader in their midst. His unique blend of irascibility, unpredictability and sentimentality is well-documented, as was his fondness for a bet, based on tips he claimed to have received from an unseen tipster named 'Jackie lad' (whom some thought an entirely imaginary figure). Peter Roebuck would recount the tale of having been sent out to place five pounds on number three and being berated when he handed over the unexpected windfall, having mistakenly placed three pounds on number five. On another occasion, he gave a young Ian Botham a dressing down for effecting a superlative run-out with a direct hit while there was no one backing up the bowler's end. Botham was told in no uncertain terms that he was never to risk overthrows again under his captain's watch. As for Brian's own

Brian Close – instilled a winning mentality in his young charges
COURTESY OF IVAN PONTING

performances, they were outstanding: so much so that they led to a further Test recall at the age of forty-five. Once again, he stood up to the bombardment of the West Indian pacemen with unflinching courage, though the old reflexes were not what they had been and some feared for his life. During the fruitful autumn of his career with Somerset, he played in 142 first-class matches, scoring thirteen centuries for them and averaging 39.41 with the bat. His seventy-four wickets came at 34.94 apiece. As an indicator of his longevity, his first Championship innings had been against Somerset, and had ended when he had been caught off the bowling of Horace Hazell by Arthur Wellard, a man who had made his Somerset debut back in 1927. Brian left Somerset fifty years later, in 1977.

He had observed that 'before I retire I want to win something for Somerset'. Alas, that was not to be, but each of the men who took them over the line and landed the county's first silverware in 1979 was firmly of the view that Brian Close had without doubt been the catalyst for change, the man who had instilled a winning mentality.

After leaving the county he went on to play briefly for Todmorden CC in Lancashire League cricket. He was also an England selector from 1979 until 1981 and, in 1984, returned to his native Yorkshire, where his roles included coaching and chairmanship of the cricket sub-committee and that of President, in 2008-09. He had played his last game of first-class cricket at the age of fifty-five, leading D. B. Close's XI against New Zealand at Scarborough and falling just shy of a career aggregate of 35,000 runs to sit alongside 1,171 first-class wickets and 813 catches. Judged by any standards it had been a remarkable career. Somerset cricket will be forever in his debt.

He died in Baildon, Yorkshire, on 13 September 2015 at the age of eighty-four.

466
Kerry James O'Keeffe
1 May 1971 v. Leicestershire, Leicester

Kerry O'Keeffe has enjoyed and sometimes endured a life in which he has at various times hit rock bottom, but has also found fame as a Test Match leg-spinner and later as a talkative and much talked-about commentator on ABC Radio. Born on 25 November 1949 in the Sydney suburb of Hurtsville, he was the son of Jim O'Keeffe, a survivor of the notorious Changi prisoner of war camp. Kerry's mother was Ngaire (née Chant), a striking woman who hailed from Wellington in New Zealand. Jim worked in a sports shop and Ngaire was Secretary of the local RSL Club for retired and serving members of the military. The marriage was an unhappy one, characterised

Kerry O'Keeffe – already fast-tracked into the Australian team by the time he arrived at the County Ground COURTESY OF JOHN LEE

by heated arguments and by excessive drinking on Jim's part. Kerry reveals that, 'On the eve of my Year 12 Higher School Certificate, mother announced she intended returning to New Zealand and to her first husband.'

A man prone to self-deprecation, he admits to being somewhat of a 'nerd' with a taste in his early years for board games or – better still – inactivity, enjoying his first experience of cricket at the age of twelve, after some paternal prompting. In his own words, he was to be found repeatedly 'bowling at a stump until nightfall'. He attributes his commitment to practising all hours in part to a wish to escape the turmoil at home. Uncoached, he bowled leg-spin but gripped the ball as an off-spinner would, imparting less spin but bowling at a fairer lick than might be expected. At the age of fifteen he was watched by Australian cricket legend Bill O'Reilly who told him: 'If they tell you you're bowling too quickly, thank them for their advice and forget it immediately.'

Educated at Marist College, a Roman Catholic school in Kogarah, he played for the local St George team and was given his break at sixteen, when the First XI leg-spinner retired and Kerry joined seasoned veterans such as former vice-captain of Australia, Brian Booth. Although he made an immediate impact, he now regrets that he allowed youthful arrogance to cloud his judgement and prevent him from adopting the disciplined approach of the senior players. He is neither the first nor the last cricketer to have embraced the more bacchanalian aspects of a life in cricket.

In December 1966, he took part in an Australian Schoolboys tour of India where he continued to build on his reputation but also suffered from a cyst 'the size of a golf ball' that, after its removal, left him with a scar on his neck that 'looks like a map of the Burma Railway'. Back in Australia, he would enjoy his first taste of professional cricket when offered employment by a pub side with the remuneration stretching to fifty cents for each wicket and five dollars for every half-century. The standard was not high and his piggy bank soon filled. Kerry recalls with great mirth his frustration when an inebriated number eleven batsman slumped to the ground and fell asleep as he walked to the crease, thus denying him an easy fifty cents. Standards rose inexorably as he raced towards a first-class career with New South Wales, making his initial appearance at the age of nineteen. The following season, he established himself as a regular with thirty-five wickets and by the 1970-71 campaign he was being talked about as a potential Test player. Selection was more or less assured when he performed strongly for New South Wales in a four-day match against MCC.

In January 1971, he arrived in Melbourne to take part in the Fifth Test and was immediately welcomed to the fold in the Cricketers' Bar of the Windsor Hotel by Messrs Walters and Marsh, at the time the Test side's most notorious imbibers. His captain was Bill Lawry, a strong believer in the merits of rectitude. Bill's advice to the greenhorn was, 'Don't get involved in any prolonged drinking sessions with Doug Walters or Rod Marsh, Terry.' Kerry elected not to correct his skipper about his name and not to confess that, on the question of drinking, the horse had already bolted from the stable. The match itself was not a great success for the new-join, who came away wicketless. Perhaps his abiding memory was being greeted on his arrival at the crease by Colin Cowdrey, who strode forward from first slip and offered an encouraging, 'All the best, young man.' Unsure whether to refer to the Englishman as Colin or Mr Cowdrey, the youngster mumbled, 'Thank you, Kipper.'

There would follow two English summers at the County Ground in Taunton. Somerset had tried without success first to entice Greg Chappell back to his old hunting ground and then to lure Ian Redpath. Both had declined and so they opted for the promising young leg-spinner, now developing into a useful all-rounder. In his first season he took seventy-seven wickets, often bamboozling opposing batsmen, but then his form fell away dramatically, despite exhortations from Brian Close, his captain in that second year, who liked the 'funny stuff' the Aussie bowled but felt that he worried too much about everything. In Kerry's words, 'the yips had set in' and Brian was of the view that his bowler's confidence had been drained by the mauling he had received at the hands of Garry Sobers, at Adelaide. Kerry in turn observes of Brian Close that, 'His was an uncomplicated mind that served him well.' By the end of the 1972 season Kerry persuaded Somerset to release him a year early from his three-year-contract so that he could regroup in Australia. With forty-six first-class appearances for his adoptive county under his belt, he had claimed ninety-three wickets at 30.82 apiece and had averaged 20.75 with the bat. He retains fond memories of his time with Somerset and continues to pore over the County Championship scores, willing on his former team.

He would represent Australia twenty-four times, but there is a sense that he never quite fulfilled his early promise. His number of appearances was curtailed in part because of the breakaway World Series Cricket of which he was a part. But perhaps his taste for post-match refreshment stood in the way of his continued development as a player. His Test career ran from 1971 until 1977 and was punctuated by a further spell in England playing for East Lancashire, based in Blackburn. Here, he acknowledges his debt to Dave Walsh, a man who took one look at Kerry and decided he was in urgent need of a personal trainer. Possessed of a stammer and a tendency, according to Kerry, to spray those he spoke to with a shower of saliva, Dave kept Kerry sufficiently on the 'strait and narrow' for him to amass a sizeable haul of wickets and a thousand runs. They remain great friends.

At the age of thirty-one and by now suffering from arthritis in his right knee and spinning finger, he retired from first-class cricket. He describes himself as being 'single, lonely, unemployed – to some unemployable – and running out of money' at that time. The truth is that his fondness for a pint and a punt

Kerry O'Keeffe – his performances as a leg-spinner fell away sharply in his second season at Somerset COURTESY OF IVAN PONTING

on the horses had not served him well. For a while he worked as a security man for Armaguard, picking up and delivering money, but he resigned when a group of colleagues were held up at gunpoint, causing a rethink about his career choice. Out of regular work, he turned increasingly to alcohol and speaks with candour about having crossed the line from someone who enjoyed a drink to someone who relied on alcohol as a prop to get through life.

Marriage followed in 1987 and the presence in his life of Veronica, a legal secretary, proved the making of Kerry. He describes her as 'everything I was not – hard-working, reliable, balanced: I have never heard her say a bad word about anyone'. The arrival of their children would help him to continue on the path to redemption, as he tried to ensure that his offspring were never prey to something akin to his own 'somewhat desolate childhood'.

After spurning the life of a security guard, Kerry tried his luck on the trading floor of the Sydney Stock Exchange. Strangely, the man who was confident to the point of recklessness when staking money on the horses encountered another case of the 'yips' as a trader and soon admitted defeat. He was offered some work as a coach at the Australian Cricket Academy by his former teammate Rod Marsh, but was still struggling to pin down a career worthy of the name. What followed was as serendipitous as a perfectly-flighted ball that lands on the spot and turns the perfect distance. It was as if he had been training for his breakthrough all his life. While honing his skills as a raconteur in favoured drinking holes, he had returned home to review clips of Australian cricket, obsessively studying the actions, the strengths and the weaknesses of each player. These skills blended harmoniously when he was invited to try his luck as a radio commentator and there followed many happy years as a highly regarded commentator for ABC Radio. Working alongside the likes of Jim Maxwell and Somerset's Peter Roebuck, he built up a reputation as an engaging and entertaining pundit, noted for his unexpected observations and his infectious laugh, described by one listener as 'the noise that would be made by a bronchial hyena'. He remained with ABC Radio until 2016. Kerry was also in demand as a television quiz show guest and has latterly resurfaced as a radio commentator with Triple M Radio.

In his youth he had attracted predictions of a successful career. After a period in the wilderness, he found his feet, although it is perhaps typical of the man that this should have been in an entirely different capacity to that which everyone had envisaged.

467
Hallam Reynold Moseley
26 May 1971 v. Derbyshire, Derby

Hallam Moseley was an enormously popular member of the Somerset team for twelve seasons, always with a beaming smile on his face and possessed of endless patience, taking time out to talk with supporters. Whether or not they all understood his rich Bajan tones and he in turn grasped the nuances of the West Country accent is an entirely different matter. Vic Marks observes wryly in his *Somerset County Cricket Scrapbook* that 'on arriving at Taunton one colleague asked Hallam whether he batted left or right handed, only to receive the bewildering answer, "Half past ten."' Nor was mastering the local idiom the only learning experience for Hallam. In the words of Vic again, 'In a benefit game he strolled innocently into a large clump of stinging nettles to retrieve the ball, with disastrous but hilarious results.' The crowds took to him with opposing fans also confessing to being fond of him.

Born on 28 May 1948 in Providence, Christ Church, Barbados, the son of Eustace and Sheila Moseley, he was educated at Providence Boys' School and The Rural Studio Secondary School, graduating to the Barbados team at the age of nineteen. Whether

Hallam Moseley – a great favourite with the crowds, he played the game with a smile

bowling or fielding, his play was characterised by an easy grace, and by 1969 he was invited to be a member of an International Cavaliers side led by Ted Dexter. He also gained further experience of English conditions when joining a late season tour with Barbados and making occasional appearances for Nottingham Second XI, at the recommendation of Garry Sobers. Indeed, it was Garry who extolled Hallam's virtues to Somerset, who were seeking an up-and-coming pace bowler to strengthen their attack. Bill Andrews duly took a look at Hallam and was quickly won over. He is quoted as saying that:

> *I was so impressed with him the first time I saw him play that I insisted on carrying his heavy bag to Taunton station. It may not always have been easy to decipher what he was saying when he arrived, but he was the nicest guy I ever met in the game. I never once saw him lose his temper when things were going wrong, or bowl a bouncer. Everyone liked him.*

He was welcomed into the fold with open arms and brought sunshine and *joie de vivre* to the County Ground. His fielding was a revelation. None of the faithful could recall ever having seen a man attack the ball in the field and fire it back at pace to the wicket-keeper with an underarm sling, all in one fluid movement and a flick of his wrists, catching many a batsman unawares. This was, in hindsight, a glimpse of the shape of fielding to come, one of the many strengths of the great West Indian sides of the 1970s and 1980s. The pity for Hallam was that he was eclipsed by some of the finest pace bowlers in history and was never able to secure selection for his national side. His bowling was consistently accurate and most observers concur with Bill Andrews and struggle to recall having seen him send down a bouncer. Perhaps Hallam was too lacking in a mean streak to hit the heights. As for his batting, it was rather more hit-and-miss although when he did hit, the results could be spectacular, such as his five sixes off the bowling of Peter Willey in six consecutive deliveries.

If the West Country weather was not to his liking, he never complained. And nor did he ever grumble when faced with a line of autograph hunters. He was happy to converse with fans as he fielded at the boundary rope and had no airs or graces. If he felt stung or displaced by the arrival of Viv Richards and Joel Garner, whose presence meant that as a third overseas player he was less in demand, then it never showed. Viv in fact lodged with Hallam for a spell and the three men would frequently get together to enjoy a taste of home, with Joel more often than not the one cooking up a Caribbean feast.

Married in 1975 to Marcia (formerly Caddle), Hallam would have a daughter, Charmaine, who later taught drama. He always had one foot in London and would reside there after his departure from the first-class game. That came in 1982 and happened earlier than he had expected – not least because he had enjoyed another of his excellent seasons in List A cricket – although he took the news with good grace. Over the course of his Somerset career he had played in 205 first-class matches, taking 547 wickets at 24.10 apiece and averaging 12.41 with the bat. His efforts had been awarded with a Testimonial Year in 1979.

From 1986 until 2008, Hallam was employed by the Ministry of Defence as a security officer, but his accumulated cricketing wisdom was sought out and he has latterly been a member of the coaching staff at the MCC Cricket Academy at Lord's, as well as overseeing his local Brentham CC Colts for a period. He remains ensconced in Greenford with his wife and daughter and is still fondly remembered at the County Ground.

1972

"Because they were not used to going all out for victory
as a matter of course, the players were not geared to the
intensity of concentration I regarded as the norm."

Brian Close

Championship Position: 11 of 17

Brian Close took over the captaincy and shouldered much of the responsibility. Once again the county's leading run-maker, he was offered able support by long-serving left-hander, Mervyn Kitchen, and, on his rare appearances, Brian Rose. Tom Cartwright was predictably the most successful bowler with 863 overs of metronomic accuracy and a haul of ninety-eight first-class wickets. Sadly, there was a sharp falling away in the form of opening batsman Roy Virgin and leg-spinner Kerry O'Keeffe. This would precipitate both of their departures.

Close and controversy were never far apart. In the match against Glamorgan at Swansea, he was upbraided for his side's slow scoring and his delayed declaration. The crowd were offered their money back but, as it transpired, this was one Close gamble that worked out perfectly. He scored a century and even brought himself on for one over and bagged the important wicket of Alan Jones, ending the opener's stubborn resistance. Glamorgan were twice bowled out on a deteriorating wicket, succumbing to the wiles of Cartwright, Langford and O'Keeffe. The Somerset skipper – as was his wont – derived enormous satisfaction from having been proved right, though less delight from the fact that only three other games were won in a generally forgettable season.

Although the debutants in truth made no lasting impression on the club's fortunes, pace bowler Bob Clapp would enjoy one memorable season (in 1974) with a record-breaking haul of wickets in limited-overs cricket.

468
Richard Claude Cooper
17 May 1972 v. Nottinghamshire, Nottingham

Born in Malmesbury, Wiltshire, on 9 December 1945, Richard (or 'Coops', as former teammates still refer to him) was in every sense a larger-than-life character. The youngest of nine children of Richard William Cooper, an engine driver based at Malmesbury Station, Coops and older brother, Gerald, were the product of Richard Snr's second marriage, to Margaret (née Archer). His other siblings were all stepbrothers or stepsisters. Shirley Cooper, the wife of Gerald, observes that her brother-in-law was 'a lovable rogue' who grew up largely unsupervised: his father had died when Coops was in his early teens and his mother had been obliged to work long hours as a hospital cook. No doubt partly as a result of this, the son remained unmanageable and dismissive of authority throughout his short but interesting life. Former teammates express a mixture of bashfulness and relish when recalling his exploits on the basis that, to quote one source, 'most of them are unprintable'. The adjectives called upon to describe him include 'colourful' and 'mercurial'. A fearless batsman, prepared to take on bowlers, regardless of their reputation, he was never short on self-belief.

Following his education at Bremilham School in Malmesbury (since merged with the Grammar School and now Malmesbury Comprehensive), he was soon in trouble with the law. As an amply-built young man, he had been taken on by a loan shark and twice endured a spell in prison for 'demanding money with menace'. He appears to have learned two great lessons from this sobering experience. The first was that he would be better served by more conventional employment and the second was that when it came to the 'management' of his own debts (most of them as a result of gambling), it was advisable to become invisible. One former player at Malmesbury CC confirms that shady characters were often to be seen arriving at the ground in large cars and that Richard would quickly disappear from view while his teammates covered for him. Guided by older brother, Gerald, he joined Autonumis, a vending machine company, servicing machines in the region. By then he was attracting more positive headlines for his sporting prowess as a cricketer and footballer for his native Malmesbury. It was his batting for Wiltshire which brought him to Somerset's attention. In particular, his performance against Somerset Second XI at Taunton in 1970 was noted. He had savaged the home bowling attack with a century in each innings (only once dismissed).

He was offered a three-year contract in 1972, but the rigours of the first-class game did not appeal to him. Never prepared to toe the line, he was admittedly not alone in having an at times strained relationship with his Somerset captain, Brian Close. One former teammate at Malmesbury relates the tale of Richard, while a member of the Somerset squad, being instructed by his skipper to 'go and fill the bath for me, lad' and responding by telling Close to run his own bath.

His highest score came in his very first outing for Somerset when his swashbuckling 95 in the Benson & Hedges Cup saved Somerset from what would have been an embarrassing defeat at the hands of Minor Counties South. He would only ever enjoy one first-class outing, with scores of 4 and 0. The second-innings duck was the second of Bar-

Richard Cooper – a larger-than-life character, brimming with self-belief
COURTESY OF IVAN PONTING

ry Stead's hat trick deliveries. Having been dismissed, he was asked by the incoming Brian Close what was happening to the ball and Richard revealed that it was swinging like a boomerang. Undeterred and defiant as ever, Brian Close took an almighty swipe at the next delivery and was caught for a golden duck by Nirmal Nanan. Richard was duly castigated by his skipper – never one to own up to an error of judgement – and informed: 'You didn't warn me it was seaming, too, lad.'

Richard would appear in thirteen List A matches for Somerset, where his batting average of 28.58 is a fair reflection of his ability. Writer David Foot observes that 'for a roly-poly man, [he] was no slouch in the field or when chasing singles'. He was also an occasional bowler. In *Somerset County Cricket Scrapbook*, Vic Marks relates the tale of one of Brian Close's 'inspired gambits':

> *Close decided to bowl Richard Cooper, a rotund hitter from Wiltshire, in a Benson & Hedges match at Gloucestershire. Richard, a confident man, assured the captain that he bowled off spinners fairly regularly for Malmesbury. Off a two-pace run up he bowled a couple of no balls, followed by a massive full toss which Mike Procter contrived to mis-hit to cover. The catch unfortunately was dropped: a Close coup had just failed.*

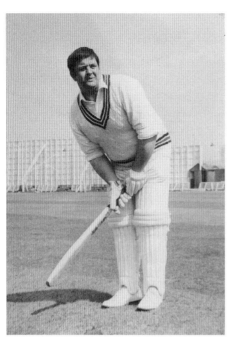

Richard Cooper – a 'lovable rogue' apt to land himself in hot water

Having parted company with Somerset at the end of the 1974 season, Richard returned to the fold with Malmesbury and Wiltshire, whom he represented right up until the end of the 1989 season. Richard Mosdell, a young man when he began his playing days at Malmesbury under Richard Cooper's captaincy, recalls often having to drive his skipper back in a venerable Jaguar as characterful as the owner, who had invariably drunk too much to take the wheel. 'I learned a lot from him,' he confirms, 'including how to set fields with a plan in mind, reacting to what the batsmen were trying to do, and how to bowl to the plan and why.'

Perhaps the example set off the field of play was less instructive, with various narrow escapes as Richard's fondness for drink, women and gambling repeatedly landed him in hot water. Having departed from the Autonumis vending business, Richard – always more comfortable at the helm than taking instruction from others – ran two businesses. He was the proprietor of the Abbey News newspaper and confectionery shop in Malmesbury and also owned Abbey Labels, manufacturing printed labels. Although he was never married, his long-term partner (the woman to whom he became engaged) was Judith Ann Foxwell, known as Judy, a talented sportswoman whose first love was tennis. Inveterate organisers, the pair made noteworthy contributions to the social life of the town, overseeing dances and the like. They lived together for a number of years in Crudwell

Richard's full and colourful life came to a sudden and spectacular end at the age of only forty-four, when he died of a heart attack while working out alongside Judy at the Physique and Fitness Health Studio in Malmesbury on 14 March 1990. Although his business ventures had left him notionally a rich man, his longsuffering brother, Gerald, assigned the task of putting his brother's affairs in order, soon found out that he had remained in debt to varying institutions and disreputable individuals to the very last. Coops had made waves while he lived and the ripples were still felt after his death.

469
Stephen George Wilkinson
24 May 1972 v. Yorkshire, Taunton

Steve Wilkinson [signature]

Dubbed 'Aggro' when he sported short hair and braces for a brief period on first arriving at Taunton, Steve Wilkinson has always been an easy-going, humorous soul. He was a popular member of the Somerset squad for five seasons from 1970, graduating to the first team in 1972. Initially, he shared a flat in Taunton with Australian Kerry O'Keeffe, who describes him as 'tremendous company and a wise sounding board'. Born in Hounslow on 12 January 1949, Steve was the son of George Wilkinson, a Physical Education teacher who was married to Pat (née Mallinder), who taught infants. He attended Isleworth Grammar School before joining the MCC ground staff at Lord's for four seasons from 1966 until 1969. Middlesex took a good look at him but he never advanced beyond their Second XI. A tall, slim, right-handed No. 3 batsman, he began his first-class career brightly with some useful knocks. His erstwhile flatmate writes that 'Aggro possessed a sound stroke range but ... fieldsmen got in the way of his best shots too often for his career to flourish.'

In his memoir *Sometimes I Forgot to Laugh*, Peter Roebuck included a jaunty but not entirely accurate piece about the man he describes as 'my particular friend among the small group of batting pros'. He wrote that Steve was not a man intent on grinding down bowlers and relentlessly building an innings and that, having reached a half-century for the Second XI, he would happily yield up his wicket on the basis that no members of the Committee were watching but they would now read his name in the local papers. Peter observed that Steve was content to spend the rest of the day focussed on the latest issue of *Sporting Life*.

For his part, Steve recounts his experiences at Somerset with a healthy dose of self-deprecating humour. Triumph and adversity are recalled with equanimity. Witness the occasion when, on 'a disgraceful pitch at Colchester in 1972' he was hospitalised by a bouncer from West Indian paceman, Keith Boyce, before returning to the crease the following day only to be greeted by an equally fearsome bouncer. 'I was face down on the ground and semi-conscious but I could sense that the Essex players were all standing around me, pretty worried,' Steve remembers. 'Then I heard 'Tonker' Taylor saying in a relieved voice, "He's all right, lads, I just saw his leg twitch."' He laughs in the face of such near-death encounters.

As well as his useful contributions with the bat, Steve had a reputation as an excellent fielder. 'It was all that training when I was at Lord's,' he suggests. 'They put you

Steve Wilkinson – left the game to become a bookie COURTESY OF JOHN LEE

through your paces with endless fielding drills.' On one occasion, though, things went not quite according to plan. 'We were playing a JPL game up in Yorkshire and I was summoned down to Taunton to captain the Club & Ground side. Kerry O'Keeffe was driving and I dozed off. Next thing I knew I looked out of the window and we were heading in completely the wrong direction, six miles from Luton. Eventually I got us home in the small hours and I'd had less than two hours' sleep. Of course, the first delivery of the day came to me at first slip and I missed it because I was barely awake. It rapped me on the knee and I was in agony.'

There is universal agreement among his former teammates that he was an amusing companion who was blessed with an enormous amount of ability as a batsman, but that he lacked the single-mindedness to establish a long-term career in the first-class game. In this he differed from his cousin, Phil Bainbridge of Gloucestershire, who enjoyed rather more success and over a longer career span.

His fellow cricketers also note his fondness for the horses and greyhounds and observe that his tips were not always infallible. Peter Roebuck has written, in jest, that 'Brian Close liked to discuss the racing prospects with him, which may have prolonged his career' but the relationship with their captain was not always as cosy as Peter supposed. Steve recalls an incident in a friendly match against Oxford University when he called for a quick single on a wet pitch that left his skipper lying face down, muddied and well out of his ground. After an expletive-laden rant at his batting partner, Brian hauled himself to his feet and marched off in high dudgeon. 'For the next half an hour, I got my head down as never before,' Steve confesses, adding that, 'I was determined not to lose my wicket until he'd had a chance to calm down in the dressing room.'

He came away from his time at Taunton with a store of fond memories and a first-class average of 20.54 from eighteen appearances. He would enjoy a longer career in the arena that was perhaps his true passion. Having taken out a bookmaker's licence in 1975, he operated on most of the major courses in the country, including the likes of Royal Ascot and Newmarket, until his retirement thirty-nine years later, in 2014. His career as a bookie was interrupted briefly in the early 1980s when he spent two years as a cricket coach, enjoying a spell in Bangladesh overseeing the development of young players as part of an initiative funded by the British Council. 'A wonderful time,' he says. 'It was great to see their enthusiasm and it was better paid than being a bookie, too!'

Now in his late sixties and ensconced in Twickenham, the former bookie has turned punter again and is once more able to relax while perusing the day's racing tips and enjoying the odd flutter. He has retained his links with Taunton. His ex-wife, Jean (formerly Bibby, née Klukarski), to whom he was married in 1974, still resides in the town. 'I walked into a night club and thought straight away that she was the one,' he reveals, 'but as it transpired, Jean preferred living in Taunton and I preferred living in London, so we went our separate ways after a while.' Steve continues to follow the fortunes of his former team, though to date he has resisted the temptation to place any sizeable bets on their winning the County Championship.

Steve Wilkinson – lacked the single-mindedness to establish a long career in the first-class game COURTESY OF IVAN PONTING

470
Robert John Clapp
26 August 1972 v. Kent, Glastonbury

Bob Clapp has been a keen supporter of Somerset cricket since boyhood. The West-on-super-Mare Festival proved the catalyst for a lifelong love affair. 'Those matches were the highlight of my summer holidays,' he reminisces. 'I loved watching Fred Rumsey thundering in off his long run and then covertly refreshing himself at the end of each over by putting his head under the cold water tap handily placed at fine leg.' He also remembers the 'groan and growl' of the Somerset crowds – the combined groan when a home wicket fell and the collective muffled debate that followed in a West Country burr.

Born in Weston-super-Mare on 12 December 1948, he was the son of a well-known local farmer, Fry Clapp, who was married to Joan. Educated at Queen's College in Taunton, Bob failed to earn a place in any of the school's junior teams, but constant practice during any free time with his best friend, Rudi Hommes, using a cherry tree as the wicket, combined with a growth spurt of six inches in a year to a height of 6 feet 4 inches at the age of fifteen, saw him emerge as an effective pace bowler. Bob eventually became captain of the school First XI in his final year.

He then left to complete a degree in Geography and Sociology at the University of Sheffield, where he also took up lacrosse with great success, having been drafted into the all-conquering Sheffield University XII, mere months after taking up the sport. Bob then went on to Loughborough for his PGCE in Physical Education. Having played for the Somerset Under-19 side in 1967, he began appearing for the Second XI from 1969. In 1971, he took up his first teaching post at Trent College in Long Eaton, between Derby and Nottingham, thus limiting his appearances for Somerset.

He recalls his first-class debut in 1972 with great clarity. 'It was a case of joy unconfined. I was fulfilling my dream of playing for the county I'd watched and supported for so long.' He relates how, on his arrival, he bumped into Colin Cowdrey who, ever the gentleman, 'wished me well on my debut and added that he hoped I'd score a century'. Bob confesses that, 'I thought to myself, "Little does he know about my batting" as I graciously thanked him for his encouragement.' Later, as Colin walked towards the pavilion, having declared on reaching an unbeaten century, the Kent legend apologised for his gaffe and added, looking the gangly newcomer up and down, that he should have guessed he was a bowler. In the drawn game, Bob did well enough, claiming three Kent wickets, all bowled.

By 1974, he was being called on more regularly and would find himself forced to choose a career either as a cricketer or as a schoolmaster. The decision to opt for cricket appeared to have been a sound one when that season proved his *annus mirabilis*. Bob claimed the record number of wickets in a John Player Special League season, with thirty-four victims and also, at the time of writing, still holds the Somerset record for the highest number of List A wickets in a season, with fifty-one in total. He had played a significant part in a successful year in which the county had reached the semi-finals of both the Benson & Hedges Cup and Gillette Cup and ended as runners-up in the John Player Special League. His most colourful memory from that year was the Benson & Hedges Quarter Final, when Ian Botham and Hallam Moseley were clawing their way

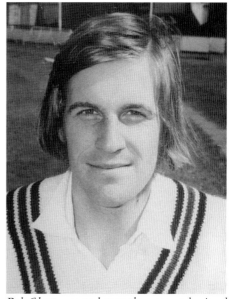

Bob Clapp – came late to the game and enjoyed a record-breaking year in 1974

back from the jaws of defeat against Hampshire, with Bob the only batsman to come. He watched as Ian took the full force of an Andy Roberts bouncer and was spitting out teeth and blood. 'Apparently Andy had two bouncers, one quicker than the other, and I've no idea which one he bowled. Nor did Ian,' he jokes. Bob watched the drama unfold as Ian recovered and set about steering his side to victory, only to hear the familiar 'groan and growl' that greeted the fall of Hallam's wicket with the side still six runs shy of their target. Bob takes up the story. 'I heard someone shout "You can do it, Bob" to which I was tempted to reply "I'm not so sure about that", as my top score was about four at that stage of my career. Hallam passed me and gave me some advice in his wonderful mellow Bajan tones that I couldn't make out and then Ian tried to give me some instructions, but his mouth was in such a state that I couldn't understand a word. The long and the short of it was that I was about to face Andy Roberts and do the best that I could. This was new territory. Batting for Burnham-on-Sea Cricket Club hadn't prepared me for this. All that I remember about that first ball was that I'd barely moved into my back lift when the ball smashed into my pad and raced towards fine leg and Ian screamed at me to run. The first crisis had been averted.' On the final ball of that over, realising that they needed a one or a three to ensure that Ian retained the strike, the pair set off as if their lives depended on it. Bob takes up the story again. 'We ran the first two and then, as I turned for a third, I caught a glimpse of the Hampshire fielder about to pick up the ball. Suddenly I felt as if I was running through treacle and I realised that my only chance of beating the throw was going to be by diving. As the ball came closer, I took to the air and landed in a cloud of dust, sprawled across the crease. Every Hampshire player roared an appeal for a run out but, after what seemed an eternity, the umpire gave me not out and the Somerset supporters erupted. Ian then hit a sumptuous cover drive for four to win us the match and embark on his stellar career. I sat quietly in the corner of the dressing room, stunned by what had happened in the preceding hour or so, but basking in the warm glow of having been involved in something special.'

Bob would remain with the county until his release at the end of the 1977 season. Deployed primarily as a one-day bowler, the format in which he enjoyed most of his success, he would appear in fifteen first-class matches, taking twenty-five wickets at 29.36 apiece and averaging 4.45 with the bat. His seventy-six wickets in List A cricket at 17.00 each reflect his importance in the limited overs game. Bob's erstwhile captain, Brian Close, would describe him as 'a nice, genuine lad [who] looked like a world-beater in the nets, but out in the middle he couldn't relax'. Peter Roebuck has argued that at times Close 'drove too hard' and that those such as Bob who 'needed gentle encouragement ... were apt to freeze upon being cursed'. Certainly he was at ease in Second XI matches, entertaining colleagues and opponents with practical jokes, such as the time he came to the crease po-faced, only to break into a broad smile at the moment of delivery, revealing a plastic set of Dracula teeth.

Bob had met his future wife, Patricia Ashcroft, on their very first day at Loughborough and, married in 1973, the couple would have a son, Matthew, and a daughter, Catherine. 'It's nearly fifty years since I first saw Patricia and we continue to enjoy our life together,' Bob observes. With a family to provide for, he resumed his teaching career, initially at Hugh Sexey Middle School at Blackford, near Cheddar, before enjoying seventeen years, from 1980 until 1997, at Rossall School, where he taught Geography, PE and French. For five of those years he was the housemaster of Liam Botham, who demonstrated his father's unyielding will to win on the sports field. Bob is described in the valedictory in the school magazine as 'an inspirational housemaster' and 'always supportive and fair'.

Between 1997 and 2007 he taught at Bradfield College, but his time there came to an abrupt end when he was diagnosed with Acute Myeloid Leukaemia. He survived thanks to months of chemotherapy, a week in intensive care and, most importantly, a stem cell transplant from his sister, Liz. Bob observes that he may well have not been alive today, had Ian Botham not raised many millions of pounds for Leukaemia Research through his charity walks. In recognition of all that Ian has done, Bob and his family joined the former Somerset and England all-rounder on part of his walk in 2012 and played their part in raising a sizeable sum for the cause. To aid his recovery, he took up golf and was elected Captain of the Goring & Streatley Golf Club in Berkshire in 2015.

Having retired to Oxfordshire, he has lost none of the enthusiasm he felt about 'living the dream' and playing for the team he has always supported. He is proud, too, to have appeared alongside several of the county's all-time greats.

Bob Clapp – an enthusiastic supporter of Somerset cricket since boyhood
COURTESY OF IVAN PONTING

1973

"The travelling was tiring for what wags on the circuit were dubbing 'Dad's Army'."

Derek Watts

Championship Position: 10 of 17

It was a poor summer in terms of the weather. Performances, likewise, lurched too often towards mediocrity. Skipper Brian Close could be by turns an inspiration or a liability. In the Second Round of the Gillette Cup, he conspired to pluck defeat from the jaws of victory. With Leicestershire at one point on the rack and seven wickets down, Close insisted on taking the gloves, after Jim Parks sustained an injury to his thumb: this, despite the fact that Brian Rose was available and a competent keeper. Furthermore, Close soon decided that gloves would be an unnecessary adornment when keeping to Allan Jones, one of the fastest bowlers in county cricket. Jonah was incensed and bowled even quicker than usual, sacrificing accuracy in the process. Brian Close was out of his depth, struggling to take the ball cleanly, but unprepared to relent. Chris Balderstone kept his cool and guided Leicestershire home. Anyone else would surely have been hauled before the Committee, but 'Closey' was not the sort of man you could upbraid for such profligacy.

There was a distinctly vintage feel to the team. The three principal contributors could boast an average age of over forty. And the supporting cast included the likes of Merv Kitchen, Peter Robinson and Graham Burgess, all in their thirties.. Little wonder, then, that the players were referred to by some as 'Dad's Army'. Jim Parks, lately of Sussex and England, and Brian Close were the run-makers-in-chief and Tom Cartwright was again by some distance the most successful bowler. Graham Burgess and the up-and-coming Hallam Moseley offered useful support with just shy of fifty wickets apiece.

The arrival of Jim Parks had certainly added class to proceedings and the other new-join, the irrepressible Dennis Breakwell, would prove a valuable addition.

471
James Michael Parks
2 May 1973 v. Essex, Taunton

Jim Parks

Jim Parks belongs to Sussex and deserves his place in that county's folklore, as do other members of the talented Parks dynasty, but he came to Somerset to enjoy the final three seasons of an outstanding career. Brian Close, touring with Jim in 1972 for an International Wanderers XI in Rhodesia (now Zimbabwe), struck while Jim was in the midst of an uneasy contractual discussion with Sussex and persuaded him to enjoy a swansong at the County Ground. It made sense. He was a class act, still with plenty of runs in the tank. He had links with Taunton, too. His second wife hailed from the town and back in 1951, his uncle, Harry Parks, had been invited down to coach the Somerset side before serving for many years in a similar capacity at Taunton School.

Jim was born on 21 October 1931 in Haywards Heath, the son of Jim Parks Snr and Irene (née Heaver). Jim Snr and his brother, Harry, were both fine all-rounders and the son would be blessed with outstanding ability as a sportsman, taking to any game from football (which he played successfully at amateur level for many years) to table-tennis. In 1936, shortly before Jim's fifth birthday, his mother succumbed to tuberculosis, which meant that the two main female influences in his life would be his maternal grandmother, who stepped into the breach, and his paternal grandmother, Ellen, who is described as a 'touchline termagant' and lived to the age of ninety-nine. Rather than moping, Jim Snr set about opposing bowlers and batsmen with complete abandon the following season, racking up an incredible 3,000 runs and 100 wickets in the season. It is a record unlikely ever to be matched, although Bill Alley would come close for Somerset in 1961.

Jim Jnr attended St Wilfrid's Primary School in the town and here he would meet Irene Young, known as Rene, who would become his first wife and the mother of Bobby, who went on to become a first-class cricketer with Hampshire and Kent. At home as a young boy, Jim had benefited from having a net in the back garden and a father and uncle capable of mentoring him. From the outset he was encouraged to go for his shots. As Derek Watts records in his entertaining biography, *Young Jim*, 'One summer in the Thirties, he shattered twenty-seven windows in neighbours' houses. Jim Snr paid up with good grace and a smile.'

Having won a scholarship to Hove County School (later the County Grammar School) in 1942, such were his talents as a cricketer – at the time a batsman and leg-spinner – that he was elevated to the First XI at fourteen and was soon at the

Jim Parks – a classy wicket-keeper-batsman who enjoyed a swansong with Somerset

top of the batting and bowling averages. There was little doubt where his future lay and, immediately on leaving school, he was offered employment as a member of the ground staff at Sussex, enjoying an early taste of first-class cricket when he came onto the field as twelfth man and promptly caught Arthur Wellard under the sight screen, much to the chagrin of the watching public. As Jim would observe, he 'fared less well as the drinks carrier, coming on at the wrong moment'.

He was an outstandingly athletic cover point – many thought the best in the country – and a sparkling attacking batsman, soon making valuable contributions. His footwork and timing were impeccable and, in the words of Ted Dexter, writing many years later, 'You could pick [him] out from a mile away, open stanced with his hands high on the handle.' Test recognition came in 1954, but only for one match. The pivotal moment in Jim's career was his captain Robin Marlar's decision in a match against Essex in 1958 – one which came as a surprise both to Jim and to the man he replaced, Rupert Webb – to instruct Jim to keep wicket. The press were informed, falsely, that the change resulted from injury. For his part, Webb's opinion of his captain was jaundiced, but he felt no animosity towards his replacement. Jim recalls that the following day he struggled to get out of bed and that 'my stomach muscles and the backs of my legs were in agony'.

He soon learned the craft of wicket-keeping, although there were clearly other players regarded as superior technicians. During the winter of 1959-60, there was widespread bemusement that he had not been selected to join the tour of the West Indies. Instead, he took up a coaching post in Trinidad. He was therefore in the right place when the call came, as the England side became ravaged by injuries. Arriving in time for a tour match, Jim played as a wicket-keeper-batsman, 'using [Keith] Andrew's bat and pads, [Colin] Cowdrey's gloves, [Ray] Illingworth's trousers, [Brian] Statham's cap and [Ted] Dexter's thigh pad'. As Derek Watts observes, 'For the life of him, Jim cannot remember whose box he used.' Selected for the Fifth Test, Jim shone with the bat and would remain a regular choice until being supplanted by the irrepressible Alan Knott. By then he had made forty-six appearances for his country.

Back in 1960, he was enjoying success both on and off the field. His autobiography *Runs in the Sun* was published, albeit with more than a little help from John Graydon. The title was perhaps unfortunate, conjuring images of gastric upsets on holiday, but it marked the beginning a brief flirtation with book writing and a number of winters as a football correspondent for United Newspapers. His marriage was by then under strain and he would divorce Irene, becoming married for the second time, with Ann (née Wembridge), whom he had met while she was secretary to the journalist Ron Roberts. Their union proved short-lived.

Jim held to the view that a batsman demonstrates his true worth in the third season of his first-class career. In the first he is unconstrained by expectation and is an unknown quantity. The second is more challenging, as word of any technical flaws spreads on the grapevine. The third season separates the men from the boys. It is a useful maxim. Perhaps the rule of three applied to Jim's marriages. Certainly his marriage to Jenny (née Rogers) in 1973 can be deemed a success. They had met when Jim's off-season job as a sales rep with Whitbread took him to a pub in Staverton, Devon.

Having endured protracted contractual negotiations with Sussex, he was persuaded to throw in his lot with Somerset. In first-class fixtures for his new county he appeared as a batsman, adding the wicket-keeping role in a number of one-day games. Over the course of four seasons, the supporters were treated to some flashes of his former brilliance. Jim was also able to dispense useful advice, not least to his captain, Brian Close. In the early days of limited overs cricket, Sussex had dominated in the Gillette Cup, having, under the astute leadership of Ted Dexter, been the first team to grasp that success lay is adopting attacking instincts while batting and defensive tactics (allied to athleticism) while bowling and fielding. Brian Close had been married to the notion of all-out attack in any form of the game. He was persuaded by Jim to reconsider. Jim was perhaps the only person he would have listened to.

He left at the end of the 1976 season, sensing that at the age of forty-four, his time was up and a new life beckoned. In forty-seven first-class matches for Somerset he had averaged 30.31, including one century. After leaving the county, he continued his employment with Whitbread. Having started out years earlier as a part-time rep based in Romsey, he joined the company on a full-time basis after his retirement from cricket, and would work for sixteen years for the Heineken brand. He would also enjoy a period as Marketing Manager for Sussex CCC, the place where he grew up and where he had become a folk hero. He would continue playing cricket for the Old England XI, comprised of former stars of the game and managed by him. He finally hung up his boots in 1999 and has enjoyed a long and happy retirement back in Sussex with his wife, Jenny.

472
Dennis Breakwell
2 May 1973 v. Essex, Taunton

Writing in Dennis Breakwell's *Benefit Brochure*, Roy Kerslake refers to the spin bowler's 'boundless energy'. Indeed, Dennis added a new dimension to the term extrovert. Dubbed 'The Severed Nerve' by Ian Botham, with whom he shared a flat for a while, along with Viv Richards, it takes a man with the constitution of an ox to out-Botham Ian Botham. But even the great all-rounder sometimes hoped that his eternally restless flatmate, who indulged in little sleep but much chattering and partying, might on occasions slow down. As for Viv, at times he was obliged to seek sanctuary at Hallam Moseley's lodgings. Every dressing room needs a man to keep spirits up when things are not going to plan, to keep his teammates on their toes when time is dragging. Dennis was that man. Even when he was not on the team sheet he remained chief cheerleader-in-residence. Witness the occasion during a Gillette Cup match when Brian Rose (known to teammates as 'Harry') informed Dennis that he should pad up next, given that a left-hander was what the doctor ordered. Dennis shaped to respond. 'Don't interrupt me,' Brian insisted. 'But I'm not playing, Harry,' Dennis interjected, finally having his say, much to the amusement of the other occupants of the dressing room.

Born on 2 July 1948 in Brierley Hill, Staffordshire, he was the son of John Breakwell (known as Jack), an estimator in the construction industry, and Florence (née Talbot). Jack enjoyed a successful career in Birmingham League Cricket and was for a while captain of Dudley CC. Educated at Ounsdale Comprehensive in Wombourne, Dennis made his first appearance for Northamptonshire Second XI (coincidentally against Somerset Second XI) as a fifteen-year-old, and was offered a contract the following season. By the time he left Northants at the end of the 1972 campaign, he was already an established left-arm orthodox spinner, having chalked up sixty-four first-class appearances that had yielded 137 wickets.

His years at Somerset were joyous if sometime chaotic times. Describing their digs, flatmate Ian Botham would later observe that he, Viv Richards and Dennis tended to stock the fridge with 'fortifying liquids' rather than food, and that they would at times stumble into the house after a night on the tiles, a boiled egg for breakfast being at the limit of their culinary skills. House cleaning and cooking were anathema and, with regard to clothing, the young tyros, unacquainted with washing machines, would drive over to Yeovil with sacks of dirty kit which Ian's mother, Marie, would cheerily clean and sort, 'making sure we turned out for Somerset in matching socks'.

On the field of play, the changing demands of the game required Dennis to develop into more of a containing bowler than outright spinner of the ball. Although his Somerset teammate Peter Denning would describe him as 'the only number eight

Dennis Breakwell – a man of boundless energy

I know who managed to convince his captain that he needed a nightwatchman (on a flyer at Old Trafford)', Dennis was in fact a competent batsman, often required to sacrifice his wicket in the interests of pushing the score along. His professional career with Somerset would span nine seasons from 1973 until 1981 (although he was called up as emergency cover in each of the two succeeding seasons) and he came away with 281 wickets at 33.22 apiece and a batting average of 21.21. Among his triumphs were two Lord's final appearances, but perhaps his proudest moment was with the bat, when he surprised the home supporters with an unbeaten century against the New Zealand tourists in 1978. The event he might perhaps most wish to erase from his memory occurred during the match against Gloucestershire at Taunton when he became the second man to be hit for six sixes off consecutive deliveries in a first-class fixture. After the final deliveries of one over were despatched over the boundary ropes by Mike Proctor, the first four balls bowled in Dennis's next over met the same fate. Somerset captain Brian Rose spared him any further misery by taking him out of the attack.

In his early days as a professional cricketer, he had supplemented his wages during the winter months by working as a painter and decorator. First married in 1971 to Rosemary (née Padmore), a clerical assistant who lived in Market Deeping, he was later divorced and in 1977 was married to Susan (née Mangnall), with whom he had a son and daughter. Taunton has remained Dennis's adoptive home and, after his playing days were over, he was invited to join the coaching staff, applying his enthusiasm and accumulated wisdom by liaising with schools and helping to develop the skills of local schoolboys. His abilities were recognised by King's College (in Taunton), who offered him the post of coach and head groundsman in 1991. He would remain in that role until 2014, when he stood down and continued to work on a part-time basis, in particular continuing to oversee the summer festivals at King's that he had orchestrated successfully for a number of years. He has described the school as 'my home and my family for twenty-five years' and among his charges at the school were Jos Buttler and Alex Barrow, who both went on join the Somerset side, the pair having on one memorable occasion delighted their coach with a record-breaking stand of 340 in a fifty-over school match in 2008. Jos refers to Dennis as 'a fantastic man', noting that it was not just the cricketing fraternity who appreciated his contribution to school life at King's, and stating that, 'He was loved by all the pupils and teachers, with that consistently bubbly character and sense of humour.'

By way of relaxation, Dennis has enjoyed hobbies as varied as fishing and skittles, with one fellow skittler observing, 'I've played against Dennis and I swear he can land a skittle accurately and turn it like a cricket ball.' Widely acknowledged as a fine raconteur of Somerset cricketing tales of a mildly scurrilous nature, Dennis's infectious enthusiasm for life in general and cricket in particular remain undiminished.

1974

> "One innings was sufficient for the Somerset players to
> realise that Len Creed had unearthed a genius. Brian Close
> delivered the immortal words, 'You'll do for me, lad.'
> It was all too much for Len Creed, who was crying."
>
> *Vic Marks on Viv Richards*

Championship Position: 5 of 17

If the preceding years had been characterised by the influx of experienced old hands, then that was about to change with a vengeance. Roy Kerslake had recommended the adoption of a youth policy, with the county being scoured for young talent – players who would be coached by Tom Cartwright et al and toughened up by Brian Close. Three of the new-joins made their first-class debut in 1974. Viv Richards, Ian Botham and Peter Roebuck all arrived on the scene. Other noteworthy additions would follow. Some vintage, this was. Viv knocked Brian Close off his pedestal as the most prolific batsman and Hallam Moseley came into his own as a bowler with eighty-one first-class wickets, ably assisted by the mercurial Allan Jones. The rise to fifth place in the Championship would have been excellent news in itself for a team about to undergo a transition, but it was the limited-overs games that truly lifted the spirits of the faithful. Viv Richards's debut – against Glamorgan in the First Round of the Benson & Hedges Cup – turned out to be a Man of the Match Award-winning demonstration of the brute beauty that would become his trademark as a batsman. It was breathtaking and elicited a guard of honour arranged by the skipper. Not to be outdone, a young Ian Botham refused, later in the same competition, to be cowed either by a painful blow to the mouth from a vicious Andy Roberts bouncer or by what everyone else in Taunton regarded as the inevitability of defeat. He picked himself up off the floor, led his team to an improbable victory and garnered another Man of the Match Award for the young guns. It was brave, it was brilliant and, not for the last time, it had the national sports pages slavering about an exceptional all-rounder from Yeovil. And yet, in the context of one-day cricket, the season arguably belonged to Bob Clapp, a quiet, humorous, self-deprecating chap who bagged a record number of wickets for his side. Those wickets helped Somerset to second place in the John Player Special League.

Nothing had been won. Of course it hadn't. Somerset never won anything, did they? But the future appeared bright.

473
Isaac Vivian Alexander Richards
1 May 1974 v. India, Taunton

Best wishes

Viv Richards

Vivian Richards was a magnificent cricketer. A fine physical specimen, he was regarded by many as the greatest batsman of his generation. Adored in his homeland – the tiny island of Antigua, with a population not much greater than the town of Taunton – he was also revered in Somerset and feted around the world. His adoptive county was blessed by his commanding presence for thirteen seasons before his departure rent the club asunder.

Viv browbeat opponents into submission by sustained, controlled aggression. When the mood took him, he could happily batter a fielding side to the point that they were utterly dispirited (as he did, for example, with his 322 against Warwickshire). Seemingly nerveless, he would doze while awaiting his turn to bat. He would then delay his entrance into the playing arena at the fall of a wicket and once he came down the steps would own the field through the sheer force of his personality. He would walk to the wicket with an imperious expression and real swagger that had many opponents already on the back foot as they saw those impressive shoulders – all this at odds with his quiet and understated self-assurance in everyday life. Viv would take guard before tapping his bat handle and then pulling away to ensure that the bowler had to wait for him to be ready. He asserted his dominance in the gladiatorial confrontation. When opponents tried to sledge Viv, they only deepened his resolve. His belief was that the bowler must by definition be the one to relent, as he is obliged at some point to make his way back to his mark. It helps if you have the skill and strength to humiliate the bowler. On one occasion, as reported in his autobiography, *Sir Vivian*, he had played and missed the ball with a couple of airy shots at the start of his innings at Cardiff, when Glamorgan's Greg Thomas made the cardinal error of eyeballing him and telling him, 'For your information, it's red, it's round and it weighs five and a half ounces.' Viv smote the next ball out of the ground and into the River Taff, informing Thomas, without sparing the expletives, that since he knew what it looked like, he could now go and fetch it. Hugh Morris, fielding at first slip, was heard to say to his bowler, 'What have you done, my son?' Viv went on to score a brutal 136 in seventy minutes before being run out, arguably the only means of dismissal open to the opposition in such circumstances. It was a pity, from a Somerset

Vivian Richards – one of the all-time greats of the game

perspective, that Viv was not sledged more often.

Born in St John's on 7 March 1952, he was the son of a prison officer, Malcolm Richards, and his wife, Gretel. Malcolm was very much an alpha male, a strict disciplinarian who put religion first and sport a close second and from whom the son inherited a will to win. Viv's cricket developed with improvised games of beach cricket in the free-spirited West Indian tradition, where defensive shots are anathema and have to be coached at a later stage. His fielding was honed not by a slip cradle but by hurling stones at the stems of mangoes and catching the fruit as it fell. He attended Antigua Grammar School and it was clear from a young age that here was an exceptional talent – a fine footballer and a brilliant batsman – although not everything would go swimmingly. Having shown dissent as a seventeen-year-old, when he was incorrectly given out caught without having scored in his first match for Antigua, his actions sparked a near-riot. Reinstated, he proceeded to record two further ducks and suffered a two-year ban from competitive cricket. Things could only get better and indeed they did. In the interim, he did not lie idle, but developed his famed physique by engaging in boxing bouts with a measure of success.

Viv had started out his working life while a fourteen-year-old, serving in D'Arcy's Bar in St. John's and given every encouragement by the owner, D'Arcy Williams, who paid for his employee's cricket kit. The wider population of Antigua then clubbed together in 1972 to fund winter coaching for their two outstanding youngsters – their 'Vivi' and pace-bowler Andy Roberts – at the Alf Gover School, in London. It was a miserable experience, cold and wet, and ended with the two attending a trial with Surrey, who informed the young hopefuls that neither of them had what it takes to make it in the first-class game, a decision arguably as ill-judged as that of Dick Rowe of Decca Records, who told The Beatles that they weren't up to it.

Back in Antigua, Viv continued to make waves and word of his prowess reached Len Creed, a turf accountant and a member of the Somerset Committee, who was touring with the Mendip Acorns. Len proved to be the bookie who took a punt of his own and hit the jackpot. Having seen the extent of Viv's talent he offered him there and then the chance to forge a first-class career at Somerset. Viv leapt at the opportunity, withstanding the fury of his father. What he did not know was that Len had neither the know-how to make the necessary arrangements nor the influence to guarantee the promises he had made. Viv admits to misgivings when he arrived at Heathrow to find that, in the absence of the necessary work permit, he was in danger of being sent back home. Fortunately, Len was able to oil the wheels when it became apparent that the customs official was, like him, a freemason. Viv then saw out his residential qualification playing for Lansdown CC in Bath and impressed observers with his brilliance. He would later relate that he knew he would feel at home in Somerset when he was seated in a queue to get into a car park and became aware that the twenty-minute wait was triggered not by congestion but by the attendant's habit of spending five minutes greeting each driver as they arrived. Apart from the atrocious weather, it was as if he had never left Antigua. Making appearances for Somerset Under-25s, he played alongside a young Ian Botham. Their first game together went not quite according to plan with Ian scoring freely and proving ineffectual with the ball while Viv registered a duck and took 5 for 25 with his off-spin. The two enjoyed instant rapport and theirs became an unshakeable and celebrated friendship.

Viv announced his arrival in the Benson & Hedges Cup match at Swansea, days before his first-class debut for Somerset. He had hit 81 not out in his own inimitable style and would soon follow it up in the cup match against Gloucestershire at Taunton where the supporters were treated to a foretaste of what was to come. Facing a bouncer from Mike Proctor early in his innings he hooked the ball out of the ground. The crowd gasped and Proctor stopped short in open-mouthed astonishment. Anyone who watched cricket in the 1970s or the 1980s will be able to regale the younger generation with their own stories of how they witnessed his genius, because he was without equal among his contemporaries. Others have been greater accumulators of runs or have batted with thrilling aggression. Some, such as Barry Richards or Graeme Pollock, were denied the opportunity to prove their worth on the

Viv Richards poses after having scored a record 322 runs in one day for Somerset

international stage, making comparisons difficult, but a substantial number of bowlers and opposing captains agree that Vivian Richards was the man whose presence on the opposition team sheet they most feared. Even fans of other countries or counties were enthralled by him and wanted his innings to last. At times his greatness eclipsed all around him.

The statistics underline his genius. In 121 Tests for the West Indies (fifty of them as captain), he averaged 50.23, accumulating more than 15,500 runs when his ODI appearances are included. If there were ever the slightest doubts about his ability to perform at the highest level, these evaporated when he scored an unbeaten 191 in only his second Test. In 1976, he was imperious, with 1710 runs during the calendar year in just eleven Tests. He would score 114 first-class centuries in an outstanding career, twenty-four of those for Somerset, for whom he averaged 49.82 in 191 appearances. His off-spin yielded ninety-six wickets for the county at 44.15 apiece and his fielding was on a higher plain to ordinary mortals (most startlingly in evidence with the three run-outs he conjured in the 1975 World Cup Final). Twice he won the Walter Lawrence Trophy for the fastest century of the season, but it was his ability to perform on the big stage, to take events by the scruff of the neck, that took the breath away. As well as his century in the World Cup Final of 1979, there were his match-winning performances for Somerset, with Lord's proving a particularly happy hunting ground. After leaving Somerset, he turned out for Rishton CC, lit up the scene and repaid their investment in full. He then enjoyed a successful four-season swansong in first-class cricket with Glamorgan, bowing out by helping them to secure the AXA Sunday League title in 1993. Reports of his waning powers had been greatly exaggerated. In 2000, he was one of five players named *Wisden* Cricketers of the Century.

He expected others around him to give of their best. In the context of the peerless West Indian teams he led, he was rarely disappointed and any anger was directed at himself, if he threw his wicket away. In humbler surroundings he perhaps failed at times to see the gulf between him and the run-of-the-mill pros and thought that they were not trying, when in truth they were simply less capable than he was. It was surely his intimidating presence that cowed those who were expected to manage him. Peter Roebuck admits with great honesty in his unpublished diary of events in 1986 that he was frightened of Viv. The West Indies selectors responded negatively to his request to step down from the captaincy and concentrate on his batting. They thought he would be a disruptive team member. Viv was stung by what he saw as rejection by Lilliputians.

As for his personal life, he was married to Miriam (née Lewis), a bank clerk with whom he had a son and daughter. Although they grew apart, the retention of cordial relations remained important to them. Viv would also have a daughter with Neena Gupta, an actress, whom he met in India. He remains proud of all three of his children.

Since retiring as a player he has never had to go seeking work. He was employed by the Antiguan Tourist Board to promote the island and later became an ambassador-at-large. He has also enjoyed a number of coaching appointments, including a four-year stint at the invitation of Prince Hakeem of Brunei. He led the Antigua team at the Commonwealth Games and has also been mentor to teams in India and Pakistan. He has toured with Ian Botham as a raconteur and publishers have beaten a path to his door. Money has never been a problem, but nor has it ever corrupted a man who adheres to the tenets drilled into him in his youth. This, after all, is the man who turned down a fortune, refusing to join the Rebel Tour to South Africa. His revulsion with the apartheid regime counted for more than any financial inducements and in recognition of his principles as much as his cricketing achievements, the two nations now compete for the Sir Vivian Richards Trophy. Viv still gains most pleasure from his work with his foundation, encouraging young Antiguans to take up sport, although the honours that have been bestowed on him are inevitably also a source of pride. They include the gates that bear his name at Taunton, the stadium named after him in Antigua, the doctorate from Exeter University, among others, and any number of awards. He is now Sir Vivian, although only in formal settings.

Forget about the knighthood, though. To West Indians, Somerset supporters and fans of cricket in far-flung places, he was and still is 'The King'.

474
Ian Terence Botham
8 May 1974 v. Lancashire, Taunton

What can be said of Ian Botham that has not already been said a thousand times over? He has crammed more adventure into his life than most ordinary mortals could dare to dream of. He has at times had the country gripped by his exploits on and off the pitch, has transcended the sport he adorned and has generated more column inches than any other English cricketer with the possible exception of W. G. Grace. He is a working class hero, a scourge of the establishment, a free spirit with the heart of a lion, and a roisterer who could out-party most who came within his orbit. A gregarious man, perhaps the only thing Ian Botham ever feared, in truth, was loneliness. Bold and experimental on the field of play (as he has been in life), he was a risk-taker capable of grasping the initiative (whether with bat or ball) in devastating, explosive

Ian Botham – never far from a microphone or a camera and often in the headlines

bursts. Teammates and opponents also marvel at an unparalleled ability to dust himself down and never to dwell on failure or to countenance regret or reticence. If his great friend, Viv Richards, was indomitable, then Ian was indestructible. And plenty of people – among them tabloid hacks and the starchier element in the cricketing hierarchy – have tried to break him and failed in the attempt.

He was born near Heswall, in Cheshire, on 24 November 1955. His father, Les, worked at the time for the Fleet Air Arm and was married to Marie (née Collett), a nurse. By the age of three, Ian had been taken by his parents to live in Yeovil, where Les had secured a job with Westland Helicopters. Ian was educated locally at Milford Junior School and then at Buckler's Mead Secondary Modern, where from a young age he displayed all the characteristics that would later define him: an outgoing joker, unprepared to bow to authority, a strapping all-round sportsman, fearless in all he did, always up for a challenge and with a low boredom threshold. Facilities might have been limited, and Ian would watch from the bottom of his garden as the boys from the local Grammar School enjoyed their net practice, but his talent and resolve were sufficient to overcome any setbacks. As a thirteen-year-old, his coordination and brute strength enabled him to throw a cricket ball 63.32 metres, causing raised eyebrows among the organisers of the competition. Later, he was a good enough footballer to be offered a trial by Crystal Palace, but on the advice of his father, who adjudged him better at cricket than football, Ian opted for a career in the former, this despite a snub at Under-15 level when he was offered the demeaning role of third-choice twelfth man for an England Schools match. Those who had played with or against him in age group cricket were surprised at the decision, although they admit that it was not yet apparent that he would become a world-beater. If he had been wary of the powers that be, then this event hardened his attitude to those who betrayed too often their prejudice in favour of boys and men who hailed from the fashionable counties and had attended the 'right' schools. He was set on a course of being the outsider who raised two fingers to the establishment.

Tom Cartwright – like Ian, an outspoken rebel who never suffered fools gladly – took him under his wing and, already impressed by his clean hitting, taught him how to swing a ball. Here was a young man who needed to be in the thick of the action – as batsman, bowler or fielder – at every point in a match. He had the temperament of an all-rounder but, more than this, for a few heady years, could have walked into any side as either a batsman or a bowler, which took matters to a higher plane. Those productive sessions with Tom Cartwright were in stark contrast to a frustrating time on the Lord's ground staff. He was big, strong and able to stand up to the bullying culture but – as with other boys from the sticks – was overlooked. Ian would later write that, 'I don't fit into London.' MCC Head Coach Len Muncer would note in Ian's 'end of term' report that he 'shows a great deal of promise but does everything his own way'.

Back with Somerset, he was part of an exciting cadre of youngsters. A little older than the others was Viv Richards, already clearly a batting genius. If Viv's unremitting focus was on becoming the best and dominating opponents, then Ian was more likely to be driven by his competitive instincts at any given moment. His instinct was to belt every ball into the stands and to take a wicket with every delivery. His path to greatness was less clearly defined. The presence of Viv acted as a constant spur for Ian to get better and better. The chemistry worked wonders.

The first headline-grabbing indications of greatness-to-come were in the Benson & Hedges Cup match at Taunton in 1974 when the eighteen-year-old came in at number nine, furious at the indignity of being placed so low in the batting order and with his team looking down the barrel of a gun. Hit in the face by an Andy Roberts bouncer, he staggered but refused to fall before leading the side to an unlikely victory. Two teeth were dislodged and a further two loosened and later removed. Ian regarded this all as a mere inconvenience. The following morning he woke up, after some excessive post-match celebrations, to excruciating toothache and the first of many headlines in the national newspapers.

His rise thereafter was meteoric. At the age of twenty-one he was awarded the first of his 102 Test caps and began as he meant to go on with a five-wicket haul, set on his way with a fortuitous dismissal of Greg Chappell. It was the springboard to a spell

Ian Botham – a devastating bowler of swing in his prime, he tore into batmen and tore up the record-books

of all-round success not just unparalleled but so far ahead of the competition as to be barely believable. It took only twenty Tests to pass the milestone of 100 wickets and 1,000 runs. This was *Boy's Own* stuff. The runs and the wickets kept coming and records tumbled. There was controversy along the way. Not everyone took to his merry japes and his propensity for dunking others in swimming pools or dousing them with a water pistol was not universally welcomed. Nor did the powers that be take to his outspokenness and lack of deference. His description of Pakistan, for example, as 'a place to send your mother-in-law for a month' demonstrated that tact and diplomacy were not his strongest suits. His mother-in-law took it all in good heart, the Pakistanis less so. By the age of twenty-four, the roistering rebel who played Test cricket with an uninhibited approach that defied all the norms had been made captain of the England team. Perhaps he was unfortunate to take on the captaincy ahead of a challenging run of fixtures against the West Indies. Brian Close warned him, 'You'll have the most miserable time of your life.' But surely few young men in his position would have stood back and watched a lesser mortal take the reins. Maybe he was unlucky or maybe he was not made of the right stuff – the man to lead a charge, an instinctive cricketer, but not an analytical one. Ian himself is implacably of the view that he just happened to hit a run of bad form at the wrong time, that the weight of responsibility borne on those impressive shoulders was no burden at all – and he is ever a man of fixed views, intolerant of nuance and not one to change an opinion.

At Lord's, in the Second Test against Australia in 1981, he reached his nadir. Desperate to find a run from somewhere, he attempted to sweep Ray Bright's opening delivery and was bowled – dismissed for a pair. He was greeted by the contemptuous silence of the suited-and-tied MCC members, some of them snubbing him by burying their heads in their favourite daily crossword, their behaviour as boorish as anything the upstart they regarded as an oaf had ever been guilty of. He resigned the captaincy to avoid the ignominy of being sacked, but bounced back, of course. The

Australians were simply swept aside, the nation transfixed by Ian's heroic deeds. If there had been question marks about his ability to carry a team of eleven men under his captaincy, he was certainly able in the summer of 1981 to carry the hopes of a nation of more than fifty million people. It was exhilarating. Peter Roebuck has analysed Ian's approach to cricket in his insightful book, *It Sort of Clicks*. Peter was of the opinion that it was Ian Botham alone who transformed cricket from a game of calculation and risk-aversion to one where fearlessness has its reward. He notes that in many ways, Ian was uncoachable and ploughed his own furrow. It helps if you have superb hand-eye coordination, the strength of an ox, and the ability to wield a railway sleeper of a bat as if it were a stick. Ian Botham ignored the rules. He simply rewrote them. T20 slog-fests perhaps owe much to him, for better or for worse.

After the heights of 1981, there was inevitable anti-climax, punctured by glorious moments of greatness. The captaincy of Somerset followed. As with England, there was reluctance on the part of the decision makers, but who among us would be strong enough to stand up against so strong a presence? He led Somerset to victory in the NatWest Final of 1983 but thereafter trophies proved elusive. In 1985, his batting for the county was sensational, with eighty sixes contributing to a bumper crop of runs, notched up at an average of 91.42. At the same time, his bowling had fallen away. There were mutterings that he had become too big for his boots, that he was orchestrating the Ian Botham Show, not leading Somerset. He was relieved of the captaincy, allowed the dignity of resignation.

Then, a season on, came an angry parting of the ways, documented elsewhere in this volume (including in the summary of the 1986 season). He left having contributed as much as any man to his county's fortunes. In 172 first-class games for Somerset, he had averaged 36.04 with the bat and taken 489 wickets at 26.52 apiece. For five enjoyable seasons he played for Worcestershire, who claimed five trophies (including two Championships) in that period, while Somerset won nothing. There was then a season and a half before his retirement, helping Durham to establish themselves. His spell in Sheffield Shield cricket with Queensland had ended less happily, following a much-publicised fracas on a flight.

During much of his career, with the tabloids hungry for tales of the country's most marketable commodity, stories of swashbuckling feats on the field of play were replaced by lurid tales of drink, drugs and women. Having agreed a lucrative contract with the *Sun* newspaper, it was perhaps inevitable that other papers would come gunning for him. But there were court cases and other controversies, too. Some of his actions were ill-advised, not least allowing himself to fall under the spell of Tim Hudson, a fantasist who had his man dressed in dapper attire and touted him as the next James Bond. Advertising agencies had for a number of years understood his value, and he had endorsed many a product from Saab cars to Shredded Wheat, though

Ian Botham – embraced by a particularly loyal and enthusiastic fan

a tongue-in-cheek 'Back on the Grass' advert by Nike, planned to coincide with the ending of his ban for possession of cannabis, never saw the light of day. When not in the public eye for the wrong reasons, he was feted, quite rightly, for his gruelling and hugely successful walks in aid of Leukaemia Research – sparked by a genuine concern after a visit to Musgrove Park Hospital in Taunton – though even his charitable deeds could be mired in some controversy, such as when he pushed aside a police officer he regarded as being too officious. His appetite for a challenge was seemingly endless. He qualified as a helicopter pilot and he flew with the Red Arrows. Later, he starred for many years in panto.

With such a breathless lifestyle, he needed refuge, away from the public gaze. While he played, his soulmate, Viv Richards, a man exposed to the same pressures, was someone he could turn to. There were other confidantes, most notably Ken Barrington, whose untimely death was a bitter setback. But away from cricket there was Kath and their three children. He proposed to Kathryn (née Waller), three months after meeting her at Grace Road, Leicester, and they were married in 1976. 'He was quiet and nice and he helped me find my car in the rain,' she has observed. Kath remained his anchor in the storms. He sought refuge with the family and he found quietude in their home life, initially at Epworth, where he was protected from the media by the locals until one unknown 'snout' (to use Ian's parlance) tipped off the police about a secret stash of cannabis. All hell broke loose and they settled for a while on Alderney in the Channel Isles before a move to North Yorkshire. He remains to this day a country boy at heart. To the annual trips to Callander in pursuit of elusive salmon – it took him nine visits to land his first catch – should be added the usual field sports. Ian is trenchant – would he be otherwise? – in his defence of country pursuits and irritated by what he sees as meddling on the part of townies. He has owned a racehorse, too – named Rely on Guy. He has played football for Yeovil Town and Scunthorpe United. He appeared for eight years on *A Question of Sport*, alongside rugby international Bill Beaumont. He is equally at home with the rich and famous and the poor and dispossessed. And he has made the transition from fearless punter on the pitch to forceful pundit off it, for Sky.

It is only possible to scratch the surface of an extraordinary life in a matter of pages. Much, much more has been written about him, but treat some of what you read with caution and remember this. Here was arguably the greatest all-rounder of them all, his achievements, in his prime, superhuman. He bowled devastating spells that many a frontline Test bowler could only dream of and hit the ball harder and more cleanly than most specialist batsmen could ever muster. He stood a yard closer to the bat at second slip than most sane men would contemplate and still swallowed up remarkable catches. He fired in the ball from the boundary faster and flatter than most could hope to. But he was human, too. His dirty washing, aired in public, was dirtier than most, his indiscretions more shocking and his misjudgements more profound. His heart was bigger, too, the miles walked and the money raised more than ordinary mortals would accomplish. Whatever his faults, Ian Botham has enriched the lives of many – from those who sat and watched him in awe, fulfilling their dreams for them, to the children suffering from leukaemia. He lifted spirits and he spread hope. In 2007, the rebel was knighted for services to cricket and charity. No longer pilloried, he was now a pillar of the establishment. Yes, he could be overbearing and yes, he got some things horribly wrong, but by and large he has made the world a better place. If you are a supporter of Somerset cricket, raise your eyes and raise your glass if the cricket ever becomes too dull to hold your attention. Look up and read his name on the Sir Ian Botham stand and give thanks for his joyful brand of cricket and the trophies it helped to bring.

475
Peter Michael Roebuck
21 August 1974 v. Warwickshire, Weston-super-Mare

Peter Roebuck divided opinion and continues to do so after his untimely death. Many regarded him as an extraordinarily generous philanthropist, while others spoke of a dark side to his character. Some found him an engaging conversationalist while others thought him self-absorbed and venomous. He had friends aplenty, but most of them were inclined to admit that they did not really know him. He will be remembered for many years to come either as the man dubbed 'Judas' who sparked a civil war that split his club in two or the leader who had the courage to confront the issues of a crumbling, once-glorious empire, by then in decay.

He was born on 6 March 1956 in Oddington, Oxfordshire, into a devoutly Roman Catholic family. His parents were teachers, Jim having met Elizabeth (née Morrison) while the former was a mature student at Ruskin College. Elizabeth, for her part, was highly intelligent and fine sportswoman who was awarded a cricketing blue and represented England at lacrosse. Shortly after Peter's birth, the cottage in Oddington was gutted by fire. In earlier times this might have been seen as a premonition of a troubled life that burns brightly and is extinguished prematurely.

He took to cricket at the age of seven, by which time the family had moved (via Scarborough) to a flat in Bath, that also happened to be gutted in a fire. Coached initially by his father – who shared his son's austere approach to personal improvement, as well as some of his idiosyncrasies – Peter came to the attention of Jack Meyer, headmaster of Millfield, who agreed not only to offer the boy a scholarship but to grant teaching posts to both parents. Thereafter, the diary commitments of the promising young cricketer played a prominent role in determining the rhythms of Roebuck family life, their efforts reaping clear reward, with Peter making his first appearance for Somerset Second XI as a thirteen-year-old leg-break bowler.

Offered a place at Emmanuel College, Cambridge, he shut himself away in his room for hours at a time, studied hard and emerged as both a first-class cricketer and a man with a first-class degree in Law and a gift for an incisive and well-crafted turn of phrase. By now cast as a batsman and occasional bowler, he would make his Championship debut for Somerset in 1974 and, although he was slower to make his mark than others among his intake, his dedication and will to succeed meant that he carved out an invaluable role as a steadying influence in a star-studded batting side prone to occasional over-exuberance. Over the course of eighteen seasons he would average 38.34 in 306 first-class appearances, with thirty-one centuries to his name. From 1984, he averaged approaching fifty runs each season on a regular basis. Consistency became his hallmark, the hours spent at the crease – with his unusual hunched stance, his concentration rarely wavering – were impressive. He also contributed forty-five wickets at 54.26 apiece. He was talked about for a while as a potential Test player, but never progressed beyond an England B match against Pakistan and, later, captaincy of an England XI in the Netherlands. Many felt he would be ill-suited, temperamentally, to the sustained stresses of Test cricket. His teammates became accustomed to Peter's changes of mood. Each August, he would suffer a loss of confidence, and

Peter Roebuck – one of a number of accomplished writers to have played for Somerset, he batted with restraint but demonstrated great flair with a pen in his hand

despondency would set in as the pressures of the first-class game once again assailed him. In the early years, he sought solace recharging himself as an English teacher at Cranbrook School in Sydney, an environment where his idiosyncrasies were more likely to be embraced. Earlier, he had found brief and wholly unsuitable employment as a quality controller for a peat extractor on the Somerset Levels. A self-confessed innumerate and a young man not cut out for a career in business, he had had no idea what was expected of him. He confesses to having poked and prodded at the occasional bag and declared everything satisfactory. Writing was, of course, the alternative career at which he would excel. Somerset cricket has perhaps thrown up fine writers more regularly than great cricketers over its long history and Peter would surely find his way into most people's all-time Somerset Cricketing Literary XI.

He was, to the surprise of many, appointed Somerset captain in 1986. Acceptance of the role would prove the defining moment of his career. It is surely fair to state that his captaincy was flawed. A private man and not one to conform to social norms, the role was never likely to come naturally to him. Captaincy is a stern test for any first-class cricketer: they generally have no grounding beyond having watched others in action, no years of preparation or training, as might be expected in business. Leading a team you have grown up with is harder still, particularly if some of them have risen to greater heights than you as players. Tackling issues requires vision, courage and excellent man-management skills. He had the first two in abundance but was found wanting in the third. The decision to shed his star players (whom some felt were living on past glories, though Vivian Richards in particular would demonstrate that there was still plenty in his tank) was not his, but he led the assault. Marshalling the opposing troops was Ian Botham.

The two main protagonists were polar opposites: one studious and the other with a piratical sense of fun and adventure; one introverted and the other a raging extrovert; one cautious, the other a daring chancer. In the early years they had formed an unlikely friendship, but a lack of common ground would cause the relationship to sour as irreversibly as spoilt milk. Their differences had always been apparent. As an example, both were struck in the head while emerging cricketers by unplayable bouncers from Andy Roberts. Ian Botham picked himself off the floor, spat out a few teeth and fearlessly carved out an unlikely victory for his team. The twenty-year-old Peter Roebuck, reeling from the assault that had him taken to hospital, later shut himself in a darkened room, played some Joni Mitchell music and gathered his thoughts while he decided whether or not he wished to continue as a cricketer, whether he believed he had what it takes. He had emerged the stronger for his experience and found a way of dealing successfully with the short-pitched stuff. Here were two very different characters united in finding the idea of compromise anathema.

The civil war that broke out has been extensively documented (including elsewhere in this volume) and the wounds took a long time to heal. For a while, the need to prove his critics wrong galvanised Peter, but – worn down by the responsibility – he would hand over the reins to his good friend, Vic Marks, in 1989. And then in 1991, he departed the stage.

He was bright enough to learn from any mistakes he had made and enjoyed success when he transferred his allegiance to Devon. It helped, too, that he was Devon's star player. The invitation had come from Nick Folland at a time when Peter was already carving a successful career for himself as a distinguished writer and broadcaster. He would prove himself able to manage the two careers concurrently. Devon became serial winners, with Peter more often than not starring in the unfamiliar role of bowler. At the same time, his journalistic output, primarily for *The Age* and the *Sydney Morning Herald* won widespread praise and his radio commentary for *ABC* was frequently as arresting as his attire. As his friend and colleague Kerry O'Keeffe would write, Peter had 'the clothes sense of a blind man and shoelaces that appear[ed] twenty years older than the footwear itself'. His trademark straw hat had seen better days, too. He continued to write his books, expressing opinions with great verve.

Having purchased a house which he shared for a while with Nigel Popplewell,

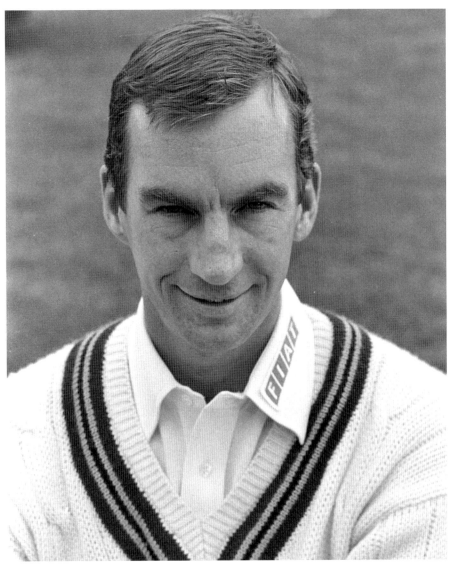

Peter Roebuck – divided opinion and continues to do so after his untimely death

Peter never bothered with niceties such as a front door key or a kempt garden. Later, he would offer lodgings to promising youngsters whom he sponsored to come over to England to further their development. Sadly, the fact that he was insistent on a regime of corporal punishment – completely at odds with societal norms – later came back to haunt him when he was pursued through the courts in 2001. He had made enemies in 1986 and many of them were more than happy to air their misgivings about him. He refused, however, to change his ways. Stubborn to the last, he continued to support youngsters in the developing world, helping to set up the Learning for a Better World (LBW) Trust in 2006 and offering a refuge to young boys in a house he had purchased in Pietermaritzburg. Rumours of an unhealthy sexual interest in his charges continually bubbled up but others felt that Peter was guilty only of naivety, too generous and open-hearted for his own good.

Houses were also purchased in Sydney, as he sought a fresh start, having successfully applied for Australian citizenship. His life continued to be chaotic, money thrown without a care at his projects while he paid scant regard to the finer things in life. In Australia, they accepted and even celebrated his oddities.

And then, in a matter of hours, it all came to naught. He was in Cape Town in his role as a Test Match commentator for *ABC*. The police came knocking on his hotel room door. The accusation hanging over him was that he had sexually assaulted Itai Gonda, a young Zimbabwean who had come to him seeking financial support. Itai remains the only man who knows precisely what had happened behind closed doors. We are unlikely ever to be able to ascertain the circumstances that led to his death, when he fell from the sixth floor of a hotel in Claremont on 12 November 2011, aged only fifty-five.

How do we summarise this complex man? He could be sharp, otherworldly, funny or exasperating in equal measure and was regarded by many, to put it more simply, as an oddball. Friendships based on wit and intellectual jousting came more easily than affection and he was happiest when in control of events, whether crafting a patient century, captaining a compliant Devon team or overseeing with a strict, unyielding regime the young dependants who benefited from his charity. Former Somerset cricketer Adrian Jones once observed that 'he just seems so bloody lonely... I think he likes to be contrary, but as soon as people react to that he doesn't seem sure whether to back down, laugh it off or come back at you.' Liked by many but uncomfortable with the idea of intimacy, he felt – wrongly, and to the lasting regret of friends and family – that he had no one to turn to. Peter had written of 'the joys to be found in nature, music, friendship, literature and humour' but had also confessed that, 'I fear love for its intrusion of privacy.' His rejection of love in all bar exceptional circumstances offered a shield for fifty-five years, but it also destroyed him. It was perhaps part and parcel of a wider fear of failure, which he had earlier confessed to, observing: 'Perhaps the insecurity of batting, sharpened as it is by being my career, has caused me to concentrate on the avoidance of failure rather than accepting the challenges.'

'I'm not perfect,' he also wrote, shortly before his death, 'but I think the good outweighs the bad.'

1975

"Struggling in the field, with an attack suddenly appearing threadbare, Somerset could at least rejoice in the strides made by their youngsters, especially Botham and Slocombe."

Peter Roebuck

Championship Position: 12 of 17

Hopeful signs have often presaged exasperated sighs for the Somerset faithful. It had ever been thus. There was a disappointing falling away in each of the four competitions. A shoulder injury sustained while attempting a catch put paid to Tom Cartwright's season: it was a devastating blow to the player and to the club. Graham Burgess suffered injury, too. Ian Botham proved to be the leading wicket-taker, his bowling showing rapid improvement under Tom Cartwright's tutelage. He was supported by Allan Jones and Hallam Moseley, both with more than fifty first-class wickets. Brian Close leapfrogged Viv Richards to register most runs, although Viv, Peter Denning and Brian Rose all topped 1,000 runs, as did Derek Taylor, now blossoming as a wicket-keeper-batsman, and Phil Slocombe, in his maiden season.

The roll call of talented debutants was again impressive. Vic Marks would go on to gain Test honours and both Keith Jennings and Phil Slocombe made important contributions over the forthcoming years.

The recruitment policy was inevitably costing the club, adding to its annual losses and, as a result, there was a strong drive to raise funds ahead of what was the centenary year for the club, founded back in 1875 as a result of the efforts of Reverend Alexander Colvin Ainslie and his acolytes. Supporters voted overwhelmingly in favour of a near doubling of the subscription from £4 to a heady £7.

476
Philip Anthony Slocombe
30 April 1975 v. Sussex, Taunton

England's hugely successful rugby coach, Eddie Jones, identifies Phil Slocombe as the man who inspired him to enter the coaching profession. Eddie had come under Phil's orbit in the nets in Australia and acknowledges that the informed advice he was given transformed his understanding of his strengths and weaknesses and enhanced his performance. Eddie resolved thereafter to pursue his career as a coach – optimising the performance of elite sportsmen – rather than as a teacher and school principal.

Born in Weston-super-Mare on 6 September 1954, Phil was the son of Anthony William Slocombe and Margaret Amelia (née Bath). Educated at Weston-super-Mare Grammar School and then Millfield School – memorably described by Stephen Brenkley as a place 'which produces county cricketers like a tree produces leaves' – he showed promise from a young age and was given his first taste of Second XI cricket with Somerset at fourteen. He finally broke into the first-class game as a twenty-year old and made an immediate impact with a score of 61 not out in his first innings and a century in his third Championship match. He would go on to exceed 1,000 runs in his first season and the future looked bright, with some observers predicting a possible Test career. Alas, it was not to be. Tom Cartwright would opine that:

> *He had talent and there was a single-mindedness about his batting that meant he would get hundreds. But I always felt he was a coached player, very schooled, very chiselled. There were days when that bore fruit, but he didn't have the natural look of the others. If you rely on the stereotype, there will be periods of play in matches that will take you into places that you're not equipped to deal with.'*

Phil's technique was indeed sound and Peter Roebuck describes his teammate as 'a neat, quick-footed batsman'. Peter goes on to reveal in *Sometime I Forgot to Laugh* that he and Phil 'had to fight for the last batting position'. He adds that, 'frustrated by his inability to secure a regular place in the one-day team in Somerset's glory years, Phillip [sic] tried to change his game, went beyond its boundaries and paid the penalty'. 'It was dog eat dog,' Peter recalls, although Phil perhaps viewed the situation with greater equanimity. As late as 1978, Phil was outperforming Peter both in terms of batting average and runs accumulated. It is also worth adding that although Phil's technique was suited to the longer form of the game, he made telling contributions as a superb outfielder, even drafted into the England team as twelfth man (substitute fielder) on two occasions in 1977 and 1981, which he modestly attributes to the persuasive powers of his Somerset team-mate, Ian Botham.

Phil always had an eye on ways in which he could supplement his wages both in the short and long term. There were his spells as a club professional and coach in Sydney (with Stockton CC in 1976-77 and Randwick CC in 1977-78) and a tour with the Derrick Robins XI to South Africa in 1976. A useful foot-baller, when not spending the winters in the Southern Hemisphere, he turned out for Weston-super-Mare FC, in the Western League. He also tried his luck with a number of business ventures, starting a small mail order business in Taunton and then an antiques shop, the latter based on an interest he shared with his partner, Susan Pamela Shepherd, to whom he was married in 1981.

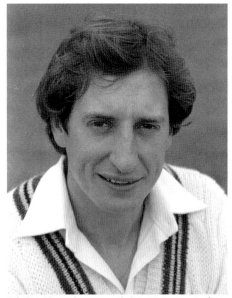

Philip Slocombe – exceeded 1,000 runs in his first season

Over the course of his career with Somerset, he played in 139 first-class games, averaging 27.63, with seven centuries to his name. He also bowled his medium-pace deliveries on a very occasional basis and claimed three wickets at 18.00 apiece. When he departed the scene in 1984, having at last claimed his place in a Lord's final, in the NatWest Trophy win against Kent in 1983, he was emphatically not one of those men who subsequently flounders or loses their zest for life. He already had ideas aplenty for life beyond the game. There was his family – including his stepson, Dylan, and daughter, Sasha – and a passion for the finer things in life that would prove the inspiration for further business ventures. Within six months of retiring as a player, he and his family had moved to Dallas, Texas, opening an antiques shop in the heart of the Design District. Phil recounts that, 'For five years I had to rely heavily on Susan's expertise but we concluded that the brashness and money orientation in Dallas didn't really suit us.' In 1990, the family moved to Brittany in France, where Phil and Susan set up a small hotel and restaurant – Le Manoir du Rodoir – with Dylan working as head sommelier. 'Susan spoke the language fluently, but it was a challenge for me,' Phil observes, although he clearly overcame any linguistic hurdles. The hotel proved a success and continues to thrive but, as Phil explains, 'We felt like slaves to the business: it was exhausting and we sold up in December 1994.' Phil and Dylan had by then developed an enduring passion for French wines and in 1995 they created The

Rare & Fine Wine Company Ltd, which he relocated to London, following the tragic loss in 2008 of Susan – whom Phil still refers to as 'my soulmate'. He continues to manage the company as its Chief Executive and, having initially sourced wines from the leading domaines and chateaux in France – covering Bordeaux, Burgundy, the Rhone and Loire Valleys and Champagne – he has recently added fine wines from Italy and Spain to the range. Latterly, he has administered the Millfield Wine Society, which invites members to purchase fine wines and join tours, with 10% of proceeds going towards the Millfield Foundation (chaired by Olympic gold medallist, Duncan Goodhew), which offers Millfield School scholarships to talented youngsters with no other means of financial support. Perhaps his efforts will result indirectly in the un-earthing of a Somerset cricketing star of the future.

Summing up his time at the club, Phil observes that, 'Although I was frustrated that I didn't achieve more in my cricket career, my lasting memories of the team success, the camaraderie and the awesome support we received still bring a smile to my face.'

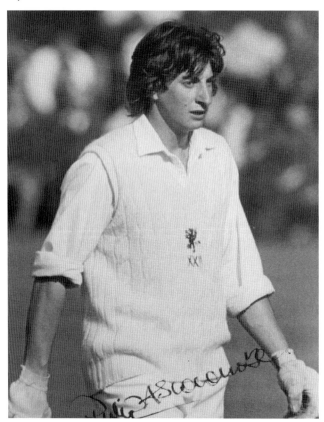

Philip Slocombe – 'he had talent and there was a single-mindedness about his batting that meant he would get hundreds'
COURTESY OF
JOHN LEE

477
John Stanley Hook
28 May 1975 v. Oxford University, Oxford

John Hook (signature)

John Hook grew up with the Weston-super-Mare cricket ground at the bottom of the garden. He still has within his extensive collection of cricketing books a copy of *The Hand that bowled Bradman*, penned (with the patient assistance of David Foot) by that other denizen of Weston-super-Mare, Bill Andrews. It bears the inscription, 'For John, hoping it won't be long before he plays for Somerset as well, Bill.' Bill Andrews was an enthusiastic and outspoken champion of his young charge, whom he had seen develop through school, club and county age group cricket. Playing for the Somerset Under-15s at Devonshire Road in his home town, John had delighted the locals – Bill Andrews included – with a return of 7 for 12 against Hampshire Under-15s. He was invited on occasions to captain a star-studded Under-19 side, leading the likes of future Somerset skippers Peter Roebuck, Ian Botham and Vic Marks. Little wonder, then, that Bill Andrews had tipped his charge for great things. Indeed, a feature appeared at the time in the *Western Daily Press*, describing him as a potential successor to Brian Langford. 'I suspect that was drafted by Bill,' John observes, with a wry smile.

For generations, John's family had called Weston-super-Mare their home. Having survived everything the enemy had thrown at him in Gallipoli and Egypt – his diary of events now in the possession of the Imperial War Museum – John's paternal grandfather, Stanley, was killed while serving with the Home Guard during a bombing raid on Weston in 1942. John's father, Follott Edward Hook, known as Ted, was by that time serving in Ceylon (Sri Lanka), before settling for a quieter life as a local government officer in Weston and then as Lands Officer for the Central Electricity Generating Board, whose offices were in nearby Bristol.

John's mother, Marjorie (née Worth) was the granddaughter of Cecil George Oxley, who, along with his brother William Henry, had established a renowned jewellery business in the town. C. G. Oxley was known far and wide for his rolled gold and bead pieces and appears not to have been unduly worried about revealing the secrets of his success, having published his booklet entitled *How to make Rolled Gold Wire Jewellery*. His confidence was certainly not misplaced. Having enjoyed its heyday in the early half of the Twentieth Century, the company survived long after his death before being wound up in the early 1990s.

John Hook – an off-spinner who describes himself as 'never remotely tough enough to survive in cricket'

COURTESY OF IVAN PONTING

Born on 27 May 1954, John was obliged to overcome the early setbacks of an ear infection – that rendered him entirely deaf in one ear – and a diagnosis of epilepsy, after it first manifested itself when he was ten. The condition has been managed successfully throughout his life. Educated at Ashbrooke House Preparatory School and Weston-super-Mare Grammar School, he went on to study for a degree in French & German at Southampton University. Here he formed a potent bowling partnership with John Southern (a slow left-armer who joined Hampshire). Also in the attack was Oliver Blunt, who would become an eminent QC, his cross-examinations proving even more penetrative than his seam bowling. John would forsake his studies at Southampton in 1974, after what in cricketing terms were two successful years that saw him selected for the combined UAU side. 'Exams got the better of me,' he explains in relation to his decision to quit his degree prematurely, although the offer of professional terms by Somerset was surely a sweet-tasting palliative.

A tall man, at 6 feet 2 inches, John bowled right-arm off-breaks and, although he had his moments in the sun for Somerset Second XI, he failed to press on. With his usual self-deprecation, he states that, 'I was never remotely tough enough, emotionally or mentally, to succeed in cricket, irrespective of any technical shortcomings.' Peter Robinson suggested on occasions that, 'You should be more like Ian Botham and start believing in yourself.' As John points out, not everyone is blessed with self-belief such as Beefy had in spades. We cannot fundamentally change who we are.

John is described by teammate Peter Roebuck as 'a tall, gentle and slightly deaf off-spinner, with whom it was impossible for captains to lose their temper'. We are informed in *Sometimes I Forgot to Laugh* that:

> They might bellow across the field or roar accusations of incompetence, but he'd simply cup his ear and politely ask for the message to be repeated. After dropping a catch once, and desperate to redeem himself, he dived full-length after something much more difficult and watched from a prostrate position as the ball bounced over him and went to

the boundary. After an appropriate period of mourning, even the bowler laughed.

The passage delights John. 'Yes,' he confesses, 'that happened at Exmouth, against Devon.' On first reading the piece, he dropped a line to Peter and a response duly arrived, littered with the author's usual misspellings. It is typical of John that he should feel flattered to have been remembered so fondly. Tom Cartwright would suggest that he was 'too nice to be a professional cricketer'. Tom notes that during their time together, after some error or other, John would 'give me that flaming peace sign with his fingers in a V. And he had one of those haircuts that wasn't particularly short. He used to drive me mad.'

His initial taste of first-class cricket was as twelfth man against Gloucestershire at Bristol in 1975. Coming on to field for two overs while Allan Jones repaired a broken bootlace, he took an excellent catch (that Jonah might well have spilled) at mid-on to remove Tony Brown. In John's words, 'Dennis Breakwell was delighted and came over to congratulate me, but Brian Close was shouting at me to get off the field so that Jonah could get back on.'

In his one full first-class appearance, John took 0 for 29 in twelve overs and scored 4 not out and 3 with the bat. There was a further appearance as twelfth man and another rollicking from Brian Close against Surrey at Bath. 'I was taking the drinks out on a scorching day and I'd just crossed the boundary rope when Dasher and Beefy descended on me and I started pouring them a drink. Then I heard Close bellowing, "Bring 'em 'ere." I nearly dropped the lot.'

After leaving the County Ground, John was invited to work as a stock-keeper by a family friend who ran a jewellery shop – Rossiter & Sons – in Weston-super-Mare. After three years, he moved to London to undertake similar work for Mappin & Webb. He had continued to enjoy success in club cricket, for Weston-super-Mare CC and subsequently for Mitcham CC. 'As well as taking wickets regularly, I managed to make a few runs and even became a decent slip catcher, especially off the quicks,' he confirms. 'But in the early 1980s I suffered a case of the yips and completely lost any confidence. I'd stopped enjoying the game and so I called it a day in 1986.'

His professional life had by then taken on a new direction. Determined to undertake work where he could 'make a difference', John joined Christian Aid, administering donations and gift aid. In 1986 he was offered the role of administrator for an Arts and Community Centre in Uxbridge before he returned in 1990 to Christian Aid. There followed spells with Amnesty International and, finally, CAFOD (the Catholic Agency for Overseas Development).

He retired in 2016 at the age of sixty-two, but has remained active as a volunteer, a lifelong love for natural history and the environment having been the spur to become involved with restoring wildlife habitats. Finally married in 2010 to Chris, a former civil servant, who had been his partner for the previous twenty years, John lives in Slough but still watches Somerset when he can. Not long ago, he was seated in the crowd at the County Ground when he spotted Vic Marks. Diffident as ever, he was reluctant to introduce himself but Chris encouraged him to step forward. 'Hello, Vic,' he began, 'I don't know if you remember me. I'm John Hook …' 'Remember you, John? How could I forget you after I did you out of a job?' Vic replied.

It is typical of John that he should still underestimate himself. He was blessed with more ability than most and has achieved more in his life than many, as well as showing more courage than the majority in his choices and in the manner he has overcome setbacks. Peter Robinson might have exhorted him that he should be more like Ian Botham and start believing in himself. But then again, being with and talking with this gentle, unassuming man is a pleasure. Why would anyone have wanted him to change?

Catching practice for the young guns (left to right): Vic Marks, John Hook, Ian Botham, Viv Richards and Peter Roebuck. COURTESY OF JOHN HOOK

64

478
Keith Francis Jennings
18 June 1975 v. Leicestershire, Leicester

K Jennings [signature]

When Tom Cartwright was appointed to the role of Somerset coach, he set out with a vision to scour the county for talent that would otherwise have slipped through the net. It was an idea that bore fruit with a serendipitous coming together of a group of young players who, with a sprinkling of overseas stars to assist them, would lead the county to their first trophies. As he explained to Stephen Chalke (their conversations having been recounted in *The Flame Still Burns*), his goal was to get 'about fifty kids of real quality together' in an attempt 'to produce a team within five years'. Clubs around the county were invited to send promising young players along. The first session was held on a Tuesday evening at the indoor cricket school in Bath, run by Peter Wight. Dispiritingly, only a photographer and a journalist deigned to attend. The next session followed on the Thursday, this time at Taunton and in Tom's account, there was just one attendee, a promising youngster named Keith Jennings. 'I'll bowl at you, and you can bowl at me,' Tom suggested and his career as Somerset coach was thus launched in earnest. In truth, Keith was already established as a member of the Lord's ground staff. 'To be honest, I can't remember the event,' he confesses. 'I would have only been nineteen at the time and so my memories are a bit hazy.' He is in no doubt, though, that he always felt the benefit after each session in the nets with Tom.

Born in a nursing home in Wellington on 5 October 1953, Keith was one of three sons of Francis Basil Jennings, a carpenter and joiner, known as Basil, whose home and business was in the village of Milverton. Basil was married to Jean, who served customers for many years at the Co-op store in the nearby town of Wiveliscombe. Brought up in Milverton, where his father was for a while chairman of the village cricket club (of which Keith's mother and Keith himself would later become committee members), he attended Kingsmead School and, although he received no formal coaching, showed promise as a schoolboy cricketer and rugby player. He was indeed a good enough rugby player to be invited to play for Somerset Colts. 'I was fortunate,' he says, 'to be encouraged by people such as Roger Masters, a teacher at Kingsmead, and Brian Jennings, a relative and a useful sportsman, who both influenced me greatly.' Selected on a number of occasions for Somerset in age group cricket, he was sent by his school to Lilleshall to receive further coaching. 'It was a last-minute decision,' Keith confirms. 'I was actually the school's second choice, and only heard I was going when another boy had to pull out.'

Keith Jennings – a medium-pace bowler who rarely strayed from a good line and length
COURTESY OF IVAN PONTING

Invited to join the Lord's ground staff directly on leaving school, Keith would remain there for five seasons, returning on occasions to play for Somerset Second XI. During the off-season, he learned the skills of the joinery and carpentry trades and played club rugby for Wiveliscombe RFC, where his father helped to oversee the up-and-coming youngsters. Having been offered a contract with Somerset in 1975, in the early part of his career he was selected primarily for limited-overs matches, although by 1978 he was being chosen on a more regular basis for Championship games and in fact enjoyed his best season that year, with forty wickets, including a match-winning 5 for 18 against Sussex at Hove. He bowled at medium pace and proved hard for opposition batsmen to get away, rarely straying from a good line and length. He was thus an important ingredient in Somerset's limited-overs success and his performance in the Gillette Cup Final of 1979 is perhaps typical. Viv Richards and Joel Garner quite rightly gained the plaudits, but Keith had proved the most parsimonious of the Somerset bowlers, conceding only 29 runs in his allotted twelve overs: his contribution had been vital and his teammates were in no doubt as to his worth. Opponents who hoped to open their shoulders once Joel Garner had been rested would soon learn that they could not do so. In the latter part of his career, Keith was beset by back problems but, like many a player before him, bowled through the pain. When he parted company with Somerset at the end of the 1981 season, he had claimed ninety-six first-class wickets in sixty-eight matches at 35.44 apiece and had averaged 10.63 with the bat.

For a while he walked away from the game, taking his place in the family business – gradually increasing the focus on joinery in the workshop, rather than carpentry work on construction sites – and he continued to play club rugby as a back, combining strength and speed. He was subsequently persuaded to come to the aid of the Milverton cricket team. His family had long been leading lights at the village club, whether as players or committee members, with Keith's mother, Jean, also working tirelessly making teas and fund-raising. He would captain them for a number of years, later helping out with the administration of the club and the upkeep of the ground. Obliged to give up rugby after an operation for a prolapsed disc in 1989, he continued to play cricket for Milverton.

He is in many ways a representative of a bygone age when there was less science and rigour applied to finding the next generation of players, and when schoolboys who emerged from the state sector were reliant – as in his case – not just on their talent but on guidance often from unpaid mentors.

The one-to-one coaching session at the County Ground on a Thursday evening in 1972 recalled by the late Tom Cartwright was indicative that things were about to change.

Keith remains as down-to-earth as ever, his head never having been turned by his spell in the spotlight. Glamour and fame hold no allure for him. 'Mind you, it wasn't that glamorous,' he observes. 'I often chose to cycle to the County Ground for training or practice sessions.' He laughs at the suggestion that his bicycle was surely replaced by a courtesy car during Somerset's so-called 'Glory Years'. 'There was no sponsorship car for me,' he asserts. He still cycles along the country lanes around Milverton as a means of keeping fit. Keith really has not changed one iota. And he continues to go about his chosen craft as a joiner with quiet efficiency and precision. Just as he went about his craft as a bowler, during his playing days.

Keith Jennings – opponents who hoped to open their shoulders once Joel Garner had been rested would soon learn that they could not do so
COURTESY OF IVAN PONTING

479
Victor James Marks
26 July 1975 v. Hampshire, Weston-super-Mare

[signature]

Vic Marks was and still is a man for all seasons. The farmer's boy-cum-classicist remains universally popular and at ease whether mingling with Oxbridge types or the hoi polloi. Major Pridham, a former Somerset Stragglers stalwart and sometime author, recounts an anecdote concerning the great Somerset side of the early 1890s. Their captain, Herbie Hewett, had come up with the novel idea of keeping his close fielders on their toes by challenging them to decline opposing batsmen's names as if they were Greek substantives. Wicket-keeper Archie Wickham and Hewett's fellow slip fielders Bill Roe and Venus Challen had found themselves flummoxed by Baldwin. Shortly thereafter, Baldwin offered a chance which Challen spilled. Hewett remarked with his usual drollery that Challen had at last learned how to decline Baldwin. It is not difficult to imagine Vic comfortable in such company, as at ease as he was in the more rumbustious Somerset dressing room of the late 1970s and early 1980s, or with his England teammates, where Bob Willis had suggested the nickname Skid, a scatological wordplay – perhaps best whispered in polite company – that he tolerated with great forbearance.

Vic was born on 25 June 1955 in Middle Chinnock, the son of Harold Marks, a farmer, and his wife, Joan (née Farthing). Harold managed three hundred acres of primarily dairy farm and Joan was a farmer's daughter, originally from Glastonbury. Although he was the couple's only child, Vic had a brother and sister, John and Susan, the product of their father's earlier marriage. Tragically, their mother had died in the late 1940s, shortly after the birth of her second child.

Young Vic would possess the phlegmatism required of any farmer in order to survive what fortune throws their way, but he was destined to apply it in other walks of life. He recalls his early years with great fondness, having noted that, 'As a young boy in the 1960s, I scored a few runs in the backyard of the [Middle Chinnock] rectory against the vicar's two sons and, occasionally, his daughter.' At Blundell's School, in neighbouring Devon, he would star as a rugby scrum-half, enjoying a successful partnership with Jeremy Lloyds, his fly-half. When it came to cricket, he was regarded at this stage as a batsman and occasional off-spin bowler. Erstwhile Somerset President, Michael Hill, would recall a conversation with Tom Cartwright, who informed him: 'There's a South Somerset lad at Blundell's School who shows some promise.' A degree of understatement that might readily be associated with Vic himself. Victor Marks has always demonstrated the self-deprecation that is the hallmark of those confident of their worth, the quiet modesty that comes with knowing that you have nothing to prove.

Somerset would have to wait before offering their young hopeful a full-time contract. Vic had been awarded a place to study Classics at St John's College, Oxford. There he would gain cricketing blues in four successive seasons, captaining the side in 1977 and 1978. His successes were many, not least among them securing the hand in marriage in 1978 of Annabelle Stewart, known as Anna, a Zoology student at Oxford who would go on to work in education and with whom Vic would have two daughters, Amy and Rosamund (Rosie). After thirty-three first-class matches for the university side, he had also come to be

Vic Marks – a good all-rounder and all-round good egg

regarded as an off-spin bowler who could bat, rather than the reverse. He had also won praise from his teammates for his captaincy skills.

Back at Somerset, having made his debut in 1975, he was by now an integral part of the young team which was blossoming into greatness. Inevitably, lasting friendships were forged between a group of disparate characters who shared a dressing room and a talent for the game. Vic and Peter Roebuck became particularly close. Their mishaps as they toured the length and breadth of the country – often in Vic's clapped-out black VW Beetle – are documented in Peter's *It Never Rains*, arguably his most engaging piece of writing. The bumbling efforts of two bright but absent-minded cricketers trying to find directions are a highlight, with Vic often tumbling out of the car to ask the way, only to forget what he had been told by the time he returned.

In the early years, he taught each winter. Three years back at Blundell's were followed by one at Taunton School. If growing up on the farm had crystallised the view that he had no wish to follow in the parental footsteps, then a taste of the teaching profession had a similar effect on him.

As the Somerset team's reputation and support spread beyond the West Country, Vic (alongside Peter Roebuck) sat somewhere between the superstars and the unsung heroes. It's a great place to be if, like Vic, you're happy to let others take the plaudits.

Ian Botham, in particular, was implacably of the view that Vic's contributions were underestimated and banged the drum loudly for his inclusion in the England team. In the event, Vic would be awarded six England caps and appear in thirty-four One Day Internationals. An instinctive and free-flowing but not an aggressive batsman, he was unlikely to leave alone any ball outside off-stump and was unconcerned by hidden trickery such as the wrong 'un. His bowling was equally uncomplicated and involved bowling a full length at the leg stump unerringly, supported by a heavily-loaded leg-side field. Surprisingly economical for a spin bowler and capable of five-wicket hauls, he stepped into the breach on occasions with the bat and steered his team home when the big guns had overreached themselves and left the side in an unexpectedly parlous state. The 1984 season in particular would prove a triumph, with 1,262 first-class runs at an average of over fifty and eighty-six first-class wickets. It was a momentous year in other respects, too. Vic had begun to establish a career as a writer. A steady output of books began with his whimsical *Somerset County Cricket Scrapbook*, published in 1984. His later books have included, among other titles, *The Wisden Illustrated History of Cricket* and *Marks Out of XI*, an account of the England tour of India and Australia in 1984-85. Perhaps the most important milestone on that tour was Vic's baptism as a *Test Match Special* summariser. With a tense end suddenly and unexpectedly on the cards in the Delhi Test and Mike Selvey laid low as his gut fauna waged war with unexpected microscopic Indian invaders, Peter Baxter stuck his head into the England dressing room and alighted on Vic, who rose to the task with aplomb. A future as a *TMS* summariser beckoned.

The decision to appoint Ian Botham as Somerset's captain ahead of the 1984 season had been flawed but understandable. England made the same mistake – the error of assuming that star performers make great leaders, that charisma trumps strategic thinking. The decision to then appoint Peter Roebuck as Ian's successor came as a surprise to many. Perhaps Michael Hill and the Committee had misinterpreted Vic's natural diffidence as a lack of self-confidence. Maybe they saw the man who had twirled his hair when he had it in abundance, or rubbed his ear or tugged at his beard when he sported one, and thought that this betrayed nervousness rather than thoughtfulness. His world-weary demeanour as he sloped to the middle, dragging his bat behind him, or his apologetic manner when he took a wicket, were subtle signals – perhaps unwitting ones – that often caused opponents to underestimate his skills. Perhaps they blinded the Committee, too. Had Vic Marks been made Somerset captain in 1984 or in 1986, then civil war might not have broken out. Calm would have prevailed. Compromises would have been sought. With a few astute signings and some careful diplomacy, success could have continued. As it happened, when all hell broke loose, Vic was on the other side of the globe, plying his trade for Western Australia in what proved a successful all-round campaign. Rod Marsh had invited him over for a season of Sheffield Shield cricket – 'I think I was the third choice,' Vic says, with his usual modesty, 'some way behind Pat Pocock.' He had earlier been blooded in the rough and tumble world of Grade cricket, enjoying an eye-opening season with Bayswater Morley CC in Perth, where sledging was as much a fact of everyday life for a cricketer as sunshine.

After a Benefit season, he became Somerset's captain for one year in 1989 (when Peter Roebuck could take the strain no more) before handing the reins to Chris Tavaré, who had walked through the portals of St John's College on the same day as Vic, fifteen years earlier. By the time his playing career ended, Vic had played 275 first-class games for Somerset, averaging 30.53 with the bat and taking 738 wickets at 32.88 apiece. Although he

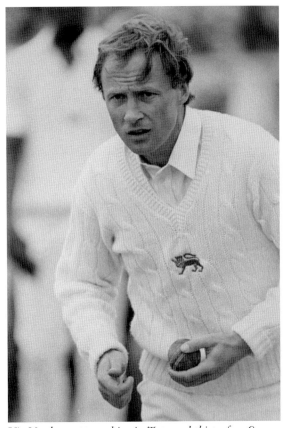

Vic Marks – appeared in six Tests and thirty-four One Day Internationals

would ideally have stayed at the County Ground for one further season, a better offer had come his way. Already writing for *The Observer* on an occasional basis, he was given the opportunity to become their lead cricket correspondent. A new chapter had begun in which, his playing days behind him, Vic would write both for *The Observer* and *The Guardian*, and his would become a familiar voice on the BBC.

He enjoys life as somewhat of an elder statesman, his roles having included that of Vice President of the Cricket Society and for a while Chairman of Cricket at Somerset. He remains as personable as ever. As Viv Richards has written, 'You would never hear him say anything bad about anyone.' And how do his teammates and colleagues see Vic Marks? Not one of them has a bad word to say of him, either.

1976

"It is, no doubt, Somerset's destiny to continue to enchant us by just failing to win anything."

Alan Gibson

Championship Position: 7 of 17

With Viv Richards away on international duty amassing copious amounts of runs for the West Indies, dominating the England attack and delighting even die-hard England supporters with his brilliance, it was left to others to ply their trade for Somerset. In the event, there were once again signs of hope. Brian Rose had hit the heights. His 1,624 runs were, in the words of David Foot, 'composed with genuine élan'. Peter Denning also topped 1,000 runs, as did Ian Botham, maturing into an outstanding all-rounder, capable in the opinion of locals of going all the way to the top of his profession. Ian indeed claimed most first-class wickets – sixty-six of them – with Hallam Moseley also making inroads with fifty-eight victims. The season was a memorable one for Brian Close, called up unexpectedly at the age of forty-five for three Test appearances.

Somerset's seven Championship wins, leading to seventh position, were encouraging, but, for most supporters of the club, the defining moments of the season were the last few balls of the final John Player Special League match of the season – against Glamorgan – when the team failed by one run to secure the tie that would have landed them the Sunday League title. After more than a century, silverware – whether first-class or List A trophies – remained beyond their grasp.

Perhaps even more of a concern than the inability to get over the line was the loss of Tom Cartwright, a man of unbending principle who felt slighted after a disagreement with club officials over his readiness to return from injury. He left for Glamorgan. With the benefit of hindsight, his impact on the club's fortunes – particularly as a coach and mentor – is inestimable. All his charges – 'Tom's boys' – are agreed on that. Among the crop of youngsters breaking through in 1976 were two local lads, Colin Dredge and Trevor Gard, both of whom would become part of the fabric and folklore of the club for many a year.

480
Trevor Gard
26 May 1976 v. West Indians, Taunton

Trevor Gard was a homegrown wicket-keeper who served Somerset cricket royally and loyally for eighteen seasons, for many of those as a patient deputy, first to Derek Taylor and then to Neil Burns. An immensely popular team man, he was happy to play a supporting role but even more delighted to enjoy some moments in the sun. The highlight of his career was undoubtedly the NatWest Final against Kent at Lord's in 1983, when his two lightning leg-side stumpings proved decisive in a match that Somerset won by twenty-four runs. 'I still vividly recall those stumpings and the shocking bright yellow gloves Trev was wearing,' his good friend and former teammate Julian Wyatt jokes.

Trevor was born in West Lambrook on 2 June 1957 and remains a true countryman, rooted in the Somerset countryside. The son of David Gard, a truck driver, and Brenda (née Clarke), who worked as a seamstress, he was educated at Huish Episcopi Secondary School, where he was fortunate to come under the aegis of Reg Pitman, who drew him to Somerset's attention. 'There was no proper infrastructure in those days. It was a matter of luck,' Trevor says. 'If you went to a state school, you were reliant on being at the right place at the right time. I was fortunate to have that encouragement from Reg Pitman and then to learn from the likes of Tom Cartwright and Derek Taylor.'

At sixteen, he was given his first airing with the Somerset Second XI. Known to teammates affectionately as 'Little Grump', Trevor went about the business of wicket-keeping with quiet efficiency. At 5 feet 7 inches he was a compact and nimble keeper. Having been advised by Tom Cartwright to obtain a qualification outside of cricket, he began a four-year engineering apprenticeship with Westland Helicopters Ltd. The company was hugely supportive of Somerset cricket and of Yeovil Town FC, releasing apprentices at the end of each off-season while they qualified. They were one of a number of such businesses in the region. Trevor thus trained as a lathe turner.

He waited patiently in the wings as deputy to Derek Taylor, playing regularly for the Second XI and enjoying some forays into the first-class arena from 1976, but he finally became Somerset's first choice keeper in 1983. In the intervening period,

Trevor Gard – a selfless and immensely popular team member for eighteen seasons

Trevor had left Westland Helicopters and gone on to work in the off-seasons for an engineering firm, Cerdic, based in Chard. He had also undertaken casual farm work on occasions. Very much a man of the country, his hobbies beyond the world of cricket included the rearing of pheasants and chickens and the breeding of ferrets. If his fourth prize with a chicken at the Devon & Exeter Show was a source both of some pride and of gentle ribbing by his colleagues, then his contribution to his county's success in 1983 drew unqualified praise from his teammates. His five catches in the NatWest quarter-final against Sussex had earned him a treasured Man of the Match award (ahead of Joel Garner, who had played an equally critical role with figures of 4 for 8 in 11 overs). Ian Botham had guided Somerset home in the semi-final against Middlesex in a tight game where scores were tied, but Somerset won on the basis of fewer wickets lost (although with 3 for 23 from 11 overs, Joel Garner was yet again unlucky to miss out on the Man of the Match award). In the final, Trevor turned the tide with two superb stumpings and Vic Marks guided Somerset to victory with useful runs and 3 for 30, although once again Joel Garner was unfortunate not to be considered Man of the Match with a return of 2 for 15 from 9 overs. It was Trevor, though – the man who had waited so long to lay his hands on a trophy – who insisted on sleeping that night with the trophy in his bed.

Ian Botham would express displeasure at his friend's being replaced and returned to the Second XI by Peter Roebuck, as Somerset rebuilt after the 'civil war' of 1986. Ian and Trevor had known each other since their youth, having both grown up in South East Somerset, often playing against one another during their schooldays and joining the staff at the County Ground at a similar time. Ian was not alone, though, in ruing what he saw as scant regard for Trevor's loyalty and his fine performances behind the stumps. In his defence, Peter Roebuck was looking to bolster the batting with Trevor's replacement, Neil Burns, a man capable of compiling first-class centuries. 'I'd hoped they might have at least given me the chance to be first choice in 1987 and put the onus on me to keep my place,' Trevor observes, 'but I don't dwell on these things: they did what they felt they needed to do.' He remained affable and the consummate professional, with Neil Burns for one expressing gratitude that his predecessor demonstrated not an ounce of resentment. In Neil's words, 'He wished me every success for the season and offered me his assistance at any time.'

Married in 1979 to Amanda (née Bailey), known as Mandy, who worked in the local government offices at Yeovil, he would have no children and the couple were later divorced. Despite having appeared only for the Second XI since 1986, he was granted a joint Benefit Year (with Dennis Breakwell) in 1989. This unexpected honour was lauded by the club's supporters as a welcome gesture and a fitting reward for Trevor's years of uncomplaining service. He would in fact make two final first-class appearances in 1989. Over the course of 112 matches, he had averaged 13.75 with the bat, including three half-centuries, and had effected 217 dismissals. Back in 1983, against Sussex, with the victory for the visitors a formality, captain Brian Rose caused amusement by handing Trevor the ball. Opener Gehan Mendis, undeterred by the risk of being despatched in humiliation to the pavilion, duly sent two deliveries to the boundary. Sussex had won by ten wickets, Trevor came away with career bowling stats of 0 for 8 in two deliveries and a select few diehard supporters can claim, 'I was there when Trevor Gard bowled for Somerset.'

Trevor confesses that although he loved playing the game, he was never an avid watcher, although he has attended reunions at the County Ground on a number of occasions. Since leaving the game, he has enjoyed a long career as a truck driver. After a spell with Pattemores, based in Crewkerne, at the wheel of dairy tankers, he spent a further nineteen years hauling grain for Patten Brothers, located in Ilminster. Having been made redundant in 2014, he returned to Pattemores. Whereas in the past he drove around Europe, he now completes local runs. 'I'm done with sleeping in trucks,' he says. 'I'm too old for that these days.'

His interests are still very much centred on the countryside he loves and knows intimately. A fine shot, he enjoys few things more than bagging a pheasant or two for the pot, but says his real passion these days is his ponies. He keeps four of them – three of the four being rescue animals. He joins the ranks of those Somerset-born players whom the supporters were able to relate to as one of their own. While others might have attracted more headlines during the trophy-laden years of the late 1970s and early 1980s, Trevor, one of the quiet members of the squad, is still remembered with fondness by the rank and file and teammates alike.

481
Nicholas John Evans
5 June 1976 v. Worcestershire, Worcester

Nick Evans has the distinction of having taken the field for England against India, albeit as twelfth man, while he was on the ground staff at Lord's during the 1971 season. He had also earlier enjoyed an airing as twelfth man in the England Young Cricketers match against their West Indies counterparts, the previous season. Nick had joined the ground staff in 1970, directly on leaving Uphill Secondary Modern School. Initially encouraged by his sports master – Gerry Williams – who saw his young charge's potential, he then came under the wing of former Middlesex and Glamorgan player, Len Muncer, at the time head coach at Lord's.

Born in Weston-super-Mare on 9 September 1954, Nick was the son of Peter John Evans, an electrician, and Rosemary (née Sara), a hairdresser. Having been raised in the county and introduced to club cricket at the age of twelve, Nick's progress had been noted by Somerset. After his two-year stint at Lord's, he was offered a contract with his home county and played regularly for the Somerset Second XI and Under-25s. He describes those years as 'the best time of my life' and learned an enormous amount, not just from wily old pros such as Peter Robinson, Brian Close and Merv Kitchen, but also from 'playing in the same side as some of the best cricketers on the planet'. The flipside of being in elevated company was that the chances of a place in the First XI diminished as the likes of Ian Botham and Viv Richards and later Joel Garner

Nick Evans – a fine club cricketer from Weston-super-Mare, who played only one first-class game for Somerset

became established. Nick made his only first-class appearance, against Worcestershire in 1976, not troubling the scorers with the bat and claiming no wickets while conceding 62 runs. At the end of the 1977, season he left to join Glamorgan for two-years but, dogged by injury, was then forced to retire.

He would continue to enjoy success in club cricket with Weston-super-Mare CC, including a return to his old stamping ground of Lord's for the William Younger Cup final of 1986, against Stourbridge. He remained a member of the team until the age of forty. Married in 1979 to Linda (née Say), who also hailed from Weston-on-super-Mare, he would have two daughters, one of whom, Samantha, played cricket for Somerset CCC Women while the other, Kelly, now lives in Australia.

Since retiring from the first-class game in 1979, Nick has enjoyed a number of spells as a National Accounts Manager, overseeing the sales function for a disparate collection of companies. After a six-year period with Patrick Sports, a Belgian sportswear company, he enjoyed a long period in the horticultural industry with Monsanto and then Arthur Bowers. Following a brief spell in kitchen supplies he has been employed latterly by Kings Seeds, who have been supplying seeds (and more recently plug plants) since 1888. Whilst not quite able to claim such longevity, Nick continues, at the time of writing, to enjoy his career in sales at the age of sixty-three.

A likeable man, clearly comfortable in and well-suited to his role as a salesman, Nick is now a proud grandfather, still a follower of Somerset cricket, still delighted to have played cricket for the county he loves and ready to regale his Australian-born granddaughter, Scarlet, with stories of how he took the field for the old enemy, England.

Nick Evans at the centre of a galaxy of star jumps: the Somerset players being put through their paces are Bob Clapp, John Hook and Derek Taylor, Keith Jennings and Nick Evans, Andy Wagner, who now coaches at Radley College, and Jeremy Lloyds, Dennis Breakwell (back to camera), Andy Ashfold, who has latterly played for Somerset Over-60s, and Allan Jones, Graham Burgess and Peter Denning (back to camera) COURTESY OF JOHN HOOK

482
Colin Herbert Dredge
16 June 1976 v. Worcestershire, Bath

Col: Dredy

Known to teammates as 'Herbie', he was dubbed 'The Demon of Frome' by writer and commentator Alan Gibson. There was irony in the idea that such an even-tempered man should have been so named. Colin Dredge was a huge favourite with the fans and the sort of man any captain would welcome into the fold. Although his delivery became more streamlined over the years, he was never blessed with the most aesthetically pleasing of bowling actions, but was nonetheless effective and never gave anything less than heart and soul for Somerset. Here was a man who refused to allow trifling matters such as the pain barrier or exhaustion to daunt him: he would have walked through walls for his various captains. In the words of David Foot, 'Frome never produced a better workhorse.' One one occasion, Joel Garner felt moved to intervene, berating his captain, Peter Roebuck, for persisting with 'Herbie' when he was on the verge of collapse. One volume of the *Benson & Hedges Cricket Year* cites the 'constant professional application by a fine seam bowler', adding that 'he represents all that is good in county cricket'.

Others might have gained the plaudits but his teammates knew his worth, not just on the field of play but off it, too, as one of the side's jesters. He is said often to have been the last to arrive at the County Ground after a commute from Frome. There would be a crashing noise and 'Herbie' would stagger into the changing room, clutching his head and claiming to have cracked it on the lintel. The joke continued to amuse his teammates, as did the times when the mood was leavened whenever the newspaper he was reading would seemingly spontaneously combust. His old jokes were his best.

Born in Frome on 4 August 1954, he was one of ten offspring of Frederick and Kathleen Dredge. He was brought up, along with his seven brothers and two sisters, in the town where his father worked for the venerable printing firm, Butler and Tanner. Educated at Milk Street Primary School in the town and then Oakfield School, Colin grew into a useful all-round sportsman, 6 feet 5 inches tall and a 'beanpole', in the words of Viv Richards, whom he caught and bowled with his first delivery in a match between Lansdown CC and Frome CC, when the pair were still unknowns. 'I only caught it because it was coming at me like a bullet and otherwise might have killed me,' Colin would later quip. In truth, he had a safe pair of hands and would hang on to many a catch in the outfield in his first-class career.

He had never planned for a life as a professional cricketer. He might have been

coached by Somerset cricketing legend, Peter Wight, but, for a brief period, Bristol City FC had a good look at
the tall striker, hard to defend against
with his height and ability to head the
ball. As it happened, he would play six
times for Bristol City FC Reserves without scoring. 'I did hit the post with a
header once, though,' he observes, smiling. He would settle for an enjoyable
career in Western League football with
Welton Rovers FC, among other sides.
Meanwhile, he served an apprenticeship
with Rolls Royce, commuting to Patch-
way, Bristol, until taking lodgings for a
while with Merv Kitchen. Merv express-
es doubts about Colin's talents as an
engineer, noting that his lodger proved
adept at taking his faulty vacuum clean-
er apart, but found it an insurmountable
challenge to reassemble it.

Colin Dredge – The Demon of Frome

In 1975, Colin and his Frome CC team, comprising in the main members of the
Dredge family, had a wondrous year, with Colin claiming 115 wickets and nearly
1,000 runs. A right-arm opening bowler, he batted left-handed with a style more
free-flowing than his bowling. Tom Cartwright would talk of Colin's 'ungainly action – all elbows and legs – drawing gasps of horror from the purists', adding that
'his head almost hit the floor when he bowled: it was one of the great achievements of
my coaching that I managed to get it up a bit.' Although Colin had begun appearing
for Somerset Second XI, he was pleasantly surprised to receive the call to play for the
First XI at Bath, in the absence of Brian Close (on international duty) and Ian Botham
(who was injured). He soon claimed the prized wicket of Glenn Turner – who accumulated runs the way Bill Gates accumulates money – with one that nipped back. It
was an early indication that he might add value to the Somerset side. As a footnote,
normal service was quickly resumed and Glenn Turner went on to score 135 not out
in the second innings. But that day would presage years of unstinting service on the
part of 'Herbie'.

In 1987, he was awarded a Benefit Year by Somerset, with many observers noting
that the tradition was made for such unsung heroes and loyal servants of any club.
In the case of the Demon of Frome, such was the folklore surrounding him and so

Colin Dredge – would have run through brick walls for his beloved county

loud the singing about his 'unsungness' that the term 'unsung hero' has proved strangely inappropriate. Over the course of thirteen seasons, toiling up the slope or into the wind for over upon relentless over, he would appear in 194 first-class fixtures, claiming 443 wickets at 30.10 apiece, his highpoint being a return of 6 for 37 against Gloucestershire in 1981. He would also claim a further 253 scalps in 209 List A games. No mug with the bat and a clean striker of the ball, his first-class average of 13.98 was boosted by four stirring half-centuries. Former England Test bowler, Geoff Miller, would remember one incident in which Colin despatched the ball into the pavilion at the County Ground through the window of the lounge where the players were relaxing around the snooker table. Ian Botham promptly appeared and lobbed out a red snooker ball, inviting Geoff Miller to try bowling with it as 'Herbie' wouldn't be able to hit it quite so far.

Married in 1978 to Mandy (née Simpson), with whom he would have three sons, all of whom would in time turn out for Frome CC in the tried and tested family tradition, Colin spent much of his career commuting from Frome to Taunton, before finally buying a property in the county town in 1985, albeit he would remain there only fleetingly. Since parting company with Somerset he has played club cricket once again with Frome CC and after more than a decade working as a toolmaker for Rolls Royce, he has latterly deployed his engineering skills working in signals and technology for National Rail. Thirty years and more after his retirement from the first-class game, the locals still remember with great fondness the man who would have run through brick walls for his beloved county.

483
David Roberts Gurr
10 July 1976 v. Derbyshire, Chesterfield

Prowess as a sportsman boils down to marrying a natural aptitude with hard graft. A successful player combines analytical thinking with the ability to deliver what is required. The purpose of practice is to embed the physical response so that the analysis is all about the desired outcome and not the mechanics. The performance should be set so deep in the muscle memory that it happens unconsciously. Practice, as they say, makes perfect. And yet, many players suffer at times a loss of confidence or a case of 'the yips'. Here is how Somerset and England's Vic Marks described in *The Guardian* what happens in such circumstances:

> *The problem is that your fingers suddenly feel like pork sausages, sweaty pork sausages at that. Meanwhile the ball somehow acquires the qualities of a melon; it will not fit in your hand. The batsman, miles down the other end, has a bat the size of a barn door and it seems that you have only seven fielders out there to defend those incredibly short boundaries.*

Vic Marks's career was not foreshortened by such problems. He was able quickly to brush aside any setbacks. Others, including his teammate, David Gurr, have been less fortunate.

David was born in Whitchurch, Buckinghamshire, on 27 March 1956, the son of a print compositor, Percy Gurr, and his wife, Mary (née Lambie), known as Maisie, who worked as a medical secretary at Buckinghamshire Hospital. David was educated at Aylesbury Grammar School, where he enjoyed academic and sporting success and was made head boy. Offered a place at Regent's Park College, Oxford University, where he studied first Theology and then Geography, he was selected to play for the Varsity side under the captaincy of Vic Marks. Having come away wicketless and slightly dispirited from his initial first-class match (against Gloucestershire), he had assumed that his career was now over and was therefore surprised when Vic informed him that his place in the team was secure. His captain's faith was rewarded when David claimed five Middlesex wickets for 73 runs in the next fixture. He remained a fixture in the Oxford University attack throughout the 1976 and 1977 seasons and was awarded a blue each year. He was a right-arm fast bowler, at times capable of hurrying a batsman. His wicket-keeper at the time, Paul Fisher, observed that David was noticeably quicker than his fellow Oxonian speedster, Imran Khan.

David Gurr – devastating when on song, his career was foreshortened by a serious case of 'the yips'

Having called time on his studies, David would leave Oxford before the completion of his degree and his efforts as a bowler and competent batsman had by then been noted by a number of admirers. He had played for Middlesex Second XI in 1975 and Middlesex were in fact one of fourteen first-class counties who made enquires, but he had been persuaded by Vic Marks that there was a likelihood of more regular first-class appearances at a county side who lacked a penetrating attack at the time.

David reflects on his time sharing the Supporters Club flat with Dennis Breakwell with something between fondness and horror. Sited a short walk from the County Ground, it was, in David's description, 'the only place I've lived in with rising damp everywhere on the ground floor and descending damp throughout the first floor. It came as something of a shock after the well-equipped facilities at Oxford.' Sadly, the only part of the house lacking moisture was the hot water tap. Tenants were obliged to make their way to the ground for a shower. The wider cricketing community knew about the flat and regarded it as a convenient source of free lodgings. David would more often than not return to find the floor littered with uninvited guests in sleeping bags. 'There was no way I could keep up with the partying,' he admits.

Ensconced at Somerset, David remained at times a devastating bowler. When he describes his approach it is clear that he was a thinker, who did not try to take a wicket with every ball but attempted to outwit the batsman, mapping each over in his head and modifying his approach in the light of events. Even during his school years, though, he had at times unexpectedly found himself conscious of the mechanics of the process, overcome by doubts, and bowling wides. 'I admired players like Both [Ian Botham], who could send down a bad ball, shrug it off and then bowl a perfect delivery,' he confesses. On his day – and consistently in the nets – David would be on fire. The testimony of Greg Chappell has made its way into Somerset cricketing folklore. Having returned to his old hunting ground, Greg was practising on the square at the County Ground with a net erected as he prepared for a Single Wicket competition. David was unplayable and, not having encountered him before, Greg had assumed he must be 'on the boat to Australia' for the forthcoming Ashes tour. And yet, at other times, David began to wonder whether or not he would even release the ball as he ran towards the wicket. Dennis Breakwell would observe that he knew what lay in store as early as the start of his erstwhile roommate's run-up.

David was astute enough to know that his capacity for analysis, which so often interrupted the flow of his bowling, could be put to more effective use. Perhaps the increased competition for the opening bowling berths had added unconsciously to his anxiety as Colin Dredge and Joel Garner established their places. But Somerset knew they had a potential match-winner on their hands and were patient as he tried to iron out his issues. It was David who made the call to end his days as a professional cricketer. 'I was aware,' he explains, 'that once you've turned thirty, your options are limited if you have no expertise beyond cricket, so I needed to begin thinking about a career before it was too late and I walked away from the first-class game on amicable terms.' The decision coincided with his marriage in 1979 to Jane (née Poole), a Taunton-based chiropodist, with whom he would have two children.

In total, he had played in twenty-four first-class games for Somerset, taking sixty-four wickets at 30.48 apiece. It is a credit to his skills as a batsman that in twenty-six innings he was only dismissed nine times. Often left high and dry, he averaged 17.88 with the bat.

After David's departure from the County Ground, a supporter of Somerset cricket pointed him towards a vacant role in Taunton with Legal & General. By accident rather than by design, he had embarked on a career that embraced initially life assurance and later fund and pension management. Having worked for companies such as Axa, Old Mutual and Deutsche Bank, he built up an impressive level of expertise, particularly in relation to legal frameworks, and in 2014, having by then opted for early redundancy, set up his own company, Diminimis Ltd, through which he trains advisers in best practice.

Away from work, David had been awarded his Level 3 coaching certificate in 2003 and he worked for a while with the late Bob Woolmer, overseeing the development of Warwickshire's Under-16s. He has also continued to coach young people in business, latterly as a volunteer for the Prince's Trust mentoring scheme.

Having returned with Jane to the outskirts of Taunton, his involvement in Somerset has been rekindled through his role as Secretary of the county's Former Players' Association, a position he has held since 2013.

1977

"I spent many happy days amongst those green hills of
Somerset and made a host of real and important friendships.
I badly wanted ... to repay a little to the county which
had given me such a warm and sincere welcome when my
cricket career seemed shattered. Unfortunately I failed in
the end but we had fun – and a few near misses."

Brian Close

Championship Position: 12 of 17

The 1977 season was notable for the absence of Brian Close and the arrival of Joel
Garner. A devastating fast bowler, Joel would form part of the trinity – Richards,
Botham and Garner – who would in time make Somerset the kings of limited-overs
cricket and render the sleepy market town of Taunton a place of excitement, glamour
and raucous celebration. Such heady days still lay in the future. For the present, the
side slipped to twelfth in the Championship table, with runs coming more readily
than wickets. Viv Richards, by now regarded by most commentators as the finest
batsman in the world, amassed 2,161 runs at 65.48, with seven centuries. Peter Denning, Brian Rose and Merv Kitchen would all exceed 1,000 runs. Ian Botham was
once again the most successful bowler, with seventy victims. The season also marked
the start of Ian's extraordinary Test career. He was straight into the action with a
five-wicket haul, but none could have foretold what was to follow. Brian Rose, too,
would be called up by England, for the winter tour of Pakistan and New Zealand.

Viv Richards's exhilarating batting apart, there were a few bright moments scat-
tered among the gloom – the victory over Australia at Bath, for example, or Peter
Roebuck's maiden century for Somerset, or Peter Denning's two centuries against
Gloucestershire – but by and large it was a disappointing time: the calm before the
storming of the citadel.

484
Joel Garner
18 May 1977 v. Australia, Bath

[signature: Joel Garner]

Joel Garner was a world class fast bowler, at times almost unplayable. 'Big Bird' was in every sense a colossus, a metaphorical giant of the game and, standing 6 feet 8 inches tall, he used every inch of his wingspan to deliver his well-aimed missiles at despairing batsmen. Former captain of Australia, Greg Chappell, has stated that, given free rein to select a limited overs side, Joel's would be the first name on the team sheet. Greg articulated the problems even the finest of batsmen had in facing the affable Barbadian. 'Good batsmen … evaluate the length of a delivery from the angle at which it leaves the bowler's hand and react accordingly. This is more difficult to do against Joel as every ball leaves the hand at an angle which suggests it will be short. Consequently, twenty years of pre-programming is wasted … He is undoubtedly one of the truly great bowlers that the game has seen.' And yet the path to greatness had not always been assured.

He was born on 16 December 1952 in Enterprise, Christ Church, at that time, in Joel's own words, 'a scattering of houses among fields of sugar cane', his family's own home being 'located at the top of a marl lane running down to the beach'. His mother, Myrna Garner, and her partner, Hutson King, left home and emigrated to Canada and the United States when Joel and his younger brother were still young, on the basis that this was their only means of finding employment. Joel and his brother were left in the care of their maternal grandmother and grandfather, Editha and Vincent, and brought up happy but impoverished. Editha was very much the head of the house, a formidable but compassionate woman whom Joel adored, despite his frequent beatings at her hand for his many misdemeanours and lapses, usually as he played cricket when he should have been undertaking various tasks. 'She wielded a mean whip,' as he put it. The family survived by managing a small kitchen garden and the chickens, pigs, goats and sheep kept in their backyard. Joel learned his cricket with improvised balls and with bats fashioned from branches of 'clammy-cherry' or coconut trees. He played on the only flat surface available to him and his friends – the main road between the cane fields, which was essentially a rolled dirt track.

Educated at St Christopher's Boys School, where lessons were held in the local church and then at Foundation Boys School, he suddenly shot up in height as his

Joel Garner – played a critical role in Somerset's success in the late 1970s and early 1980s

thirteenth birthday approached and kept growing until he reached his full height by his sixteenth birthday. At his secondary school, Joel had his first stroke of good fortune when he came under the tutelage of three West Indian greats in quick succession, viz. fast bowler Manny Martindale, followed by Sir Everton Weekes and Seymour Nurse, both stylish batsmen. At the time, Joel was an all-rounder: a batsman who tried to avoid bowling wherever possible on the batsman-friendly tracks. He was informed by Seymour Nurse that he was far too tall to be a batsman and should be bowling – fast. His second stroke of good fortune was being sent to attend coaching classes led by Charlie Griffith, which he would later call 'essays in seriousness and application'.

Having left school, Joel applied for a job with Cable and Wireless and was pleasantly surprised to receive an offer. Unbeknown to him, Wes Hall had been instrumental in securing him the role and welcomed Joel into the Cable and Wireless cricket team as his opening bowling partner. What better coaches could a young fast bowler have had than the inimitable Hall and Griffith?

Barbadian society was at the time class-ridden and, coming from a poor background, Joel found it hard to break through. On the advice of Collis King, he joined the YMPC [Young Men's Progressive Club of Barbados], where Collis played, and Joel's claims for representative honours began to gather pace. Then came an offer to expand his cricketing education with a contract at Littleborough in the Central Lancashire League in 1976, as Garry Sobers's replacement. It was a step into the unknown for the Bajan from the sticks, but he was welcomed into the fold in Lancashire. With his engaging personality and a haul of 110 wickets and 507 runs in his first season, the locals loved him and dubbed him 'Little Bird', Joel noting with droll good humour that the moniker 'was refreshing after some of the things I was called on some of the other grounds'. He would, of course, later become more widely known as 'Big Bird'. Somerset knew a good thing when they saw it and leapt in to secure a contract for Joel from the 1977 season.

If the Barbadian authorities had been dilatory about promoting Joel's cause, the same was not true of the members of the West Indies team and Alvin Kallicharran and Clive Lloyd persuaded him to join them as participants in the breakaway World Series Cricket orchestrated by Kerry Packer. Although the players were jeopardising their Test careers, there was no hesitation. Here was money that Joel could only ever previously have dreamed of and a chance for him to provide for the grandmother who had nurtured him. He was a huge success both for the West Indies and for Somerset. His achievements are extraordinary.

It is widely acknowledged that batsmen win you limited overs matches and bowlers are the ones to secure victory in the longer form of the game. Which renders Joel Garner's performances exceptional. Consider this. In the Prudential World Cup Final of 1979 he took 5 for 38 in 11 overs. Only Viv Richards's imperious century denied Joel the Man of the Match award. A couple of months later, in the Gillette Cup Final, he took 6 for 29 in 10.3 overs but was once again pipped to the Man of the Match award by Viv. History repeated itself in the Benson & Hedges Final in 1981. 5 for 14 from 11 overs and once more Viv plucked the Man of the Match Award from under Joel's nose. Even his 2 for 15 from 9 overs in the 1983 NatWest Trophy Final was not enough to win him the Man of the Match award. All of which goes to show that bowlers can win one-day matches, even if adjudicators are sometimes inclined to overlook the fact and favour the batsmen.

Joel's statistics speak for themselves. As well as appearing in fifty-eight Tests as part of the fearsome foursome who terrorised opposing batsmen, his ninety-eight ODI matches yielded 146 wickets at only 18.84 apiece. For Somerset, he played in ninety-four first-class matches and claimed 338 wickets at 18.10 apiece. In 128 List A matches, he claimed 206 victims at 15.15 apiece and could boast an astonishingly good economy rate of 2.89 an over. As for his batting – a source of wry amusement to teammates as he vowed continually that he would curb his attacking instincts, only to abandon all thoughts of defence after a couple of deliveries – his average of 18.00 was compiled with some lusty blows as he swung the bat in an enormous arc.

He was a popular figure with a lovely, laid-back Bajan demeanour and a great sense of fun. There is a well-worn anecdote about the time a female admirer summoned the courage to ask him if he was 'all in proportion', to which Joel responded with his uninhibited laugh that if everything were in proportion, he would be ten feet tall. Down-to-earth, he enjoyed socialising and he loved driving, thinking nothing of commuting up to Lancashire and back in a day to catch up with old friends, always happy to take responsibility for cooking – another of his passions. Nor did he ever forget his humble beginnings. Former England cricketer Derek Pringle recalls being taken to a food stall in Barbados, run by Joel's former dinner lady. Joel

insisted it offered the best food on the island, apparently adding that, 'I been eating this since I was six. How else you think I got this big?'

Towards the end of his time with Somerset he was blighted by injuries that curtailed his appearances. If, as some have argued, his time was up, then it is certainly the case that those he served so well could have and should have handled events with more sensitivity. Joel is not one to bear grudges, but when asked about the background to his departure, he lays the blame firmly at the door of Peter Roebuck. He described his erstwhile Somerset captain at the time as, 'a man who lacks sensitivity

Big Bird – one of the most effective limited-overs bowlers in history

and good sense. I've never met a man who's read so much and knows so little ... He is an incredibly moody man; but we accepted him as he was ... He is representative of that force in English cricket that is seeking to drag down others to accommodate itself instead of raising standards.' Strong words from a forthright and honest man who gave everything for his adoptive county and one who cared enough to come along to the infamous showdown at Shepton Mallet, although he had the good grace to keep his counsel.

After leaving Somerset, he continued to play in Barbados and also starred for a season as the pro at Oldham CC, taking ninety wickets for them in a reprise of his earlier adventures in Lancashire League Cricket. In 1993, he returned to Somerset to play for Glastonbury CC, his £6,000 salary paid for by local sponsors. He later agreed to become President of the club. Back in Barbados, he has since 2007 been President of the Barbados Cricket Association and in 2010 stood in as West Indies tour manager. Joel is still feted wherever he goes – nowhere more so than in his beloved homeland. He was married back in 1986 to Heather, and their daughter, Jewel, is a popular figure on the island, awarded the title of Miss Barbados in 2007 and representing the island in the Miss Universe pageant. She retained the title for nine years, attending numerous formal functions, and is now an attorney.

Players have arrived at the club and have gone some way towards filling the gap left by Viv Richards and Ian Botham. Jimmy Cook amassed runs. Graham Rose took games by storm with his muscular, all-round pyrotechnics. But no one has ever come close to filling the void left by Joel's departure. Some might argue that, for all the brilliance of Viv and Ian, without Joel their efforts might well have been in vain.

Joel Garner – a popular figure with a lovely, laid-back Bajan demeanour and a great sense of fun

485
Martin Olive
15 June 1977 v. Glamorgan, Cardiff

How many of us are able to tell our grandchildren that we once partnered one of cricket's all-time greats? Martin Olive regards it an enormous privilege to have opened the batting on a number of occasions during the 1980 season with Sunil Gavaskar. It is easy to be overawed, walking out to the wicket with a hero at your side, but the modest Sunny was able to put his junior partner's mind at ease. 'He was so supportive,' Martin recalls, 'and such a gentleman.'

Born in Watford, Hertfordshire, on 18 April 1958, Martin was the son of Dan Olive, at the time an architect, and Margaret (née Bulley), a teacher. The family moved to Somerset when Dan opted for a career change and trained as a Church of England priest, becoming Rector of Mells, near Frome. Sent to Wells Cathedral Junior School, Martin was encouraged to apply for a sports scholarship to Millfield School by the Wells Cathedral School cricket coach, Alan Whitehead (formerly of Somerset and later a Test umpire). Arriving in his new surroundings in April 1970, he progressed through the county junior and English schools ranks and was selected for the England Under-19 team in 1977. By then he had already established himself as a batsman for Somerset Second XI, appearing alongside a number of players who would graduate to the First XI. Also among his teammates at that time was the Australian, Trevor Chappell, brother of Ian and Greg, the latter having graced the Somerset scene in the late 1960s.

Having been fortunate enough to enjoy the tutelage of Alan Whitehead, Martin then benefited from the mentoring skills of Tom Cartwright, who drove him regularly during the winter months from Mells to the Indoor Nets at Taunton, which were led by Tom, working alongside Peter Robinson. Having left Millfield in 1979, Martin began studying for a teacher training qualification at St Paul's College in Cheltenham but after two terms heeded the advice of Ken Palmer, who informed him that if he was serious about the idea of a first-class career, he should join the Somerset playing staff without further delay. In the event, Martin's career never quite progressed as he might have hoped, with only occasional appearances, the majority of them in the 1980 season, during which, against Yorkshire at Weston-super-Mare, he registered his only half-century, a feat upstaged by his opening partner, Sunny Gavaskar, who had notched up 155 not out in the first innings.

Martin left the County Ground in 1981. In seventeen first-class appearances, he had mustered a batting average of 15.56. Having forsaken a career in teaching – a decision over which he harboured no regrets – Martin joined the Western Counties Building Society and after three months was appointed manager of the company's new flagship store in Exeter. The sparkling new edifice proved enticing not only to customers but also to felons. In the financial world's equivalent of being faced with a bouncer from Jeff Thomson in your first over as a batsman, the premises were the subject of an armed hold-up on day one. Martin held his nerve. Those years as a steadfast opener had not been in vain. He enjoyed two successful and mercifully less eventful years with Western Counties before joining AXA Equity and Law, initially

Martin Olive – regards it as a privilege to have opened the batting with Sunil Gavaskar

as a sales consultant and then in increasingly senior roles. In the earlier years he continued to play cricket, for Devon, but having been married in 1980 to Catherine Powell, known as Cathy, with whom he would have four sons, the demands of a career and of raising a family meant that after 1987 he stood down from Minor Counties cricket.

After three years as a Key Accounts Manager with AXA, he enjoyed a further ten years as Key Accounts Director for the newly merged AXA Sun Life business. After a subsequent spell with Sun Life Financial of Canada, he joined Partnership Assurance in 2011 and then from 2013 he was employed in a senior role by Now: Pensions, the UK arm of a huge Danish pension provider.

Having retired in 2017, Martin, very much a family man, has now found himself able to spend more time with his wife and four sons and their children. These days, he is more likely to be holding a golf club than a cricket bat but he retains fond memories of a brief first-class career with Somerset in the metaphorical firing line as an opening batsman and rather less fond memories of his very first day quite literally in the firing line as he embarked on a successful twenty-five year career in the financial services sector.

1978

"Last Summer put years on me."

Brian Rose

Championship Position: 5 of 17

Brian Rose was handed the captaincy, making him the youngest man among the counties in the role. Some doubters wondered about the wisdom of choosing the quiet and often forgetful horticulturalist. Not the team, though. And the doubters would be proved wrong. Brian would become the most successful captain in the club's history, capable of channelling the efforts of his collection of stars and supporting cast and bringing the best out of them. Perhaps only after he had gone would everyone begin to understand his worth.

Viv Richards was in sparkling form, and Brian Rose and Phil Slocombe both scored well in excess of 1,000 runs. Despite being away on Test duty, Ian Botham was once more the leading wicket-taker, although in 1978 there was a strong supporting cast – Colin Dredge, Hallam Moseley, Dennis Breakwell and Keith Jennings – all chipping in with a decent haul of wickets.

Fifth place in the Championship was a worthy return for the team, with nine games won. But the season was defined by the final weekend when the Gillette Cup Final was lost as Sussex turned the screw and then, the very next day, Somerset went into the final round of John Player matches as red hot favourites to win the title but fell an agonising two runs short of triumphing. Tears were shed in the dressing room and Viv famously smashed his bat in frustration.

Hurt by their failure to land the prizes, emboldened by the unwavering support of the crowds, bonded as a result of having grown up together – many of them since they were young boys – and united in their love of the club, the team were determined to learn from their bitter experiences and become winners. As Ian Botham wrote at the time, 'I enjoy playing for England, of course, and I enjoy success with England, but nothing could beat being part of the first Somerset team to win a trophy.'

With a settled squad in situ, there was no need to call on any debutants.

1979

"No longer will critics write Somerset down as underdogs: they have at last built a team which will rise to greater heights."

Graham Burgess

Championship Position: 8 of 17

If Graham Burgess was able to bow out of the first-class game with a winner's medal after thirteen seasons of hurt, then younger members of what was now an outstanding team could look forward to further glories. The frustrations of the final weekend of the 1978 season were more than matched by the heady feeling of landing two titles – the Gillette Cup and the John Player Special League – in 1979. It had all started so badly. The bookies' favourites for the Benson & Hedges Cup, the team had made an ill-judged decision – perhaps stemming from their fear of falling at the last hurdle – to secure their passage from the group stage with an unsporting declaration against Worcestershire that preserved their run rate. The opprobrium of the cricketing establishment and the team's ejection from the tournament served to galvanise the supporters and team alike. In the words of Brian Rose, 'The whole experience strengthened the backbone of the team. We were hardened by it. It made us a lot more resolute, less like the Somerset of old.'

Viv Richards, with a century, and Joel Garner, with six wickets, stole the headlines at Lord's, but others had paved the way to the final, too. A day later, at Trent Bridge, the vital victory (while elsewhere, Kent stumbled) was secured by a workmanlike team effort with everyone contributing one way or another. The team might have had everything under control, but the nerves of the supporters were shredded. The joy that followed was unconfined.

In the Championship, the team coped with the absence for half their fixtures of Ian Botham, away on Test duty. Brian Rose, Peter Roebuck, Peter Denning and Viv Richards all topped 1,000 runs and Vic Marks, Joel Garner and Dennis Breakwell all took a significant number of wickets, in Joel's case at a parsimonious 13.83 apiece. But too many matches – fifteen of them – were drawn on tracks too placid.

The two debutants – Jeremy Lloyds and Nigel Popplewell – were both successful additions to the bumper crop of talent already unearthed in a heart-warming and ultimately uplifting decade for Somerset cricket.

486
Jeremy William Lloyds
23 June 1979 v. Cambridge University, Bath

[signature: Jeremy Lloyds]

Jeremy (or Jerry) Lloyds was born on 17 November 1954 in George Town, Penang, Malaysia, the son of Edwin William and Grace Cicely. His father oversaw the Royal Dutch Shell oil tankers in the Far East, based in Singapore. His mother had worked in the Cypher Office in the War Rooms and had been a member of Harold Macmillan's staff. The couple had met after the Second World War in Chungking (Chongqing) in China. After twenty-five years working overseas with Shell, Edwin returned with his family to England in 1961.

Educated at primary level in Somerset before going on to Blundell's in Devon, Jeremy starred at school alongside Vic Marks at both cricket and rugby. A fly-half to Vic's scrum-half, Jeremy would go on to captain Taunton RFC during the 1977-78 season. An all-rounder, he batted left-handed and bowled right-arm off-spin. Vic would write during their playing days that 'his off-spinners, it is embarrassing to relate, have a tendency to spin more than mine' and nor is this false modesty on Vic's part. Tom Cartwright, who coached them both, agrees, although, as Tom would write, 'Vic acquired good changes of trajectory and flight.' Initially viewed as one of 'Tom's boys' – the group of talented youngsters who broke through in the mid-1970s – Jeremy was already appearing for the Somerset Second XI as an eighteen-year-old in 1973, but the county were reluctant to offer a contract. For eighteen months he worked – appropriately enough – with Lloyds Bank, but decided that a career in cricket was his preferred option, handing in his notice when he was offered a place on the Lord's ground staff in 1975. He would remain there for four seasons, honing his skills. Jeremy is nothing if not determined to succeed in his chosen path and tenacious in reaching his goals. Finally, after a winter coaching at St Stithian's College in Johannesburg, Jeremy was belatedly given his chance at Somerset, although he would not be offered a full-time contract until 1980, at the age of twenty-five. His friend and schoolmate, Vic Marks, has suggested that the only reason Somerset procrastinated for so long was that he was thought to be 'too chancy or too casual at the crease', although he certainly tightened up his technique once given his opportunity in first-class cricket. Perhaps he had begun to apply the skills he had passed on to others as a coach.

If Jeremy's flirtation with the world of banking was brief, then his commitment to a career in cricket was correspondingly resolute. A lifetime in the game awaited. He would remain with Somerset until 1984, playing for the county in one hundred

Jeremy Lloyds – a successful all-rounder who left for Gloucestershire in 1984

first-class fixtures and coming away with a batting average of 28.42, including five centuries. Two of those hundreds had come in one match against Northamptonshire in June 1982 when he scored 132 not out and 102 not out. It was a bizarre drawn game in which only one Somerset wicket fell and Jeremy notched up two thirds of the runs accumulated by his side, Peter Roebuck stubbornly holding up the other end. His bowling yielded 133 wickets at 34.84 apiece with six five-wicket hauls. But any personal triumphs were dwarfed by the pleasure of being on the winning side in the NatWest Final of 1983.

He expressed his wish to leave the club at the end of the 1984 season. Determined to utilise and develop his talents rather than to settle for a future on the fringes of the team, he asked to be released, with a heavy heart and some honest observations about how the running of the club could be improved. He duly departed – though, sadly, his warning that the club was headed for choppy waters went unheeded.

He would then spend seven productive seasons with Gloucestershire, where there was more scope to apply his all-round skills as batsman, bowler and a fine slip fielder, who would claim 229 first-class catches. He would appear for his new county in 166 first-class fixtures, here taking his career tally up to 333 first-class wickets and over 10,500 runs.

His appetite for the game seemingly insatiable, Jeremy had continued to play and coach abroad each off-season (barring the winter of 1985-86 when he felt a pressing need for a short break from the game).In addition to two seasons at St Stithian's, he enjoyed a number of spells in various Australian states and a season in Cape Town. During the 1980s, he was selected on occasions for the Orange Free State side and was the leading run scorer in Western Province league cricket in 1988-89.

Once his playing days were over, he enjoyed a number of years coaching in South Africa. In 1992, he set up a Youth Programme in Western Province and then in 1995 enjoyed a reprise of his role as coach at St Stithian's College in Johannesburg, a role he remained in until 1998. He was married in 1997 to Janine, an Orthopaedic Nursing Sister at Constantiaberg Clinic who had a daughter, Kaeli. Soon thereafter, he entered the third phase of his cricketing odyssey, joining the Umpires List. Having earned his spurs, he officiated in his first County Championship matches in 1998 and would go on to become a Test Umpire in 2004. He rose immediately to the challenge. If Jeremy had hoped for an easy entrée then he was to be disappointed. In his very first delivery, Pedro Collins of the West Indies rapped the pad of Bangladesh's opener, Hannan Sarkar. Pausing for a moment, Jeremy raised his finger. He had been thrown in at the deep end but video replays showed his decision to be spot-on. Could his mettle be put to a sterner test? Yes. In the following Test, exactly the same scenario was played out. The first ball of the innings. Pedro Collins was the bowler. The ball struck Hannan Sarkar's pad. The finger was again raised. Another heart-stopping moment, but once more he was proved correct. As Jeremy later reflected, 'Dav Whatmore, the Bangladesh coach, came up to me at lunch and said it was a brave thing to do and not everybody might have done it.' It takes nerves of steel as well as technical know-how to be a Test Match umpire. He would officiate in five Tests and remains at the time of writing a first-class umpire. He also continues to coach during the off-season, latterly at Radley College.

Jeremy lists golf among his main interests outside the world of cricket and has also developed into somewhat of a connoisseur of fine wine, influenced by having worked for much of his adult life in established wine-growing regions. Like the choice wines he is happy to imbibe, Jeremy was slow to mature as a young cricketer, but has subsequently stood the test of time. Much-travelled during his career as player, coach and umpire, he now resides in Gloucestershire.

487
Nigel Francis Mark Popplewell
28 July 1979 v. India, Taunton

Born on 8 August 1957 in Farnborough, Kent, and brought up for a brief period in Chislehurst and then in Buckinghamshire, Nigel was the son of Oliver Popplewell (later Sir Oliver) and Margaret (née Storey). His father had played cricket for Cambridge University as a wicket-keeper-batsman but was more noted as a high court judge who, among his other duties, chaired the enquiry into the fire at Bradford City's Valley Parade ground, where fifty-six lives were lost in 1985.

Nigel attended Radley College and captained the First XI in his final year there, leading from the front with 720 runs at an average of 45.00 and sixty wickets at 10.18. Offered the opportunity to read Natural Sciences at Selwyn College, he first enjoyed a gap year, employed on a temporary basis in Macclesfield, working in the pharmaceutical industry, before lodging in Hampshire with his good friend, Mark Nicholas, and indulging in two summers of cricket there. At Cambridge he not only appeared in twenty-five first-class matches but also encountered Peter Roebuck, who played his part in poaching the promising all-rounder. Having written to Nigel, Peter received a self-deprecating response that if Somerset were interested in signing a 'Mickey Mouse all-rounder', then he was happy to give it a go. Peter facilitated an indoor trial at Somerset in the early months of 1977, but the catalyst for the offer of professional terms was his performance for Cambridge University against Somerset at Bath later that year, when he took 3 for 18 and then scored forty-four of his team's ninety-eight runs in their second innings. Two weeks later, he was phoned by Peter Robinson and offered a contract. After a period in a 'lonely bedsit in Galmington', Nigel was invited to share a newly-acquired house in Monkton Heathfield with his

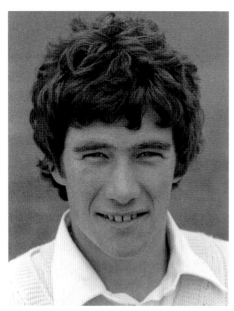

Nigel Popplewell – his sometimes exhilarating performances were combined with an unfailing zest for life

fellow Cantabrigian, Peter Roebuck. Peter's otherworldly existence is the stuff of legend, but Nigel garnered first-hand evidence of a lifestyle that verged at times on the chaotic, noting that on one occasion Peter left for Australia having omitted to lock any doors.

After two years as Peter Roebuck's lodger, Nigel was married in 1982 to Dr Ingrid Halfyard, a medic who specialised as an anaesthetist at Musgrove Park Hospital and later became a General Practitioner. The couple had originally met at Cambridge and, having set up home in Lydeard St Lawrence, they would have two sons and a daughter.

A young man utterly at ease in his own skin, unaffected and able to turn dishevelment into an art form, Nigel quickly became a welcome member of the set-up at the County Ground. His telling and sometimes exhilarating performances (in particular with the bat) and his athletic fielding whether at short-leg or in the deep, were combined with an unfailing zest for life. His qualities were amply demonstrated when he plunged into the waters of the River Avon during the Bath Festival, to the amusement or bemusement of the assembled corps of pressmen and teammates. The following day, he was plundering a forty-one-minute century from the Gloucestershire attack, which should by rights have won him the Lawrence Trophy for the fastest hundred, but he was toppled from that throne by Steve O'Shaughnessy's ton, later in the season, fed by a diet of declaration bowling. This was one of Nigel's four first-class centuries in a total of 118 matches in which he averaged 28.18 for his adoptive county. His highest score was achieved in 1985 with an innings of 172 against Essex, when he was involved in a first-wicket stand of 243 with Peter Roebuck. He also took seventy-eight first-class wickets at 39.60 apiece, bowling at medium pace. In addition, he made regular contributions to the team's success in limited overs cricket during those heady days when they became acquainted with winning ways. It has been noted that his bowling was rather less muscular than his batting – surprising, perhaps, in a strong man with a propensity for ending exercise routines with two eye-catching sets of thirty one-handed press-ups.

During his time at the County Ground, he taught Biology in the off-season at

Taunton School. Fellow teacher, John Hill, describes him as 'a lovely guy with a smile as big as his talent and very modest, too. Shivering on a cricket pitch on a Monday in April wasn't a big attraction to him. He had the personality, intelligence and people skills to have been a great captain for Somerset, but cricket was always a game for him and not a career.'

In January 1986, having decided that it was time to pursue his chosen destiny, Nigel confirmed that he no longer wished to remain a professional cricketer or indeed a teacher, but had opted to become a solicitor. Peter Roebuck would write a touching tribute to his friend and former teammate, mourning Somerset's loss.

> *Nigel retired because cricket was not in his blood. As a boy, he did not yearn to represent Somerset, it was something which arose, a way of delaying his entry into the world of collars and ties. It was a life he enjoyed while it lasted, one he left with lots of marvellous memories but very few regrets. Somerset will miss him.*

Peter Roebuck's loyalty was rewarded when Nigel took to the platform at Shepton Mallet, the scene of a revolution less bloody but just as venomous as the Monmouth uprising of 1685, crushed a few miles to the west, in Sedgemoor. The decision to speak was a last-minute one. Concerned at the way in which opposing factions had become polarised, Nigel focussed on the facts. Essentially, he saw the decision to terminate the contracts of Viv Richards and Joel Garner as the correct one, although he still questions the manner in which they were released.

Wishing to pursue a career in the legal profession but 'wanting to bring up a family in Somerset', he qualified as a solicitor in London, before spending two years as an articled clerk with Clarke Willmott in Taunton, working alongside Somerset stalwart Roy Kerslake. In 1990, he qualified as a tax specialist and after nine years was ready to use his expertise in a bigger pool, advising larger companies. Thus in 1999 he joined Burges Salmon LLP in Bristol as a partner and remains there at the time of writing. In 2015 he was invited to become a judge, overseeing tax tribunals, a recognition of the extent of his know-how.

A propos Nigel's 'brilliant 171 in Southend', Peter Roebuck wrote of 'a thousand pities that Nigel does not have it on tape to remind himself, when he is contemplating some dense legal difficulty, of how good he was at this game'. Invited by the family of the late Peter Roebuck to deliver the eulogy at the mournful occasion that was his memorial service, Nigel was able to recall some of his erstwhile teammate's important contributions.

He retains his links with Somerset cricket, his son, Harry, having played for Taunton and for the county's Second XI. Somerset had felt instantly like home to the bright-eyed student who was welcomed into the fold back in 1977. Nigel may be immersed in arcane matters of taxation these days, but his sunny outlook and zest for life remain undimmed. As does his love of the county.

1980

"Everyone assumed the season would be something of an anti-climax ... but despite the unscheduled worries over selection and the lamented absentees, Somerset still finished equal fourth in the Championship."

David Foot

Championship Position: 4= of 17

Somerset expected to tread water in 1980. However, with Viv Richards and Joel Garner starring for the West Indies and Ian Botham and Brian Rose also on Test duty, others stepped up to the plate. As Brian Rose, the team's horticulturist-in-chief, could have told his men, prune hard and there's every chance that you will encourage new growth. Brian and his England captain, Ian Botham, topped the batting averages on their infrequent appearances for the county. Brian Rose's two centuries at Worcestershire expunged any unhappy memories of his personal nightmare of the previous season's ill-judged early declaration in the Benson & Hedges Cup. Ian Botham's double-century against Gloucestershire at Taunton was a delight: fearless, violent and compelling. More sedate but mesmerising in their own way were the occasional flashes of genius from the most noteworthy of the debutants, stand-in overseas signing, Sunil Gavaskar. Peter Denning stood alone in reaching the milestone of 1,000 runs, although in the normal course of events he would have been joined by the Test players. Colin Dredge, ever willing, was able to claim sixty-three first-class wickets. There was valuable support from Vic Marks and Hallam Moseley. Not to be ignored were the contributions of the estimable Derek Taylor, a man of quiet competence and considerable know-how.

The greater surprise, though, was the runner-up slot in the John Player Special League. Viv Richards and Joel Garner had only been available for five matches and Somerset had won all of those. Supporters of the club were left to ponder what might have been, had the superstars all been in regular attendance. Nothing had been won, but nor was there any sense of a loss of momentum.

488
Sunil Manohar Gavaskar
24 May 1980 v. Gloucestershire, Taunton

Sunny Gavaskar took the cricketing world by storm in the West Indies in March and April of 1971 when, having missed the First Test, owing to the surgical removal of a whitlow from a finger, he was given his Test debut and, over the four Tests in which he played, compiled an average of 154.80. His performances had raised expectations to fever-pitch in his home country. Sunny would prove that his countrymen's hopes were well-founded. Over the course of 125 Tests for India, he would average 51.12 and in 348 first-class games he would average 51.48. But for the intervention of an eagle-eyed relative, Narayan Masurekar, things would have turned out very differently.

Sunny was born in Mumbai on 10 July 1949, the son of Manchar Keshav Gavaskar, a cotton textile executive and a talented club cricketer, who was married to Meenal Manchar, sister of the former Indian wicket-keeper, Madhav Mantri. On his first visit to see the newborn baby, a relative noticed an unusual little hole near the top of the boy's left earlobe. On the second visit, he noticed to his alarm that the hole was missing. A frantic search of the hospital ensued and Sunny was found in a cot beside a fisherwoman. The babies had been swapped inadvertently while being bathed. Sunny Gavaskar could very easily have been brought up as a fisherman, never holding a bat in his hand. Instead, he would enjoy a life of relative privilege. We should all join Sunny in rejoicing that the world was not denied the fruits of his talent.

After his schooling at St Xavier's High School he went on to gain his degree in Economics and Political Science at St Xavier's College, affiliated to the University of Mumbai. From the outset, he showed the skill and determination never to yield his wicket that would set him apart. As a youngster – much to the shame of the generous man of later years – he quite literally took his bat and ball home if he felt he had been dismissed unfairly.

His infamous 36 not out in 174 balls (while 'chasing' an England total of 334) in a World Cup match speaks of a man ill at ease with the one-day game. His Test career, on the other hand, places him among the greats of the game.

Accompanied by his wife, Marshniel (née Mehrota), whom he had married in 1974, and by their young son, Rohan, named after Rohan Kanhai, he was welcomed to Taunton as a temporary replacement for Viv Richards. It helped that Rohan's hero was Viv and the boy's love affair with Somerset was cemented when Viv presented him with the bat with which he had scored his masterful 138 not out in the 1979

Sunil Gavaskar – a superb batsman who enjoyed god-like status in India

World Cup Final at Lord's. For his part, Sunny took a while to adjust to the chilly weather of an early English season, fortifying himself, in the testimony of Dudley Doust, with full English breakfasts which in turn necessitated the consumption of his more familiar crushed betel nut to aid the digestion. Ever the perfectionist, Sunny found himself having to adjust to the conditions and altered his grip to allow him to play the ball later, even ordering new bats, five ounces lighter than his customary ones, to help with his technique. Normally inclined to create a shell around himself in the Test arena, he adopted a more relaxed air during his time with Somerset. As ever, he was unfailingly polite to supporters and the press and he also invested time in helping the young players in the squad to iron out flaws. Although there was evidence of his greatness, it came only in flashes and his season on the English county circuit was perhaps the least successful of his career, his fifteen first-class matches yielding a batting average of 34.30, a modest figure by his standards.

In India, he has godlike status. As is the way of these things, he has even had a hit song, which went down well with his fan base, and a starring role in a film – *Savli Premachi* – which was arguably not his finest hour, although the main dance sequence is riveting in its own way. Since his playing days ended, Sunny has been much in demand as a commentator and pundit, working across the continents, most familiarly to English listeners as part of the BBC's *Test Match Special* team. He has also written four successful books and has served on high-profile committees, including a spell as Chairman of the ICC Cricket Committee. As a key member of the BCCI Committee, he has also spent time overseeing the Indian Premier League. Inevitably, various honours and awards have come his way. Among them has been the naming of a stadium in his honour in his homeland and – more surprisingly – the naming of the S. M. Gavaskar Cricket Field in Louisville, Kentucky. He has been given the keys to the ground by the Mayor of Louisville, though one wonders if he is every likely to avail himself of the facilities except perhaps in the direst of emergencies.

He is remembered with great fondness by those Somerset supporters who encountered him. His unfailing courtesy won him many admirers, as did the occasional flash of his undoubted genius.

489
Hugh Edmond Ivor Gore
28 May v. Surrey 1980, Kennington Oval

Hugh Gore was born in the Antiguan town of St John's on 18 June 1953, a year after Viv Richards. The two of them – both folk heroes on the island of their birth – have remained lifelong friends. Hugh's father, Leonard Edmund, known as Leo, had played for the Combined Leeward & Windward Islands side after the Second World War, following his return from active service, and would also be for a while the Commanding Officer of the Antiguan Defence Force. Whereas Viv went on to study at Antigua Grammar School, Hugh enjoyed his secondary education at the Lodge School in Barbados, where he was placed in the care of Harley Mosley and his wife.

Having left school in 1971, he was appointed captain of the Combined Islands Youth Team in 1972 and would go on to represent Antigua (alongside Viv Richards), the Leeward Islands and the Combined Islands teams. A right-handed batsman, he was a left-arm seam bowler, described as fast-medium in his prime. He gained experience of English conditions while spending a season with Kent Second XI in 1975 and enjoyed a spell with Border Second XI in South Africa. Recommended to the club as a short-term replacement by his friend, Viv Richards, who was unavailable owing to Test duty, Hugh is recalled with great fondness by his former teammates, Brian Rose noting that he is 'particularly remembered for his genial character'. Sadly, though, as can be the case with pace bowlers, he was troubled throughout the 1980 season by injuries and was never able to enjoy a prolonged spell in the team. Indeed, this would prove his last adventure in the first-class game. He left Somerset having

Hugh Gore – 'particularly remembered for his genial character'

played in eleven games, his best performance being a haul of 5 for 66 against Surrey at The Oval. In total he took fourteen wickets at 47.78 apiece and averaged 8.00 with the bat.

His appetite for the game would remain undiminished, but as a coach, back in Antigua. For many years, he mentored not only his native Antigua team but also the Leeward Islands side, latterly combining the roles of coach and manager. A popular and well-known figure, he was the recipient of the inaugural Egen Warner Humanitarian Award in 2016. Seeking the spotlight has never been his goal and he was a reluctant recipient of all the praise lavished on him at an event to which the great and the good of the local sporting scene were invited. His hair is white these days and he sports a beard, looking every inch the kind and avuncular figure he is. But he is also a strong believer in speaking out and his forthright views are often to be heard.

He might have been a popular character during his brief and injury-blighted stay at the County Ground, but he is very much a man of Antigua who has offered wise counsel to many an up-and-coming player over the years.

490
Neil Russom
27 August 1980 v. Glamorgan, Taunton

[signature: Neil Russom]

Neil Russom was born on 3 December 1958, the son of Dudley Russom, a Chief Hydrographer in the Civil Service, and Geraldine Sheila (née Clarke), a teacher. In 1967, when Neil was eight years old, his father was offered a transfer from offices in Cricklewood to the newly established UK Hydrographic Office in Taunton. Educated at Huish's Grammar School (the source of a number of Somerset cricketers over the years), Neil performed sufficiently impressively as a schoolboy all-rounder to be invited to play for the Somerset Second XI team at the age of sixteen. He won a place to study Law at St Catharine's College, Cambridge, from 1978 until 1981 and, batting right-handed and bowling right-arm medium pace, he would play in twenty first-class fixtures for Cambridge University. He was awarded blues in 1980 and 1981 and averaged 38.13 with the bat while taking thirty-three wickets at 45.87 apiece. In his final year, he opened the bowling with England all-rounder, Derek Pringle. He would also make one first-class appearance for an Oxford & Cambridge XI against the visiting Sri Lankans. A highpoint of his career as a student cricketer was a Benson & Hedges Man of the Match Award for his 5 for 40 for the Combined Universities against Northamptonshire in 1980, when he dismissed Allan Lamb for a duck and bowled four other batsmen, though sadly it was not enough to avert a thumping loss. More controversially, he was a member of an Oxbridge side, who, under the moniker *Jazzhats*, were the first significant team to tour South Africa after the imposition of sanctions. Their involvement would lead to a temporary ban for the participants and whereas Derek Pringle's response was to observe that 'we were being used for propaganda: I will never return there', Neil would later make the country his home.

His performances for Somerset Second XI were at times outstanding. The 1980 season was a particular highlight, when he enjoyed a run of success in his seven Minor Counties Championship matches that yielded a hatful of wickets and a batting average of 208.50. His four first-class appearances for Somerset were spread very thinly, with one match in each of four seasons from 1980 to 1983, and would yield a batting average of 13.66 and five wickets at 33.00 each. In the off-season, he coached cricket during the final two years of his contract, but he had the good sense to realise that a career in the game was unlikely to prove lucrative. Instead, he headed in 1983 for South Africa, making Port Elizabeth his home. After working in what he describes as his 'first real job' – in Logistics – for three years, Neil embarked on what would prove a long and successful career with General Motors. His initial role was to increase the company's export business into neighbouring countries, the opportunity having opened up as a result of what he describes with understatement as 'improving relationships between the South African Government and the rest of the world'. Other roles over the years have included strategic planning, purchasing and managing supplier quality. Neil had been with the company for twenty-eight years when General Motors announced their exit from South Africa in 2017.

Married in 1986 to Linda (née Strydon), he would have a son and daughter. For fifteen years, Linda owned an estate agency, supported by Neil, who undertook much of the administrative work, also assisting with viewings in the evenings, as and when his work with General Motors allowed. The business was eventually sold on and Neil and Linda remain happily ensconced in Port Elizabeth, enjoying the proximity of their grandchildren (who number three at the time of writing).

Those early-season fixtures at Fenner's on dank April days and his brief spell as a professional cricketer at the County Ground seem a long time ago, a world apart from the life he enjoys in South Africa.

Neil Russom – awarded two Cambridge blues, but played in only four first-class matches for Somerset

1981

"Suddenly, as I recall, Viv skipped to square leg and cover drove
Nigel Cowley for a skimming, unbelievable six into the New
Pavilion. That astonishing stroke, it seemed to me, transformed
the match. It galvanised {Ian Botham} into violent batting action
of a sort I have never seen equalled ... The gigantic power, the
certainty of selection, the cleanness of the strokes, to all parts,
for ball after ball, was quite astounding."

Eric Hill

Championship Position: 3 of 17

O nce in a while, someone comes along and, through their heroics and the sheer
force of their personality, claims a year as their own. If 1066 belongs to William
the Conqueror, then 1981 was Ian Botham's year. His heroics in an unforgettable
Ashes series were scarcely believable, though several column miles of print confirm
the tales to be true and render any further description here redundant. The pity of it
was that he was only available for ten of Somerset's Championship matches.

An exhilarating run of seven victories in the final nine Championship matches
helped the team to third position. Viv Richards amassed 1,718 first-class runs, with
seven centuries. Peter Denning, Peter Roebuck and Brian Rose all topped 1,000 runs.
Joel Garner enjoyed his best Championship season with eighty-eight wickets, despite
missing five games. Colin Dredge, Hallam Moseley and Vic Marks chipped in with a
significant number of wickets, too.

Somerset landed their first Benson & Hedges Trophy. At the Lord's Final, Joel
Garner took 5 for 14 in eleven unplayable overs. But Viv Richards secured the Man
of the Match award with his innings of 132 not out.

The team ended the season as runners-up – yet again – in the John Player
Special League, though those who witnessed the match against Hampshire at Taunton in
August (including Eric Hill, quoted above) were still talking, long afterwards, about the
partnership between Viv Richards and Ian Botham that yielded 179 runs in 67 minutes.

This was looking at last like a proper county cricket club. Even the smart new
pavilion spoke of their progress. With little need for new faces, only Richard Ollis
was offered a first-class debut.

491
Richard Leslie Ollis
29 August 1981 v. Gloucestershire, Bristol

Born in Bristol on 14 January 1961, Richard was the son of Richard Frederick, who became a haulage contractor, and Barbara Ann (née Elston). Richard Snr, known to many as Dick, was generous in his support of local sports. Fry Club Junior FC were indebted to him when, during difficult times for them, he not only allowed them the use of a field adjacent to his haulage yard on Pixash Lane in Keynsham, but also set aside a lorry to transport the youngsters to away matches in the days when such unorthodox arrangements were not deemed a risk to life and limb.

Although ultimately destined for a career in the family business – named Ollis Transport and the source of his dressing room nickname of Haulage – Richard Jnr was a talented all-round sportsman and promising enough to capture the attention of Somerset, while a schoolboy at Wellsway Comprehensive in Keynsham. As a footballer, he would enjoy an amateur career as Brislington FC's goalkeeper.

At 6 feet 1 inches tall, he was a correct and stylish left-handed batsman, drafted into the Somerset Second XI in 1978 and coming under the tutelage of the county's coach, Peter Robinson, whom he cites as a major influence. Richard also bowled occasional right-arm medium pace and was a capable wicket-keeper if circumstances required it. During the off-season, he was being prepared for greater things in the family business, working his way up the company, initially as a trainee assistant to the distribution manager. His progress through the ranks at Somerset was less assured. After his debut in 1981, he remained on the fringes of the first-class game until the World Cup in 1983 enforced the absence of a quartet of players – Botham, Garner, Marks and Richards – providing a window of opportunity for Richard, with thirteen first-class appearances. In the first match of that season, things had started brightly, if frustratingly, with a score of 99 not out against Gloucestershire. Despite agreement from David Graveney that Gloucester would bowl an extra over after the allotted time had elapsed and the game was already drawn, Richard remained marooned one short of a maiden first-class century.

For much of his time at Somerset, Richard – a fine fielder – found himself selected as twelfth man. He has noted that more often than not it was Viv Richards or Joel Garner, both partial to the physio's table, whom he stood in for. 'I never minded getting on the pitch,' he observes, 'because it meant you didn't have to run the baths, make the drinks and help with the lunches.' Perhaps Richard's most decisive intervention came in the final moments of the 1984 season. Having wrapped up their final game, Essex watched and waited, knowing that only a Nottinghamshire win at Taunton could deny them the Championship. In the interests of fair play, laced with a modicum of devilment, Ian Botham set Nottinghamshire a 'gettable' total of 297 off sixty overs and then set his spin bowlers, Vic Marks and Stephen Booth, to work. Clive Rice seemed well set to take Notts over the line but, on 98, was denied a six when substitute fielder Richard caught him on the boundary. Notts continued their chase. They had no other option but to do so. With Mike Bore batting in a way that made a nonsense of his surname, they were nine wickets down, needing just four runs off Stephen Booth's final two deliveries. Mike hit a lofted drive to long on. It looked for all the world like

Richard Ollis – a correct and stylish left-handed batsman

the winning hit, when Richard unfurled to his full height and plucked the ball out of the air. Joy was unconfined in Essex. Nottinghamshire were crestfallen. Richard would later confess that his overwhelming feeling was relief, not so much that he had held on to the catch but because he had earned himself (and his colleagues) a much-needed win bonus. Mike Bore would complain until his sadly premature dying day that he had recurring nightmares of the scene. As a postscript to these events, it has been noted that when Somerset played Essex the following season at Southend-on-Sea, Richard was dismissed for a duck, caught by Keith Fletcher off the bowling of John Lever. As Richard walked back to the pavilion, Derek Pringle observed, 'That's no way to treat the man who won us the title.'

He was released by Somerset at the end of the 1985 season, but not before he had played his part in Viv Richards's record-breaking 322 runs in one day against Warwickshire with a stand of 174 to which he had contributed 55. In thirty-seven first-class appearances, a century had narrowly eluded him, but he was able to return to club cricket with Brislington CC, safe in the knowledge that he had amassed more than a thousand runs at an average of 18.14.

Richard then focussed on the family business in Keynsham, assisting his father and rising in time to become a director of Ollis Transport, which later became RONO Holdings (based on the names of Richard's father and his uncle, Nicholas, a builder by trade). Richard would later be appointed a director of the Avon Lodge Truck Stop off the M5, replacing his father as head of the company in 2011. The enterprise offers an affordable, no-frills stopping off point for long-distance lorry drivers.

Married in Bath in 1990 to Helen (née Edwards), he would have a daughter and son. He continued to enjoy local club cricket for many years as a player and administrator with Brislington CC. Latterly, his son, William, a useful opening batsman and wicket-keeper, shows every sign of taking on the mantle. Richard is at the time of writing a Vice President of Brislington FC. In many ways, his exploits are akin to those amateurs of yesteryear whom Somerset so often called on: local businessmen, many of them very good cricketers and all-round sportsmen well above the average, but never able to impose themselves on the first-class game.

Richard Ollis catches the ball, watched by (l to r) Gary Palmer and Simon Turner

1982

"Viv is quite simply the greatest player I have ever been
fortunate enough to watch and play with, and surely in
a few years' time, when most of the present Somerset
players have retired to the bar, they will be reminiscing
about the days they played in the same side as him."

Brian Rose

Championship Position: 6 of 17

Viv Richards again topped the county's batting averages and Brian Rose, alone
among the others, reached the target of 1,000 first-class runs. With Joel Garner
struggling to overcome injury and Ian Botham a regular absentee on Test duty, it fell
to Vic Marks to shoulder the main burden of the bowling. He completed more than
660 overs and took sixty-five wickets. The all-round performances of Jeremy Lloyds
were of note, a high point being his unbeaten century in each innings against Northamptonshire. The team's captain, Brain Rose, remained very aware that, for all the
excitement surrounding the limited-overs success, the big prize was continuing to
elude Somerset. He observed that, 'The Championship is the competition our players
would most like to win, but with key players missing or injured over the last few
years, it properly is the most difficult to attain.' Among the debutants were Mark
Davis, Gary Palmer and Nigel Felton, all of them capable of some sterling performances, though none of them likely to lead their side to that elusive Championship
title.

The John Player Special League campaign proved a disappointment but the securing of a second successive Benson & Hedges trophy ensured that winning ways were
maintained. In a one-sided final, with Nottinghamshire defeated by nine wickets, the
Man of the Match Award went to Vic Marks, with 2 for 24 in eleven overs, including
the valuable wickets of Derek Randall and Clive Rice, although Joel Garner, with an
analysis of 3 for 13 from his 8.1 overs was unfortunate to miss out on the prize once
more.

492
Russel John McCool
12 May 1982 v. Derbyshire, Derby

Russel McCool [signature]

Although Russel McCool was born in Taunton on 4 December 1959, he is in every way barring a technical sense Australian. His father, Colin, married to Dorothy (née Yabsley), was a noted all-rounder and a member of the Australian 'Invincibles', captained by Don Bradman. Colin played in fourteen Tests after serving in the Second World War as a pilot, flying in active service against the invading Japanese forces. He later played for Somerset for five seasons in the autumn of his career, making his debut for them in 1956, when he was already thirty-nine years old. Any thoughts that he might be cruising gently towards retirement or that his competitive zeal was waning were soon dismissed when, in the words of an earlier volume of the *Somerset Cricketers* series, he 'set an unflinching example' for the rest of the team to follow. With Colin's hugely successful first-class career finally drawing to a close at the end of the 1960 season, Russel was a babe in arms, less than a year old, when he was taken 'home' to Australia. English winters had bitten deep and when asked on one occasion what he planned to do on his return to his homeland, Colin replied, 'I'm going to grow pineapples, lad. I bet you don't know what they are, do you?' The jocular remark led to a myth (unfortunately promulgated in *Somerset Cricketers 1946-1970*, but subsequently corrected by Russel) that Colin had set up a market gardening enterprise. He had in fact re-joined the Public Service until his retirement at fifty-eight. He had also continued to be employed for a while as a pro in Grade cricket at Belmont CC – the first man to enjoy that status in the Newcastle cricket competition.

Russel would grow up surrounded by the sights and sounds of the surf coast and verdant hinterland of Umina Beach in New South Wales, eighty miles north of Sydney. Educated at nearby Woy Woy South Primary School and Woy Woy High School, he followed the example of his father and became a leg-break bowler. While playing his club cricket in Sydney, Russel also worked in the New South Wales Public Service after leaving school in 1978. During the 1980-81 season, he was selected to play for New South Wales Colts (Under-23s) and would represent them again for two further seasons. In 1981, he made the pilgrimage to England under his own steam, hoping to further his cricketing education in English conditions. Having been told that there were no opportunities at Somerset, he benefited from an intervention by 'the kindly Peter Denning'. Brian Rose was persuaded that Russel should be given a trial in a friendly against Glamorgan at the County Ground. He started well, dismissing their seasoned opener, Alan Jones, having deceived him with a flipper, but three days later suffered a dislocated knee while batting in the nets. He underwent some pioneering surgery and physiotherapy back in New South Wales but believes that, with the benefit of hindsight, his return was 'a little too premature'.

Perhaps because of the change to rules regarding the covering of wickets ahead of the 1982 season, allied to the hope that the Taunton-born son of an Australian great might perform heroics for the county of his birth, Somerset decided to offer the young leg-spinner a one-season contract. Having initially been informed he would be allowed to 'settle in', he was told at short notice, and much to his surprise, that he had been included in the team to play Derbyshire on 12 May. It would prove his only first-class appearance. Although

Russel McCool – born in Taunton but brought up in Australia, he enjoyed a brief spell back in Somerset

disappointed by how things turned out, Russel still remembers the game well, not least for 'the sound of Beefy Botham's ghetto blaster in the changing room that could be heard across the other side of the ground'.

There followed an extended run in the Second XI, where the wickets were much slower than the hard tracks that had suited his bowling back in Australia, making wickets hard to come by. He parted company with the county at the end of the season. In his only first-class appearance, Russel had taken no wickets at a cost of 63 runs and scored 7 and 12 in his two innings. He remains upbeat about his time in Somerset. 'I enjoyed it,' he says, 'and took the opportunity to play in the Taunton League each weekend for Milverton CC. And I have good memories of playing alongside the likes of Ian Botham, Vivian Richards and others, of course.'

Returning to New South Wales, he continued to play Grade cricket in Sydney and was selected to be part of the New South Wales Sheffield Shield squad. Sadly, a second knee injury in 1984 served as a catalyst to forsake cricket as a career option. Thereafter, he would enjoy the game for pure pleasure while he held down jobs in insurance, automotive finance and for a while as a grain handling operator at the docks in Newcastle, New South Wales. Finally, he settled on the career as a teacher that has remained his vocation.

Married to Rodalyn and with two children, Bridget and Colin, he has enjoyed a long career in the teaching profession with spells at Newcastle Grammar School, Knox Grammar School, Melbourne Girls' Grammar School and time overseas in Thailand, the Philippines and the United Arab Emirates. He is now ensconced at King's School Parramatta in Sydney, Australia's oldest independent school, founded in 1831 at the behest of King William IV. Russel teaches Year Six children in the preparatory school and is noted for an innovative and engaging approach to the profession, embracing technology as a means of making education more interactive. He talks with enthusiasm about the impact of gamification – taking the elements of game-playing and applying them to the classroom. He describes himself as 'an educator, father and a lifelong and life-wide learner' and sees it as his mission to help his charges embark on a similar journey where learning is a joy and never a chore. He coaches the preparatory school First XI at King's School in what he describes as 'the Australian way, encouraging younger players to enjoy the game and not to change their style of play, whilst keeping their heads in the books for academic achievement'. He practices what he preaches. A knowledgeable student of the history of cricket, he is a keen book collector and has also used his technical know-how to help contacts in the cricket book industry – whether publisher or bookseller – to construct their websites.

His brief return to Taunton, the town where he was born, proved a pleasurable interlude for him in a varied and interesting life.

Russel is listed incorrectly in a number of sources as 'Russell'. He confirms that his name has always been spelt with one l.

Enjoying a knees-up (back row, l to r) are Colin Dredge, Nigel Popplewell, Mike Bryant, Russel McCool, Hallam Moseley and Andrew Jones (cropped): in front of them (in white track suit) is Dermot Reeve, who joined the squad in 1984 for two practice sessions on the recommendation of Peter Roebuck, but was not offered a contract

493
Mark Richard Davis
19 May 1982 v. Worcestershire, Worcester

[signature: Mark Davis]

Mark Davis came to Somerset's attention when his mother entered him for a *Somerset County Gazette* 'Search for a Star' competition, where schoolboys were invited to bat and bowl against Ian Botham. Left to his own devices, Mark would happily have continued terrorising opponents of his village side as a young fast bowler. He and fellow applicant Andy Robinson were successful, although Andy opted for a career in rugby union, going on to win renown as an international player and coach.

Born in the village of Kilve on the Somerset coast on 26 February 1962, Mark was the son of a builder, Robert, known as Bob and married to Penelope (née Stevens), who worked in a secretarial role at Kilve Court. A member of a cricketing family who filled most of the slots in the Kilve CC side and could indeed field a whole team of family members, had they had the inclination to do so, Mark was introduced to the club side at the age of twelve. He observes that his Somerset teammate Colin Dredge was able to claim membership of a similar dynasty of Dredges in the vicinity of Frome and a Davis Family versus Dredge Family match was occasionally mooted, although it never transpired.

It was clear at a young age that Mark was destined to be a useful left-arm pace bowler and he was offered a scholarship to Millfield. Despite parental encouragement, he dug his heels in and declined, on the basis that he wished to remain with his friends at West Somerset School in Minehead and later at Bridgwater College, to complete his A-Levels. He was then offered a one-year professional contract by Somerset, which he signed with alacrity, and was mentored by Hallam Moseley. His progress was sufficient for his contract to be renewed and he would remain with the county until 1987, playing in seventy-seven first-class fixtures. Over that period, he enjoyed some devastating spells and Peter Roebuck describes Mark in *Sometimes I Forgot to Laugh* as 'a hustling and bustling left-armer whose deliveries cut away and often took batsmen by surprise'. Roebuck then goes on to say:

> *Repeatedly Davies {sic} took wickets with the new ball, which made life easier for captains and colleagues alike. Had his second spells been as effective he might have played for his country, for the West Indies were running riot and a change of angle had its merits. Alas, Davies {sic} lacked stamina, athleticism and dedication and swiftly faded.*

Mark had indeed enjoyed a superb season in 1984 when, despite missing six Championship matches through injury, he was still able to claim sixty-six wickets.

Mark Davis – 'a hustling and bustling left-armer whose deliveries cut away and often took batsmen by surprise'

Between 1982 and 1987, he would take a total of 149 wickets at 35.62 and – ever a self-effacing and honest man – he attributes the falling away of his form to his becoming disillusioned with the game in general and his skipper in particular. His captain at that time, Peter Roebuck, was not noted for his man-management skills, although Peter would learn from his mistakes and later captain Devon with much more flair and emotional acuity.

An easy-going man – clearly too easy-going in the eyes of his erstwhile captain – Mark had by that time shrugged his shoulders and looked to new horizons. An offer came to join Sussex, but he declined it. Somerset was his home and Somerset the team he had always supported. The idea of playing for another county was anathema to him. Instead, he spent two years as the pro at Llangennech CC, across the Bristol Channel and joined his father's building firm in Kilve. There were appearances for Wiltshire in 1989 but Mark was increasingly drawn to the idea of coaching, spending time as a professional player and mentor at the Taunton Vale Sports Club, before being offered the opportunity to coach cricket at Millfield School, where he would be employed from 1997 until 2014. During his time there, eighteen future first-class cricketers would come under his tutelage – a reflection both of Millfield's commitment to cricketing excellence and to Mark's talents. Each coach brings a unique perspective to the art and science of performance and Mark is firmly of the view that individuality is something to be built on and enhanced, whereas some others might take the view that differences should be ironed out.

Married in 1985 to Elizabeth (née Healey), known as Liz, Mark was subsequently divorced and his partner for many years has been Kim Rogers, whom he first met while she was working in the Marketing Department for Somerset at the County Ground and with whom he would raise his family. Since parting company with Millfield School, he has managed his own freelance professional coaching company, named Cricappeal. In regular demand at a number of local schools – including Queen's College and King's College, both in Taunton, and King's School, Bruton – this personable former player continues to contribute to cricket in the county he loves and still lives in. He is the co-author of two *Wisden* books on coaching, notable for their clarity: *Batting* and *Bowling*. In addition, he has been an analyst in the BBC Bristol cricket commentary team for twenty years. An enthusiastic supporter both of Somerset CCC and his beloved Bristol City FC – both of whom are more likely to elicit exasperation among their followers than they are to win major prizes – it is perhaps a good thing that he is such a phlegmatic character. Mark accepts whatever comes his way with the happy-go-lucky fatalism that characterises a majority of West Countrymen.

Michael Bryant

5 June 1982 v. Essex, Chelmsford

Mike Bryant was born in Beacon, Camborne, in Cornwall, on 5 April 1959, the son of William Lewis Bryant, who served for many years in the Royal Navy before becoming the village sexton, and Rose (née Rogers). One of nine children growing up in the small village on the outskirts of the town of Camborne, Mike attended Treswithian County School and cut his teeth as a cricketer with Beacon CC, opening the bowling in tandem with an elder brother, John.

They are made of tougher stuff than normal in places like Beacon. Back in 1906 the cricket club had been set up by Joe Thomas, the man who owned the local grocery store. Concerned that the young lads in the village were idling away their days with limited prospects for employment since the tin mining industry had lurched into terminal decline, he had been the leading light in the club's early years. The team were strong boys, too, moving their pavilion around from ground to ground as they attempted to establish a permanent home before settling on an old field 'scarred by mine burrows' that they worked hard to improve. The poverty of the soil proved a blessing, though, when it was one of a handful of cricket grounds in Cornwall deemed unfit for ploughing and giving over to vegetable crops during the Second World War. When the Bryant brothers emerged, they were typical of that breed of tough competitors long associated with the club. Writing in *The Thorn Between Two Roses*, Malcolm Lobb would observe that 'the cricketers of Beacon are fighters, accustomed to living off scraps and hardened to the struggle for survival. Out of this has arisen a loyalty between Beacon's players and their community.'

The word 'fighter' might certainly be applied to Mike, who at times demonstrated a short fuse. One former teammate recounts the tale of the occasion when Mike was asked by his brother John (captain on the day) to bowl from the less favoured end. Taking umbrage, Mike allegedly argued loudly before and between each of his first three deliveries before throwing the ball to the ground and deserting the scene. The ten men of Beacon were obliged to continue without him. Disconcertingly quick by club standards, Mike's bowling was regularly devastating but often wayward. John was the steadier of the two brothers who opened the bowling for Beacon CC. As with their bowling, so it would prove in life. Where John settled down to life as a carpenter, Mike left home a relative innocent but would 'go off the rails', later described as the black sheep of the family. By 1978, at the age of nineteen, he was taken on by

Mike Bryant – offered a contract with Somerset on the basis of some devastating fast bowling for his native Cornwall

Gloucestershire but never broke through into the first-class arena. One former team-mate reports that he allegedly borrowed Gloucestershire coach Graham Wiltshire's car and crashed it while under the influence of alcohol. Not perhaps the best way to earn an extension to one's contract and Mike duly left the county after one season. 'He was a young lad who got in with the wrong crowd and lost his way,' a family friend laments.

Back playing for Cornwall, Mike put in some hostile spells of bowling, not least against Somerset Second XI, where among his impressive performances were a 5 for 25 and a 6 for 62. On the basis of the evidence before them, Somerset offered Mike a one-year contract. He arrived a newly-wed, having been married in April 1982 to Mandy (née Cook) and would spend most of his time in the Second XI but was selected for two first-class matches. On his debut, against Essex, he opened the bowling with Ian Botham but, having proved expensive in the first innings, was not called on to bowl in the second. In total, over his two appearances, he would take two wickets at 79.00 apiece and average 3.00 with the bat.

Writing in the *Somerset Year Book*, Second XI coach Peter Robinson observed that 'Michael Bryant suffered from a lot of injuries [and] had a no ball problem which he failed to overcome, and tended to bowl too short,' all of which pointed to a man straining every sinew to bowl as fast as possible, sacrificing accuracy in the process. He tried his luck with Warwickshire, where he was given a trial game in their Second XI in September 1982, but no offer was forthcoming and Mike returned to the fold in Cornwall.

He found work where he could, employed for a while as a coal delivery man and undertaking building work and then left Cornwall to begin a new life in France with his wife, Mandy. He would later return to the county of his birth but friends and family talk of their despair as alcohol came to rule his life. In time, Mandy and he parted. His is a sad story of a talent blunted by drink, a tale of what can befall a young man who strides out into the world with high hopes, stumbles and loses his footing.

495
Nigel Alfred Felton
31 July 1982 v. Hampshire, Bournemouth

Nigel Felton was a gritty left-handed batsman who still feels fortunate to have played for Somerset at a time when they were enjoying a spell of unparalleled success, although, sadly, he also witnessed the disintegration of the club in 1986. Born on 24 October 1960 in Guildford, Surrey, he was the son of Ralph Felton and Enid (née

Peters), a clerical secretary. Ralph, who worked as a printer, had emigrated with Enid from Cape Town in order to escape the apartheid regime, under which he had played football and cricket alongside Basil D'Oliveira as a so-called Cape Coloured.

The family moved to Kent while Nigel was still young and he was educated at Hawes Down Secondary School in West Wickham before being offered a Sixth Form Scholarship to Millfield School on the basis of his prowess as a cricketer. He had already represented England Schoolboys at Under-15 Level and would go on to captain the England Young Cricketers (Under-19s) on their tour of Australia in 1978-79. On the books at Kent, he asked to be released by them once he had embarked on a degree

Nigel Felton – a gritty left-handed batsman who proved a consistent accumulator of runs

in Physical Education and Sports Sciences at Loughborough University, qualifying as a teacher there. Already well-known to Somerset from his time at Millfield, he joined the county in 1981 on a summer contract, opening the batting during the academic year for the Loughborough side before decamping to Taunton in June.

Having broken into the Somerset First XI in the fixture at Hampshire in July 1982, three days after he had compiled a century against the same county's Second XI, he would render valuable service for seven seasons, proving a consistent accumulator of runs and complementing some of the more stellar names. His first century (173 not out) was memorable not only as a landmark but also because he completed it in only his second first-class game and in partnership with fellow-centurian, Viv Richards. His eighth and last century for Somerset was against Gloucestershire in 1988, in what was his final innings for the county. He had by then made 108 first-class appearances and averaged 28.83. He had also played as a pro for Wanneroo CC in Perth during the winter of 1985-86, although he summarises his extra-curricular employment during his time at Taunton as having been a combination of 'teaching, digging holes and working with the Somerset CCC marketing department'.

Having been released by Somerset on an amicable basis, he joined Northamptonshire, whom he represented for six seasons, enjoying his best canpaign in 1990, when he amassed 1,538 runs. He also gained a NatWest winner's medal in 1992.

Between the years 1991 and 1993 he achieved fulfilment on a wider scale when, in the post-apartheid era, he ran a coaching programme in the townships around the Cape, assisted by six young English cricketers. Having forsaken the teaching profession for which he had once trained, he became Commercial Director at Northants CCC in 1999 and remained in the role for three years, later becoming a board director of Northants Cricket Holdings, the limited company formed to place the county's cricket on a better financial footing.

A shrewd businessman who goes about his work with the quiet efficiency and tenacity with which he once went about constructing an innings, Nigel has run a successful company named Sports and Stadia since 2002. His wife, Jill (née Kennedy), whom he married in Bishops Lydeard in 1989, is a fellow director and the Company Secretary. The enterprise offers a variety of innovative solutions for protecting sports venues from rain, frost and snow and he has helped to improve the facilities at places as varied as Cheltenham Racecourse and Twickenham rugby stadium. Systems have been devised for well-known football clubs as well as top teams from both rugby codes.

Nigel remains a prime example of a player sufficiently talented and committed to have enjoyed a prolonged first-class career and bright and driven enough to have created and managed a lucrative business once his playing days were over.

496
Gary Vincent Palmer
21 August 1982 v. Leicestershire. Taunton

Gary Palmer was blessed with enough self-belief not to feel the burden of being touted as the young all-rounder who was going to lead Somerset to new heights, and nor was he broken by the experience of falling short of the wildly optimistic hopes that surrounded him as a teenager. He also had the skill and determination to establish himself later as a highly-regarded cricket coach, able to apply his know-how as readily to seasoned Test players as to aspiring schoolboys.

Born into a Somerset cricketing dynasty on 15 November 1965 in Taunton, he was the son of Somerset and England all-rounder Ken Palmer. If cricket ran in the Palmer genes, with Ken's brother, Roy, also having represented Somerset as a lively quick bowler, then Gary's mother, Joy (née Gilbert), who taught at Castle School in Taunton, also deserves recognition for having passed on her skills as a fine squash player.

Educated at Queen's College on the outskirts of the town, Gary was soon at-

tracting attention as a schoolboy batsman and right-arm medium pace
bowler. His 'double whirl' bowling
action was unusual but effective: not
the straightforward, upright, side-on
delivery beloved of coaching manuals.
Guided by his father (who worked for a
while as groundsman and coach at Millfield School), Gary would soon begin his
ascent through the county age groups.
In conversation, he is quick to cite his
debt to his father, acknowledging that,
'He spent hour after hour coaching me,
feeding the bowling machine. His hard
work and excellent advice were paying
off and helping me towards my dream
of becoming a professional cricketer and
carrying on the family tradition.'

Gary Palmer – a promising young all-rounder
who later became a successful coach

By the age of fourteen, Gary was not
only drafted into the Somerset Second
XI but was offered professional terms, making him one of the youngest players to
have been awarded a contract by a first-class county. He would also be invited to
represent England Under-15s, England Under-19s and Young England. When he
stepped up to the Somerset First XI, he was, by his own admission, initially overawed. 'It was an amazing feeling,' he confides, 'being on the same pitch as players I'd
idolised, previously queuing up for their autographs. It was definitely nerve-racking
for the first few games.' He was only sixteen at the time of his first-class debut for
Somerset, with a bright future predicted. As it transpired, he would play in fifty-four
first-class matches between 1982 and 1988 before being released by the county. He
had averaged 15.30 with the bat and taken ninety-two wickets at 44.64 apiece. He
also appeared in eighty-three List A fixtures in which he claimed a further seventy-seven wickets. He would go on to represent Bedfordshire and then Oxfordshire in
Minor Counties cricket.

For a while, Gary coached squash at Millfield School, but it is as a cricket coach
that he has made a name for himself since hanging up his boots as a player. Former
Middlesex player Mike Selvey once begged the question in his column in the *Guardian*: 'Do the credentials to be an elite coach … demand a previous career of high
achievement at that level?' Responding to his own query, he wrote that 'the answer, of
course, is an emphatic no', citing examples from other sports such as Nick Bollettieri

in tennis or Jose Mourinho at football. Assimilating all the lessons learned in a career and having the skill to articulate those is a talent every bit as valuable as prowess at a sport. Gary has demonstrated his abilities as a coach to great effect. His big break came when he was offered the role of Head Coach at the Eastern Province Cricket Academy, where a whole cadre of promising young South African cricketers, including Mark Boucher and Ashwell Prince, came under his wing. Most of that crop went on to enjoy success as professional cricketers and Gary came away with his reputation as a coach secured and his belief in his own methods enhanced.

Married in 1997 to Kathryn (née Donaghy), he has latterly made Oxfordshire his home. For fifteen years, he has offered his services to private schools and at various times he has enjoyed everything from long-term appointments (such as being made Oxford University Head Coach) to consultancy work as a freelance. Able to adapt his approach, he has worked with men and women, aspiring youngsters and seasoned internationals, individuals and teams. Latterly, he has managed the Palmer Cricket Academy, based in Oxfordshire. A particular specialism – calling on his own personal odyssey – is helping players to bridge the gap between Minor Counties and first-class cricket. Among his clients have been nine first-class counties as well as the Indian, Sri Lankan and Australian touring teams. In 2017, he joined the England Lions Tour to Australia as the batting consultant.

Individuals as various as Jos Buttler and Ian Bell of England, Kieran Powell of the West Indies and Shan Masood of Pakistan have all benefited from Gary's input. His crowning achievement, though, has undoubtedly been his three years as personal coach to Alastair Cook, helping the former England captain to iron out issues, to rediscover his form and to improve his technique. 'For many years I stuck to my guns about batting, because I could see that many players needed to open their stance much more than is generally advised,' he observes. 'I'd seen the results in action and knew what needed to be done. After the work with Alastair, many more people really began to take notice of what I was saying.'

Gary has also found time to write a guide entitled *Batting Mechanics* and remains a regular contributor of articles on the subject of coaching. Throughout it all, he has gained a reputation for embracing innovations in a constant quest for self-improvement. 'I think it's important to have the humility to accept that there are things to learn. My own bowling action for example was too complicated. It's also important to know when to stick to your guns and not just follow fads as a coach.'

Early predictions of unbridled success on the pitch could have turned the head of the young Gary Palmer but in the end, he has surprised observers by carving out a hugely productive career as a thoughtful coach rather than as a player. His passion for developing both young cricketers and established ones and drawing out every last drop of their talent remains undiminished and his success stories continue to flow.

1983

> "Brian has been as fine a captain as has ever played for Somerset ... Ian's appointment will bring a different brand of leadership. Never a man to shrink from a challenge, he will lead from the front."
>
> *Michael Hill (Chairman)*

Championship Position: 10 of 17

Back problems curtailed captain Brian Rose's season and vice-captain, Ian Botham, stepped into the breach, when not on Test duty. It was an unsettled sort of season that never quite got going. The World Cup robbed Somerset of its brightest stars, although, in their all-too-infrequent appearances, Viv Richards and Ian Botham delighted the faithful with their pyrotechnics. Peter Roebuck – more circumspect and gaining in stature as a batsman – amassed 1,235 first-class runs for the county. There were other occasional highlights, such as Nigel Popplewell's swashbuckling forty-one-ball century at Bath. Those uncomplaining troopers, Vic Marks and Colin Dredge, bowled many an over and claimed fifty and forty-eight wickets respectively. Tenth position was about par for a mediocre season. Among the new-joins, Julian Wyatt's contribution would be the most lasting as a doughty batsman and later in a coaching capacity.

The John Player Special League title slipped from Somerset's grasp on account of their having won fewer away games than Yorkshire, who ended with the same points tally. It was the sixth time they had ended as runners-up in eight seasons. They did, however, secure their first NatWest Trophy. They had been dragged into the final in a nail-biting finish against Middlesex when, with the scores tied, Ian Botham had shown remarkable restraint. Knowing that his side had conceded fewer wickets, he saw them home in the last over with some stoical and uncharacteristic blocking, resisting all temptation to secure the four runs that would have landed him his century. In a tense, low scoring final, Vic Marks steered the side home against Kent. The County Ground hosted its first One Day International on 11 June 1983, when England played Sri Lanka in the Prudential World Cup. Expectations were high with two local heroes performing. Sadly, Ian Botham was run out for a duck and went wicketless, but an impressive return of 5 for 39 from Vic Marks helped to secure a comfortable victory for England.

497
Peter Hugh L'Estrange Wilson
30 April 1983 v. Nottinghamshire, Nottingham

Hugh Wilson

For a brief while, when he was with Surrey, Hugh Wilson, known to teammates and supporters as 'Flea', was talked of as the young quick bowler England should turn to, but the selectors opted instead for Graham Dilley. Thereafter, Hugh would fade into the background, although only metaphorically so, given that he is a great bear of a man. At 6 feet 5 inches tall, weighing fourteen and a half stone and charging in looking uncannily like Bob Willis, he must have had the more timorous batsmen quaking in their boots. The likeness between 'Flea' and 'Goose' Willis is unsurprising, given that Bob helped to coach a young Hugh.

Born in Guildford on 17 August 1958, he was the son of Lieutenant Commander Peter Sydney Wilson of the Royal Navy and Heather Margaret (née Grant). Educated at Wellington College, for whom he once scored 192 not out against Haileybury, Hugh took a while to find his feet as a first-class cricketer, turning out initially for Hampshire Second XI and working in estate agency and as a teacher at Highfield Preparatory School in Liphook. He joined Surrey in 1978 and enjoyed an initial first-class appearance against the touring Pakistan side, teaming up for the first time with his opening bowling partner, the left-armer David 'Teddy' Thomas. Thomas would later become wheelchair-bound and increasingly afflicted by multiple sclerosis and Hugh would brave the New York marathon in 2000 in order to raise money for research into the condition that had beset his friend and former teammate. Sadly, David Thomas died in 2012.

Hugh certainly had his moments in the sun at Surrey, most notably in the Benson & Hedges Cup Final of 1979 when he bowled with real fire and pace, although his four wickets were insufficient to prevent an Essex victory. If his bowling caused palpitations in the breast of the odd opponent, then his batting was unlikely to do the same. Hugh jokes that he must surely be the only cricketer who has performed with the bat in front of television cameras on three occasions and been dismissed each time for a golden duck. One of those occasions had been the Benson & Hedges Final.

There followed a winter with Northern Transvaal, MCC tours to Bangladesh and Central and East Africa, together with three more seasons with Surrey, before a parting of the ways. 'Things didn't quite work out,' as Hugh put it. Somerset felt that he would add some menace to their bowling attack and offered him a contract. Over the course of two seasons, he played in fifteen first-class matches for Somerset, taking thirty wickets at 33.76 apiece and averaging 10.00 with the bat. The well-spoken Old Wellingtonian might perhaps have repeated his refrain that 'things didn't quite work out'.

After leaving Somerset at the end of the 1984 season, he settled on a career in insurance with Willis, Faber & Dumas, where he began by providing crime-related insurance around the world. In 1990, he transferred to Los Angeles, helping a number of West Coast offices to access the European insurance markets. While there, he was persuaded to try his hand at softball and had found that while he could strike the ball a prodigious distance, catching anything while wearing a mitt had proved problematical.

Having returned to London (for business reasons rather than his efforts at softball), he continued to enjoy success but was headhunted in 2002 and, in his words, 'in a moment of madness'

Hugh Wilson – a pace bowler with an imposing physique COURTESY OF JOHN LEE

went to work with another Lloyd's broker. In 2006, after four years away, he re-joined Willis as part of a newly-created Financial and Executive Risks team. He remained with the company for a further nine years before leaving once more to join Alwen Hough Johnson as a Divisional Director.

Married in 1985 to Michele, the daughter of England cricketer, Raman Subba Row, he has a son, Harry. 'You always wonder if your children inherit the cricketing gene,' Hugh jokes, 'although in our case we always hoped it would go down the maternal line.'

If his response that 'things didn't quite work out' was applicable to his spells as a first-class cricketer, then the same cannot be said of his career in the arcane world of insurance, which has turned out rather well.

498
Julian George Wyatt
2 July 1983 v. New Zealand, Taunton

[signature]

Julian Wyatt has been known to describe cricket as 'a simple game complicated by intelligent people who lack common sense'. It is certainly the case that his approach as a batsman and later as a coach has always been straightforward and uncomplicated. When discussing his own efforts as a batsman, he describes himself self-deprecatingly as a 'blocker', but a more generous interpretation is that he had an excellent temperament, a sound technique and his innings rarely involved unnecessary risk-taking. Although his approach was initially more suited to the longer form of the game, he was able to adapt to the demands of limited-overs cricket and in his last season compiled some substantial innings – in particular, quick-fire half-centuries against Surrey and Yorkshire – at an impressive strike rate.

Born in Paulton on 19 June 1963, he was the son of Christopher Wyatt, a farmer, and Dinah (née Porch). Educated initially at Farrington Gurney Primary School, he went on to study at Wells Cathedral School, where he starred at rugby and table-tennis, as well as captaining the cricket team in his final year. He had earlier been a keen footballer and retains fond memories of being ferried to Fry Junior Club FC's Under-12 and Under-13 away matches in a lorry provided by Dick Ollis, father of Somerset cricketer, Richard Ollis. 'I'm pretty certain it wouldn't be allowed these days on safety grounds,' Julian observes.

Passionate about Somerset cricket, he was a late developer – 'a shy farmer's boy,' he suggests – who first made an appearance with the Under-16s but was no more than a fringe player until he joined the Under-19s, by then impressing with his unfussy batting and athletic fielding. Having left school in 1980 he worked for Brandon Tool Hire but by the spring of 1983 he had made the decision to hand in his notice and pursue his dream of playing for the county he supported. Offered a contract in 1983, he soon broke into the First XI and looked comfortable in the elevated company. By the following season he was into his stride. Early in 1984, he registered his first century against a dispirited Oxford University side, whom Somerset put out of their misery by declaring at 365 for 1. Among three first-class centuries, his most laudable was arguably his match-saving innings against Hampshire in 1985, when his hundred was crafted patiently over six hours and twenty minutes. His finest hour, though, must surely be his resolute stand in 1984 against a West Indies attack that included Malcolm Marshall and Courtney Walsh. Holding his nerve while all around

Julian Wyatt – a batsman with an excellent temperament and a sound technique

him were losing theirs, he accounted for more than fifty-five per cent of his side's runs (excluding extras), with two brave innings of 45 and 69. During the winters, he gained wider experience with spells as a pro and coach in Australia with Kew CC in Melbourne and Manly CC in Sydney. For all his strengths and undoubted application, Julian was never able to hit the heights and his playing contract was terminated in

1989. Over the course of sixty-nine matches he had averaged 25.35 with the bat and taken three wickets at 32.33 apiece with his occasional right-arm medium pace. His batting might at times have been measured and unlikely to have had the faithful on the edge of their seats, but he had a ready wit. When asked (by the compilers of *The Cricketers' Who's Who*) what changes he felt would benefit the game, his response was a droll suggestion that the 'LBW law and slip fielders should be abolished'.

Julian's association with Somerset cricket would continue when he was given the role of Schools Development Coach and, from 1995, Youth Development Officer. Having spent thirteen seasons (including in his formative years) playing club cricket for Keynsham CC, he subsequently turned out for Tiverton Heathcoat CC, before hanging up his boots in 2000. He also played between 1993 and 1995 for Devon, afforded the opportunity to develop his skills as a bowler as well as a batsman, although not always in the manner he wished. 'I remember bowling against Simon Ecclestone in a pre-season friendly. I'd let him lodge with me for a while, back when he was getting established at Somerset. He bludgeoned the first three deliveries of an over for six. That's gratitude for you! Fortunately, he didn't manage the six sixes he was hoping for.'

From 1996 until 2001, Julian was Somerset Second XI Coach and Academy Directory and for three years from 2004 until 2007 he worked as the coach and Chief Executive of the Mid-Canterbury Cricket Association in New Zealand. While residing in New Zealand he was married to Rebecca (née Wood) in Akaroa in 2005, with fellow Somerset cricketer Ricky Bartlett doing the honours as best man.

Latterly, he has been the Director of Cricket at Exeter University and has set up the Julian Wyatt Cricket Academy, offering one-to-one coaching, primarily at local schools, including Blundell's, Wellington School and Plymouth College. Julian's approach is thorough but not prescriptive, tailored to the unique needs and differing style of each pupil. He has plans for courses that he hopes to run at the Desert Springs resort in Almanzora, Spain, unencumbered by the English weather, though his ambition to establish his name as a writer has proved a pleasant distraction from his charted course. As with any coach worth his salt, he has reflected on his own experiences. 'I've thought about why I didn't push on as much as I'd hoped as a player,' he says, with candour. 'Often, it's niggling doubt rather than technical flaws that can hold a player back. Fortunately, these days there's a much greater understanding that technique and psychology go hand in hand.' Certainly, that shy farmer's boy who had entered the portals of Wells Cathedral School had developed into a player unprepared to be cowed by a hostile West Indian attack and these days he attempts to instil that inner strength in his young charges.

Devon might be his home now, but his commitment to his beloved Somerset cricket remains undiminished.

499
Stephen Charles Booth
27 July 1983 v. Northamptonshire, Northampton

Steve Booth was born in Cross Gates, Leeds, on 30 October 1963, the son of Eric and Katheen (née Lupton). Educated at Boston Spa Comprehensive (as it was then named), he enjoyed success both at cricket and football, although enjoyment was not the operative word when in 1982 his spleen had to be removed following a calamitous collision. Fortunately, his enthusiasm for the game of cricket was not affected. A left-arm orthodox spin bowler who batted right handed, he was a member of the Lord's ground staff in 1983 (having joined them straight from school as a seventeen-year-old), when he was invited early in the season by coach Peter Robinson to appear in two games for Somerset Second XI and, in Peter's words, 'showed enough promise to be offered a contract in the middle of June and given a run in the first team in the latter part of the season'. The hope was that here was a left-armer who would complement the right-arm off-spin of Vic Marks.

Still only nineteen years old when he came to Somerset, he took up the contract he had been offered at the County Ground with alacrity. With his boyish looks and his northern tones, he was dubbed 'Heathcliff' by Peter Roebuck, though Steve is not by any stretch of the imagination an anguished character in the manner either of Heathcliff or, indeed, the late Peter Roebuck. Writing in *It Never Rains*, Peter includes jocular references to his teammate's characteristics, not least his parsimony when feasting on '20p's worth of chips, good Yorkshireman that he is'. David Foot observes in *Sixty Summers* that Steve was 'pushed too far, too soon, and he remains the classic case of the over-exposed slow bowler'. He certainly bowled a lot of overs – on average, approximately thirty per match – but here was a young player eager to be in the action and to be handed the ball. He settled in well on debut, claiming the wicket of the mighty Kapil Dev – one of two players he bowled in the match. Kapil Dev would suffer the same fate in the return fixture, though not before he had flayed the Somerset attack on that occasion.

Married to Jane (née Kilby) in 1984, he counted among his wedding guests members of the Somerset team, including his captain, Ian Botham – never one to miss a lively celebration. Steve had been offered work in Taunton in the off-season and would remain with his adoptive county for four seasons, having to make do with life in the Second XI in the last of these, his role as the left-arm spinner having been supplanted by Rob Coombs. In Steve's own words, he 'lived the dream for four years'

Steve Booth – a Yorkshire-born left-arm orthodox spin bowler, dubbed 'Heathcliff' by Peter Roebuck

and recalls his time in first-class cricket as a joyous period. As clear in the memory as his moments in the sun – such as his 3 for 21 and 4 for 26 against Middlesex at Lord's in 1981 – are sharing the field with some of the greats of the game. He recalls with a smile being sent out as nightwatchman to 'protect Viv Richards from the bowling' and being asked the rhetorical question, 'Why do I need looking after, man?' During his time at Somerset, he appeared in thirty-three first-class matches, taking eighty-seven wickets at 36.31 apiece and averaging 10.63 with the bat.

Having been released by Somerset, he was in discussion with Worcestershire but opted instead to take up the offer of employment back in Wetherby in West Yorkshire. His first-class career had ended while he was still only twenty-one. He has enjoyed a varied career involved in anything from the sale of floor tiles to supplying woven labels and ticketing to the clothing industry, when he was responsible for the UK operations for Nilorn, a post he held until 2008. Thereafter, he has been employed as Operations Manager for a company who manufacture and install safe rubber surfaces for play areas and the like. Most recently he has worked in a similar role, overseeing operations for Trico, a Bingley-based company who produce vitreous enamel signage.

Steve's enthusiasm for the game of cricket and his eagerness to be handed the ball at every opportunity remain undiminished. For many a year he has turned out for Collingham & Linton CC in the Airedale & Wharfedale League, enjoying a period as club captain. He also plays for the Yorkshire Over-50s team. He may be a veteran these days, but in the thrill of the moment when another wicket is claimed, it is possible to feel once more like that nineteen-year-old who, on his first-class debut, had the temerity and the ability to bowl Kapil Dev. Or the youngster with the unbridled exuberance that had him offering to shield Viv Richards from the bowling.

Messrs Bail, Booth and Botham – seated in strict alphabetical order – endure Somerset's annual photocall

1984

"For a successful club, it was hard to swallow missing out on a trophy, but the experience gained for a comparatively young side was invaluable."

Martin Crowe

Championship Position: 7 of 17

It is a measure of just how far the club had progressed in a few years that it should come as an unpleasant surprise to go a whole season without winning anything. Was this a temporary blip or must all good things come to an end? Brian Rose had handed on the captaincy to Ian Botham, but he was absent for much of the season on Test duty. Martin Crowe had arrived from New Zealand as cover for Viv Richards and Joel Garner, both unavailable. After a slow start, he was prolific with the bat, scoring 1,870 first-class runs. Peter Roebuck was consistently among the runs, too, with seven centuries to his name. There was valuable support from Nigel Popplewell, but this was a year of outstanding all-round achievement for Vic Marks, with 1,262 runs at an average of over fifty and eighty-six wickets at 25.96 apiece. Only Mark Davis came close to that haul of first-class wickets, with sixty-six victims. Six wins were never enough to threaten for honours, though.

Martin Crowe declared himself surprised at the indiscipline at the club and did his best to instil good habits in the up-and-coming players. The performances of the new arrival had been a revelation, but some felt that cracks were appearing, and that the outstanding batting of the New Zealander had merely papered over them. Perhaps more noteworthy than any incoming talent was the list of the departed. Seasoned campaigners Hallam Moseley and Peter Denning had gone. Phil Slocombe and Jeremy Lloyds had left, too, both of them among the crop of talent nurtured by Tom Cartwright. The death of Peter 'Jock' McCombe – jester, confidante and factotum – came as a blow to many of the players.

As Jeremy Lloyds was at pains to inform the Committee before he walked through the door, all was not well.

500
Martin David Crowe
28 April 1984 v. Yorkshire, Taunton

[signature: Martin Crowe]

Martin Crowe's first-class and Test records stand as a lasting testament to his greatness as a batsman. So it is worth recalling that, at the time of his appointment, he was still only twenty-one and Somerset were taking a risk with a hugely promising but as yet unproven player, accused at the time by his New Zealand captain, Geoff Howarth, of being a 'show pony'. Martin had been drafted in as cover for Viv Richards and Joel Garner, both touring with the West Indies. He arrived still suffering from the debilitating effects of salmonella poisoning, contracted during a tour of Sri Lanka with New Zealand, and struggled in the early matches to find his feet (apart from a century against a very weak Oxford University side). But by the end of the season, he had silenced any doubters with 1,870 runs at an average of 53.42 and forty-four useful wickets with his medium-paced in-swingers. As with Greg Chappell and Viv Richards before him, Somerset had demonstrated a fine eye for an emerging batsman of genuine class. Martin had rewarded Somerset's faith in him and the experiences had in turn served him well, acting as a springboard to a superb career.

Born on 22 September 1962 in the suburbs of Auckland, New Zealand, he was the son of Dave and Audrey Crowe. An exceptional family, were the Crowes. Both parents were talented at sports – Dave playing first-class cricket and Audrey a successful tennis player. Martin's older brother, Jeff, would captain New Zealand at cricket and their cousin, Russell Crowe, would enjoy global fame in the film industry. From the outset, Martin stood out not just on account of his skill, but also because of his intensity. Some of this was driven by the determination to keep up with a brother four years his senior and some by his innate will to win. Enjoying his first taste of cricket when batting as a five-year-old, he survived a few gentle deliveries in oversized pads that rendered the taking of a single impossible and came away with a score of 0 not out, perhaps hinting at a future in which he never yielded his wicket lightly.

At Auckland Grammar School, he and his close friend and classmate, future All-Black, Grant Fox, were clearly both destined for greatness in their chosen spheres and Martin was determined to outdo brother Jeff, knuckling down to his studies while focussing on relentless improvement as a cricketer. By the age of fifteen he had graduated to the national Under-20s team, at seventeen he was playing first-class cricket for Auckland and at nineteen he won his first Test cap. Martin would later pin his well-deserved reputation for being at times remote and irascible (and always single-minded) on a childhood bypassed, describing himself as a 'record holder for

Martin Crowe – a brilliant cricketer, uncompromising in his quest for excellence

grievances … a disconnected spirit and soul overwhelmed by the ego and the emotional instability created from my unfinished teenage development'. He also described his brother, Jeff, as 'the nicer guy'.

By the time he came to Somerset, Martin had established himself in the New Zealand side without having set the world alight. The prospect of stepping into the shoes of Viv Richards, whom he considered, along with most observers, as the outstanding batsman of the previous eight years, might have caused a lesser man to wilt. But, having recovered from the setback of salmonella poisoning, he established his presence with centuries in four successive matches. Somerset's captain at the time was Ian Botham and, for a while, Martin had shared a flat with him. The bacchanalian lifestyle and constant partying favoured by the skipper proved too much for Martin and it is perhaps no coincidence that his form picked up once he had been offered calmer quarters with Nigel Felton. Beefy might have had the constitution of an ox, but not everyone is so blessed.

Having left Somerset at the end of what proved on a personal level a successful season, Martin would go on to enjoy a hugely successful Test career that would ultimately see him become the highest run maker in his country's history with an aggregate that included a record seventeen centuries.

He had retained his links with Somerset with guest appearances in 1985 and 1986 for the Second XI and for a team named the Young Nags (comprised of a group of young pros and colleagues whose favoured watering hole was The Nag's Head), but found himself in the centre of a storm as Somerset lurched towards civil war. By now one of the most talked-about cricketers in the world, it was inevitable that other counties would express an interest in him and indeed, Essex asked permission of Somerset to sign him as their overseas player. Unbeknown to Martin, this precipitated the decision to release Viv Richards and Joel Garner. Forced to make a choice, Somerset had opted to bring Martin on board. With something to prove, Martin set about rewarding Somerset's faith in him and the statistics demonstrate his worth. His second spell was, however, a more fraught time than his first. There was a huge weight on his shoulders to quell the unrest and turn the county's fortunes around. In the Benson & Hedges Cup quarter final against Northants he aggravated a stress fracture at the base of his spine while bowling his allotted eleven overs and was obliged thereafter to focus on his batting which he did with undoubted success, accumulating 1,627 first-class runs during the 1987 season at an average of 67.79. In the wider context, he would exceed 4,000 runs across Test and first-class cricket in 1987, one of only a handful of men to have achieved the feat in a calendar year.

Dogged by injury the following year, he was obliged to curtail his stay. In truth, the second spell with the county had been at times a frustrating one for him. By his own admission, he regretted that his loyalty to Somerset had meant that he was obliged to watch while Essex went on to greater glories, while he was at times alone in setting the highest of standards at his adoptive county. There was also a sense of discomfort that he had been a pawn. In Martin's own words, spelled out in his book *Out on a Limb*, 'the Somerset Committee should have taken the winter to discuss the situation with everyone involved, and I should have gone to Essex. If they had determined that their future lay with a new captain or overseas player, they should have given Viv and Joel the best possible send-off, then searched for the most suitable replacements.'

It became apparent in time that Martin had never fully recovered from the salmonella poisoning he had suffered earlier in Sri Lanka but after a period of recuperation he was back at his brilliant best and his Test career went from strength to strength. In the 1992 New Year's Honours List, he was awarded an OBE for his services to the game. However, his reputation as a loner and a generally abrasive presence in the dressing room continued to grow to the point that, in 1992, he was about to be dropped as New Zealand captain. He dug in his heels. If New Zealand's star player was going to be stripped of the captaincy then he was not prepared to offer his services. Sanity prevailed and, with a point to prove, he led the national side superbly to the semi-finals of the 1992 World Cup, being named Player of the Tournament.

He made his last Test appearance in 1995, leaving the international arena secure in his position as one the game's greats, having bettered more or less every record available to a New Zealand batsman. In many ways there was a sense of release for a man who had borne so much responsibility and had set himself exacting standards since his teenage years. Married for the first time in 1991 to Simone Curtice, an interior designer, whom he referred to as Simmy, their union was later dissolved and he had a daughter, Emma, with a subsequent partner. He was married again in 2009 to Lorraine Downes, who had won the title Miss Universe in 1983. Spared the pressures of the constant need to prove himself as a cricketer, he had mellowed. He was able to pursue his passions, which included the delights of fine wine and dining and designer clothes, as well as the pleasure he derived in writing. Not for Martin Crowe any ghost-written books: his was a fluent and excoriatingly honest style. He also worked for a number of years for Sky Television, quite happy to speak his mind and prepared to arouse opposition. He worked hard to establish a shortened version of the game of his own invention – Cricket Max – which was rendered redundant when T20 was established. In many ways, Cricket Max is the more interesting of the two formats, but T20 had the advantage of simplicity. He also spent a brief period in 2008 as Chief Cricket Officer with Royal Challengers Bangalore. He became an outspoken critic of sledging, writing in *Wisden* in 2014 that, 'We have all been guilty of taking cricket too seriously. Instead we should consider the consequence of winning at any cost. Sport is an athletic activity, not a religion or a ritual. It's not about life or death.

It needs to be natural, light, free, healthy and humane.'

In 2012, he was diagnosed with follicular lymphoma. He was deemed to have been in remission when the illness returned in 2014. Having already borne his chemotherapy once with great fortitude, he opted on the second occasion to accept his fate and live his remaining days in the bosom of his family. He died on 3 March 2016 in Auckland. His wife, Lorraine, would write that, 'He was the most honest man I have ever met. He wasn't afraid to stand up against any injustice, whether it concerned himself or anyone else.' His fearlessness and honest analysis of his own failings had stood him in good stead as a cricketer and had prepared him to face his untimely impending death with great courage.

501
Murray Stewart Turner
13 June 1984 v. Lancashire, Bath

Murray Turner.

Murray Turner was born on 27 January 1964 in Shaftesbury, Dorset, the son of John Peter and Kathleen (née Steers). John was employed at GCHQ and his work subsequently took him to Taunton, while Kathleen worked as a secretary at Castle School, in the town. Educated at Huish's Grammar School (now Richard Huish College), Murray is described by David Foot in *Sixty Summers* as 'a lively and successful club cricketer in the Taunton area, his progress having been monitored from early schooldays'. At 6 feet 5 inches tall and with long flowing locks in his younger days, he was an imposing all-rounder who bowled right-arm fast-medium seamers but was capable of adding left-arm spin to his armoury as his party piece. He made his debut for Somerset Second XI as a seventeen-year-old in 1981 and became a regular in the side in the ensuing seasons. By 1984, he was knocking on the door for elevation to the First XI and when he completed an innings of forty-five and took nine wickets in the match against Worcestershire Second XI at the start of June, he was given his chance. In the event, he was never able to command a regular place in the first-class game and would appear twelve times over three seasons, averaging 18.00 with the bat and taking fifteen wickets at 52.53 apiece. Murray had left the permanent squad at the end of the 1985 season and the following year played and was paid on a match-by-match basis, which offered nothing in the way of financial security for a young man who was still, in the words of coach Peter Robinson, 'the pick of the bunch' among the Second XI bowlers and a strong enough batsman to score seventy-eight not out that season against Warwickshire Second XI. He had discussions with other counties

Murray Turner – a lively all-rounder and an imposing presence

ahead of the 1987 season and received offers of contracts but concluded that there were better ways to earn a living. During the winter breaks he had found work where he could, spending time at the service reception desk at a Ford dealership, but it was time to secure full-time employment.

In March 1987, he joined the RAF and would remain with them for twelve enjoyable years, during which time he was married in 1992 to Sally (née Cowe). 'Being in the RAF was much more fun than being a cricketer,' he says, although he left in 1999 to join Whitbread as team leader in their Food Logistics function. Since 2011, he has worked as a team leader for Blatchfords, a long-established company specialising in aids to personal independence, with products ranging from prosthetics to wheelchairs.

He was married for second time in 2015, to Helen, has two children and is settled in Hampshire. An ebullient character during his playing days, the passing of the years has not dimmed his appetite for life. With thirty years involved in one way or another in logistics, he can now safely be deemed an expert, but no one can accuse him of becoming a staid businessman or of slowing down. 'I still try to get to as many music festivals as I can fit in each year,' he confesses. 'Murray's a bit wild, but he's basically kind, too,' one teammate observes. 'Lively', David Foot wrote of him. The label still fits.

502
Simon Jonathan Turner
7 July 1984 v. Hampshire, Taunton

Simon Turner was born in Cuckfield, Sussex, on 28 April 1960, the son of Derek Edward Turner, the Sales Director of an engineering company, and Doris Lilian (née Watts). After living for a while in Sussex and then Worcestershire, where younger brother and fellow Somerset cricketer Rob was born, the family settled in Weston-super-Mare. Educated at Broadoak Comprehensive School in the town, Simon had been inspired from a young age by sport and all things mechanical and went on to gain his City and Guilds Technical Certificate in Engineering, taking up a post as an apprentice with Westland Helicopters as a production controller and playing his part in overseeing the Gazelle Aircraft production line. He would remain with Westland Helicopters for ten years, having in the interim retrained as a computer programmer. During 1984 and 1985, he would be offered a contract with Somerset and released by his employer for the summer months.

He played his club cricket as a left-handed wicket-keeper-batsman for Weston-super-Mare CC and enjoyed his first outing for Somerset Second XI in 1982, in what was for him very much a home fixture against Wiltshire at the Westland Sports Ground in Weston. By the start of the 1983 season, he had established a more regular place in the Second XI and to this day he recalls the stress of arriving late for the opening fixture against Hampshire Second XI at Dean Park, Bournemouth, owing largely to the woeful navigational skills of his passenger, Clarence, the team's scorer, whose grasp of statistics was greater than his map-reading abilities. He recovered quickly enough to take three catches in rapid succession that had their opponents reeling.

Having been offered a professional contract, his debut for the First XI came in the 1984 NatWest fixture against Hertfordshire, when Somerset scraped home on an awful wicket at St Albans. Vic Marks, writing in the *Bristol Evening Post*, would observe that, 'Thanks to Weston-super-Mare wicket-keeper Simon Turner, we won one of the most nerve-racking limited overs games I can remember.' Vic went on to say that the uneven track 'required a high standard of wicket-keeping and Simon provided that'. Having been summoned after first-choice Trevor Gard had broken a finger, plaudits continued to come his way following his first-class debut, with the *Western Daily Press* reporting that, 'One of the features of the day was the athletic and very safe wicket-keeping of twenty-four-year-old Simon Turner.' Over the course of six first-class matches during the 1984 and 1985 seasons, he would average 28.00 with the bat and effect nineteen dismissals, before returning to club cricket, where he played a central role in Weston-super-Mare CC's march to the final of the William Younger Cup at Lord's, where they fell at the last hurdle to Stourbridge CC.

After leaving Westland Helicopters in 1987, he was employed for a number of years in information technology for the grocery chain Somerfield plc, as a project manager and in various strategic roles. In 2000, he left Somerfield to work as a consultant for Aspective (now part of Vodafone), recommending ways for businesses to enhance their performance by exploiting new technology. His career as an IT consultant continued with spells at Oak IT Management Services

Simon Turner – a proficient wicket-keeper who stepped up to the plate when his county needed him

Limited and then Canon. Some cynics have been known to regard management consultants as bloodsuckers (though Simon's clients would surely disagree with such an analysis). It is therefore perhaps ironic that more recently he has worked for NHS Blood and Transplant, managing the business changes brought about by the modernisation of their core systems.

Married in 1986 to Jacqueline (née Sims), they would have three children together, although he is now divorced. Simon is certainly not the sort to have ended any relationship on a whim, if his forays into the car market are anything to go by. He is passionate about old vehicles and still owns the 1969 Triumph GT6 that he bought at the age of seventeen and formerly drove to matches, home and away. It is a measure of his mechanical skills and technical know-how that his beloved car still serves him well. These days, he resides in a characterful cottage in Middlezoy, accompanied by his motor car and the woman he describes as 'my lovely partner, Sam'. A man of many talents, he plays the piano and guitar, though he claims modestly that he does so very badly 'largely due to the number of broken fingers while keeping wicket'.

His younger brother, Rob, cut from the same cloth and also a tall wicket-keeper-batsman, might be more familiar to Somerset supporters, but Simon – never a man to trumpet his achievements, and one who, by his own admission, takes delight in fixing things – stepped up to the plate and fixed his county's problems when they needed him. And did a sound job, too.

1985

"Somerset's history is laden with paradoxes but not too many compare with what happened during this miserable, confusing season."

David Foot

Championship Position: 17 of 17

The ignominy of a team with a star-studded cast propping up the Championship should have led to some soul-searching. Instead there was some surface-scratching. It was extraordinary that a team for whom Ian Botham and Viv had amassed a combined total of over 3,000 runs, despite the former's limited availability, should have earned the wooden spoon. There were runs aplenty, including five Botham centuries and an average of 91.42, with 480 of his runs coming in sixes (eclipsing Arthur Wellard's record by some distance). There were nine centuries for Viv Richards, including his astonishing 322 in a day against a demoralised Warwickshire attack. There were more batting bonus points than any other team mustered. But there was only one victory and seven matches were lost, including the first three fixtures, which had set the tone for the season. Joel Garner was hampered by injuries and Ian Botham's ability to impart prodigious amounts of swing appeared to be in rapid decline. Vic Marks alone enjoyed repeated success with the ball. He bowled 812.4 overs and bagged seventy-two wickets to add to his 885 runs. Among the debutants, local boy, Richard Harden, had what it took to establish a long and productive career in first-class cricket.

The John Player Special League campaign was mired in mediocrity, apart from a handful of cameos from Viv Richards. More games were lost than won and the August fixtures were all abandoned without a ball being bowled.

It was becoming clear how much the calm, thoughtful leadership of Brian Rose was missed. Ian Botham relinquished the captaincy 'by mutual agreement'. Some wondered if he was becoming a law unto himself. Vic Marks, who had stood in gamely in the skipper's absence for all bar eleven games, was widely expected to replace Ian. The Committee chose, instead, to hand the reins to Peter Roebuck. 'I am very honoured,' Peter observed, 'but I'm also very surprised.' He was not alone in that.

503
Andrew Paul Jones
27 April 1985 v. Nottinghamshire, Taunton

Andrew Jones is much-travelled, his time with Somerset accounting for fewer than three years in the life of a man who embraced Antipodean culture long enough to have gained dual British and Australian citizenship and who now works in the Netherlands. Born in Southampton on 22 September 1964, he was the son of Paul Jones, a fuel injection engineer employed by Hendy Lennox Ltd, and Patricia (née Bole), a computer operator for Ford Motor Company.

Andrew attended Toynbee Secondary School and Barton Peverell College, both in Eastleigh. 6 feet 2 inches tall, he was a right-arm bowler at the quicker end of medium-pace who played for his native Hampshire at Under-16 level and on occasions for their Second XI. Asked how he came to Somerset's attention, Andrew reveals, 'I was at the West of England training camp at Exeter University and bowled at Vic Marks, and was watched by Bob Cottam.' Both men were impressed by what they witnessed and he was duly offered a contract. Lodging with teammates Julian Wyatt and Mark Davis, he enjoyed his three seasons at the County Ground – 'hanging out with my peer group' – and was part of the Young Nags group, the select bunch of acolytes taken under the wing of Martin Crowe, whose goal was to bring the best out of Somerset's up and coming players. Their name was derived from their get-togethers at the Nag's Head pub. A regular in the Second XI, Andrew would make only three first-class appearances for Somerset, taking three wickets at 47.33 apiece and averaging 1.50 with the bat. By the time he and Somerset parted company, he had begun studying for a BSc in Geography & Sports Science at the West London Institute of Higher Education (later merged into Brunel University), graduating in 1988. He would also play on two occasions for Middlesex Second XI, while enjoying his club cricket with Richmond CC. A good all-round sportsman, he had represented Hampshire at golf as well as appearing for British Colleges at both golf and basketball. But it is not just his athletic prowess that has stood Andrew in good stead. He was offered his first step on the business ladder with Cavendish Consultancy, a corporate entertainment company, before pursuing a career in the drinks industry, calling on his abilities as a fine communicator, bringing the best out of sales forces. In 1992, he joined Courage Breweries, who were later taken over by Scottish & Newcastle. He then emigrated to Australia, where he joined Lion Nathan, a sizeable Australian food and drink distributor (with their headquarters in Sydney) who carry within their

Andrew Jones – a medium-fast bowler who played three times for Somerset

portfolio both local and international brands. Here he took on the role of Sales Capability Director, ensuring the right sales team was in place, armed with the right skills. He remained based in Sydney until 2007, when he took on a similar role within the Scottish & Newcastle business empire before their takeover by Heineken and Carlsberg, who split the various brands and markets between them and apportioned jobs for their new employees accordingly. Taken on by Heineken, Andrew's role, at the time of writing, is that of Senior Capability Leader, overseeing the company's global sales academy, based at their head office in Amsterdam.

In 1995 he had been married to Sarah (née Morgan), whom he met while she was working as a trade marketer at Courage, but was later divorced and married in 2002 to Chris (née Albin), who worked in recruitment and with whom he now has a son, Joshua, and a daughter, Georgia. With his dual citizenship, a family he adores, a successful career and the knowledge that many happy hours on the course await for this skilled golfer when the time finally comes to retire, the fact that he is a former first-class cricketer is mere icing on the cake.

504
Richard John Harden
8 May 1985 v. Australia, Taunton

There is some truth in Peter Roebuck's assertion that Somerset's home grown players blooded in the 1970s were by and large a success and that those introduced in the 1980s struggled to make their mark in the same way. Perhaps it was one of those quirks of fortune. Maybe the departure of Tom Cartwright, by any measure an outstanding coach, heralded a change. Or had a healthy rivalry, with Viv Richards and Ian Botham laying down markers, spurred a group of players to greater feats? If the trend is true in general terms, then Richard Harden stands out as an exception. Judges as sound as Viv Richards, Jimmy Cook and Peter Robinson all predicted early that here was a young batsman who had what it takes to survive the rigours of the first-class game. To thrive requires a combination of skill and temperament and the latter was certainly tested when Richard endured the most dispiriting of welcomes to the first-class arena. As he walked towards the wicket he was greeted by Australia's Craig McDermott. In Richard's words, 'The first two balls whistled past my nose … and McDermott finished his follow through with some encouraging words, "I'm going to knock your ------ head off, you little pommie ----" … I then proceeded to glove the fifth one to the keeper. I remember thinking: how was I ever going to get any runs.' As it happens, he would amass 13,338 of them in the first-class game, the vast majority for Somerset.

Known to friends and fellow cricketers as Dick (although his teammates in New Zealand gave him the moniker 'Floppy'), he was born in Bridgwater on 16 August 1965, the son of Chris Harden, and Ann (née Cottle). Richard attended King's College in Taunton, coming under the aegis of former West Indies and Hampshire bats-

Richard Harden – one of the mainstays of the Somerset batting line up, regularly among the runs, refusing to yield his wicket without a fight

man, Roy Marshall, and captaining the cricket, rugby and hockey teams, whilst also representing the school at squash. Although he had played for Somerset in age group cricket, no contract was offered when he left school. Instead, he decided to embark on a career in the insurance industry, but soon found himself hankering after life as a professional cricketer. He therefore spoke to Peter Robinson, who was overseeing the Second XI and who confessed that no money was available. Such was Richard's determination to make a go of things that he agreed to appear whilst being paid only a meal allowance and travelling expenses. Peter was further impressed by his charge's audacity in insisting that there was little point in sending him to bat in the middle order as he would be denied the opportunity to prove his true worth to the club. To his undoubted tenacity should be added the further virtue of self-belief.

Perhaps the county's initial reticence stemmed from Richard's approach to batting, which was effective rather than orthodox and not always pleasing on the eye. Where others might have stroked the ball elegantly through the covers, Richard, playing with a lot of bottom hand, accumulated the majority of his runs with strong shots off the back foot or by paddling the ball behind, much to the exasperation of opposing spin bowlers. He worked assiduously to hone his technique, building on his strengths rather than attempting to alter his approach. Further experience was gained each winter. After one season in South Africa, he would enjoy seven winters in New Zealand, with Nelson in South Island becoming a second home to him as he spent time there as a player and coach, first with New Plymouth Old Boys CC and then Wakatu CC, also appearing for Nelson representative sides and Central Districts. He would take a step towards making New Zealand his permanent home when he was married in1992 to Nicki Patterson, with whom he has a son, Joel.

Back in Somerset in 1985, his first innings might have proved nightmarish but he was soon into his stride with a confidence-boosting century against Cambridge University in his third appearance. By 1990, he was considered one of the mainstays of the Somerset batting line up, regularly among the runs and refusing to yield his wicket without a fight. Ken Palmer would recall the match against Leicestershire at Weston-super-Mare in 1995 in which he was umpiring, observing that, on a turning pitch, 'for two overs, Dick couldn't lay a bat on the ball', providing much amusement to all bar the batsman himself. But he knuckled down, bided his time and grafted his way to a score of 124. The innings was typical. His fielding, whether at short-leg or in the covers, was surprisingly athletic, it has been noted, for a well-built man. Over the course of 233 matches, he would average 38.90, with twenty-eight centuries. His bowling – which he delivered left-arm at an unthreatening pace: 'dobbers', he calls them, self-deprecatingly, the term being synonymous with the buoys that float on a fishing line, devoid of momentum – yielded sixteen wickets at 56.18 apiece. It is a measure of the respect in which he was held across the first-class game that when he and Somerset called it a day in 1998, two years after his Benefit season, Yorkshire offered a two-year contract. It is a rare thing for Yorkshire to show interest in a Somerset-born player, though many a cricketer has migrated in the other direction. Sadly, his time there was blighted by injuries, including a broken finger.

For a number of years after his last winter season in New Zealand – 1991-92 – Richard had worked each off-season for Pennine Dataforms, a company based in the North West whose specialism was printed stationery compatible with the computers of the time. The plan had been for Richard to act as a sales rep, building up the business in the South West, in readiness for the setting up of a subsidiary, in Taunton, that he would manage on his retirement from the game. But things moved on both for the computing industry and for Richard, and he settled instead in Nelson. Since moving there, he has worked as a financial adviser, setting up his own company, Richard Harden Investment Services, in 2002, managing investments for individuals, companies and trusts. He specialises in UK pension transfers for those wishing to follow his lead and emigrate to New Zealand. Since 2010, he has been a director of Professional Investment Associates, an invitation-only group of like-minded individuals who come together to share best practice. Richard has always been committed to making the most of his talents: single-minded, but prepared to listen to those with good advice to offer. In 2017, he joined forces with two other financial advisers to form Totara Wealth Management, based in Nelson. He was married for a second time in 2017 to Rachel Reese.

During his career he garnered an outstanding reputation for accumulating runs while avoiding any unnecessary risks. These days, he applies those attributes with the same rigour to the protection and enhancement of his clients' wealth.

505
Paul Andrew Clayden Bail
29 May 1985 v. Yorkshire, Leeds

Born on 23 June 1965 in Burnham-on-Sea, Paul was the son of John Bail, the commercial manager of a property business, and Erica (née Slater-Poole). With his father for a while President of the Somerset Cricket League and Paul a pupil from 1978 until 1984 at Millfield School – a rich source of talented cricketers – there was little or no prospect of his slipping under Somerset's radar. Indeed, he was given his chance in the Second XI in 1983 and would make a number of further appearances as a batsman

Paul Bail – a talented Cambridge undergraduate, awarded multiple blues at cricket and football, he opted for a career more lucrative than cricket

and occasional off-break bowler in his final two years at Millfield. Having shown signs of great promise with performances such as his 194 for an England Schools Under-19 side and his double century against Lancashire Second XI that contributed to his being second in the national Minor Counties averages in 1984, the future looked bright. Having won a place at Downing College, Cambridge, to study for a degree in Economics, he would go on to represent his Varsity side for four seasons, gaining blues in each of his first three years there and being lauded by *Wisden* as one to watch in both senses of the expression. The high point was undoubtedly his 174 against Oxford University in 1986. He would also win two blues at football, having previously played for the English Public Schools football team for two seasons.

By the time he graduated, his career with Somerset was over. He had played in only seven first-class games for the county and had come away with a batting average of 22.90. If the high point was his seventy-eight not out while opening against Kent in 1985, then the nadir came against Warwickshire three months earlier, when he was struck a blow in the head from a vicious bouncer from Gladstone Small and was obliged to retire hurt, making way for Nigel Felton who was promptly dismissed by Small for a golden duck. Enter Viv Richards. Uncowed by anything Gladstone Small or any other member of the Warwickshire attack could come up with, Viv made his imperious 322 in a day that had everyone bar Paul, Nigel and the eleven men of Warwickshire delighted to have been there.

Bright, numerate and with his Economics degree under his belt, Paul embarked on what would prove to be a successful career in the financial industry, cricket remaining an enjoyable pastime rather than an end in itself. He found his way in time to club cricket for Richmond CC in the Middlesex League, having made Minor Counties appearances over the course of three seasons for Wiltshire.

Employed after graduating by Hill Samuel, a subsidiary of the TSB Group, he managed the relationship with a selection of the bank's corporate clients before spending time in the TSB headquarters as a member of the strategic development team.

Then, for an eight year period, he was with Bank of America, taking up senior roles in leveraged finance – for the uninitiated, perhaps best summed up as matching those wishing to invest money with those who are likely to deploy it to generate profit. There followed a spell with Barclays Bank, for whom he became a Senior Director in 2007. A subsequent two-year tenure with Investec as a director in their debt advisory business – arranging refinancing deals for companies or raising capital – then led to Paul's time at Robert W. Baird & Co, a US-based company with offices in Finsbury Circus in the City of London. Initially hired as a director in their debt advisory business, he has subsequently taken on a role as a managing director in their mergers and acquisitions team, his remit covering Europe. Married in 2003 to Amanda (née Simpson), with whom he has a daughter, Paul remains with R. W. Baird at the time of writing.

In *Sixty Summers*, David Foot asks: 'Might Somerset have persevered longer with him?' Perhaps. But it appears that Paul had bigger fish to fry. Some fortunate souls who have the talent to survive in the first-class game are happier thriving in more lucrative environments.

506
Richard Edward Hayward
8 June 1985 v. Gloucestershire, Bath

Until his retirement in 2016, Richard Hayward had enjoyed a long association with Nelson Cricket Association in New Zealand's South Island. The association has worked its way into cricketing parlance with the term 'Nelson' applying to a score of 111, a number regarded with dread by many batsman of a superstitious bent, supposedly heralding the likelihood of a dismissal. Some have attributed the myth to the ill-luck of Admiral Horatio Nelson's ending his life in possession of one arm, one eye and one other unspecified body part. The most likely explanation for the name, though, lies in the fortunes of Nelson CA during their formative years. In both the very first and very last innings of their brief brush with first-class status, they had scored exactly 111 runs. Given that the city was named after the eponymous admiral, the proponents of the more fanciful explanation are not entirely wrong.

Born not in the country that became his home, but in Hillingdon, Middlesex, on 15 February 1954, Richard was the son of Alec Henry Francis Hayward MBE, a company managing director who had served with the Royal Artillery and risen to the rank of major, and was married to Sylvia (née Thoroughgood). There was some crick-

Richard Hayward – came to the aid of a Somerset side beset by injuries and did not disappoint

eting pedigree in the Hayward family. Richard's father – at one time a wicket-keeper in club cricket – later became Chairman of Ickenham CC. His uncle presided over Civil Service cricket and the Kent Association of Cricket Clubs. Educated at Latymer Upper Grammar School in Hammersmith, Richard was selected to play for the England Schools side in 1970, but then spent six years as an executive officer in the Civil Service. Over that period, he made a number of appearances for Middlesex Second XI as an all-rounder, batting left-handed and bowling left-arm medium pace, before then throwing in his lot with Buckinghamshire, also being selected for the combined Minor Counties XI, making his first class debut against India.

He gained his first taste of New Zealand cricket in 1979, as a member of a Cricket Club Conference side who also toured Australia, Singapore and Hong Kong and the following year, he was invited back to spend the winter as Nelson's professional coach, taking over from Billy Ibadulla. This proved the springboard to his career in the first-class game in England, initially with Hampshire, where his debut in July 1981, against the touring Sri Lankans, could hardly have gone much better, with an unbeaten century followed by a half-century in the second innings. At the age of twenty-seven, he had been late to the party, but it had been worth the wait. He spent three seasons with Hampshire, but his association with Nelson in New Zealand would prove more long-standing. By 1985, he was well established and had been invited to captain the Central Districts side when the call came unexpectedly for him to come to the aid of a Somerset side beset by injuries, a number of top order batsmen having broken fingers. In nine matches he would average 30.88, with one unbeaten century to his name. That same year he was married in August at Curdworth, Warwickshire, to Susan Anne Harper, a teacher, based at the time in North London. Apart from a brief spell with Hampshire as Assistant Coach from 1992 to 1994, his future lay in New Zealand. He captained and later coached Nelson until 2002, when he was offered the role of High Performance and Coaching Director of Canterbury CA, with whom he would remain until 2014. During his tenure Canterbury Cricket's international ground, Lancaster Park, was destroyed in the earthquake that devastated much of Christchurch on 22 February 2011 and threw the lives of many into chaos. The aftershocks continued for more than a year and the city was ruined. The earthquake caused a major upheaval in the lives of Richard and Sue, their home having been severely damaged. It took five years for them to receive the settlement from their insurers which enabled them to move on and buy a home in Nelson. In Richard's own words, 'Living through it all was very traumatic and scary, a life-changing time.'

In 2014, Richard was welcomed back into the fold as General Manager of the Nelson Cricket Association, at a time when they were cementing the reputation of their new Saxton Oval ground as a venue for One Day Internationals. He played a leading role in the organisation and running of three matches in the 2015 Cricket World Cup at Saxton Oval. The event was deemed a huge success and has provided a lasting memory for all Nelsonians. An indoor cricket school was also in the throes of construction – all a vast improvement from the days when Richard had played for the association. A mere two years later, though, in 2016, he announced that he was retiring from the game he loved and that he and his wife, Sue, would be moving to a newly-built home in Nelson, a base from which to explore the beautiful country they call home.

507
Jonathon Colin Mark Atkinson
10 August 1985 v. Northamptonshire, Weston-super-Mare

Jonny Atkinson was born in Butleigh on 10 July 1968, the son of Colin Atkinson and Shirley (née Angus). Colin was at the time headmaster of Millfield School, having retired a year earlier from a career in the first-class game that had included three seasons as Somerset captain, a period in which he had led the county to their first Lord's final in the Gillette Cup of 1967. Colin would go on to play a prominent role as President of Somerset CCC, while enhancing the reputation of Millfield by building on the foundations laid by the mercurial Jack Meyer. Like his father before him, Jonny was born to lead. But whereas Colin was by nature a reserved man, the son was extroverted, tall (at 6 feet 4 inches) and unfazed by the fact that his father was head of the school.

Educated first at Edgarley Hall (the Millfield Junior School) and then Millfield Senior School, Jonny was a member of the First XI for five years and captain for the last two of these. There was never a question of any nepotism. On the contrary, it has been noted that on one occasion, Jonny was summoned to his father's office to explain the overly exuberant behaviour of his team when visiting a rival school in Taunton. An all-round sportsman, he played in the hockey First XI for three years, representing the county and the region. As a member of the rugby First XV for two seasons, he was that rare beast, a place-kicking number eight.

He made his first appearance for Somerset Second XI a week after his sixteenth birthday and was soon making a name for himself as a forceful batsman and bowler of quickish medium pace. Drafted into the Somerset team for his first-class debut at seventeen, his first two appearances were notable. Having been invited to play at Weston-super-Mare after a penetrative bowling stint for the Somerset Colts at Chippenham, the previous day, he announced himself in the game against Northamptonshire by blasting 79 runs in an exhilarating display of uninhibited hitting alongside Ian Botham. The pair would enjoy a partnership of 177 in double-quick time, with Beefy amassing ten sixes during his innings and Jonny contributing three maximums. As he would later observe, 'I think T20 would have suited me rather well.' In the following match, it was his turn to be on the receiving end. Having had to borrow one of the team's two communal helmets, on the advice of Colin Dredge, he was obliged to don ill-fitting headgear. It is a moot point whether the protection was a help or a hindrance as Jonny faced Wayne Daniel of Middlesex, whom he describes understatedly as 'a bit quicker than I was used to' and was promptly hit square between the eyes, dislodging a bolt that hit Clive Radley at first slip. Radley kindly screwed it back in place. The helmet at least did its job and Jonny recovered to piece together a score of 25, hitting Wayne Daniel for a straight six a few balls later before being told to calm down by Vic Marks, on the basis that it was advisable 'not to annoy him'. Although his maiden knock would prove his best for the county, Jonny was impressing the powers that be sufficiently to be drafted into the Young England (Under-19) side in 1986.

His career with Somerset would span six seasons, but he would make only fourteen first-class appearances for them over that period, averaging 28.13 with the bat and taking four wickets at 107.00 apiece. He also played in eight List A matches for the county. A major reason for his peripheral role was his absence while an undergraduate. Having been offered a place at Downing College, Cambridge, to study Economics, he would be awarded blues in each of his three years there, playing twenty-seven first class games for Cambridge, although his first Varsity match – in 1988 – was abandoned as a wash-out. He played eleven games for a strong Combined Universities side who defied expectation by reaching the quarter finals of the Benson & Hedges Cup in 1989. Among his teammates were future England captains Mike Atherton and Nasser Hussain. Ahead of the quarter final, Jonny was interviewed at Fenner's for *Grandstand* and asked what it would be like to be playing against his own county at Taunton. He has never been allowed to forget his response that, 'It will be nice to go

Jonny Atkinson – 'I think T20 would have suited me rather well'

home and get some washing done.' In the event, the Combined Universities fell an agonising three runs short of the Somerset total in a pulsating game.

He captained Cambridge in 1990 and the fact that he cites the former team's victory over Sussex at Hove as a highlight, despite having been run out for a duck, confirms that Jonny was a team man. He confesses to having found the politics of the Somerset dressing room 'sometimes volatile and juvenile, but always interesting'. Perhaps the experience had served him well when it came to his own leadership of a more harmonious bunch of players. In an earlier age, he might have been asked to follow in his father's footsteps and take on the task of leading the county. But on graduating, he opted for a career in the insurance business, enjoying eighteen years from 1991 as a broker, initially with J & H Insurance, where he specialised in professional liability, and latterly, based primarily in London but with a five-year spell in Bermuda, as a partner with JLT and then Willis. Since 2011, Jonny has been the Global Head of Distribution and Marketing for the Aspen Insurance Company.

Married in 1996 to Alice Blount, whom he describes as 'a beautiful Norfolk girl and farmer's daughter I met at a dinner party thrown by Richard Pyman [who played for Cambridge University, Somerset Second XI and Dorset and was Jonny's best man]'. The couple would have four sons and Jonny states that, 'My family means more to me than any of my other achievements by some margin.' Although now ensconced in London and enjoying occasional games of cricket for the prestigious Hurlingham Club in Fulham, even setting a record of thirteen sixes in one innings, Jonny retains fond memories of his upbringing in Somerset 'including the ever-present smell of Friesian cows on The Levels'. He must be one of a limited number of well-heeled Londoners who remains unwavering in his support for Bristol Rovers FC as well as Somerset CCC, following their fortunes in their good times and in their bad, though he has had to witness rather more of the latter over the years. In his own life, by way of a contrast, things have turned out rather well.

508
Simon Alexander Ross Ferguson
14 August 1985 v. Middlesex, Weston-super-Mare

Simon Ferguson was born in Lagos, Nigeria, on 13 May 1961, the son of Iain Alexander Waverley Drysdale Ferguson, a company director, and Marjorie (née Dean). Educated at Framlingham College in Suffolk, having previously attended the college's prep school, Brandeston Hall, he initially played his club cricket for Chelmsford CC, close to where his parents then lived. He went on to Lancaster University, where he captained the team for two seasons. A right-handed batsman and occasional bowler of medium-pace, he led his side to two indoor UAU (Universities Athletic Union) titles. Having notched up three consecutive centuries for the English Universities, he was invited to captain the British Universities Sports Federation side against Essex Second XI, impressing observers with scores of 80 not out and 73. There followed a period with Essex, with Simon topping the county's Second XI averages in 1983. He also appeared for Suffolk and, during that time, he combined his playing with two years working in the fashion industry during the off-season.

His move to Taunton came in 1984, when he captained the Staplegrove CC team and played regularly for the Somerset Second XI. He recalls his trial with the Somerset Under-25s side with amusement. 'I'd arrived on the 4 am milk train from London in my blue blazer and grey trousers – the regulation dress at Essex – and the Somerset boys were looking askance at me, but fortunately I scored ninety or so [91] and then had to sleep on the snooker table because I couldn't afford a hotel.' His form for Staplegrove was excellent and he performed strongly for Somerset Second XI in 1985. Simon was rewarded with his only first-class appearance in August 1985. Playing against Middlesex at Weston-Super-Mare, he scored eight runs in his one first-class innings. Having subsequently suffered from a back injury, he recovered sufficiently to play in Sydney during the winter of 1985-86 but thereafter opted to focus on his business career.

Married, for a brief period to Caroline (née Jeffery), who hailed from Corfe, Simon would continue to enjoy considerable success as a batsman in club cricket with Hampstead CC and Richmond CC, captaining Middlesex Cricket Union and representing the England Amateur XI. While at Hampstead, he was a teammate of Andy Caddick, and one of those banging the drum that he was ready to step up to the first-class game. Subsequently, based near Cape Town in South Africa, Simon enjoyed further triumphs with Claremont Constantia CC and was a member of the side who won the Supersport National Club Championships. He serves as an example of a player dominant at club level – who over the course of his playing days would be able to make the claim of having scored a century of centuries – but unable to make his mark in the first-class arena.

Beyond the world of cricket, his journey through life has not always run smoothly. Embroiled in a legal dispute over alleged fraud that dragged on for more than a decade, Simon was finally found to have been a victim rather than a perpetrator. Somewhat of a wheeler-dealer, whose investments have not invariably proved sound, he admits to errors of judgement. Fingers – his own and those of others – have been burned along the way. Sadly, his supposed crimes were widely reported but his subse-

Simon Ferguson – a batsman dominant in club cricket but unable to impose himself at a more elevated level

quent exoneration passed by barely noticed, perhaps reflecting the taste of journalists and readers for the sensational.

The misadventure began in 1996 when he was persuaded to invest in Hemingway plc. and given the role of negotiating with scientists at City University (as it was then known) in London. Hemingway planned to market an emulsifier – Aquasolve – that would allow cars to run more cheaply, cleanly and efficiently on a mixture of diesel and water. The negotiations collapsed after thirteen weeks, the Hemingway bubble burst, and, bruised by his experiences, Simon left for South Africa, in large part to indulge his passion for cricket in Constantia. Not long afterwards, he was approached by a company named Lifeline, who had acquired the patent and were, they confirmed, prepared to sell him the South African licence. By 1998, the original product had been sufficiently modified and enhanced by a South African cosmetics manufacturer to acquire a fresh patent for an alternative named Olpex. A new company, Whetstone Industrial Holdings, was listed in 1998 on the Johannesburg Stock Exchange but very soon a seemingly viable business had proved a chimera. Many lost fortunes overnight, Simon among them. It has subsequently emerged that one man, a once well-regarded attorney, had stood to gain most from the shenanigans. But for many years, stories, leaked to the media, suggested that Simon had been a serial fraudster, an egregious character who had escaped bail and fled to South Africa. After a harrowing time during which his assets, including his family home were sequestrated and auctioned off, he was finally exonerated with his then lawyer found to be the instigator and perpetrator of the lies told about him. Simon was able to start his business life afresh. In his own words, 'I've lost a great deal of money, but the greater loss has been suffered by my family – the humiliation of having your home auctioned off and the gossip.'

His parting shot to journalists at the end of his ordeal was, 'I'll be back.' True to his word, Simon has now set up a company – named Sutrex Defense – with five fellow partners. Based in Montenegro, he flies the flag of the defence industry on behalf of UK and US arms manufacturers. This company has become one of the most successful of its type in the industry. Sadly, he has suffered more recently from ill health and is undergoing treatment for cancer, another battle that he will face with courage and determination. Beside him in his struggle will be his daughter, Anna, whom he describes as 'the light of my life' and Aksana (née Belush), whom he was finally married to in December 2018. 'I should have done it a long time ago,' he confesses. Aksana has been his partner for many years and, in Simon's words, 'a source of love and strength' throughout his trials and tribulations.

509
Robert Vincent Jerome Coombs
14 August 1985 v. Middlesex, Weston-super-Mare

Rob Coombs was late to the first-class game, the offer of a professional contract with Somerset coming suddenly and unexpectedly, just as he was about to embark on a teaching career. Sometimes one serendipitous moment changes everything – in his case, a beautifully-flighted delivery to the advancing Ian Botham.

Born on 20 July 1959 in Barnet, Hertfordshire, he was the son of John Michael Coombs, known as Michael, a life assurance manager, married to Dena (née Steeds). Rob attended King's College in Taunton, as his father had done before him. After leaving school, the son began working in Poole as a motor claims negotiator for Norman Frizzell (latterly subsumed into LV). A tall, left-arm orthodox bowler, he played club cricket for Bournemouth CC and from 1979 onwards turned out regularly for Dorset in Minor Counties cricket.

Four years were enough to convince him that his future lay elsewhere than in the insurance industry and he left for St Luke's College (University of Exeter) to qualify as a teacher, taking a B Ed degree in Education, Chemistry and Science. While at St Luke's, he was a member of the side invited to play Somerset at the County Ground in a warm-up match. Rob recounts the tale. 'I was having a good day and Martin Olive couldn't get me away. Ian Botham was at the non-striker's end and getting frustrated that the score wasn't moving along and so, when he finally got to face me, he'd already decided that he was going to show Martin how it's done. The first delivery I bowled to him, he came down the wicket and tried to plant the ball in the stands, but I beat the edge of the bat and he was stumped. To tell the truth, it wasn't even a proper stumping. Our keeper fumbled it and it bounced off his pads and knocked the bails off.' Ian Botham was instrumental in ensuring that Somerset secured Rob's services when he became available in June 1985. A five-wicket haul on his maiden appearance for Somerset Second XI was followed by a similar feat on his first-class debut, when he took 5 for 58 in Middlesex's only innings in a drawn match at Weston-super-Mare. He then appeared the following season on a regular basis, without ever managing to establish himself in the First XI for a prolonged period. Perhaps his most vivid memory of that time is of the match against Gloucestershire at Bristol, when he came in at number eleven with Mark Davis valiantly holding up one end. The pair attempted to avert the follow-on, faced by a rampant Courtney Walsh. They had managed to put

Rob Coombs – the offer of a professional contract came suddenly and unexpectedly, just as he was about to embark on a teaching career

together a partnership of twenty-eight – the largest in the Somerset innings – when calamity struck. Rob takes up the story. 'I'd snicked a couple of fours between the slips and gully and so I knew what was coming next. I was wearing a helmet that didn't fit me properly. I'd borrowed it from Richard Harden. The bouncer duly came and removed the helmet from my head, landing on the stumps, so that I was out hit wicket for eighteen. Fortunately, the helmet absorbed all the impact so I was none the worse for the experience, just disappointed that our heroic efforts had left us seven short of avoiding the follow-on.'

At the end of the 1986 season, with Somerset ringing the changes, he parted company with them, opting instead to embark on his planned teaching career. In total, he had appeared in thirteen first-class matches, taking thirty-two wickets at 34.75 runs apiece and averaging 5.33 with the bat. That same year, he was married to Jill Gauntlett, whom he had first met when she was serving behind the bar at Bournemouth CC. Jill and Rob would have five children, their three sons becoming successful club cricketers. Sadly, Jill died of lung cancer in 2013. The youngest of their children was in his mid-teens at the time, but Rob and his family worked through the pain of their loss. He has subsequently found happiness once more with his second wife, Helen Saunders.

Back in 1986, Rob had been offered a post as a primary school teacher at Winton Junior School (later amalgamated into Winton Primary School). At the time of writing, some thirty years later, he is still there, on a part-time basis. At 6 feet 4 inches and with a voice suitably authoritative and sonorous, maintaining discipline and the rapt attention of his pupils has never been a problem for Rob, whom most friends and colleagues would describe as a gentle giant, as indeed would those of his young pupils familiar with the term. He has retained his links with Bournemouth CC, at various times as captain of the First XI and then the Second XI, spending time as the club's chairman. 'I carried on playing for Dorset until 1990, but I'm afraid I suffered from the yips for a while. It's a debilitating thing, not knowing how the ball will come out of your hand, but I was happy to watch the progress of my sons, one of whom still plays for Bournemouth,' he says.

Rob plays golf these days – 'badly', he insists, with his usual modesty – but he can look back fondly on his brief spell as a first-class cricketer and enjoy his status as a member of a select band of bowlers who tamed Ian Botham.

*   *   *   *   *

Royston Cyril John Sully

Making his only List A appearance for Somerset in 1985 was Roy Sully. Roy was thirty-four at the time and had played on occasions for Somerset Second XI, his appearances limited by work commitments. When asked by team captain, Ian Botham, what his view of the selection decision was, Peter Roebuck responded (as noted in *The Power and the Glory* by Simon Wilde) that he believed 'the lunatics had taken over the asylum, which put my cards on the table'. On another table – the physio's – lay Roy, struggling with a groin injury he had failed to declare, having been determined not to miss his chance. This was, after all, a dream come true for a man who had supported the club since boyhood.

Born on 10 April 1951 in Taunton and raised in nearby Bishops Lydeard, he was the son of Percival, a boilerman at Sandhill Park Hospital who had earlier worked for the Great Western Railway, and Sylvia Jean, known as Jean, whose many and varied jobs included a spell at the Lethbridge Arms in the village. Roy attended Kingsmead School in nearby Wiveliscombe. He was from his early days a confident, ebullient character and enjoyed success in club cricket and as a forward for Taunton Town FC, among others. Perhaps his greatest feats of endurance involved his ability to match Ian Botham's capacity for alcohol, though Roy points out that rumours of his selection for Somerset being based solely on their friendship are wide of the mark. 'To be fair,' he observes, 'I took more than 550 wickets in the local Premier

Roy Sully – a confident, ebullient character who enjoyed success in local club cricket and football

League at nine runs apiece.' A medium-pace bowler who made useful runs at club level, he had started his club cricket with Bishops Lydeard CC before going on to play for Taunton Nomads CC and Taunton CC. 'I was fifteen when I made my club debut,' Roy recalls. 'I can tell you the date, too. 30 July 1966. I was playing at Dene Court [Bishops Lydeard CC's ground at that time] when I'd have rather been watching England playing West Germany in the World Cup Final.'

In the John Player Special League match on 12 May 1985 against Glamorgan, Peter Roebuck carried his bat, Ian Botham bowled brilliantly and Roy mustered a score of two and took 0 for 15 in his two overs before limping out of the fray. Glamorgan won by two wickets. Although already selected for the following game – against Kent in the Benson & Hedges Cup – Roy was forced on this occasion to withdraw because of the extent of his injury.

He garnered further headlines in the local press a few years afterwards when, at Minehead, he came to the defence of a policeman who had been attacked and stabbed by two assailants, both under the influence of drugs. He was widely feted as a 'have-a-go hero' and presented with an award for his bravery. For many years, Roy was an Area Sales Manager for Arthur David, a fruit and vegetable wholesaler based in Bristol. He continues to work on a part-time basis, while golf has replaced cricket and football as his sport of choice. At the time of writing, he is captain of the Oake Manor Golf Club near Taunton, still as cheerily positive in his late sixties as he was when he supported Somerset as a young boy.

1986

"I can cope with the 'superstars' in our team ... Most of
the senior players have been together a long time now –
Viv Richards, Vic Marks, Ian Botham and myself all joined
the county at the same time. We go back a long way and
we have been friends a long while. I see no reason
for that to change now."

Peter Roebuck

"Judas."

Attributed to Ian Botham

Championship Position: 16 of 17

The trajectory of the season was rendered inconsequential by what followed, but,
for the record, the fare on offer was less spectacular than the previous season's, the
results marginally less dispiriting. Five men – Peter Roebuck, Viv Richards, Richard
Harden, Vic Marks and Nigel Fenton – exceeded 1,000 runs. Ian Botham would have
done, too, had he been more readily available. He had, in truth, become a fine batsman who turned his arm, whereas the reverse had once held true. Vic Marks's haul of
wickets was the greatest, with Joel Garner not far behind. Among the debutants, Jon
Hardy and Ricky Bartlett would both turn in some useful performances with the bat,
but neither man would impose himself on the first-class game.

If the performances on the field too often failed to stir the blood, then the same
could hardly be said of the internecine fighting that engulfed the club. The club officials were faced with the need to revivify a team suffering ailing health. Some felt that
the younger players were intimidated by the likes of Viv and Ian. Others felt that the
problem was simply a dearth of new talent. Where was the next generation of serial
winners? In the event, their hand was forced. Martin Crowe was by then one of the
world's leading batsmen. Essex wanted him, but he felt he owed a debt to Somerset
and offered them first refusal. Viv and Joel would be unavailable two seasons down
the tracks. The Committee acted decisively. The two West Indian superstars were
informed that their services were no longer required. Had they not both enjoyed

bumper Benefit Years? Was the account not even?

There has been a tendency when analysing Somerset cricket's disintegration and descent into civil war to focus on the players as the main protagonists, when the fault surely lay with those who were at the helm of the club. It is easy to forget that a majority of sportsmen, though fine specimens who seem to have been in the public eye for an eternity, are in fact relatively young and often unversed in the nuances of man-management. Hard-nosed planning for the future – the tricky decisions in the present – should arguably fall to the club managers and not the players. Times have changed in the three decades that followed. In the mid-1980s, those running the club had been complacent or reticent and assumed or hoped that the good times would last forever. But Somerset had in truth reverted to type, a happy-go-lucky club propped up by spellbinding cameos. And when belatedly they tried to rectify their errors, Peter Roebuck bore the brunt of the opprobrium. Ill-equipped at the time for the role of captain, he combined admirable intellectual integrity with a dearth of emotional intelligence. It would take years for the club to recover from its self-inflicted admission to Intensive Care.

We should be grateful, with the benefit of hindsight, that social media was at the time no more than a gleam in the eye of the two-year-old Mark Zuckerberg. There was polarisation and vitriol enough back then, positions hardening as the clock

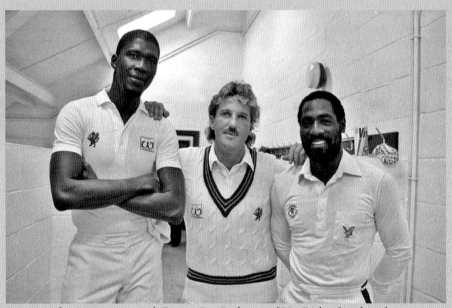

Somerset's three superstars – Joel Garner, Ian Botham and Viv Richards, whose departure sparked something akin to civil war

165

ticked towards a showdown at Shepton Mallet, normally a sleepy sort of place where the most exciting event each year is the Royal Bath & West Show. Not in 1986. Metaphorical dirty washing was aired, some home truths exposed. The rebels lost the day. The three superstars were lost to Somerset cricket. The whole exercise had been managed with an absence of wit or diplomacy. Viv Richards would return triumphantly with Glamorgan. Ian Botham would win trophies aplenty with a strong Worcestershire side. Joel Garner would enjoy a successful return to league cricket. Peter Roebuck would later leave for Devon, revelling in his newly-found freedom and leading the Minor County to greater glories. Somerset turned to outside help to bolster the squad, as had always been the case from the dawn of the club's Championship history. They had years of solid and unspectacular achievement ahead, punctuated by flurries of excitement. Yes, the days of glory had been and gone.

The three departing heroes eventually made their peace with the club. Personal enmity lingered rather longer. Peter Roebuck, blamed by some for the debacle, at least deserves credit for his full, frank and fair-minded account of events in his history of the club, published in 1991.

Four supporters of Somerset's 'Big Three' voice their opinion with more eloquence and subtlety than some others mustered, though, sadly for them, the power of the carefully-crafted anagram proved insufficient to win the day

166

510
Jonathan James Ean Hardy
19 April 1986 v. Oxford University, Oxford

[signature: Jon Hardy]

Jon Hardy has arguably had a greater impact on the game of cricket as a result of his inventiveness and business acumen than through his time as a player. Born on 2 October 1960 in Nakuru, a city in Kenya, he was the son of Ray and Petasue Hardy. Ray hailed from Yorkshire and was a useful club cricketer and Jon's maternal grandfather, John Stapleton, had played rugby for Leicester Tigers before leaving England to farm in Kenya, penning a diary of his experiences in a book entitled *The Gate Hangs Well*.

After attending Pembroke House Preparatory School in Gilgil, Jon came to England to complete his education at Canford School in Dorset. Having left with a good crop of O- and A-Levels, and having allowed himself only one term to sample university life, he set about pursuing a cricketing career. Known as 'J.J.', he was a left-handed batsman, 6 foot 3 inches tall and with a sound technique. For a decade he would follow the sun and divide his time between England and South Africa, enjoying a peripatetic existence. Having previously appeared for Pirates in Durban in 1981, the South African adventure later began in earnest with Cape Town CC, before periods with Pirates CC in Durban, and Paarl CC and then Cape Town CC again, this time as their captain, when he led them to the South African National Club Championship. From 1987 until 1991, he made first-class appearances for Western Province. Indeed, when Jimmy Cook arrived from South Africa to star so memorably for Somerset over three seasons, he confessed that the only Somerset player of that time whom he had heard of was Jon Hardy. Jon also played his part in settling Jimmy into the club when lending him a spare outfit, given that the newcomer's kit had not arrived.

Back in 1980, Jon had been offered a contract with Hampshire and the initial signs were promising when he notched up a score of 94 not out on his Championship debut, ironically against Somerset, who clearly liked what they saw. Having pondered his future competing for a place in a star-studded batting line-up, he transferred his allegiance to Somerset in 1986 and would remain with them until the end of the 1991 season. Over the course of eighty-seven first-class appearances, he would average 27.63 runs, with one century and twenty-four half-centuries. He also completed two centuries in List-A matches for the county before then joining Gloucestershire for one year and subsequently enjoying a number of seasons in Minor Counties cricket, with

Dorset. For the bulk of his time in the first-class game, he had been obliged to live with the effects of bilharzia (schistomiasis), an at times debilitating tropical disease he had contracted in Africa.

Jon was married in Cape Town in 1987 to Janet (née Lindup). As early as 1988,

Jon Hardy – a tall, left-handed batsman with a sound technique, he played eighty-seven first-class matches for Somerset

he had begun preparing for life after his days as a professional cricketer when he set up a company in Cape Town manufacturing cricket helmets at a time when they were beginning to become more widely used. Having earlier suffered from a blow to the head when facing Sylvester Clarke, Jon had set about designing a helmet intended to be lighter and safer than the pioneering models in use at the time. A stainless steel grille replaced the existing polycarbonate and heavy, coated steel grilles. He adopted the brand name Masuri – a Swahili word meaning 'excellent'. A shipment arrived in England in 1989 and Jon's first three high profile clients were David Boon, Dean Jones and Geoff Marsh of the visiting Australian tourists, who were playing at the County Ground in May of that year. With such a positive endorsement, the remainder of the batch of a thousand helmets was ordered by a Cheltenham-based retailer, who sold every last item in a matter of weeks.

Jon's direct connections within the cricketing world meant that Masuri helmets became popular with players at all levels, including household names from Graham Gooch to Brian Lara. Over the years, he has adhered steadfastly to a number of principles, including a constant striving for improvement and outspoken opposition to any contractual agreements or sponsorship deals that oblige players to wear any particular brand. Jon's view is that batsmen should have complete freedom of choice in such a life-or-death matter. He has also resisted any approaches to pay high-profile cricketers to wear his products. In his mind, the equipment must stand on its own merits. Furthermore, a central tenet is that there should be no compromise in striving to maximise safety, comfort and visibility. Over the years, developments have included a titanium grille, a fielding visor and a wicket-keeping helmet. Latterly, a state of the art 'Vision' series has been patented. No system of protection is infallible, as the career-ending injury to Craig Kieswetter and the tragic death of Australian Phil Hughes demonstrated. Phil was at the time wearing one of the earlier models of a Masuri helmet but was struck below the ear by a delivery from New South Wales paceman Sean Abbott in a freakishly rare set of circumstances that no helmet available at the time could have protected him from.

With the manufacture of helmets having been moved to Basingstoke, Jon has over the years embraced linked ventures, including custom-made team strips and cricket bats. More recently, he found himself in disagreement with partners he had brought into the company and he left to start over again. Remarried in 2013, it was a time for fresh starts and, unable for contractual reasons to manufacture cricket helmets, he has invested time and money in developing a polo helmet under the brand name Instinct. 'The signs are good that it will do well,' he confirms, pragmatic about the prospects, but optimistic, too, as any entrepreneur should be. Whatever the future holds, he can rest happy in the knowledge that he has contributed hugely to the safety of batsmen the world over.

511
Richard James Bartlett
19 April 1986 v. Oxford University, Oxford

[signature: Richard Bartlett]

The sleepy village of Ash Priors has an early link to Somerset cricket. Much of the land there – that, at least, which was not part of the common – was purchased by the Winter family at the time of the dissolution of the monasteries. They also came into possession of the priory at Taunton, which would enjoy a reincarnation as the Somerset Cricket Museum, and the seven-and-a-half acres of meadow that would become the County Ground. When occasional Somerset cricketer John Arundel Winter found himself haemorrhaging the family fortune, he decided to shore up his finances by leasing the land at Taunton to the newly formed Somerset County Cricket Club (along with other sporting groups).

As with John Arundel Winter 115 years earlier, Ricky Bartlett hailed from Ash Priors, though his background was more modest. Born on 8 October 1966, Ricky was the son of a Post Office Telephones engineer, Richard, known as Dick, and Barbara (née Hurle). Selected on account of his connections rather than his ability, Winter's first-class debut went badly, with only four runs to his name. He was not invited to play again. Ricky, in contrast, arrived with a bang. When he became, at the age of nineteen, the first Somerset player since Harold Gimblett to score a century on his initial first-class appearance, hopes were sky-high that the youngster – a local boy to boot – might go on to hit the heights. Sadly, he would not kick on as hoped.

Ricky had attended Taunton School, where he had starred alongside fellow future Somerset cricketer, Nick Pringle, in an outstanding side who had enjoyed a particularly successful season in 1985. No one doubted Ricky's talent, and a string of fine bating performances saw him elevated to the Somerset Colts and England Under-19s, for whom he scored three half-centuries in five innings against the team's Sri Lankan counterparts. He was awarded the Gray Nicholls Trophy in 1985 as the most improved schools cricketer. A further string to his bow was his ability at hockey, where he played for the Somerset Under-21 team.

Although offered a place at Swansea University, Ricky opted instead to try his luck as a professional cricketer. In the event, he would remain with Somerset for seven seasons, playing in fifty first-class matches and sixty List A fixtures. Apart from an extended run during the 1988 season, his appearances for the first team would be sporadic. In 1990, he must have felt a mixture of pride and frustration when he was awarded the Rapid Cricketline Second XI Player of the Season Award.

From the outset, Ricky always found employment where he could to supplement the modest wages granted to county players. He had worked for the shirt manufacturer Van Heusen and for British Gas as an office clerk and he also undertook bartending. He even worked for five months in a Bingo club but – more relevantly in terms of the trajectory of his life – he began to spend winters playing as a pro for two seasons with Manly CC in Sydney, Australia, and then around Wellington in New Zealand, with Johnson CC and Wellington CC. It was the beginning of a love affair with the latter country.

Ricky Bartlett – scored a century on debut at the age of nineteen

He parted company with Somerset at the end of the 1992 season, having averaged 24.28 with the bat, including two centuries. He also took four wickets at 36.25 apiece, with his occasional off-spin. In summarising Ricky's career, David Foot has written that he 'was never able completely to shake himself free of pre-innings tensions', adding that he 'brilliantly patrolled the covers and the outfield', making him a useful member of the side in limited-overs matches. After a further season with Cornwall, where runs came freely from his bat, he left to begin a new life in New Zealand. Here, he met his future wife, Donna (née Weston), at the time a deputy principal of a primary school. They were married in 2004 and Ricky has a stepdaughter and stepson and, at the time of writing, three grandchildren - Tai Mana, Amaia and Tukaha.

Since settling in New Zealand, he has worked in a variety of jobs. After three years in computer sales, he tried his luck as a travel consultant in Paraparaumu. A subsequent four-month stint as a financial advisor was enough to convince him that this was not the life for him. There followed a spell of a little over a year selling advertising for Wellington Newspapers, before he was back in the cricketing fold. Appointed Cricket Development Officer for the Horowhenua-Kapiti Region with New Zealand Cricket, he enjoyed what he describes as 'an amazing four years working with clubs, schools, parents and players'.

What followed was arguably a more amazing but also gruelling year – or 362 days to be precise – during which Ricky completed a round of golf on every course in

New Zealand in order to raise approximately NZ$50,000 for a number of charities. The beneficiaries – Amnesty International, Cancer Society, Ronald McDonald House and the SPCA – were a varied bunch. Having begun with a handicap of three, Ricky found this slipping at one point to seven. He was not helped by a nightmare round of 106 on the Kaitoke Dunes links course on Great Barrier Island, described in the official blurb as 'unique and challenging' and including a seventh hole gleefully termed 'The Black Hole', which Ricky can confirm is an apt moniker. Having regrouped, he ended his tour with a handicap of four. No major damage done. He put his changing fortunes down to exhaustion and the dubious nature of some courses, with putting a particular problem on greens frequented by seemingly incontinent sheep. Ricky recounts his most unexpected encounter when, whilst shaping to putt, he was assaulted from behind by a sheep that had 'made contact with an electric fence, flown across the green and upended me'. Asked which course the incident occurred on, Ricky responded that it was all a haze and 'it could have been any one of about sixty-odd with sheep grazing on them'. If this trauma was the cause of hilarity, then the reception granted at the Chatham Islands course near Canterbury was dour in the extreme. The only course among 422 where the waiving of the green fee (of NZ$15) was

Ricky Bartlett – played in fifty first-class matches for Somerset before emigrating to New Zealand COURTESY OF SOMERSET COUNTY GAZETTE

refused, the course itself was overrun by sheep and littered with evidence of their presence, forcing guests to tread carefully. The tour had begun at the Kauri Cliffs course in Northland and ended with Ricky's triumphant homecoming at his local Paraparaumu Beach course.

Back in the world of commerce, Ricky worked for one year in advertising sales for a newspaper publisher before taking up a post selling real estate in the Kapiti Coast area. In 2014, having already worked in the sector for various companies for a total of seven years, he joined Tall Poppy Real Estate, who champion an honest, value-for-money approach to the business of selling property.

As for his cricket, he played for Kapiti Old Boys from 1993 until 2004 and then, five years later, was talked out of retirement to captain the side. But golf is now his sport of choice. Reflecting on a life where he seemed, briefly, to have the world at his feet, Ricky observes that, 'With the benefit of hindsight, there's sadness, knowing how things could have been with a little more knowledge or help. But all paths lead somewhere and mine has led to an amazing country and a wonderful family and so there are no regrets.' He recalls his upbringing in Somerset and his exploits as a young cricketer with great fondness, but shows no inclination to uproot from his adoptive home on the Kapiti coast. Who in their right mind would?

512
Rayner John Blitz
19 April 1986 v. Oxford University, Oxford

Born on 25 March 1968 in Watford, Rayner Blitz was the son of Anthony and Jean (née Shucksmith). Educated at Gaynes School in Upminster, London, Rayner came through age group cricket with Essex, enjoying success as a wicket-keeper-batsman. Blessed with natural talent, he has always seen cricket – or any other sport – as something to be enjoyed. The discipline and hard graft sometimes called for are less to his taste. He lives in the moment. In one junior match, he came to the crease to join fellow Essex batsman and future England captain, Nasser Hussain, who was two short of his maiden century with fifteen runs required for victory. Through sheer devilment, Rayner proceeded to stroke the next four deliveries to the boundary before being chased back to the pavilion by an irate Nasser, apoplectic at having been denied a significant milestone.

On leaving school, he was offered a contract with Essex and played for the Second XI throughout the 1985 season. His progress as a wicket-keeper was not helped by

Rayner Blitz – blessed with natural talent, but discipline and hard graft were not to his taste

the presence of Neil Burns, who took the keeping berth, leaving Rayner to play as a batsman, and, it should be noted, an outstanding outfielder. Neil would also later to go on to play for Somerset and the two form an interesting contrast – Neil earnest and committed to squeezing every last drop of his ability and Rayner an easy-going party animal. Following his first (and only) season with Essex, Rayner was playing in Sydney as the pro with Waverley CC when he enjoyed a sparkling innings against a side that included Peter Roebuck, who immediately informed the Somerset hierarchy that they should sign him ahead of the 1986 season as deputy to Trevor Gard.

Determined not be downcast by the miserable weather that curtailed his debut at Oxford, Rayner surprised some teammates by arriving for breakfast not from his hotel bedroom but from an all-nighter. Here was a young man, diminutive in stature at 5 feet 4 inches but with a giant appetite for enjoyment and a determination to live life to the full. 'A colourful character, is Rayner,' one former colleague observes. Playing more often for the Second XI than the First XI, he would make only five first-class appearances before parting company with Somerset. He had averaged 6.60 with the bat and taken eight catches behind the stumps. In other circumstances, that might have represented the end of his relationship with the county of Somerset, but things would in fact turn out differently.

Having appeared for Derbyshire Second XI in 1987, he 'came back for a weekend in Ilminster'. The weekend became something more akin to a lifetime. Initially relying on friends for a place to lay his head, Rayner would soon make the town his home. In 1992, his father, Anthony, sadly died at his home in Brentwood. Divorced from Jean by then, he left his property and a substantial sum of money to his two sons, Rayner and Mark.

Since then, Rayner has enjoyed a hedonistic lifestyle, dealing in property as a means of supporting a lifestyle that might be the envy of those hidebound by convention. For many years he has turned out for Ilminster CC, contributing something in the order of 15,000 runs. In time, he handed over the gloves to fellow Somerset wicket-keeper, Sam Spurway. Journalist and sometime Ilminster player Craig Rice observes that 'Rayner was blessed with the natural ability to time the ball beautifully, whether he was playing cricket, tennis or squash.'

Never married and without family commitments, he has enjoyed travelling in the Far East during the winter months, with trips to Thailand and India, where, in keeping with his free-spiritedness, he favours travelling around on a motorbike. In Thailand, he has played for the Southeners Sports Club, based in Bangkok. The club was set up initially as a rugby outlet for ex-pats and Thais, with the All Black Zinzan Brooke instrumental in their early success. Cricket was soon added to the roster and a report by Tony Munro in February 1999 notes that, 'Southerners has been one of the form teams so far this season, with the appropriately named middle-order batsman and first-change bowler, Rayner Blitz, one of their key players.' Batsman, outfielder,

wicket-keeper and bowler. Versatility is clearly one of Rayner's virtues.

Like a swallow, he returns home early each summer to Ilminster to be among his teammates, turning out for the club whenever they need him and still a lively presence. His 'weekend' in Ilminster became a lifelong love affair with the place. Perhaps even a man as free-spirited as Rayner Blitz needs somewhere to call home.

R. J. Blitz – 'a colourful character, is Rayner'

513
Nicholas Simon Taylor
19 April 1986 v. Oxford University, Oxford

Nick Taylor was born in Holmfirth, Yorkshire, on 2 June 1963, the son of Ken and Avril (née Hadfield). Ken Taylor was a hard act to follow. A down-to-earth Yorkshire-man, modest but possessed of extraordinary talents, he played cricket for Yorkshire and England, starred as a centre-half for Huddersfield Town, coached at cricket and football, studied at Slade School of Fine Art and became an art teacher and subsequently a professional artist. His brother – Nick's uncle, Jeff Taylor – also played for Huddersfield Town and studied at the Royal College of Music before becoming a professor at the Glasgow Academy of Music and an opera singer. Anyone seeking a fuller account of Ken's life and times is advised to read Stephen Chalke's beautifully crafted *Drawn to Sport*.

When Nick was four, his father was offered the opportunity to teach art at Rondebosch High School in Cape Town and thus began the son's fragmented education, where he would attend eight schools across three continents. Within eighteen months, Ken had taken on a new role, sponsored by the Rembrandt Tobacco Company and based in Pretoria, orchestrating football coaching across the country. This latter move was not a success (in part because of the problems of conducting business in Afrikaans) and the family would seek a fresh start. Having endured life at an Afrikaans-speaking school, Nick spent a brief spell at Gresham's Prep School in Holt, Norfolk, before the family upped sticks once more, heading this time for Hamilton, in New Zealand, where Ken taught briefly. They then returned to Gresham's, where Ken was appointed Head of Art. Nick confesses to having had 'a brutal time of it' at his various schools. 'Always being the outsider was a real challenge,' he admits and 'bullying was rife, until I grew big enough to look after myself.' He found salvation in sport, not only performing exceptionally well as a cricketer but also excelling at squash. He would take part in the British Under-19s Open Championship. His regular practice partner was James Hunt, who went on the win more fame as a Formula One Champion. Having thus honed his skills, Nick entered the senior British Open, where in the second round he came up against Jahangir Khan, perhaps the greatest player in the history of the game. 'I managed to get six points off him, which is six more than some,' Nick jokes.

A promising fast-medium bowler, 6 feet 3 inches tall and strongly-built, he won national recognition as a schoolboy as a result of his at times devastating pace bowling. His big breakthrough came when he entered a competition in his native York-

Nick Taylor – 'that year at Somerset was the most enjoyable of my career'

shire. With the county struggling in an era when other sides were benefiting from the influx of overseas stars, Ray Illingworth had in 1981 initiated a laudable attempt to unearth exciting young talent. In a competition sponsored by Berger Paints, the quality of entrants proved extraordinarily high. Among a raft of future first-class players – all hoping for equipment to the value of £100 and a greater prize for the winners – were Richard Illingworth and Ashley Mallett. But Nick and fellow pace bowler Paul Jarvis were the two young men who emerged victorious after a final two-hour session in the nets at Headingley. Nick first appeared for Yorkshire Second XI in 1981 and was offered a contract with his native county.

Having finally been given his chance in the First XI against the Indian tourists, he describes walking through the gates at Headingley with his father as 'the proudest day of my life'. He shaped well, taking the wickets of Gundappa Viswanath and Ravi Shastri, both caught behind by David Bairstow, but he remained with Yorkshire for only two seasons, spending much of his time playing for the Second XI whilst making eight first-class appearances before his release at the end of the 1983 season. He had by now gained experience in the Southern Hemisphere during the winter months. A season with Hawthorn CC in Melbourne would be followed with similar engagements in New Zealand, South Africa and then a return to Australia with St Mary's CC. 'That was a tough experience,' he reveals. 'You were given lodgings and the loan of a car and expected to turn out for two matches and take two coaching sessions each week, but had to pay your way. I found work wherever I could. I was laying paving slabs or working on building sites and I've spent a fair amount of time as a bouncer.'

In the meantime, ahead of the 1984 season, he was approached by Hampshire and Surrey, and opted to agree terms with the latter. Another two frustrating seasons would ensue as Nick hovered between the Second XI and First XI, before he spent a season with Somerset. Here, he was given a greater run and would play in sixteen first-class matches, taking twenty-nine wickets at 42.13 apiece and averaging 8.91 with the bat. His strongest performances were arguably in limited-overs matches, where he played eighteen times. 'That year at Somerset was the most enjoyable of my career,' he recalls, 'but when I was offered just a one-year contract extension instead of the two I was hoping for, it was hardly a vote of confidence and so I had to think about my future. I still regard it as a great honour to have played for three counties and with and against some greats of the game, though.'

During the previous winter, Nick had come second in a Mr Johannesburg competition while playing in South Africa, and this had led to a three-month modelling contract. He had also appeared, perhaps surprisingly and certainly to the envy of some teammates, on a postage stamp for St Vincent, issued in 1985, part of a 'Leaders of the World' series that included Tom Graveney and Bob Willis. As with much of Nick's subsequent career, you could not make it up. Weighing up his future, he opted for life as a model rather than as a first-class cricketer. Moving to London, he took up a position as a manager of a night club in Leicester Square, so that he had a regular income while he set about establishing himself in the modelling business. Being a well-built lad in the classical tradition, Nick found his services more in demand in places such as Germany, Spain and America. In England, casting directors were more taken by waif-like frames. A highlight was his starring role in a national TV advertisement for Latta margarine. 'I had to run into the sea and walk about,' Nick reveals. 'It took us two weeks of filming in the Cayman Islands and I stayed there for a month.' Good work, if you can find it. Having decided that his

Nick Taylor – a fast-medium bowler, tall and strongly-built

prospects were greater across the Atlantic, Nick took a flight to San Francisco in 1990.

Still an active cricketer, having kept his hand in playing for Norfolk, Nick made a tentative phone call to Ronnie Iranpur, the leading light of Hollywood CC. 'I told Ronnie about my background and he bit my hand off and said "You're in", there and then. I played for them for three seasons, taking over from Ronnie as captain for the last one, when the side won all three trophies available to them. Ronnie won't mind me describing him as a brilliant friend and a woeful captain!' Meanwhile, Nick had registered with the Judith Fontaine Model Agency and lodged with a model and actress named Kelly. The couple made an instant connection and decided to 'tie the knot' on Sunset Boulevard. Securing the right to stay and work in the USA was a bonus and they set up a consortium for producers and actors, based in Costa Mesa, on the outskirts of Los Angeles. In 1992, Nick landed a contract as a 'Bic Man', featured seated in a bath in the brand's adverts and paraded at the Super Bowl. Thereafter, though, things went awry. He relates the tale. 'Six months down the road, we were stuck in an actor's flat with three Schnauzer puppies, and Kelly and I driving each other nuts.' Invited to play cricket for the USA, those plans fell through when his divorce was confirmed and not long afterwards, Nick was involved in a serious car crash. 'I went through the windscreen. I was over the alcohol limit after a cricket match and ended up in a Los Angeles jail,' he confirms.

The helter-skelter life of Nick Taylor continued apace when, after his release, he was recommended to the William Morris Agency by the renowned actor and roisterer Peter O'Toole, whom Nick and his father, Ken, had coached at Lord's. Nick was taken on but, in what he describes as a 'totally devastating' turn of events, the company sent his portfolio to their New York offices, managing to lose it. 'All those cuttings and videos were irreplaceable,' he says. 'You couldn't readily source copies back then.'

Nick's dizzying changes of fortune were matched only by his resilience. He met a Californian woman, Kristen, and was married for the second time in 1996. Following the setback to his modelling career, Nick settled with Kristen in Kingston upon Thames while he worked as a sales executive for Rank Xerox in London. They both missed the climate and lifestyle of California, though, and in 1999 started life afresh in Palm Springs. Here Nick found work as a painter and decorator. Within two years, he had bought the company. In part, the decision was forced on him. In 2002, he broke his back when a generator he was helping to lift slipped from a van. 'I shattered a number of vertebrae. I can't run anymore and I lost an inch in height,' he says. After four years, he had a team of twenty-five employees. 'We were painting about five hundred country clubs and houses, inside and out, each year,' Nick reveals. But then came the financial crash. 'People were going bankrupt, there were empty houses everywhere and everyone pulled the plug. We had two years of work lined up and it just disappeared.' Nick's company, too, inevitably went bankrupt. With his relationship heading for divorce, Nick returned to the UK in 2008. If his first marriage ended in a crowded little flat, this one ended with Nick and Kristen, 'rattling around in this enormous house, without the kids that we once hoped to have, but it wasn't to be.'

His often chaotic life might read like a hazy, boozy decades-long party, but Nick is now based once more in sleepy Norfolk. He lives with his long-standing girlfriend, tends to their chickens and three black Alsatians and paints large canvasses which he offers for sale in a small gallery. 'I've always enjoyed art,' he says. 'When I was a kid, my father would sit me down with a pencil and paper and get me to draw while he did his paintings.' He also takes on house painting work on occasions in a reprise of his career as a painter and decorator in Palm Springs. He feels tied to Norfolk for the foreseeable future as he keeps a watchful eye on his ageing parents, who live not far away. 'I've had good times and bad, but it's been an amazing life,' he observes. Reading his life history, not many would disagree with that assertion.

514
Mark David Harman
20 August 1986 v. Sussex, Taunton

The son of Michael and Barbara (née Barrett), Mark Harman was born on 30 June 1964 in Aylesbury, Buckinghamshire, but brought up and educated in Frome. After his schooling at Frome College, he already had in mind a career beyond cricket when he went on to Loughborough University to study for a degree in Economics and Finance. Clearly a man with an aptitude for the subject matter, he would come away with a first class honours degree. As for his career in first-class cricket, this would not go quite as swimmingly as his studies. Having been given his opportunity in the Somerset Second XI, selected at the age of sixteen as a promising off-break bowler, he would wait patiently to be elevated to the First XI five years later. His debut would prove to be a miserable rain-effected draw. Close to being run out on his very first delivery, he went on to chalk up eight unbeaten runs, but the match was abandoned before he had the opportunity to bowl. Dogged by persistent lower back problems and offered only limited opportunities, with Vic Marks the incumbent in the spinner's berth, he left Somerset on amicable terms at the end of the 1987 season to try his luck with Kent. He had appeared in nine first-class matches for Somerset, his eight wickets coming at 64.75 apiece. His batting average of 13.44, with a highest score of 41, demonstrated that he was no mug with the bat. David Foot describes Mark in *Sixty Summers* as 'a quiet young man, with a natural ability to turn the ball' and 'a valuable fighter with the bat'. At Kent he would fare better with the ball but was released after two seasons. That year he was married to Maria (née Kilkelly), with whom he has two sons.

Although he would then go on to coach and play in New Zealand immediately after parting company with Kent, he now saw a future outside the game.

In 1998, he and colleagues started up a specialist corporate finance and tax consultancy in Bath, named Target. The company soon grew from a small start-up to a larger concern offering mergers and acquisitions advice and support to small and medium-sized enterprises. From 2002 onwards the business expanded quickly, in large part through a number of acquisitions, developing into a multi-disciplinary practice with four offices in the UK. Then came the financial crash in 2008, which left the business over-stretched. An attempt to rebuild the company with headquarters in Bristol never quite flew and the business was broken up and sold off in late 2011.

Back in 2000, Mark had co-founded another company, Recipero, at the vanguard

Mark Harman – has enjoyed more success in the world of finance than he did as a first-class cricketer

of offering software applications for mobile phone data analysis. Initially a shareholder and a non-executive director, he would become more involved in the day-to-day running of the company in 2012 as Chief Executive Officer, expanding the business into the US, Malaysia and the Netherlands. The company was acquired in 2016 by Callcredit, and Mark was retained as Managing Director of Recipero, charged by the owners with integrating the newly-acquired company. Since then he has also acted in an advisory role, giving guidance to Callcredit on the issue of fraud and theft in mobile devices.

In 2018 Mark, was appointed Chief Executive Officer of a new Bath-based company – i4C Software – offering banks and financial planners modelling and forecasting software applications. In addition, at the time of writing he is an advisor to the Board of Nexor – originally a cyber-technology company spun off from Nottingham University – where his expertise on business strategy and software applications is invaluable.

Away from work, he has played his club cricket for Frome CC for many a year along with Somerset's Colin Dredge, but has now passed on the mantle to the next generation. Mark has experienced the highs and lows of life as a first-class cricketer and has enjoyed or endured the thrills and spills of life as a business owner. It takes pragmatism, resilience and a relentless drive to have achieved all he has.

515
Daren Joseph Foster
20 August 1986 v. Sussex, Taunton

Born in Tottenham on 14 March 1966, Daren was the son of Vivian Foster and Sadie (née Clark). As was often the case at the time, he was sent over to Jamaica to enjoy a carefree upbringing living alongside his extended family and looked after by his maternal grandmother, while his parents worked hard to earn a living in London. After ten years, he returned to the UK in order to complete his secondary schooling, but Daren would never lose his happy-go-lucky charm, where he treats triumph and disaster with a smile and a shrug of his shoulders. After attending Somerset School in Tottenham, he left to study at Southgate Technical College. He then spent time at the Haringey Cricket College, set up for young players who showed promise but were held back by a lack of facilities. It offered students a chance to hone their skills with high class coaching under the watchful eye of West Indian Reg Scarlett. This was allied to training in wider spheres such as groundsmanship, based on the pragmatic view that only a small proportion of players can expect to enjoy a long and financially rewarding first-class career. Other alumni include England cricketer Mark Alleyne and Keith Piper of Warwickshire. Sadly, the college was obliged to close its doors in 2000 as a result of a lack of funding. With many bemoaning the falling away in the number of inner city-born players and lobbying for a reinstatement, the project has enjoyed a reincarnation as the Grass Roots Academy.

Possessed of a slim frame and sending down decidedly whippy fast-medium deliveries, Daren was regarded at the time as an all-rounder, although over time he was obliged to focus on his bowling, with too few opportunities to bat. He applied unsuccessfully to join the MCC ground staff but was instead recommended to Roy Marshall, who was on a nationwide search for a long-term replacement for Joel Garner. The plan was that Joel would mentor the new arrival for two years, although matters would turn out differently when Joel's services were dispensed with.

Having already enjoyed a brief airing in the Middlesex Second XI, and just returned from a Haringey College tour of Barbados and Trinidad & Tobago, Daren joined Somerset and was soon pressing his case for elevation into the first team with performances such as a return of 4 for 9 against Shropshire in early August 1986. Having opened the bowling on his first-class debut with Joel Garner in a severely rain-affected draw, he came away wicketless (as did Joel) and would then only operate

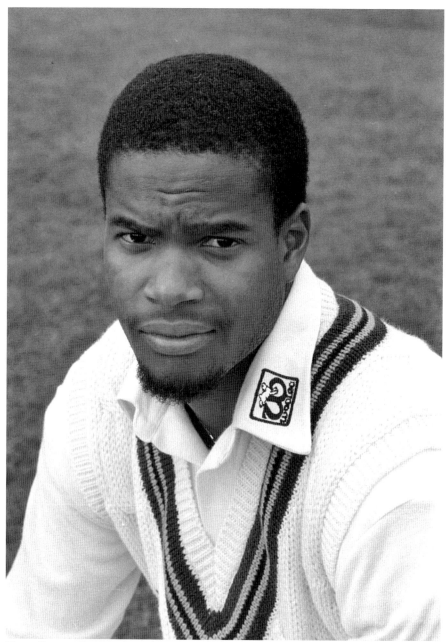

Daren Foster – Somerset 'was the county I'd always wanted to play for'

on the fringes of the First XI, appearing in twenty-eight matches and taking forty-nine wickets at 45.10 apiece. His batting average was 8.40.

An easy-going character, he quietly did what was asked of him without complaint. Somerset's John Player Special League match against Warwickshire in August 1986 offers a prime example. After the news of the rift in the Somerset dressing room had become public, he was asked to travel up from London to Edgbaston as a standby in case Joel Garner or Viv Richards failed to appear. In Peter Roebuck's account, Daren's train was stuck in a tunnel for four hours before it was returned to London and Daren was obliged to try again, finally reaching Birmingham in a car shortly before 2.30 but 'seemingly unperturbed by his misfortune'. Nor was he put out to find that Viv and Joel were both playing and opening the bowling together. A conversation with Daren reveals a complete absence of any bitterness, but a feeling on his part that it is nigh impossible for a first-class career to progress in the longer term without a leap of faith on the part of a club and a decent run for a player in Championship cricket. Not directly affected by the civil war that raged in the club, he was, however, conscious of the politics. While Peter Roebuck was captain, Daren felt valued. 'Peter was very good towards me and offered me encouragement, both as a batsman and a bowler,' he reveals. 'I found him very supportive, but after he stepped down from the captaincy, my face didn't fit for whatever reason and it was clear I had no future at Somerset, which was doubly sad, because it was the county I'd always wanted to play for.'

After not being re-engaged by Somerset at the end of the 1989 season, he was obliged to seek a new county and found temporary employment with Surrey and Derbyshire, appearing for their Second XIs. Glamorgan then offered him a two-year contract ahead of the 1991 season, and with his focus intensified by his first Championship match for them being against Somerset, he came away with a career-best 6 for 84. Although his strike rate had improved at Glamorgan, Daren decided to leave them after two seasons, having claimed a further forty-seven first-class wickets in seventeen matches. He cites his disenchantment with the county's internal politics as the reason for his reluctance to agree a contract extension.

Despite his best efforts to prolong his first-class career elsewhere, Daren made just one appearance with Essex Second XI before joining Berkshire for a season. After leaving the county game, he played club cricket for Finchampstead CC until he suffered a career-ending cruciate ligament tear. Thereafter, he worked for eighteen months as a PE teacher in a primary school in Muswell Hill before being employed in the banking sector in a clerical role with HSBC for a number of years.

Daren has children – adults now – but has never been married. These days he lives in Northampton with his partner, Jaqueline, and is in the throes of establishing a new business named 10's Sports, importing sports goods – much of the range sourced personally on trips to India – and retailing on the internet.

His has been a varied and interesting life since the time when, towards the end of his secondary education, he informed a teacher that he intended to become a professional cricketer and was told by a classmate, 'If you're lucky, DJ, you might get to clean Viv Richards's boots.' 'I never quite believed that I'd get to be my hero's teammate,' Daren says, smiling at the irony. 'Maybe it was because I went to a place called Somerset School or maybe it was because of associations with Viv and Joel and Ian Botham that made them the glamour team at that time, but the county I'd wanted to play for was Somerset, so at least I can say I ticked that one off.' His first-class career never quite took off as he had hoped. He deserves a lucky break this time around with his 10's Sports business venture. Whatever the future holds, Daren is likely to greet it with a sunny smile.

516
Nicholas John Pringle
3 September 1986 v. Worcestershire, Worcester

Nick Pringle has spent the bulk of his working life steeped in alcoholic beverages, although before anyone rushes to judgement it should be noted that his role has been one of purveyor rather than imbiber.

Born in Weymouth on 20 September 1966, he was the son of Marian Pringle and Guy Pease. Educated at Priorswood and Taunton School (where he starred alongside Ricky Bartlett in an all-conquering team), he developed into an all-rounder who bowled right-arm medium pace and was an athletic presence in the field, as effective in the covers as at forward short leg.. Given his first airing in Somerset Second XI while a seventeen-year-old schoolboy, he then went on to join the Lord's ground staff after leaving Taunton School. He continued to play, on occasions, for Somerset Second XI before being called up from Lord's for his first-class debut as a nineteen-year-old. It proved a one-sided game with Worcestershire chalking up 345 for 5 declared, before twice dismissing Somerset cheaply, with only Jon Hardy offering up any resistance. The season was memorable in other ways, too, with Nick earlier having suffered a dislocated shoulder and a broken hand.

During the off-season, he joined Mossman CC in Sydney as their pro, and that would set a trend for subsequent seasons with Napier Tech CC in Hawke's Bay in New Zealand (twice) and Harvey CC in Western Australia. His six seasons at Somerset were spent oscillating between the Second XI and First XI, with a total of

Nick Pringle – 'dominated Second XI cricket ... and denied games on a bigger stage only by those in possession'

twenty-seven first-class appearances. Nick observed that he never lost sight of what a privilege it was to enjoy a career in the game he loved and 'watched in awe as the likes of Viv Richards, Steve Waugh, Ian Botham and Sunil Gavaskar sauntered in and out of the dressing room'. Never in their rarefied league, he was nevertheless good enough as a batsman to register three half-centuries and average 16.83 with the bat while taking five wickets at 110.20 apiece. Summarising Nick's Somerset career, Peter Roebuck wrote in *From Sammy to Jimmy* that, 'Pringle and Bartlett dominated Second XI cricket, taking their team to a limited-overs final [The Bain Clarkson Trophy of 1990, in which Iain Fletcher had also played a prominent role] and were denied games on a bigger stage only by those in possession.'

At the end of the 1991 season, Nick left the County Ground and turned instead to drink, in the best possible sense of the expression. His career in the game had proved a launching pad, Nick recalling that 'all the while I was travelling the world playing cricket, I was also building up contacts in the [drinks] trade'. For twelve years he worked for ABInBev (a company formed by the merger of Interbrew from Belgium and Ambev, based in Brazil). Here he led and managed call centres and enjoyed project leadership roles before leaving in 2007 to join the Gaymer Cider Company (now Magners), having been appointed their Commercial Manager, overseeing the Matthew Clark brand in the UK while driving the establishment of the name in a number of other countries. There followed a change of direction and a year working as Business Development Director for Games Media, involved in the pub gaming industry. Then in 2011 he continued his progression from beer to cider to wine when he became Commercial Director at Accolade Wines, responsible for the Americas, Asia and the Middle East. The jewel in Accolade's crown was Hardy's Wine and Nick has continued to extol the virtues of the Australian wine, latterly as Head of China (a grand title that might have caused Xi Jinping to look askance, wondering if his position as President of the country was under threat) and then as Chief Operating Officer of Sula Vineyards, based in Mumbai. Here, Nick is conscious of the barriers to be overcome, among them the facts that import taxes on wine are high, that alcohol advertising is illegal and that wine-drinking has no established culture in the Indian subcontinent. What does a resourceful Chief Operating Officer do in such circumstances? He does what a succession of Australian captains did when needing a breakthrough and calls up Glenn McGrath. With near godlike status in India for his background as a cricketer and charity worker, and immunity from the internal politics in India that can lead to a home-grown player being loved and lauded in one state and loathed in another, Glenn was the perfect choice.

Among the other important choices in an interesting and varied life, Nick was married in 1994 to Lucinda (née Vaughan), known as Lucy, with whom he has a son and a stepdaughter. He was later married for a second time, to Lisa (née Rimmer) with whom he has a stepson. Nick has never lost his enthusiasm for his work or for the travel it has entailed and remains a sociable fellow with an easy manner. 'I establish business relationships that turn into friendships,' he asserts. For all that he has travelled the world and been to any number of exotic locations, Nick still loves Somerset, stays fit by running with his dogs in the Somerset countryside and describes himself 'happiest when watching a son playing cricket'. Perhaps his endorsement on the Sula Vineyards website says it all, informing us that 'on the personal front, Nick sets the perfect example of a well-rounded individual'.

1987

"Had I known of the extreme difficulties and bad feeling existing within the walls of Somerset CCC at the time, it is entirely fair to say that I might have signed for Essex instead. Basically, I was walking into a minefield, if not a war zone."

Martin Crowe (*in* Out on a Limb)

Championship Position: 11 of 17

Given free rein to recruit new talent, former captain and now Cricket Development Officer, Brian Rose, landed four highly capable players, all of them unfulfilled in their careers in different ways. Neil Burns, Adrian Jones, Neil Mallender and Graham Rose can all be considered a positive addition. Each would render useful service. The brief appearance of Steve Waugh as a replacement for overseas signing Martin Crowe for four matches proved inspired. He averaged 113.33 with the bat. Whatever else was wrong with Somerset cricket, they still knew how to spot overseas talent as well as or better than most. Martin Crowe was superb, amassing runs aplenty and leaving the rest of the batsmen across the counties in his wake. Peter Roebuck, Nigel Felton and Jon Hardy all exceeded 1,000 runs. Vic Marks was once more the primary wicket-taker, but he now shared the burden with Adrian Jones and Neil Mallender.

The nadir was surely the NatWest Trophy first round match at High Wycombe when Somerset were beaten by Buckinghamshire. The Buckinghamshire opening bowlers – Booden and Edwards – suffocated the visitors, taking four wickets for 26 runs between them in twenty-four overs. Where was Viv when they needed him?

There were signs of improvement and a renewed sense of team spirit. Eleventh place in the Championship was no disgrace. Fourth place in what had become the Refuge Assurance League was reassuring. But this was solid and unspectacular stuff: not the exciting fare the supporters had grown used to witnessing.

517
Neil David Burns
25 April 1987 v. Lancashire, Taunton

There has always been an unwavering intensity about Neil Burns, constantly challenging the status quo and restless in his pursuit of improvement. This striving to bring out the very best has applied equally to his own performances and to those of his teammates and – these days – to the players he coaches.

Born in Chelmsford on 19 September 1965, he was the son of Roy and Marie (née Cordery). Roy, a talented club cricketer who captained Finchley CC, gave Neil and older brother Ian every encouragement to fulfil their dreams of a future in sport. The brothers would spill out of their house and onto Chelmer Park, spending every available moment playing cricket or football. Neil set his sights early on a career as a wicket-keeper-batsman. 'Alan Knott and Rod Marsh were my heroes,' he recalls, 'and besides, I worked out that with a group of seven kids chasing around after the ball in a thirty-five acre sports ground, behind the stumps was the best place to be.' Later, he would acknowledge a need to take control, observing that the cricketing contest feeds through the wicket-keeper, who has a responsibility to help dictate the flow of energy in a game.

Educated at Moulsham High School, Neil appeared destined for a career as a professional sportsman. For a while he was on the books of Tottenham Hotspur FC and (Leyton) Orient FC, but this failed to bear fruit. He would retain his links with football, training over some winters with his beloved West Ham United FC, retaining his fitness and observing different coaching techniques, particularly those of West Ham's inspirational manager, John Lyall. His route to success as a cricketer was through the Essex age groups. He delights in recalling that, as an Under-11, he completed a hat trick of stumpings to a young leg-spinner named Nasser Hussain, and by the age of sixteen he was offered professional terms, soon making his mark with an impressive eight stumpings in a game for Essex Second XI against Kent Second XI at Dartford in 1984. 'I felt as high as a kite after that match,' he observes. 'I thought my career was going to be a walk in the park.' Inevitably, setbacks followed. He waited patiently in the wings at Essex, mentored in particular by Ray East, whom he worked alongside in the Essex CCC indoor nets some winters, as part of his terms of employment.

Although he enjoyed his initial taste of first-class cricket in 1986, it became clear that he was destined to remain the county's second choice, behind David East. His horizons had by then been broadened by a spell with Northerns-Goodwood CC in

Western Provence, where he learned a great deal about different playing conditions and developed a lasting affinity for cricket in South Africa, founding the NBC International Cricket Academy in Cape Town. Determined to develop his career, Neil responded to an approach from Brian Rose, who confirmed that Somerset were planning to offer him regular first-class cricket. The subsequent strife at the County Ground in Taunton led to inevitable misgivings but, having been persuaded by Martin Crowe (who had ironically declined Essex's advances) that Somerset had a positive plan in place, Neil made the move. Somerset were able to lay claim to a wicket-keeper-batsman of genuine class, but the move was something of a culture shock for Neil. Essex were regarded at the time as having a restless drive for trophies. At

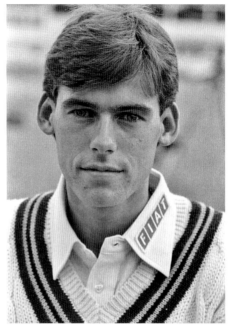

Neil Burns – never one to rest on his laurels or to accept second best

Somerset, things were less well honed. Neil was never one to rest on his laurels or to accept second best, even if that meant taking teammates out of their comfort zones on occasions. In his own words, 'I've always been prepared to stand apart from the majority opinion if I've disagreed with something. I put this down to the strength of character nurtured in my elder brother and me, within our family environment.'

He remained with Somerset for eight seasons, during which he made 150 first-class appearances for the county, averaging 30.09 as a left-handed batsman, with five centuries to his name, and effecting 333 dismissals. He was arguably unfortunate to find himself displaced by the up-and-coming Rob Turner, and if Neil felt that he had something to prove, his response was an impressive one. Having been appointed captain of the Somerset Second XI for the 1994 season, he led the team to the summit of the Rapid Cricketline Championship, bringing on some promising youngsters in the process.

Married in 1987 to Susan Anne (née Clarke), Neil was by this time well advanced with plans for a life beyond cricket, having established his sports promotion and event management business, NBC Ltd, and having also raised money for the National Holiday Fund for sick and disabled children, reflecting a continuing belief that sport

191

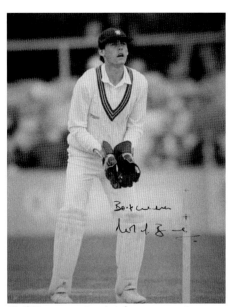

Neil Burns – *enjoyed eight seasons at Somerset as a fine wicket-keeper and accomplished left-handed batsman*

can be a force for wider good. He had also found time to write a column for the *Sunday Independent* (and remains to this day an enthusiastic blogger and inveterate networker). Having left Somerset, he was offered the role of player-coach with Buckinghamshire, subsequently being appointed Director of Cricket, affording him the opportunity to implement a number of ideas in a root and branch review of cricket in the county. There followed an unexpected and welcome return to the first-class game in 2000 with Leicestershire, facilitated by Jack Birkenshaw, where he brought his experience to bear and led the list of wicket-keepers in terms of dismissals in both the 2001 and 2002 seasons. Age had proved no barrier to success. His time at Leicestershire ended as unexpectedly as it had begun when, having been verbally offered a further contract, Neil was let down when internal politics engulfed the club. Stung by the injustice and unprepared to let matters rest, he would successfully claim compensation from Leicestershire in a landmark judgement.

Having left the first-class game, Neil focussed on his business ventures. To speak with him for any length of time is to be struck by how much thought he gives to every action, from the minutiae of technique to the wider context of understanding oneself in order better to be equipped to play sport at the elite level. He is apt to dissect every aspect of the game, from the ways a successful team can avoid complacency to the techniques used by the best players in the gladiatorial contests between batsman and bowler. He also embraces wider ideas such as Tai Chi. His career in the first-class game has allowed him to observe at close quarters some of the finest players in history. When he re-established and re-invented London County in 2004 (the original having been the cricket club founded by W. G. Grace in 1899), Neil's mission was to bring together elite sportsmen, leaders from other walks of life and academics, in order to create a melting pot of ideas and best practice. Supported by a number of household names, the business has transformed the performance of many individuals and changed lives. Careers – and not just cricketing careers – have been reinvigorated and talent unearthed. In the first category sit the likes of Nick Compton, who worked closely with Neil to achieve their shared goal of a place for Nick in the England Test team. In the second category, the biggest success story is arguably Alex Hales, whose raw and unique talent was spotted by London County through their 'Search 4 a Star' scheme.

When asked about his hopes and plans for the future, Neil replies: 'I'll keep doing what I'm doing, motivated by my love of the game, trying to learn from others, trying to pass on everything I know. I'll hopefully grow wiser with each passing year.'

He certainly appears to have alighted on the profession he was born for.

518
Graham David Rose
25 April 1987 v. Lancashire, Taunton

Graham Rose.

Born in Tottenham on 12 April 1964, Graham was the son of William Rose, a useful club cricketer, married to Edna (née Fisher). Educated at Northumberland Park School in Tottenham and the famed Haringey Cricket College, Graham enjoyed his first taste of competitive cricket as an eight-year-old in the Haringey Under-11 side who took part in the inter-borough games held back then. Graham reveals that 'I was cricket-mad as a kid.' He was drawn to the role of all-rounder, observing that 'I always liked the fact that if I had a bad day with the ball, I could make it up with the bat later on [and vice versa].' Scouted by former Middlesex and England player J. D. B. (Jack) Robertson, he was first selected for the Middlesex Second XI as a sixteen-year-old in 1980 and would play for the English Schools and Young England sides. He was not, however, offered a contract with Middlesex until 1984. A former teammate has observed that, 'Because Graham came up through his own steam rather than through the usual channel of the Middlesex age groups, I'm not sure he was given the breaks his rich talent merited.' Certainly, when he was finally given his first-class debut, against Worcestershire in 1985, he made an immediate impact with a return of 6 for 41. But he would appear in only seven first-class matches for Middlesex.

In view of his success at Somerset, it is perhaps surprising that Graham was released so readily by his first club. One explanation is that, for all that he was a big man – 6 feet 4 inches tall, strongly built and oozing talent – Graham was not overly endowed with self-confidence. It was a school of hard knocks under the leadership of Mike Gatting at Lord's and competition for places was stiff. At Somerset, his reputation boosted by some early successes, Graham, was, in the words of teammate, Neil Burns, 'carried along by that wave of love that the Somerset supporters expressed

Graham Rose – his muscular exploits with bat and ball won him the moniker 'Hagar'

in their unique, vociferous way'. Neil cites two turning points in particular: Graham's 95 runs on debut against Lancashire, followed by a sustained period of excellent bowling when he took 2 for 23 in seventeen overs, and then a confidence-boosting performance against Middlesex in the Refuge Assurance League match in 1988, more likely to be remembered for Steve Waugh's masterful 140 not out. Mike Gatting had torn into Graham with four boundaries but the bowler held his nerve, refusing to be bullied into submission, and dismissed his erstwhile captain caught and bowled, setting up a Somerset victory. Over time, the support of the fans would prove transformational – another example of that enduring bond between players and the crowds in the intimate arena of the County Ground.

Graham's ursine build and muscular exploits won this gentle man the moniker 'Hagar'. Encouraged to go for his shots without inhibition by his sometime coach, Jack Birkenshaw, he proved a match-winner on many an occasion, particular in limited-overs games. His records of the fastest centuries in the history of the NatWest competition (in thirty-six balls versus Devon) and John Player Special League (in forty-six balls against Glamorgan – subsequently surpassed) are testament to his enormous power. In a later age, he would surely have gained international honours in the T20 format. Over the course of sixteen seasons at the County Ground, he played 244 times for Somerset. 1990 would prove his most fruitful campaign, with a thousand runs and fifty-three wickets, but he continued to perform well – at times superbly – until forced to retire in 2002, by which time he had become increasingly injury-prone. His body was telling him it was time to quit. 'Even bowling for the Second XI, I felt in pain each following day. Everything hurt and it felt like I would break. I had just reached the end of my natural life as a cricketer. There was no way I could do one more year,' he explains. He came away with 588 wickets at 29.83 apiece and a batting average of 31.20 (including eleven centuries).

One of those footnotes of cricketing history – called out on odd occasions as dastardly questions in pub quizzes – is that when he had run in to bowl to Anurag Singh of Warwickshire on the evening of 23 July 1997, Graham had become the first man to bowl under floodlights in a List A game.

Married in 1987 to Teresa (née Humphrey), Graham is the father of two children, Georgina and Felix, both born in Taunton. He has enjoyed or at times endured a variety of occupations. Winters early in his career were spent in the Southern Hemisphere, with spells as a pro with Carey Park CC and Fremantle CC in Western Australia and with Paarl CC in South Africa, although he confirms that he supplemented his wages in Australia with work on building sites, which his massive frame lent itself to and, perhaps more surprisingly, as a wool-tester, 'going round to all the wool brokers and taking samples for a catalogue'. Having moved to Somerset, he would later find work for a computer supplier and for Somerset County Council, before trying his luck in the financial industry, working alongside Somerset wicket-keeper Rob Turner at Rowan Dartington Stockbrokers. Having tasted life as a civil servant at the Ministry of Defence, he has finally found himself working in Information Technology with Boeing. Lest anyone should think that such a role might appear tedious in the extreme to a man used to throwing his Herculean frame into full-blooded encounters on the cricket field, Graham is clear that, in his words,

'I feel really lucky to have ended up in a job I really enjoy.'

He gave heart and soul for his adoptive county and was a great favourite with the club's at times raucous supporters. It is pleasing to hear that this gentle giant is thriving in a rather quieter environment.

519
Neil Alan Mallender
25 April 1987 v. Lancashire, Taunton

[signature: Neil Mallender]

'Ghost', as he is known, earned his moniker early in his time with Northamptonshire. On a grey, overcast late-August day at Headingley in 1980, his irrepressible team-mate Allan Lamb coined the name as Neil appeared out of the gloom with his long, fair flyaway hair. The name gained greater traction as he enjoyed spells striking terror in a number of batsmen by sending down his well-aimed bouncers. His reputation on the field was at odds with his demeanour off it. Chris Tavaré would describe Neil as mild and thoughtful off the pitch, but 'a grumpy and temperamental bowler' on it.

Neil's arrival at Somerset was a genuine coup, as the county attempted to rebuild after the travails of 1986. Peter Roebuck observes in *Sometimes I Forgot to Laugh* that the new recruit had 'tired of bowling on dreary pitches' for Northants and that former club captain Brian Rose 'flew to New Zealand to offer him terms, a gesture that impressed a man from the old school of county cricket'. It would prove an astute signing for club and player.

Neil was born on 13 August 1961 in Kirk Sandall, a village in South Yorkshire. His father, Ron Mallender, who worked in management roles in the laundry industry, was married to Jean (née Lawton), at the time a nurse. Ron's work would take the family around the country and, as a result, Neil's peripatetic education saw him enjoying spells as a star of the cricket teams at Bourne Grammar School in Lincoln, followed by two years at Westfield Comprehensive in Yeovil and finally a period at Beverley Grammar in his native Yorkshire. By then, he had shown enough promise to be selected for the England Schoolboys XI and for an England Under-19 tour of the West Indies. Neil had impressed at a series of coaching sessions in Newcastle led by Doug Ferguson, who acted as a scout for Northants, having formerly played for their Second XI. Despatched down to Northamptonshire, Neil was handed a two-year contract and asked to sign it there and then. Uncertain of what the future might hold in Yorkshire, he thus embarked on his career as a first-class cricketer. The Yorkshire hierarchy had been unable to guarantee regular first-class cricket, but were disappointed to have let Neil slip through their fingers.

Neil Mallender – an England international and subsequently a Test umpire

He would spend seven seasons with Northamptonshire, consistently claiming in the order of fifty wickets a season. By then, if he had become well-respected by the Northants establishment, he was a cult figure in Dunedin on the South Island of New Zealand. Initially recommended by Allan Lamb to Warren Lees, the captain of Otago CC, he would spend ten consecutive seasons as their overseas player, exceeding his hosts' expectations with his sustained excellence and a number of match-winning performances, most notably his 7 for 27 against Auckland in January 1985 that had the Otago faithful in raptures. Neil modestly attributes his success to the fact that Warren Lees gave him free rein to bowl with extra pace and hostility as the club's out-and-out strike bowler, rather than being charged with a containing role. Each year he decamped to the Southern Hemisphere, accompanied at times by his wife Caroline (née Russell), a nursery nurse whom he married in 1984. Neil, Caroline and their two children were welcomed into the Otago community.

Such was his reputation that the New Zealand public remained mystified that

Neil was consistently overlooked by the England selectors. He was even approached over the possibility of transferring his allegiance and playing for New Zealand, but he declined, describing himself as 'an Englishman through and through'. There would be much rejoicing when news reached the Otago supporters that a man they regarded as one of their own had finally received international honours. Selected to play for England in two Test Matches in 1992, he did not disappoint, claiming ten Pakistani wickets at 17.18 apiece. Neil would captain the Otago side for two seasons and would register his only first-class century for them against Central Districts in February 1992. Inevitably, he attributes his improvement as a batsman to others, noting that his friend and Somerset teammate Richard Harden had

Neil Mallender – a consistently good fast bowler, admired in England and revered in New Zealand

helped him by improving his grip, previously more suited to putting at golf. Neil was awarded a Testimonial Year by Otago in 1992-93, a reflection of their gratitude for his loyalty and wholehearted commitment.

Somerset would also offer him a Benefit Year – in 1994. He had represented them for eight seasons from 1987 until 1994, coming away with 329 wickets at 25.78 apiece over 118 first-class matches and averaging 17.81 with the bat. He then returned to Northants for two seasons, before enjoying a swansong in Minor Counties cricket with Buckinghamshire.

After some gentle persuasion from Ray Julian, whom David Lloyd describes as 'the most complete umpire ever', Neil joined the Umpires Panel and has stood in first-class matches from 1997 until the present day. He officiated in three Tests in Zimbabwe in 2003-04.

No one has a bad word to say about Neil Mallender. Not even those opposing batsmen he roughed up with his bouncers. Teammates universally sing his praises, among them the young guns whom he helped along the way. Former teammate Andy Cottam describes him as 'the best character' he has shared a changing room with. 'Neil was great to me. He took me under his wing and looked after me,' Andy says. Sometimes the mere statistics, however impressive, are insufficient to measure a man's worth.

520
Adrian Nicholas Jones
25 April 1987 v. Lancashire, Taunton

The parallels with Allan Jones, who represented Somerset from 1970 until 1975, are uncanny. Both known to teammates as 'Jonah', they arrived at Taunton having cut their first-class teeth with Sussex. Both of them were capable fast bowlers, devastating at times and just as fiery in their exchanges with authority. Both of them obtained something approaching cult status with the more loquacious among the fans stationed at long-leg. Once proclaimed 'the best white fast bowler in the world' by no less a judge than Imran Khan, there is a sense that Adrian never quite fulfilled his rich potential.

He was born in Woking on 22 July 1961, the son of William Jones, who was married to Emily (née Payne) and was a self-made man who ran a stationery and office equipment company and had been a useful all-rounder in Surrey club cricket, but had died while Adrian was still young. One of three children brought up by his mother, Adrian attended Seaford College and came away with a good crop of O- and A-Levels. Although he planned a career as a professional cricketer, he qualified early in his career as an NCA coach, in his words 'to guard against failure'. His first contract was with Red & White (Rood en Wit) CC in Haarlem, Netherlands, and his first-class career then began with Sussex in 1981 when he was nineteen. An imposing physical specimen at over six feet and thirteen stone, he shaped up well in his first season, taking seventeen inexpensive wickets in five games and then spent the winter in South Africa coaching at Selborne College in East London and appearing for Border. He would remain with Sussex until the end of the 1986 season when, despite his affinity for Sussex cricket, there was a parting of the ways. Here was a man of principle – a regular churchgoer but not one of a meek persuasion – inclined at times to blow a gasket if he felt hard done by. Somerset leapt at the opportunity to secure his services. He was an opening bowler of genuine pace and hostility, though, as Rob Steen observes in *Spring, Summer, Autumn*, 'The frequency of leg befores and disturbed stumps bore testimony to his pace and precision, counterbalanced by a goodly smattering of loose deliveries that cost plenty.' If his new bowling partner, Neil 'Ghost' Mallender, was the quiet assassin, then, as journalist and former Somerset cricketer Eric Hill put it euphemistically, Adrian found himself 'in occasional trouble with some authorities for his huge enthusiasm to get rid of batsmen'.

Adrian Jones – 'a dominant personality in the dressing room and very popular off the field'

Adrian soon settled into his new surroundings. Vic Marks describes him as 'a dominant personality in the dressing room and very popular off the field'. Initially, he decamped to South Africa for the winters, coaching and playing in Orange Free State in 1986 and Pretoria in 1988, although this latter spell descended into farce when his sponsor went bankrupt and Adrian was forced to return home early. Fortunately, on hearing of his plight, a vice president of Hughes & Hughes Ltd, an Essex-based company who sold laboratory equipment and pest control products, came to his rescue. He was offered a job in Wellington, Somerset, as a sales rep for an off-shoot of theirs named Jarvis-Allen, for whom he would later become a director. Married in 1988 to Liz (née Aspen), whose father, among other things, was a breeder of dogs, he would be celebrating the birth of his first child within a couple of years and the couple appeared settled in the West Country. The 1989 season was a personal triumph. He was ever-present during the Championship campaign and claimed seventy-one wickets in a season where the odds were stacked heavily in favour of the batsmen. His teammate Jimmy Cook of South Africa would express surprise that Adrian was not selected as part of the England touring party, announced at the end of the 1989 season.

Never one to give anything less than heart and soul, nor one to yield any quarter if he sensed an injustice – whether a turned-down appeal or a lack of recognition for his input – Adrian parted company with Somerset when he was offered only a one-year contract at the end of the 1990 season. Perhaps the county felt that a longer contract was a risk, given that a well-built fast bowler puts his body through enormous strain and becomes increasingly injury-prone. 1991 therefore saw a parting of the ways. Lest anyone should imagine it was an easy decision for Adrian to leave Somerset, he described it as 'even more difficult than it was when I left Hove because I'm married now, and I've got a home and family to consider … but I also know it's not too late for me to fulfil myself elsewhere. I feel as if I'm being pushed out here.'

In eighty-eight appearances for Somerset, he had taken 245 wickets at 30.72 apiece. In each of the four seasons from 1987 to 1990 inclusive, he had exceeded fifty wickets. He averaged 12.32 with the bat. Adrian was described by Peter Roebuck as 'a red-faced, huffing and puffing fast bowler' whose strong presence in the changing room derived from his preparedness to voice opinions 'hovering in the backs of the minds of more discreet colleagues'.

He was still regarded as a potent force and offers came in from Glamorgan, Kent and Surrey, but his heart said Sussex and he would spend three seasons back with them. After some success, with a haul of fifty-seven wickets in the first season following his return, he was plagued by niggling injuries and left to pursue a career in business.

In 2001, he set up Solus, a company based in Haywards Heath providing office supplies, a field in which his father, William, had enjoyed huge success, before Adrian's brother, Glynne, had taken over the reins. Bright and driven, if Adrian fell short of his ambitions as a bowler who had once dreamed, with some justification, of Test recognition, he was always likely to succeed in his new path.

521
Stephen Rodger Waugh
5 August 1987 v. Hampshire, Weston-super-Mare

In any debate about the greatest cricketer ever to have worn the Somerset jersey, Steve Waugh's name would surely be among the first in the hat. Securing his services was a masterstroke, his performances for the county exceeding all expectation. He was an uncomplicated cricketer, clear on what was required to stay at the crease, to accumulate runs and to win matches. Everything that failed to work towards this goal – flashy shots, flickers of weakness – was expunged. His career statistics speak volumes, not least among them the fact that in fifty-seven games as Australian captain, he led his side to victory on forty-one occasions.

Every branch of the Waugh family tree appears to have groaned under the weight of sporting prowess, and so most games came naturally to Steve and his (non-identical) twin brother, fellow Australian international, Mark. Steve himself has said, though, that success in the Test arena is 95% about the mind. He bemoans the fact that a majority of coaches appear to think that success is 95% about fitness and the body. Perhaps his indomitable spirit was inherited in the main from his paternal grandmother, Ella Waugh, an extraordinary woman who contracted polio at the age of eighteen and refused to accept the message delivered by doctors that she would be able neither to walk nor have children. She proved them wrong on both counts. Her son, Rodger, would develop into an excellent tennis player, as would Rodger's future wife, Beverley (née Bourne), whom he met via the game. They were married at eighteen and the following year on 2 June 1965, in Canterbury Hospital in Campsie, a suburb of Sydney, Steve was born, followed four minutes later by Mark. Writing many years later in the *Western Australian*, Doug Comley would joke: 'Forget Shane Warne, this was the delivery of the century.' Beverley has noted that, by the age of eighteen months, the twins were showing outstanding hand-eye coordination, although the course of their sporting careers did not always run smoothly. At the age of seven, they endured their first game of cricket, allegedly overseen by a couple of ladies who had even less idea about the game than their pupils. Mark was out for a golden duck. Steve then came to the crease with his pads on the wrong legs and – as mystified by the rest of his kit as his teachers were – with his box stuffed under his front pad, protecting his knee. He survived the first ball and was clean bowled with the second.

By the time they were attending East Hills Boys High School, they had extended their knowledge of the game and begun to develop their technique. Both all-round athletes – Mark excelled at tennis and Steve at football – cricket was their first love.

If Mark seemed the more stylish of the two, Steve made up for this with his sheer determination and, perhaps to the surprise of their parents, was the first to break into Sheffield Shield cricket when he was invited to play for New South Wales as a nineteen-year-old. He would also become the first, by some years, to be selected for Australia. Already established as a Test player when he joined Somerset, Steve had made useful contributions with bat and ball, sufficiently talented and gritty to retain his place, but still in search of elusive match-winning performances. He would later write that his time at Somerset proved a turning point.

With Martin Crowe unable to see out his contract for the 1987 season, owing to a stress fracture of the spine, Peter Roebuck telephoned Steve and invited him to take Martin's place. He was already based in England. Having

Steve Waugh – an unassuming man who became one of the most successful players in the history of the game

previously played for Essex Second XI, he had been plying his trade with Nelson in Lancashire League cricket when the call came. He was instantly struck by the speed of the West Indian bowlers playing in the County Championship – in particular, Sylvester Clarke, whom he encountered in his second game for Somerset. Watching some of the players around him looking defeated before they had reached the crease, he acknowledged that he needed to summon previously untapped reserves of inner strength, embrace what he describes as 'good fear', with the resultant sharpening of the senses. He stepped up to the plate and scored 111 not out. A similarly courageous stand against Courtney Walsh on 'a dodgy pitch at Bristol', as he describes it, yielded 137 not out. By the end of the season he averaged 113.33 after four matches. Asked to return and share duties with Martin Crowe the following season, he readily accepted. Although Middlesex had offered a contract, he wished to work with Martin Crowe at close quarters and learn what it took to rise to the very top as a batsman. When not playing for Somerset that season, he would appear for Smethwick, in the Birmingham & District League. In the event, Martin was obliged to end his contract prematurely and another SOS went out to Steve to play against Hampshire. Having driven down

Steve Waugh – a tough Aussie, and a thoughtful one, too
COURTESY OF BARRY PHILLIPS

to Southampton, he arrived just before lunch with Somerset reeling on 64 for 4, went in at No. 7 and scored 115 not out. Obliged to leave in mid-August to prepare for the Australian tour of Pakistan, he had scored 1,314 runs in just fifteen first-class fixtures. His first-class average in his brief but brilliant Somerset tenure was 78.76 and he had also contributed fourteen wickets at 29.14 apiece, bowling at medium pace (with the occasional quicker delivery). He was ready to take on the world and the Ashes series in England the following season would, indeed, prove a personal triumph. After notching up his maiden Test century at Headingley, he went from strength to strength. Although dropped in 1991, making way, ironically, for his twin brother, he bounced back and became for a prolonged period the rock around which the Australian XI was built. In 168 Test appearances, he amassed nearly 11,000 runs at 51.06 and contributed ninety-two wickets, leading the way in making Australia a winning machine. Surely no stay at the crease was sweeter than his fourth-wicket partnership of 231 with Mark at Kingston, Jamaica, in the 1994-95 series against the West Indies. And can any twins have bestridden a sport the way he and Mark did when they were ranked No. 1 and No. 2 batsmen in the world by Coopers & Lybrand in 1997? He would finally leave the stage to universal plaudits in 2004. By then, he had been awarded the Order of Australia (AO), not just for his services to cricket but for his charitable work, too. Always keen to immerse himself in the culture of the countries he toured (and often encouraging his teammates to broaden their horizons in the same way), he had visited Mother Teresa in 1996 and been moved by the plight of the poor and dispossessed. In 1998, with Australia having been trounced by India inside four days at Kolkata, he was approached by Shanlu Dudeja and invited to join her in visiting children suffering the fall-out of leprosy at the Udayan Resurrection House on the outskirts of Barrackpore. Galvanised into action, he set about raising the funds for an accommodation block to house the young daughters of leprosy victims.

In 1991, he had been married to his childhood sweetheart, Lynette (née Doughty), whom he had first met when she emptied a bucket of cold spaghetti over him while the Boys' and Girls' High Schools were enjoying some school-leaving japes. (Lynette's recollection, it should be said, was that she had been the recipient of the spaghetti and Steve the offender.) Having summoned the courage to mutter a few words at a school dance and later to invite her to his school's farewell ball, love blossomed. Steve would describe the ordeal of his first date and his initial meeting with his future parents-in-law as 'like facing Curtly Ambrose without a helmet – you couldn't afford to make a mistake because you wouldn't get a second chance.' They would have three children together, one of them, Austin, having graduated to the Australian Under-19 team at the time of writing. Lynette would join Steve in giving much of her time to charitable work, refusing to be daunted after the setback of a serious stroke at the age of forty from which she has mercifully recovered. Together, they help to run the Steve Waugh Foundation, founded to support children and the under-25s who slip through the net of other charities. Steve has also set up a successful commercial enterprise. His company, Waugh Global, facilitates investment in the Indian property market for clients around the world.

His advice is continuously sought by those wishing to improve their performance. In 2008 he was appointed Australia's Athletic Liaison Officer for the Beijing Olympics. Articulate and with a keen sense of history – these days he has built up an impressive collection of cricketing memorabilia – he has written extensively, eschewing the very idea of a ghost writer. His *Tour Diaries*, beginning in 1993 and accompanied by many of his own photographs, were well received and his autobiography *Out of my Comfort Zone* is a veritable tome. He remains an example to any sportsman. He has harnessed every ounce of his considerable talent, and fame has never gone to his head. Rather, his quest for self-improvement has been unremitting and his humanity undiminished.

A tough Aussie and a thoughtful one, who believes we should learn from our mistakes – not dwell on them, but act on them – he has an uncompromising 'no regrets' view of life. He made very few mistakes when he turned out for Somerset. But those who saw him play might quietly regret that he was with the county for too short a while.

522
Robert George Woolston
9 September 1987 v. Derbyshire, Taunton

A left-arm orthodox spin bowler, Robert Woolston was invited to the County Ground as a direct replacement for Rob Coombs. Born in Enfield, Middlesex, on 23 May 1968, he was the son of George and Patricia (née Thornton). After his schooling at Enfield Grammar School, he completed a BTEC course in Graphic Design at Ware College. He arrived at Somerset having been scouted by Peter Robinson, who seemed at the time to be intent on unearthing emerging talent from the capital. Robert had spent a year as a member of the Lord's ground staff, combining this with any work he could find, such as trying his luck as a building worker and as a sales demonstrator. He had also been given trial matches with both Middlesex Second XI and Worcestershire Second XI in 1986, but no offer had been forthcoming. He arrived at the County Ground in June 1987 and would go on to enjoy a hugely productive season in the Somerset Second XI, by some distance the most successful bowler, amassing sixty wickets across the Second XI and Minor Counties Championships. Second XI coach, Peter Robinson, would observe that Robert 'gave the attack a much needed variety'. It would be Somerset's last season in the latter competition. The majority of first-class counties had long since withdrawn their Second XI sides from the Minor Counties Championship. Somerset had been the last ones standing when they were replaced by Wales ahead of the 1988 season.

Robert's only first-class appearance came at the end of the 1987 season, in the home fixture against Derbyshire, as a result of his sterling efforts for the Second XI. He claimed two wickets at 53.50 apiece, one of them New Zealand opener John Wright, who had already bagged a century. In stark contrast, Robert made a duck in his only innings.

The following season was one of relative disappointment with thirteen wickets in six appearances for the Second XI. He was released at the end of his second season and Peter Robinson would note in the *Somerset Year Book* that 'the search for a slow left arm bowler will continue'.

On a personal level, Robert's time, both with the Lord's ground staff and then at Somerset, was not a happy period for him. Social interaction did not come easily, the cut and thrust of debate was not his forte. It is a reminder of the difficulties an introverted young man is faced with when obliged to forsake his roots, in the interests

Robert Woolston – his only first-class appearance came as a reward for his outstanding season with the Second XI

of pursuing a sporting career. Some have an easy charm and confidence that ensures that they are welcomed into established cliques. Others are not so blessed and remain outsiders. Robert's former teammates typically describe him as 'hard to get to know' and somewhat of a lone wolf, a man who 'kept himself to himself'. After leaving Somerset, he made no further appearances in first-class cricket, but has turned out for a number of club sides, including Enfield, where he was born, and Sawbridgeworth, in Hertfordshire, where he now lives a quiet existence, averse to any publicity.

1988

"[I] did not want to preside over an ordinary team, one
forever promising jam tomorrow, or over a club ruled by
outdated committees, the banishment of which had
been promised during the 1986 turbulence."

Peter Roebuck

Championship Position: 11 of 17

This was another humdrum season, overshadowed once more by off-the-field rum-
blings that would lead to another mini-revolution at the year's end. 1988 heralded the introduction of experimental four-day matches, an innovation that was here to
stay. It became apparent early in the season that Martin Crowe was seriously off colour
and he was later diagnosed with salmonella poisoning. Steve Waugh stepped into the
breach and proceeded to dominate the county's batting with 1,314 runs at an average
of 73.00. No one else at Somerset came close to amassing 1,000 runs. Not so Worcestershire's Graeme Hick, who chalked up a score of 405 at Taunton in May. That game
apart, the bowlers performed creditably. The evergreen Vic Marks was once more the
leading wicket-taker with seventy-six victims, but Graham Rose, Adrian Jones and
Neil Mallender were all among the wickets. The addition to the ranks of off-spin
bowler Harvey Trump meant that Somerset had a potential replacement to step in
due course into Vic Marks's shoes.

Peter Roebuck had suffered a loss of form, in part because he was troubled by injury, but also perhaps because he had become increasingly vexed by the club's seeming
inability to adapt to changing times. Further blows came with the news that popular
club Secretary, Tony Brown, was leaving to take up a post with the Test & County
Cricket Board (TCCB) and the announcement by the Chairman that neither Brian
Rose nor any other member of the Somerset set-up would appointed as his replacement. This latter news went down as well as might have been expected. Brian Rose
left the club. Peter Roebuck let it be known that he was fed up with the ponderous
bureaucracy and acceptance of mediocrity that enveloped the place and resigned the
captaincy.

523
Matthew William Cleal
14 May 1988 v. West Indians, Taunton

Born in Yeovil on 23 July 1969, Matt was the son of Michael Gordon Cleal, an engineer who worked at Westland Helicopters, and Diana Alma (née Shire), in her time a hairdresser and dinner lady. He was educated at Preston Comprehensive in the town. While a schoolboy, he had proved a successful all-round athlete and a good enough footballer to have been on the books at Bristol Rovers FC. An engaging character, his enthusiasm was infectious. Former Somerset wicketkeeper-batsman Neil Burns recalls a pre-season tour to Bahamas. 'Somerset and Worcestershire were invited over there to celebrate the opening of a new ground, in part because they wanted to pitch Ian Botham against his old club. The teams got on well. Beefy was, of course, a charismatic character who attracted his acolytes but, when he met Matt, it was almost the other way around, really. Beefy was taken by this exuberant young lad from Yeovil [where he, too, had grown up] who probably reminded him of how he was when he was a kid. Matt was leading the singing on the coach with the two of them chanting *We are Yeovil* and the like.' Neil also recalls that: 'Everyone was fond of Matt. He was a genuinely open and funny guy.'

At 6 feet 3 inches, well-built and with a wholehearted approach to the game, there seemed to be every indication that this likeable crowd-favourite would find his way into the Somerset folklore in the way that other home-grown players had done. Some even saw him as the new Ian Botham, an opinion based primarily on blind optimism allied to their similar physiques and backgrounds. Matt remains the source of many an anecdote, having arrived at the County Ground a wide-eyed innocent. It is claimed that, having joined the team as twelfth man for the Championship fixture against Middlesex at Uxbridge and blissfully unaware of the proximity of Heathrow airport, a young Matt Cleal asked Brian Rose, 'Where are all these planes coming from, Harry?' As Peter Roebuck would note, Matthew, utterly without guile and eager to learn, was happy to play the role of team clown. It masked an enquiring mind in a lad who had forsaken his studies while he honed his skills as a sportsman.

Offered a baptism of fire against the West Indies, he had been drafted into the side at the eleventh hour when Neil Mallender was called away for the birth of his first child. Prior to his first-class debut, Matt had gained experience in the Second XI, having first appeared as a sixteen-year-old. He had subsequently been invited to take part in the Seven Nations Youth Festival, held in Ireland, where he received

Matthew Cleal – an exuberant team member and 'a genuinely open-hearted and funny guy'

the Bowler of the Tournament award. Having previously worked as a delivery man and embarked on an alternative career as an apprentice painter and decorator, he was confident enough of a first-class career to take up the YTS (Youth Training Scheme) position at the County Ground, his wages supplemented by a sponsorship deal with the *Somerset County Gazette*. Later, he was despatched up the M5 on a regular basis on

Saturday afternoons to play for Smethwick CC, when an agreement was made that he would appear for them in Birmingham League cricket as a replacement all-rounder whenever their overseas pro, Steve Waugh, was appearing for Somerset.

His first-class debut was a triumph, with Matt taking 4 for 41, but this would prove his best return in a career cut cruelly short by recurring back problems. Another high point that sticks in Matt's memory was smashing an almighty six out of the ground off Jack Simmons as Somerset successful chased down a target in the Championship match at Old Trafford in1988. 'To be honest,' Matt jokes, 'it wasn't a case of great shot selection. More a question of trying to get the job done before Wasim Akram came on at the other end. I was thinking, "I need to get this over and done with."'

He was obliged to leave Somerset at the end of the 1991 season having played in fifteen first-class games, taking twenty-six wickets at 34.96 apiece and averaging 9.16 with the bat. In the early years, he spent the winters playing football as a central defender, initially with Bristol Rovers Youth Team and then for a period with Yeovil Town FC. He also spent one winter with Wanganui CC in New Zealand, before opting to spend his winters playing for Westland FC, having failed to secure a place in the Yeovil Town FC team. The foreshortening of his cricketing career might have broken a lesser man, but Matt is nothing if not resourceful. He resolved to get back to basics, which meant revisiting his schooling and building up his qualifications from scratch. In the words of Peter Roebuck, he 'studied alongside boys five years younger than him'. Matt admits with great candour that his re-entry into the world of education involved some chicanery on his part. 'Yeovil College were concerned that I lacked the academic rigour needed to study, so they asked me to write a summary of my life and cricket career, I presume to check my written work,' he confesses. 'To cut a long story short, I got Roeby to write it for me and when I handed it in they were mightily impressed by my efforts and I sailed in.' A resourceful young man, indeed.

Thereafter, success was down to Matt's own hard work. Having achieved the required grades, he was offered a place at the University of Wales Institute, Cardiff (later Cardiff Metropolitan University), where he qualified to become a teacher. He continued to play football both for UWIC and for Wales at student level, while gaining his FA coaching qualifications. After coaching for a brief period at Millfield School, Matt joined the staff at Malvern College, where he has coached both football and cricket. He has seen the facilities develop markedly, with the completion of a new Cricket Centre, opened in 2009 by Michael Vaughan.

Matt was married in 2001 to Jacqueline Anne (née Cox), a hairdresser, with whom he has two sons, Jarvis and Isaac. Jarvis, the elder of the two, has inherited the paternal footballing skills and has been a member of the academy at West Bromwich Albion for six years. At the time of writing, Matt is the lead football coach at Malvern and oversees the cricket Second XI, working alongside head coach, Mark Hardinges, formerly of Gloucestershire and Essex.

Peter Roebuck was not a man who handed out praise very readily, but he wrote with unguarded warmth about Matt Cleal, fondly recalling those occasions when a voice could be heard at the end of the telephone, all ebullience and brimming with *joi de vivre*. In Peter's words, 'Most conversations [began] with, "Roeby, you're not going to believe this, but …"', whereupon he'd outline his latest academic endeavour.' Peter Roebuck's warm tribute is echoed by others. None of Matt Cleal's teammates has a bad word to say of him. His charges at Malvern College continue to be inspired by his enthusiastic example.

524
Timothy John Adam Scriven
15 June 1988 v. Sussex, Bath

The Scriven family can claim some sporting pedigree. Tim's grandfather, Herbert Richard Scriven, known as Bert, was for many years Southampton FC's goalkeeper before becoming the licensee of the Bear and Ragged Staff pub in Michelmersh. Tim's father, John Richard, who worked for many years in the pharmaceutical industry and was married to Hilary Margaret (née Davies), played cricket for Buckinghamshire, as would Tim and Tim's younger son, Jack.

Born in High Wycombe on 15 December 1965, Tim was educated at the Royal Grammar School in the town. Encouraged by a father who had played for Hampshire Second XI as well as Buckinghamshire, Tim was offered terms by Northamptonshire and would remain with them for four seasons without ever breaking into the First XI. A tall, left-arm orthodox bowler, he was approached by Somerset as they continued their search for a left-arm spinner, having concluded that Robert Woolston – offered only one first-class outing in 1987 – was not the answer to their prayers. As it transpired, Tim would spend much of the 1988 season in the Second XI and appear in only two first-class fixtures before departing the scene. During the preceding winters, he had found work as an insurance clerk and had spent time as a groundsman at a sports centre. He had also been taken on as a pro by Marists CC in New Plymouth in the Taranaki District of New Zealand. After leaving Somerset he spent a further winter in New Zealand with Marists CC, next opting to travel and see something of the world prior to settling down to a more conventional career.

Having returned to England, he had responded to an advertisement placed in the *Daily Telegraph* by a German wine company seeking applicants to oversee the export of their product to the UK, when he received a call out of the blue from Peter Robinson. Peter informed him that Somerset needed his services at Bath. 'I was stony broke with not a penny to my name, so when I was offered a daily fee and expenses I grabbed the opportunity with both hands,' he reveals. 'What I didn't dare admit was that I hadn't played or even had any time in the nets for weeks and I had no idea what was about to happen when I held a bat or ball.' Fortunately for Tim, Jimmy Cook and Chris Tavaré spent the opening day putting the Lancashire attack to the sword and so he was able to slip away and work off the worst of his rustiness with some discreet net practice. Having been spared the ignominy of batting, he succeeded in taking four wickets during a match which Lancashire

Tim Scriven – 'I didn't dare admit that I hadn't played or even had any time in the nets for weeks'

won, owing to a sporting declaration by Chris Tavaré. Thirty years on, Tim is finally able to spill the beans. His three first-class matches for Somerset over two seasons had yielded seven wickets at 56.00 apiece and a batting average of 5.50.

From 1986, ahead of his brief spell with Somerset, he had appeared on occasions for his native Buckinghamshire and would continue to turn out for them until 1999, for a while as captain, working in tandem with Neil Burns, also previously with Somerset but by then Director of Cricket for the Minor County.

Tim's speculative application to join the wine trade had proved successful. Now focussed on a career that he had happened upon by good fortune rather than any prior plans, he built up his expertise with a further spell importing wines for another company. He was married, meanwhile, in 1990 to Sheena Montague, with whom he would have a daughter, Annie, and two sons, Bradley and Jack, both of whom have proved to be useful cricketers.

In 1995, Tim made the decision to branch out with his own wine merchant's business and formed Chalgrove Wines, now based in Thame, with a further offshoot in Liverpool. Tim talks about himself with light-hearted humour and a refreshing degree of self-deprecation, surprised that anyone should be interested in his cricketing exploits. Asked about the experience of playing first-class cricket for Somerset, he responds by saying that, 'It was enjoyable and I was in some elevated company,' adding with a chuckle, 'but I was at the other end of the spectrum.' Twenty-three years after its formation, his company continues to thrive. His taste of first-class cricket was brief, but his adventures in the wine trade have proved substantially more enduring.

525
Harvey Russell John Trump
23 July 1988 v. Nottinghamshire, Taunton

Harvey Trump was born in Taunton on 11 October 1968, the son of Gerald and Jackie (née Betty). He was blessed with good cricketing genes, his father having captained both Somerset Second XI and Devon. A man of considerable talent and energy, Gerald had taught at Millfield School (recruited by Jack Meyer, shortly before the departure of the school's maverick founder). He had specialised in helping dyslexic pupils, before founding not one but three specialist schools – at Edington, then Shapwick, both near Glastonbury, and finally at Shrewton, near Salisbury – each of the institutions being subsequently bought out as going concerns.

Harvey attended Edgarley Hall Prep School before moving up to Millfield Senior School, where he is described as having been a model pupil – 'well-mannered, diligent and quiet' – who transformed into an ultra-competitive athlete on the field of play. That combination of talent and a will to win led to his representing Somerset at all the age groups up to Under-19 level at both hockey and cricket. He was also selected for the England Under-19 tour of Sri Lanka and for the inaugural Youth World Cup in 1987, sponsored by McDonald's and held in Australia. The England Under-19s, led by Mike Atherton, were defeated by the hosts at the semi-final stage.

An accomplished off-spin bowler, Harvey was a fine fielder, too. A specialist slip or gully, he was also, in the words of erstwhile teammate and experienced judge of the game, David Graveney, 'the best fielder off his own bowling I've ever seen'. He was given his debut with Somerset Second XI in 1986 while still a schoolboy, although that would prove a sobering experience, with the Hampshire Second XI batsmen engaging in a runfest. He left Millfield in 1988 to study for his degree in History & Physical Education at Chester College of Higher Education (part of Liverpool University). While in the North West, he played for Chester Boughton Hall in league cricket and, on returning to Somerset in June 1988, was granted his first-class debut, a more uplifting experience than his first appearance in the second tier had been. Bowling fourteen overs in tandem with Vic Marks, he took 2 for 17 before, his confidence now boosted, he scored forty-eight runs. That would prove his highest first-class score, but he would continue to develop as a bowler, enjoying his most fruitful period in the 1991 and 1992 seasons, with a combined total of 100 wickets. The highpoint of his career was a return of 7 for 52 in each innings against Gloucestershire in 1992. There were a further seven five-wicket hauls in a first-class career that stretched from

1988 until 1996, by which point he was struggling with back problems. For a prolonged period, he was understudy to Mushtaq Ahmed, so that opportunities were limited, but Harvey is insistent that he welcomed Mushy's arrival and learned a great deal from the man who became for a while his mentor. His 106 first-class appearances yielded a batting average of 12.54 and 242 wickets at 38.76 apiece.

After graduating, he taught for six years at the Stamford Endowed Schools, an unusually structured establishment, where pupils of both sexes are taught together at junior and sixth form levels but separated during the intermediate years when hormones are generally raging, just at the time when exams require most focus. This far-sighted institution released Harvey to play cricket each summer and he in turn taught History, PE and PSHE, coached rugby and hockey and ran an indoor winter cricket programme. In 1991, during his time teaching in Lincolnshire, he was briefly married to Nicola (née Towle), a fellow teacher.

Harvey Trump – an accomplished off-spin bowler and a fine fielder
COURTESY OF JOHN LEE

He returned to Taunton to teach at King's College. Appointed a house master, he taught History and PE, coached the hockey First XI and worked alongside the irrepressible Dennis Breakwell in nurturing the cricketing talent. Having remarried, he has two sons (born in 2003 and 2006) and he is happy to encourage their ambition to become professional sportsmen, though their sports of choice appear to be football and tennis. Harvey remained at King's College until 2004, at which point he took up an appointment as deputy headmaster at Tettenhall College in Wolverhampton. He worked concurrently as a lecturer, tutor and mentor, helping members of the teaching profession in schools in the surrounding area to improve the boarding experience for their pupils. This was the stepping stone to his first headmastership at St Dominic's, an independent school in Staffordshire. Then, in 2015, he was offered the role of Headmaster of the Regent International School in Dubai, before going on to become a vice principal in Oman, and he has since been appointed a member of the leadership team in GEMs Education, who are responsible for a chain of schools in the Middle

East. At the time of writing, he has recently taken up the post of Deputy Principal at a college in Kampala, Uganda.

Harvey talks with conviction of the need to instil 'character, core values and leadership' in his charges. His own will to succeed is evident in his every action – whether giving of his best on the cricket field or knuckling down to complete an MA in Education at Edge Hill University in his spare time, between 2008 and 2011. He is just as determined to eke out the very best of the unique talents in each pupil. If his personal ambitions were at times frustrated as a first-class cricketer, he has certainly more than made up for that in a teaching career that had gone from strength to strength.

Harvey Trump – for a prolonged period he was understudy to Mushtaq Ahmed
COURTESY OF IVAN PONTING

1989

"Vic [Marks] should have been made captain in 1983.
If he had, the miserable years might never have occurred."

Peter Roebuck

Championship Position: 14 of 17

It was a season of false dawns. In the first County Championship match, all was set fair when Jimmy Cook and Peter Roebuck built an opening partnership of 143 against Hampshire, but that match fizzled out into a draw. In the Refuge Assurance League, Chris Tavaré entertained with a masterful 120 not out, but the match, once more against Hampshire, was lost. After a sparkling first round win over Essex in the NatWest Trophy, with centuries for Chris Tavaré and Peter Roebuck, that campaign ended in the next round. Only in the Benson & Hedges Cup was there a sustained run. The side reached the semi-final, where they went down fighting to Essex, despite another unbeaten century by Chris Tavaré.

Vic Marks had taken on the duty of pilot of not quite a sinking ship but one not yet strong enough to impose itself on the prevailing winds and currents. South African recruit, Jimmy Cook – another of those inspired overseas signings that Somerset kept pulling out of the hat – was brilliant and could not stop accumulating runs in eye-watering quantities. Fellow new signing, Chris Tavaré, long a friend of Vic's, from their university days, showed his class, as did the redoubtable Peter Roebuck. Another important recruit was the widely-respected Jack Birkenshaw, brought in as Cricket Manager, to work in tandem with new Chief Executive, Peter Anderson, an excellent leader whose background lay in policing rather than cricket. For once, the new captain was not the principal wicket-taker. That honour fell to Adrian Jones, who enjoyed a productive and injury-free season and claimed seventy-one victims. Neil Mallender offered support with fifty wickets.

526
Stephen James Cook
20 April 1989 v. Hampshire, Southampton

[signature: Jimmy Cook]

Jimmy Cook would enjoy three extraordinary seasons with Somerset. A return of 10,652 runs in all forms of the game in such a short time was beyond his adoptive county's wildest expectations. His first-class average in seventy-one matches was 72.41 (and his two wickets at 34.00 apiece a mere curiosity). The wonder of it was that he had first appeared in the County Championship at the age of thirty-five. When asked why this should have been the case, he replied that no one had ever asked. When Brian Rose rang Jimmy in South Africa, inviting him to come to the County Ground and offering generous terms, he consulted his friend and compatriot Clive Rice (who had thrived at Nottinghamshire for many seasons) and was informed that he should take up the offer with alacrity. A gentleman of the old school, who always found time to talk patiently with supporters or to help the young players with their technique, he made it his habit to enter the opposition changing room and shake hands with those with whom he was doing battle. The respect was mutual, with instances recorded of the likes of Michael Holding and Malcolm Marshall approaching him at the close of play and thanking him for the challenge he had afforded them. There is a mistaken view that Jimmy Cook was merely an accumulator of runs, but this is far removed from the truth. He was a team man, prepared to accelerate and take risks when needs must. More concerned with results than personal glory, he even urged his captain Chris Tavaré to declare when he (Jimmy) was on 313 not out and just short of Viv Richards's all-time record for a Somerset batsman. The pity of it was that he was supported by a relatively feeble bowling attack at Somerset, who could not take advantage of the opportunities he created. Not so with his performances for Transvaal, who were the dominant cricketing province in South Africa at the time.

Jimmy was born in Johannesburg on 31 July 1953. He was of British stock, although his father, Buddy, had been born in Bombay (Mumbai) and had arrived in South Africa as a teenager, going on to teach and coach young boys (including Jimmy and his brother, Brian) at sport at Rosebank Primary School in Johannesburg. By the time the sons went on to Hyde Park High School, Jimmy had already developed an insatiable appetite for batting and would spend his free time in the nets. This paid dividends when he was drafted into the Transvaal Under-15s team with whom he came under the influence of coach Dickie Bird, who would later find fame as a much-respected, and at times eccentric, umpire. In the meantime, Jimmy's skill as a footballer was being noticed and at the age of sixteen, a trial with Wolverhampton Wanderers was mooted but declined. He would continue to play the game in South Africa for Witwatersrand University until hanging up his boots in 1985.

Jimmy was playing for Transvaal from the age of nineteen, and, like many of his generation, was denied the opportunity to play in official tests during his prime, although he was a shoo-in to the national side in the Rebel Tours that elicited a mixed response and reprisals for some of the participants. On a personal level he found the apartheid regime abhorrent, but felt that cricket was at the vanguard of integration and that South Africa's isolation was counterproductive.

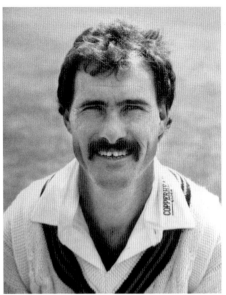

Jimmy Cook – exceeded all expectations over the course of his three seasons at Somerset

Having enjoyed more or less unbroken success in his homeland, he relished the opportunity to test his mettle in English conditions but was determined that his wife, Linsey, should be happy with the arrangement and that the education of their two sons, Stephen and Ryan, should not be compromised. There was an additional hurdle to overcome. For seventeen years he had been associated with Fairways Primary School in Johannesburg as a coach and teacher, but the Education Department informed him that he could not be released for the English summer. In the event, he was offered a coaching role and the freedom to travel by the Rand Afrikaans University and the family would take instantly to life in Taunton for six months of the year, with the boys continuing their schooling, their progress seemingly unharmed.

Jimmy adjusted very quickly to English conditions. A relative weakness against spin was soon rectified by assiduous practice in the nets with the help of Jack Birkenshaw and Peter Robinson. Teammates were soon waxing lyrical. Peter Roebuck, writing in *The Sunday Times*, would record that, 'At the crease he is peaceful, durable and solid, gentle with bat and ball, certain of his own mind ... Cook has a range that includes dominance and obduracy.' Vic Marks would write in *The Observer*: 'Statistics will record Jimmy's tremendous batting achievements, but there is far more to tell. Off the field, he offers a great example to our less-experienced players which will benefit the county for years to come.' By the end of the season, Jimmy Cook had confounded any doubters with 3,143 runs for Somerset in all forms of the game. As the *Somerset County Gazette* reported:

Munch! Bill Alley takes another bite out of the humble pie he's been eating since suggesting on these pages that Jimmy Cook probably wouldn't succeed at Somerset this season. As one of life's more unfortunate predictions, it's up there with Chamberlain's 'peace in our time' …

If the 1989 season was an unqualified triumph, then it was bettered by events in the following season. Writing once more in *The Sunday Times*, Peter Roebuck stated: 'By seeking command and finding it with new shots, a very good accumulator has turned himself into a batsman capable of wreaking havoc.' Runs continued to flow – 3,939 of them in all forms of the game.

Unlikely as it now seems, a run drought threatened during the 1991 season, but a quiet word from Ken Palmer, umpiring in a Sunday League match at Bournemouth, was enough to trigger an immediate correction. Jimmy had, as Ken pointed out, begun to open up his stance fractionally, so that he was less side-on. It is a measure, not just of Ken's cricketing brain, but also of Jimmy's preparedness to listen, that the improvement was so sudden and so marked. Once more, he ended the year with an astonishing number of runs to his name. There were 3,570 of them in all forms of the game and a first-class average for the season of 81.02.

The departure from Taunton of Jimmy and his family was emotional for all parties. The club were grateful for his unstinting excellence and for the polite assistance offered to the ordinary mortals in their ranks. The family were delighted to have been welcomed into the bosom of Somerset cricket. Back in South Africa, with the national team finally returning from the wilderness, Jimmy had the distinction of facing the first ball for his country in the new era. Controversially, he was given out caught by Sachin Tendulkar at slip for a golden duck. Convinced that the ball had not carried, Jimmy nevertheless returned to the pavilion without complaint, ever the gentleman, unruffled even in the most trying of circumstances. There was redemption when his and Linsey's elder son, Stephen, went on to represent South Africa, first appearing as an opening batsman for them in 2016 and scoring a century on debut. Misty-eyed romantics in Somerset would have been disappointed to see Stephen surfacing at Chester-le-Street rather than at Taunton, in 2017.

In the autumn of his playing career, Jimmy turned his hand increasingly to coaching, returning each season to Rand Afrikaans University in Johannesburg and, for a short stint, at Hampshire. He has subsequently run the Jimmy Cook Cricket Academy, based in Johannesburg, where his charges have included Graeme Smith, a batsman of similar intensity, talent and application, who also enjoyed an all-to-brief but hugely successful spell at Somerset.

Jimmy's record speaks for itself, but here is what he wrote of his time at Somerset:

Jimmy Cook – 'a very good accumulator has turned himself into a batsman capable of wreaking havoc' COURTESY OF JOHN LEE

> *From the very first day I flew in from Africa and set eyes on Taunton I have been in love with the town, the ground, the environment and the people, and over the following three years I did my best to justify the faith the club had placed in me.*

The faith of Somerset was undoubtedly well placed. The Committee's decision to offer him a contract reaped rewards beyond any reasonable expectation. The club remain proud to claim Jimmy Cook as one of their own.

527
Christopher James Tavaré
28 April 1989 v. Glamorgan, Taunton

[signature]

He was obliged to endure the cognomen 'The Tortoise' and there were those who claimed that there was more fun to be extracted from watching paint dry than enduring him keep opposition Test bowlers at bay. When Henry VIII's flagship, the 'Mary Rose', was raised from its watery grave in 1982, there was a joke doing the rounds that the first question asked by a sailor who had been trapped in an airlock for the best part of 450 years was: 'Has Chris Tavaré reached his half-century, yet?' And yet he had merely fulfilled his brief to use his skills – as a batsman with few if any technical flaws and superhuman powers of concentration – to wear down opposing Test bowlers. His Somerset teammate Adrian Jones got it right, observing of Chris that: 'He is a brilliant cricketer, better than people know. Many of our supporters think of him as scoring excruciatingly slow fifties for England, but the style he adopted in Test cricket bore no relation to the way he normally bats.' For the supporters at the County Ground, fed a diet of anecdote, his free-flowing masterclasses came as a revelation.

Born on 27 October 1954 in Orpington, Kent, Chris was the son of Andrew Tavaré, who was married to June (née Attwood). Educated at Sevenoaks School, he was offered a place to study Zoology at St John's College, Oxford, where he gained three blues from 1975 to 1977. Although he was disappointed that his good friend and fellow undergraduate at St John's, Vic Marks, was offered the captaincy ahead of him, he would graciously state that the right man had been chosen for the job.

Having made his initial first-class appearance for Kent in 1974, he soon became an integral member of the side and gained further experience in the winter months when he was awarded a Whitbread Scholarship that led to his spending two seasons in grade cricket in Australia, initially in Perth and later in Melbourne. He would play for Kent on 259 occasions, for two seasons as their captain. The Kent faithful knew his true worth, as did the England selectors, who turned to him on thirty-one occasions at a time when there was stiff competition for batting places. Asked to do a particular job and wear down opposition attacks, Chris's exploits became the stuff of legend. If his sixty-six balls to get off the mark against Australia was regarded as soporific, then his five-and-a-half-hour half-century against Pakistan that year, or an even more excruciating 35 against India in 1983, represented the acme of dogged determination. According to one memorable description, 'tall, angular and splayfooted, a thin moustache sketched on his top lip, he would walk to the crease like a stork

Chris Tavaré – 'he is a brilliant cricketer, better than people know' COURTESY OF JOHN LEE

approaching a watering hole full of crocs'. After each delivery he had successfully blocked he would 'walk gingerly towards square leg' while he gathered his thoughts. At times his efforts were overlooked. Witness his crucial runs in the Fifth Test of the 1981 Ashes series. Ian Botham rightly won plaudits for his second innings century, but it was Chris's two watchful innings (that had him outscoring Ian) that made victory possible. The fact that he was awarded twenty-nine One Day International caps to add to his thirty-one Test caps demonstrates his ability to adapt to different formats. In limited overs games, he was generally circumspect at the start of an innings but 'turned up the volume' with seeming ease, as conditions demanded it. There were flashes of brilliance in the longer form of the game, too. On one occasion, appearing for Kent, he was goaded over his blocking tactics by Ian Botham, who dared him to despatch Vic Marks into the River Tone. Chris nodded and smiled. Two hours later, he did as bidden.

Married in 1979 to Constance Vanessa Leary, known as Vanessa, who had been born in Chatham but was a died-in-the-wool Somerset supporter, Chris needed little persuasion to join Somerset when he felt that his career needed refreshing, particularly given that his friend, Vic Marks, was doing the persuading. An added attraction was that he was able to work during the winter months with the Ministry of Agriculture in Exeter. Previously he had tried his luck in administrative roles in insurance with Save & Prosper and in financial management with Schroders, but here was an

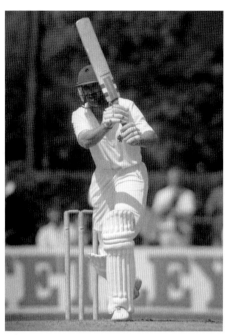

opportunity to indulge his passion for entomology. The work included analysing soil samples for pests. Chris regarded it as a welcome break from the pressures of the game, noting that 'during the summer you played so much it could get stale, but this kept me enthusiastic'.

He was welcomed into the fold at the County Ground: an elder statesman whose abilities and knowledge of the game were much valued. Vic Marks held the fort for a season before the newcomer was elevated to the captaincy. Adrian Jones describes Chris as 'a cerebral rather than a motivational captain [who] didn't need to crack the whip: we had so much respect for him, for his experience, that we knew what was needed'.

Adrian observed at the time that: 'He did a flip-chart presentation, highlighting the mistakes we made last year, primarily in the one-dayers, and what we were going to do to remedy this: no one had ever done that at Somerset before.'

Chris Tavaré – 'he would walk to the crease like a stork approaching a watering hole full of crocs'

His precision extended beyond his batting to many other aspects of life, whether the meticulous folding of his clothes when he changed or the strict adherence to speed limits, facilitated by the fitting in his car of a cruise control device, which his sometime passenger Peter Roebuck described – with his usual grasp of technology – as 'a machine that made his car tootle along at exactly 70 mph'. Peter observed of Chris that he was 'a brilliant batsman held back by the desire to retain control of every aspect of his life'. His lugubrious manner led some of his teammates to refer to him – in a nod to the downbeat inspector in the TV series *On the Buses* – as 'Blakey', a character with whom he shared more than a passing resemblance. With his dry sense of humour, Chris was happy to endure the gentle ribbing with quiet dignity.

There was certainly steady progress in Somerset's performances and these continued until his departure at the end of the 1993 season. He had also earned a recall to the England side during his time at Taunton, reflecting his personal accomplishments with the bat. In 102 games for Somerset, he would average 43.00, with thirteen centuries, taking his career total to an impressive forty-eight hundreds.

He left the first-class game to become a Biology teacher at his alma mater, Sevenoaks School, where he took great delight in coaching the pupils at cricket. The school now boasts a Cricket Academy, which, at the time of writing, he oversees, and hosts a tournament each year for local primary schools. His lessons are mercifully more engaging than his Test innings were. Chris has spoken about the bubble of professional cricket and how teaching is a more rounded pursuit. He has remained an integral part of life at Sevenoaks School since 1994. It has been a long innings, although retirement now beckons.

He was a fine batsman, destined to remain for many people a byword in obduracy at the crease, a man memorably referred to by writer Gideon Haigh as having the quality of 'making every ditch a last one'. But those who saw him liberated from the shackles will tell a different story.

528
Paul David Unwin
17 May 1989 v. Australia, Taunton

Paul Unwin's selection for the Somerset team was unexpected. A twenty-one-year-old off-spin bowler from New Zealand, he was residing in the county after having been the recipient of a scholarship set up by Martin Crowe for promising youngsters from Central Districts and was enjoying a season based at Clevedon CC as their professional. Not qualified by residence, he was unregistered by his adoptive county, not expected to make any first-class or List A appearances, but played on a number of occasions for Somerset Second XI, also enhancing his knowledge of the game as a member of the ground staff at Taunton. Paul notes with understatement that it was 'a pleasant surprise' when First Team Manager, Jack Birkenshaw, approached him shortly before the start of the tour match and asked if he would like to play. He recalls that 'I was bowling to the Aussies before the game, as were other Second XI bowlers. Unfortunately, Vic Marks's father had passed away the night before and, unbeknown to me, Somerset had been seeking special dispensation from the ECB for me to play, as we already had an overseas player in Jimmy Cook.' Having accepted the invitation with alacrity, Paul then proceeded to bag three prized wickets in Australia's first innings – those of David Boon, Tom Moody and their captain, Allan Border, the last of these for a duck. In total, he would take five wickets in the drawn match at a creditable 23.20 apiece. He scored 4 not out in his only innings. Paul had lived up to his sponsor Martin Crowe's billing.

Born on 9 June 1967 in Waipawa, near Hastings on New Zealand's North Island, he was the son of Reg and Diane Unwin. Educated at Lindisfarne College, he had

Paul Unwin – a promising youngster from New Zealand who enjoyed a season with Clevedon CC COURTESY OF JOHN LEE

risen through the ranks as a rugby player for Manawatu and played his cricket for Hastings Old Boys CC before becoming a member of the Cornwall CC team in Hastings, formed in 1989 when Hastings Old Boys merged with Whakatu Mahora CC as a means of strengthening the city's presence. Paul's father, Reg, was appointed manager of the clubrooms of the newly-formed Cornwall CC at their ground in Cornwall Park.

Known to teammates as 'Unners', he enjoyed a relatively brief first-class career in his homeland, appearing for Central Districts on twenty-nine occasions before playing for Canterbury in South Island four times during the 1993-94 season. He came away with a total of sixty-five first-class wickets to his name. For two years he coached the Central Districts Hinds women's cricket team, before embarking on an overseas career as a teacher. Never married, he has devoted much of his adult life to teaching. For two years, he taught in an American School in Abu Dhabi where he was struck by the hordes of workers from the Indian sub-continent 'playing cricket in every car park space and dusty little corner you can find'. Proud of his New Zealand heritage, and noting that the country 'is the bottom of the world and that's what makes it so special', he embraced the culture of the Middle East. He was subsequently offered a six-year contract as Principal of the English Modern School in Doha, Qatar. Paul observes wryly that although he had embraced the Arab culture, the free accommodation and absence of taxes, together with a funded flight home each year, was an offer he could hardly refuse. The only aspect of his stay that he failed metaphorically to warm to was the stultifying hot summers and he was always happy to decamp to Hastings for a taste of New Zealand winter.

His contract ended in 2015 and, keen to return to the coalface and interact once more with students, he now teaches at Hereworth School, an independent preparatory school for boys in Hawke's Bay. This was very much a homecoming for a man who has seen much of the world but has never lost his sense of identity as a Kiwi – and one who can derive quiet satisfaction at having dismissed the much-feted captain of great rivals Australia for an ignominious duck at Taunton, on the other side of the world.

1990

"I should mention that, along with the superb weather, the conditions in 1990 were weighed very much in favour of the batsmen. Bowlers were given balls with a narrow and flatter seam, lessening the swing potential, and groundsmen were ordered to prepare straw-coloured wickets."

Jimmy Cook

Championship Position: 15 of 17

It is typical of Jimmy Cook that, having made 2,608 first-class runs to add to the 2,241 amassed the previous season, he should have played down his achievements. They were phenomenal. It was, however, true that this was a season for the batsmen to fill their boots. Jack Birkenshaw would joke, 'Spare a thought for our bowlers, who toiled with balls which many a mongrel dog would refuse to play with.' Six men exceeded 1,000 runs, among them Chris Tavaré, local boy Richard Harden, who was now finding his feet, and new-join Andy Hayhurst, who had come down from Lancashire and would go on in time to captain Somerset. Three bowlers – Adrian Jones, Graham Rose and Neil Mallender – gamely conjured over fifty wickets each. Adrian Jones, for one, was unsure about some of the changes, noting that the enormous communal bath had 'fallen foul of the AIDS lobby' and bemoaning the absence of 'those delicious tea-time cakes', which had been displaced by fruit. 'Sometimes,' he observed, 'I don't know whether I'm bowling with a ball ... or a Granny Smith's.'

If Jimmy Cook's runs had been accumulated with unwavering efficiency, then Graham Rose's had come in astonishing bursts. In the NatWest Trophy he put Devon to the sword with a thirty-four-ball century before Roland Lefebvre, a new-join who hailed from the Netherlands, inflicted further misery on Somerset's neighbours with a return of 7 for 15. Less than a month later, Graham was hammering a century in forty-six deliveries off the Glamorgan attack in the Refuge Assurance League.

529
Roland Philippe Lefebvre
18 April 1990 v. Oxford University, Oxford

Roland Lefebvre must rank among the finest cricketers to have emerged from the Netherlands. The pioneering path he took to the County Ground at Taunton has since been trodden by a succession of his fellow countrymen. Born in Rotterdam on 7 February 1963, he was the son of Pierre Joseph Ernest Lefebvre, known as Ernest, who worked in insurance and later for the Diners Club credit card company. His antecedents were French Huguenots who had fled France and originally settled near Amsterdam before become involved in the whaling industry. Roland's mother, Anne Hermeliene (née Henkes), was an accomplished artist and a member of the family who had established the Henkes Jenever gin brand (founded in 1824 and bought by Bols in 1986). Although this does not read like the typical launching pad for a career in the game, Roland in truth came from a family of talented cricketers.

Educated at the Montessori Lyceum in Rotterdam and the Hague Academy of Physiotherapy, he began to make a name for himself as an all-rounder with VOC Rotterdam CC (for whom his father and brothers have also played) and the touring Flamingos CC team. Having been invited to play for the Netherlands Under-19s at the age of sixteen, he was subsequently chosen for the Dutch side at twenty and would go on to play for his country in a record-breaking combined total of fifty-four ICC matches and One Day Internationals, many of them as captain, taking a total of eighty wickets, whilst contributing useful runs and thirty catches, before his retirement from the international scene in 2003. Never insular in his outlook, Roland had looked beyond the boundaries of the Netherlands to experience different pitches and varied playing conditions. From 1978, he played club cricket in New Zealand during the winters and would later be offered a professional contract with Canterbury CC.

When Jack Birkenshaw put Roland's name forward as a possible recruit for Somerset, his reputation was already established. He had played at Lord's for an MCC side captained by Somerset and New Zealand legend Martin Crowe in a match against Ireland and was a member of the Dutch side who defeated Peter Roebuck's touring England XI in 1989.

Over the course of three seasons with Somerset, he would make thirty-six first-class appearances for them, claiming fifty-four wickets at 45.40 apiece and averaging 20.96 with the bat, with one century to his name. Perhaps his most memorable match was the astonishing 346 run NatWest victory over Devon in 1990, when he returned figures of 7 for 15. In March 1992, Roland suffered a broken arm in extraordinary circumstances while on an MCC tour of the Leeward Islands. Having playfully thrown some water over the twelfth man, Brad Donelan, in the thirty degree heat during the drinks break, he was rewarded with an unexpectedly violent kick, which he attempted to fend off. In Roland's own words, 'I could hear the break, mentioned this to the stunned players and walked off. I flew back to England two days later.' Although he was ready to return to the fold by mid-June of that year, Somerset's newly-appointed coach, Bob Cottam, was resistant to Roland's inclusion. Despite the fact that his contract was scheduled to run until 1994, Chief Executive Peter Anderson gave permission for Roland to talk to other counties. He chose Glamorgan, a decision he describes as 'a fan-

Roland Lefebvre – ranks among the finest cricketers to have emerged from the Netherlands

tastic move'. Glamorgan felt equally enthusiastic about his time with them. Between 1993 and 1995, when a serious groin injury led to his having to step away from the demands of the county game, he became a valued and popular member of the Glamorgan team. Cricket writer and historian Andrew Hignell describes Roland's signing as 'a masterstroke' and writes that, 'Week after week, the Dutch seamer bowled a full and nagging length to frustrate and contain a host of opposition batsmen.' He cites the Quarter Final of the NatWest Trophy in 1993 as an example of Roland's value to the side, given that he took 2 for 13 in eleven overs, although the Man of the Match Award went to Matthew Maynard for his 84 runs, perhaps offering further evidence for those who claim that, in matters of adjudication, the pyrotechnics of batsmen are all-too-often favoured over the unsung heroics of the bowlers. Roland was regarded as an important contributor to his side's winning of the AXA Equity and Law League in 1993, with some Somerset supporters wondering if their county had made the right decision in allowing two of the victors – Roland and his teammate, Viv Richards – to slip through their fingers.

A man of many talents, Roland is an accomplished pianist, in the classical mould. 'Not the sort of playing where I could lead the team's post-match revelry,' he con-

firms, 'although we often had dinner at Porter's wine bar, owned by a friend of Peter Roebuck, and I was sometimes persuaded to play the piano there.' Having qualified as a physiotherapist prior to his professional career, he had been able to find work as a locum. Later, while with Somerset, he and Ray Heard set up the Wyvern Physiotherapy Clinic, housed in the pavilion at the County Ground and offering a year-round service to members and the public. He was married in 1994 to Sandra (née Puttergill), known as Sandy, a South African schoolteacher whom he had met at a pre-season function hosted for Glamorgan by Andersen Consulting. After leaving Glamorgan, he became the Argentine National Coach for a year in 1996. Between 1997 and 1999, he was the

Roland Lefebvre – made thirty-six first-class appearances for Somerset before going on to enjoy a successful spell at Glamorgan COURTESY OF JOHN LEE

pro and coach at Alma Marist CC, based in Cape Town. He and Sandy also owned and ran the Palmyra Guest House, located around the corner from the Newlands stadium.

In 1999, the couple made the decision to return to the Netherlands on the basis that this would be the best place to raise their children. For three years, he worked as a sales rep for a friend, whilst also finding time to turn out for the Netherlands. Since 2002, he has been employed by the Netherlands Cricket Board (KNCB), initially as their Development Officer and latterly as the Director of Cricket. In his present role, Roland is committed to advancing the cause of the game in his country, but is aware of the challenges in a part of the world where football and hockey take precedence. He remains global in his outlook and pragmatic in his approach: all that we would expect of a man born and raised in the Netherlands.

530
Ian Geoffrey Swallow
18 April 1990 v. Oxford University, Oxford

It took a little more than one summer to make this Swallow decide to migrate back in his native Yorkshire. Born on 18 December 1962 in Barnsley, Ian was the son of Geoffrey Swallow, a useful club cricketer with Elsecar Village CC, who was married to Joyce (née Senior). At the age of two, he suffered the loss of a finger in his right hand, when it was caught in a washing machine. Most boys might have balked at the idea of ever taking up spin bowling, but Ian refused to have his horizons limited by such a setback and learned to impart off-spin. For this alone he deserves plaudits, but he is also praised by teammates as pleasant company, a dressing room joker, a good team man, and one prepared to bowl as long was required of him.

Educated at Kirk Balk Comprehensive School in Hoyland, Barnsley, he came under the influence of 'Rocket Ronnie' Hallam, an irrepressible games master who nurtured a number of professional footballers and cricketers and is said to have influenced the depiction of the PE teacher in Barry Hines's *Kestrel for a Knave* (although in truth, Hallam's undoubted will to win was not tarnished by the sadism evident in the character of his fictional counterpart). Ian then went on to Barnsley Technical College, before playing his first game for Yorkshire Second XI as a nineteen-year-old, appearing alongside two future Somerset cricketers, Paul Jarvis and Nick Taylor – the three of them part of a veritable wave of arrivals from Yorkshire that has continued for many a year at the County Ground, as the club has looked to instil some Northern grit into proceedings. His debut for Yorkshire followed in 1983 and in the early days he was touted as a great hope for the future. He had his moments – most notably a return of 7 for 95 against Nottinghamshire at Trent Bridge in 1987 – but fewer of them than he and Yorkshire had hoped. Over the course of seven seasons, Ian would appear in sixty-one matches for his native county before a parting of the ways in 1989. He had also spent two seasons Down Under with the aptly named Sunshine CC in Melbourne and in other winters was offered work as a stores clerk, nearer to home, to supplement his summer contract.

Having arrived at Somerset, already in possession of substantial experience, as a replacement for Vic Marks, Ian was never able to achieve the penetration as a bowler that his new county had hoped for. He was, however, a popular member of the team, and the source of the occasional anecdote such as the time when, with the Somerset team all gathered in the dressing room at Scarborough ahead of a Refuge Assurance game, pumped up and raring to go, Jack Birkenshaw invited Ian to tap into his

Ian Swallow – a good team man, and one prepared to bowl as long was required of him

insider knowledge and run through the Yorkshire side, giving the lowdown on their vulnerabilities. As Ian ran through the side, beginning with the opening partners, Moxon and Metcalfe, he shook his head slowly. Each of his former teammates had the potential on his day to be a world-beater. There appeared to be no chinks in their armoury. Hope abandoned all who had entered the room. They went out and promptly lost. 'Fish', as he was fondly known by his Somerset teammates, was not called upon again to rally the troops. He would remain with Somerset for two seasons. Over the course of twenty-seven matches, he took forty-two wickets at 60.19 apiece. A capable batsman, good enough to score a first-class century for Yorkshire while opening the batting against MCC at Scarborough in 1987, he averaged 21.16 with the bat during his time with Somerset. He was also regarded as a superb fielder, anointed the best in the team by Jack Birkenshaw.

Happily ensconced back in Barnsley, Ian was married in 1993 to Barbara (née Kilner), with whom he would have two sons – Thomas and James – both of whom would keep up the family tradition and play for Elescar CC.

He has continued to reside in his home town, supporting Barnsley FC in the winter months and turning out for many years for Meltham CC in the Huddersfield League, captaining the side for a number of seasons before his triumphant return to Elescar CC, the club he had first turned out for as a boy. Welcomed back as captain of the side, he immediately led them to the South Yorkshire League title in 2008.

Once he had ceased to be a professional cricketer, he had worked in the construction sector, spending ten years as a Project Manager and Operations Director with Technical Solutions Brecks Ltd, involved with building and electrical works, specialising in ATM installations. Since 2010 he has been Project Manager with DAC Environmental Ltd, involved in similar installations.

Here is a man rooted in the town of Barnsley, a Yorkshireman to his very bones, winkled out of the place, but only for two seasons with Somerset.

531
Andrew Neil Hayhurst
3 May 1990 v. Glamorgan, Cardiff

[signature]

It requires guts for a first-class cricketer to recover from adversity. More so when you err in a manner that a sentencing judge describes as a 'spectacular fall from grace'. Events in recent years have tarnished Andy Hayhurst's reputation, but an appraisal of his life serves to show that here is a man with positive qualities, too. Let the judge and jury do their judging. What of his life as a whole?

Born on 23 November 1962 in Davyhulme, Manchester, he was the son of William and Margaret Hayhurst. Educated at Worsley Wardley High School and Eccles College, he would then go on to Carnegie College of Physical Education in Leeds (now part of Leeds Beckett University) to study for a degree in Human Movement (of the athletic kind, rather than migration). He was by then already proving his worth as a batsman and useful bowler with Worsley CC and in representative games at Under-19 level, scoring 197 for the North of England against the South in 1982. He made his debut for Lancashire in 1985 and would remain with them for five seasons, making forty-two first-class appearances and producing some worthy performances with bat and ball, without ever hitting the heights.

Married in 1990 to April (née Cauldwell) shortly before his arrival at Taunton, Andy is clearly a man with a taste for a spectacular entrée, scoring 110 not on debut for Somerset (although he was rather overshadowed by Jimmy Cook, who scored 313 not out in the first innings before making way for others in the second). Andy's first season at the County Ground was a triumph, with 1,559 first-class runs at an average of 57.74, and he came to be regarded as a key member of the side – so much so that he was appointed captain in 1994, in the words of Matthew Reed 'as much for his calm and common sense as for the traditional reason of his being the best player in the team'. If the latter point is a moot one, he was certainly an important member of the side.

The first eight competitive games as captain were an unmitigated disaster – all lost – but the team rallied under his leadership and clawed their way to respectability. However, 1996 saw a precipitous falling away of Andy's form as he struggled to get bat on ball. At 10:00 am on 1 August, about to lead his side out against Hampshire, he was informed that he had been dropped from the side in favour of a young Marcus Trescothick. Peter Bowler was asked to step into the breach as captain. Marcus went on to score 178, which might have left Chairman of the Cricket Committee, Brian Rose,

Andy Hayhurst – arrived in a blaze of glory and was later made Somerset's captain

COURTESY OF JOHN LEE

relieved that his brave and ruthless call had been the right one, but would have done nothing to mitigate Andy's feelings of humiliation and disillusionment. A parting of the ways at the end of the 1996 season was by then inevitable. Over the course of seven seasons with Somerset, he had averaged 38.86 with the bat in 122 first-class games, with thirteen centuries and thirty-six fifties to his name. It represented a near-doubling of his average at Lancashire, although there had been a commensurate falling away of his bowling prowess, with sixty wickets at 55.28 apiece, as he had focussed on his batting. If his debut back in 1990 had been pregnant with promise, his end had been a disappointment. This pattern was set to repeat itself.

Andy joined Derbyshire as Second XI captain and coach and later their Development Manager. Following an appearance for the First XI against Cambridge University, he continued the progression of noteworthy debuts, his opening Championship game for Derbyshire in April 1997 (against Kent at Canterbury) ending abruptly when he tore a cartilage in what would prove his last match in first-class cricket. More detrimental to his hopes of a prolonged time at Derby was Dominic Cork's need for complete control of every aspect of cricket at the county. Having been appointed Director of Cricket in 1998, Andy left the club 'by mutual consent' in March 1999. It was another less-than-glorious ending to a chapter of Andy Hayhurst's undulating life story, but worse was to follow.

He returned to his roots, appointed in 2002 to the role of Secretary of the Lancashire Cricket Board, a role he completed successfully for eight years before being invited to become a director on the board, a position he would hold until his contract was terminated in 2013. Andy had been playing for Worsley CC, the club he had first appeared for as a boy, and had been applying successfully for grants from 2006 until

2013. Intended for the development of grass roots cricket in the county, approximately £100,000 of £107,000 had found its way into his bank account. Rumbled by the Lancashire Cricket Board in October 2013, Andy agreed to pay back in the region of £22,000 that December, but a full police investigation revealed the extent of his embezzlement. He pleaded guilty to all charges, although, given the weight of evidence it would have been foolhardy to have done otherwise. Andy was handed a two-year prison sentence in June 2015.

Life carried on for the Hayhurst family, with April having carved a successful career at Derby College and their son, Myles, enjoying success at age group cricket in Derbyshire as a talented all-rounder. Andy had been one of the blessed few able to make the leap from promising youngster to successful first-class cricketer. It is a long and sometimes arduous journey, not unlike a climb to a mountain top. To continue the analogy, his fall from the summit was swift, sudden and shocking. Redemption, if it comes, will have been hard-earned.

532
Jeremy Charles Hallett
16 May 1990 v. New Zealand, Taunton

Jeremy Hallett was born in Yeovil on 18 October 1970, the son of Glyn and Rosemarie (née Turner). Educated initially at Wells Cathedral Junior School, Jeremy then attended Millfield School for six years until 1989. His mother was school secretary at the time. In July of that year, the eighteen-year-old school leaver made his debut appearance for Somerset Second XI. Life seemed straightforward and his prospects bright when he proceeded to outshine his fellow opening bowler, Andy Caddick, with a return of 5 for 54. Those prospects went from bright to dazzling when he was selected for the England Young Cricketers Tour of Australia in 1989-90 and was deemed Player of the Series for his performances as a seamer who made some useful contributions with the bat. There were also international appearances at Under-19 level on home soil against New Zealand and Pakistan. Then in 1990, by now embarked on a degree course in Combined Social Sciences – Economics, History & Business Management – at Durham University, whose cricket team he captained, he was offered his first-class debut by Somerset. In sixteen first-class matches for his home county, he would take twenty-four wickets at 47.58 apiece. Sadly, his effectiveness was blunted as

Jeremy Hallett – injury forced him to reinvent himself as a batsman COURTESY OF JOHN LEE

he became beset by back problems that would in the end ring the death knell for his cricketing career. His batting had appeared nothing above the ordinary in the early days, but by his final first-class appearance for Somerset against Middlesex at the County Ground in September 1995, on what was admittedly a superb batting track, he proved how far he had progressed. Having scored 47 in the first innings, he was invited to open the second innings with Marcus Trescothick and proceeded to score 111 not out, carrying his bat while seven wickets fell, as Somerset hit out to set a declaration target. He had given his batting average an unexpected boost, coming away with a figure of 21.92. This change of emphasis perhaps serves as a reminder that many first-class cricketers are all-round performers, but are forced for a variety of reasons to specialise until one skill or another falls into disuse, though the underlying talent remains intact. The 1997 *Somerset Year Book* includes a warm tribute to Jeremy, noting that:

> *Jeremy Hallett has been an ever-present in the Second XI for the past two seasons as he struggled to overcome a back injury. Had everyone else displayed as much determination and professionalism as he did in trying to overcome his problem, the team results would have been better. As his bowling waned, his batting improved beyond all recognition.*

In his final years as a professional cricketer, he had overwintered in New Zealand, gaining both experience and new friends. Indeed, when he was married in County Durham in August 2005 to Sarah (née Hodgson), his ushers were all former team-mates from New Zealand. Among the guests was Marcus Trescothick, given leave to attend the wedding to 'rest his brain and body' during the epic Ashes contest that season. Marcus is said to have found himself unable to escape continued Antipodean sledging when, having taken to the dance floor with his wife, Hayley, England's open-er, noted for his lack of footwork at the crease, was greeted with a chorus of, 'Move your feet'.

Jeremy was by this time employed as a business development director with Ernst & Young, having previously spent six years with Thomson Financial as an account manager, overseeing sales of their systems solutions to companies and institutions around the globe. While with Thomson Financial, Jeremy completed an online MBA at Cardean University (now the New York Institute of Technology) and became a 'poster boy' for the course, with an advertisement noting: 'If Jeremy Hallett had his way, he would be sitting on a leafy university campus in the United States with plenty of time to contemplate the theories of business. Instead, he spends hectic lunch hours and long evenings in his office cubicle, earning his MBA. "It's not a perfect world," he says with a shrug.'

He duly gained his spurs, although, armed with his further degree, he was recruit-ed in 2004 by Ernst & Young. At the time of writing, Jeremy remains with Ernst & Young as a partner and business development leader. While working on consultancy projects for clients, Jeremy has specialised in promoting opportunities for women in business and has operated in partnership with Athlete Career Transition (ACT), working with professional athletes to prepare them for a career after retiring from sport. Statistical analysis confirms the strong correlation between success in sport and business, the drive and will to succeed often being transferable. In addition, the need for many more women in senior roles is self-evident. But it is a truism that many elite sportswomen and sportsmen know little of the world of business and require men-toring and preparing for the change in their careers. It is to be hoped that Jeremy's efforts continue to bear fruit.

One of his former teachers at Millfield recalls Jeremy as a bright and talented pu-pil who informed him earnestly one day that he was keeping a diary of his cricketing experiences in the hope and belief that his musings might eventually be enticing to a publisher. Seated in the car with them was Ian Ward, who would go on to play for England and was presumably too busy honing his batting technique to bother with a journal. Although Jeremy's cricketing career never quite worked out as planned, the story serves to illustrate his thoroughgoing approach to everything in life.

533
Gareth Terence John Townsend
23 August 1990 v. Sussex, Hove

Gareth Townsend was born on 28 June 1968 in Tiverton, Devon, the son of Terry, a teacher, and Sheila (née Madge), a teaching assistant. Educated in Tiverton, he went on to study for a degree in General Studies at Birmingham University, majoring in Sport & Exercise Science. He played his club cricket for Tiverton Heathcoat CC alongside his father and elder brother, David (a useful all-rounder who, like Gareth, would go on to represent Devon on a number of occasions).

Gareth played youth cricket for Devon from Under-13 level upwards and, from an early age, looked set to follow the trail of talented Devonians poached by a first-class county – more often than not by their neighbours at the County Ground in Taunton. He was recommended to Somerset by Terry Barwell, the former first-class cricketer turned teacher at Blundell's School, who was also an active member of Tiverton Heathcoat CC. Invited to appear for Somerset Second XI as a nineteen-year-old, Gareth's debut for them – against Hampshire Second XI – was a triumph. A first innings score of 81 was followed by an unbeaten 115 in the second innings. Dismissing the idea of a contract until he had a degree under his belt, Gareth then completed his studies at Birmingham University – whose cricket team he captained – while returning regularly to play for Somerset Second XI and working in the off-season in Birmingham, teaching PE at Park Grove School in the city and coaching cricket at the university.

Making his debut in first-class cricket in 1990, Gareth fared less well than he had done in his maiden Second XI appearance. This time he came away with a duck. His spirits would be lifted in his third appearance – in the following season – when he scored 53 against the Sri Lankan tourists, although this would remain his only first-class half-century. He would over-winter for two seasons in Australia – in Perth and then Sydney. It had been hoped that in 1992, after the departure of Jimmy Cook and Peter Roebuck, he would force his way into the team on a regular basis but, in the event, Gareth failed to do so and was released at the end of the season. In a total of twelve first-class appearances, he had averaged 20.70 with the bat, although he had performed better in List A cricket, where he had averaged 37.33 in six matches.

He enjoyed a greater run of success in Devon's march to multiple Minor Counties Championship titles under the eccentric but effective leadership of Peter Roebuck. Peter, writing in *Sometimes I Forgot to Laugh*, describes Gareth as 'a gifted player capable of lashing sixes over point or rebuilding an innings, depending on the circum-

stances'. The admiration was mutual, with Gareth retaining happy memories of that time. 'We all enjoyed our Devon playing days,' he says. 'There was a combination of young players like Chris Read who were progressing, alongside players who had finished their professional careers. For a Minor Counties side, it was an extremely talented bunch. Peter insisted that we played positive cricket, which hadn't always previously been the way.'

Gareth would appear for Devon, as and when he was available, until 2001. By then, he was ensconced at Surrey, where he had joined the coaching staff in 1994 (making a cameo List A appearance in 1995). He had applied successfully to become part of the Cricket Development team at Surrey after completing a PGCE at

Gareth Townsend – 'a gifted player capable of lashing sixes over point or rebuilding an innings, depending on the circumstances'

Bath University. In 2003, the year in which the ECB launched its academy programmes, Gareth stepped up to become Director of the Academy at The Oval, a position he still holds at the time of writing. He now coaches and manages the Under-17 and Second XI teams whilst overseeing the Performance Department for the club as a whole. Asked how he approaches his role, he responds that it is equally important to instil the fundamentals of the game and ensure a positive approach to training and play. He remains a thoughtful, equable man, offering his charges encouragement and honest feedback rather than an iron-fisted approach.

Married to Hayley (née Frith), he has a daughter – Ella – and two sons – Jack and Ben – both of whom have followed the paternal example and play club cricket for Stoke D'Abernon CC, near Cobham in Surrey. Like his father before him, Gareth has nurtured the talents of his children. In his case, he has been able to use his coaching skills in a wider domain. As Academy Director, in control of Surrey's elite development programme, he has a wonderful record of bringing through promising players both in men's and women's cricket. His judgement has proved sounder than one predecessor in a similar role in an earlier age who sent a young Andy Roberts and Viv Richards away following a trial at The Oval, informing them that they both lacked what it takes to become first-class cricketers. We are all equally guilty of having made errors of judgement, but some, to adapt the words of George Orwell, are more equally guilty than others. As far as is known, Gareth has not dropped any similar clangers.

*   *   *   *   *

Perry John Rendell

Making one List A appearance in 1990 was Perry Rendell, a right-handed all-rounder who bowled at medium pace. The limited-overs fixture against the touring Sri Lankans in September 1990 would be his only game for the county, although he would play in two Benson & Hedges Cup games for Combined Universities in 1991. Perry came away from his one game for Somerset having bowled eleven overs with an analysis of 2 for 46, which helped his side to secure a comfortable victory. He was not required to bat. His appearances were otherwise limited to the Second XI, for whom he turned out on a number of occasions.

He was born in Weston-super-Mare on 20 January 1970, the son of Colin, a music teacher, and Irene (née McKevitt), a counsellor. Educated at Broadoak School, Perry had made his debut for Somerset Second XI as a promising seventeen-year-old before going on to study for a degree in Sports Science & Recreation Management at Loughborough University between 1989 and 1992. For a while after graduating, he lived and worked in Australia but in 1994 he returned to Somerset and worked for the bat makers, Millichamp and Hall, helping them to set up and run their first retail shop at the County Ground. He remained with them for two years, during which time he often found himself roped into emergency fielding duties. 'I recall I spent more time in the field than I ever did when I was contracted to play for Somerset,' Perry quips. 'A highlight, if you can call it that, was fielding in the County Championship match against Leicestershire at Clarence Park in 1995, when Hansie Cronje scored a double century for them.' He adds that perhaps his employers were beginning to notice that he was on release more often than he was working. In 1994 he also played a number of games for Herefordshire, the Minor County having noted his performances in the Western League for Weston-super-Mare CC. At the end of the 1995 season, Perry's thoughts turned from the carving of cricket bats to the carving of a career. After studying Business Administration at City of Bristol College, he worked for two years for Learning Partnership West in Bristol, followed by a spell with BBC Science in London. A career as a creative designer then began in earnest. For three years, he was employed by Williams Lea in graphic design before branching out and setting up his own agency, Zard Creative. Among his more unusual achievements was conceiving and organising the Conkerfest in 2009, to raise awareness of prostate cancer. He remained a Director of Zard Creative until setting up a new agency business – Creative Midfield – in 2010, delivering branding, digital and print solutions in all areas of sport and working with high profile individuals, sport brands and governing bodies.

Creativity and sport have always been Perry's joint passions. He retains his fitness as a runner and a tennis player, and has latterly trained as an integrative counsellor, a discipline that draws on many aspects of therapy – appropriate for a man who is interested in holistic solutions to challenges. London has been his home for many a year, but he still returns to the West Country to visit his family and play in the Weston Exiles Golf Masters, an annual get-together for former Weston-super-Mare CC cricketers, the group with whom his cricketing odyssey began.

Perry Rendell – creativity and sport have always been his joint passions
COURTESY OF SOMERSET
COUNTY GAZETTE

1991

"Included in the current arrangements, rather a hotchpotch, is a captain who like Archdale Wickham is interested mostly in butterflies, a coach who likes Pavarotti, several fast bowlers scarcely less keen on beer than Andrews and Wellard, an aged dressing room attendant who had, he insists, a trial with Somerset in 1935 and a Dutchman who can play Mozart piano concertos. And Somerset still wins hearts."

Peter Roebuck (in From Sammy to Jimmy *(Published 1991))*

Championship Position: 17 of 17

Vic Marks had opted for a career as a journalist, leaving Chris Tavaré to captain the side. Chris welcomed an interesting and varied crop of newcomers to the fold. David Graveney, for many years a stalwart of Gloucestershire, popped by for a season and bagged fifty-five wickets. He was well supported by Harvey Trump, with fifty-one victims and Neil Mallender with forty-two. The batting was once more dominated by the peerless Jimmy Cook, with an astonishing 2,755 first-class runs at 81.02 that left the journalists running out of superlatives. Chris Tavaré and Richard Harden were also in fine form, but, once again, too many games were drawn and too few won.

The season would be Peter Roebuck's final one for Somerset. The last of that wondrous crop of youngsters nurtured in the 1970s was now gone. But, whether through serendipity or thoughtful planning, the roll-call of young debutants was an impressive one, including, as it did, the exceptionally talented duo of Andrew Caddick and Mark Lathwell, both future Test Match players, though Mark would shrink from fame. Rob Turner appeared for the first time, too. He would prove a rock for many a season as the county's wicket-keeper-batsman. And then there was Andre van Troost, on his day unplayable and one of the fastest men ever to bowl a cricket ball, though sadly not one of the most accurate.

534
David Anthony Graveney
27 April 1991 v. Sussex, Taunton

[signature]

Born on 2 January 1953 in Westbury-on-Trym, Bristol, David Graveney was the son of Ken and Jeanne (née Crew). He came with a good cricketing pedigree. His father had played for Gloucestershire from 1947 as a fast-medium bowler, forced to leave the game prematurely in 1951 as a result of recurring back problems, only to be invited back in 1963 to captain the team, a wise head brought in to guide what was seen as a talented side. In the event, they propped up the County Championship in 1964, at which point Ken and Gloucestershire decided enough was enough and that he could give more to his beloved county as a committee member. David's uncle, Tom Graveney, a stylish, attacking batsman who made seventy-nine Test appearances, had also captained Gloucestershire for a while before leaving to join Worcestershire.

Despite the fact that David was educated in Somerset at Millfield School, he was always destined to play for Gloucestershire and by the age of sixteen, he was already playing for their Second XI. He made his first-class debut in 1972 and would go on to represent them for eighteen seasons, seven of them as captain. Not a particularly athletic figure, he was tall at 6 feet 4 inches and used his height to full advantage as a left-arm orthodox spin bowler, often bowling around the wicket. Also a competent right-handed batsman, he was good enough to notch up two first-class centuries during a long career. After the 1988 season, he was replaced as captain of his county, later quipping that he had been the third Graveney to have been sacked as Gloucestershire's captain. It had become something of a family curse.

In the winter of 1989-90, he was player manager of the Rebel Tour to South Africa, which for a brief while put him at odds with the authorities. After leaving Gloucestershire in 1990, he joined Somerset for a season, with both parties aware that it was a short-term measure, a move to Durham having been planned for the following season, with that county about to be granted first-class status. His only season with Somerset proved fruitful, with fifty-five wickets in his twenty-one appearances at 39.27 apiece, although his batting, with an average of 8.42, was on the wane. David Foot notes in *Sixty Summers* that the Somerset supporters took to the 'towering, creaky-jointed figure, as he offered helpful advice to young spinners'. He had been offered the captaincy of Durham (much to the chagrin – albeit fleeting – of fellow Durham new-join, Ian Botham, who had hoped to secure the role). David had an affinity for the North East, his father having been born in Hexham, in neigh-

David Graveney – gave Somerset the benefit of his vast experience for one season

bouring Northumberland. He would remain with Durham for two seasons before finally retiring in 1993 at the age of forty. His experiences, together with his knowledge of the wider history of cricket in the county, are recorded in *Durham CCC: Past, Present & Future* (published in 1993), which he co-wrote with Jack Bannister.

Qualified during his playing days as a Chartered Accountant, David had since 1981 acted as Treasurer of the Professional Cricketers' Association. He remained for many years a member of the executive and enjoyed spells as General Secretary, Chief Executive and then President of the organization and Chief Executive of the Benevolent Fund.

Numerate, articulate, an experienced man-manager and grounded in the art of oiling the wheels of progress, he was invited by England to take on the role of Chairman of Selectors in 1997. Some questioned the wisdom of his appointment, given his lack of Test experience, but David was soon able to prove that he was the right man for the job. Whereas his predecessor, Ray Illingworth, had favoured autocracy and strong opinion over democracy and empirical evidence, David brought a more collegiate approach to bear. He also set about changing attitudes, one of his first moves being to scrap the Selectors' Dinner, an event held on the evening prior to Test Matches. His view – which only the most diehard of selectors, might have questioned – was that the needs of the players should come first. Engaging in polite conversation with strangers was hardly the best preparation for a fixture. In addition, he introduced a more thorough examination of the talent around the country where, for generations, there had been a feeling in some quarters that some counties were regarded as more fashionable than others, when it came to matters of selection. His efforts in pushing for central contracts also bore fruit. Such was David's confidence in the role that he was happy to surround himself by prickly characters, including captain Nasser Hussain and coach Duncan Fletcher. Committed to the cause, in the words of Alec Stewart he 'lived every ball England played', sometimes in a haze of cigarette smoke, at other times unable to sleep, as he agonised over issues. It is a measure both of his robustness and skills of diplomacy that he remained in the role until 2008, when he handed over the reins to Geoff Miller, advising his successor that 'if we win, the players get the credit, but if we lose, it's our fault. If you're happy with those terms, crack on'. David took up the new position of National Talent Manager, charged with overseeing the monitoring of up-and-coming players. From 2017, following a restructuring, he has been a selector for the England Under-19s. He has not, at the time of writing, shown any hint of a desire for early retirement.

Married in 1978 to Julie (née Smith-Marriott), he would have a son and daughter, the former, Adam, already demonstrating that he has inherited the Graveney cricketing genes. In 2003, David and Julie established their own company, D. J. Graveney Management, combining their skills in events management and consulting. Latterly, Julie has worked in the area of marketing and admissions at Badminton School, in Bristol. In 2005, David was awarded an OBE for his services to cricket and in 2013, a little over forty years after his first-class debut, he became a board member of Gloucestershire CCC. It is hard to imagine that any man has given more to the game of cricket in general and to his home county in particular. He has done well from the game he loves – as a player, captain and administrator – and has given back to the world of cricket in equal measure.

535
Kenneth Hervey MacLeay
22 May 1991 v. Derbyshire, Derby

These days, this former all-rounder is less likely to be concerned with the intricacies of the LBW laws than he is with the EBV – the Estimated Breeding Value – of the bulls he breeds. Ken Macleay's ancestors were notable citizens of Australia. One of them – Alexander MacLeay – had built up an impressive collection of insect specimens. Begun in the 1780s, it would prove the genesis of what was later described as 'Australia's best early private museum'. His son, a friend of Charles Darwin, had continued the process, garnering further zoological specimens and Aboriginal artefacts. Over time, forty thousand historical photographs were also added. In 1888, Sir William John MacLeay donated the photographs and what then amounted to one million specimens to the University of Sydney, where the items are housed in the

Ken MacLeay – a stalwart of Western Australian cricket who had been born in Bradford-on-Avon

MacLeay Museum. One hundred years on, in 1988, Ken's father would join the centenary celebration of the original act of philanthropy, where, incongruously, in an unexpected and thoroughly un-Scottish heatwave, the MacLeay family's Scottish roots were celebrated, led by the Sydney University Regimental Piper. Yes, such a post existed, the incumbent being Sergeant Frank Fraser. There was haggis for those who wished to try it, shortbread, which was perhaps devoured with more enthusiasm, MacLeay Duff Scotch for those in need of a tipple, and the place was draped with MacLeay tartan. The introduction of the MacLeay Miklouho-MacLay Foundation, funding a research fellow each year, was announced. A publication, *Mr MacLeay's Celebrated Cabinet*, charts the history of the collection.

Ken MacLeay's connection with Somerset cricket was genuine. Serendipitously, he had been born a short distance over the county border in Bradford-on-Avon on 2 April 1959. His father, Donald Hervey Macleay, known as Don and married to Felicity (née Cloete), had served in the Royal Navy since the age of sixteen, had subsequently qualified as an engineer, had seen active service in the Second World War and would rise to the rank of Lieutenant Commander. At the time of Ken's birth, he had been stationed at the Admiralty in Bath and Ken would live in England and Ireland for the first six years of his life before the family settled once more in Australia.

Described as 'a vibrant, learned man', Don made the decision, having retired from the Navy, that he would set up a stud farm, breeding prize Angus bulls. Asked at a later date how he had developed the skills that would make him a renowned breeder, he replied that he had 'read a book about it'. After purchasing twenty heifers and a bull from the Naranghi Stud in Victoria, he set up his new enterprise at Blackrock, not far from Busselton, near the South Western tip of Australia. What set Don apart was the way in which he was one of the earliest breeders to apply scientific method and meticulous attention to record-keeping as he set about improving the qualities of the bulls born there. No stone was left unturned, no detail overlooked in the search for perfection. One would expect nothing less of an engineer, applying his know-how to a new discipline.

Ken was educated at Scotch College, in Perth, before going on to study at the University of Western Australia, in the same city. He trained as an accountant and took up the profession in the off-season in the early years of his cricketing career. If the aptly named 'Hercules' represented the apotheosis of Don MacLeay's early breeding programme at Blackrock, then at 6 feet 4 inches and with an easy action, his son, Ken, had the physical attributes required of a useful swing bowler and batsman. The genes would have contributed to their respective success. In Ken's case, his father had appeared for the Combined Services XI, for Devon in Minor Counties matches and for the exclusive Free Foresters team. He would later invest his spare time in coaching and administration in local cricket in the Busselton region. Where Hercules the bull's success as a progenitor was consistently impressive, Ken's performances for Western Australia would prove good enough to earn him a place in Australia's One Day International side on sixteen occasions. With pitches and conditions in England more suited to a medium-paced swing bowler than those in Australia, it comes as no surprise that his crowning achievement was a return of 6 for 39 against India at Trent Bridge in the Prudential World Cup of 1983.

He had announced his arrival in Sheffield Shield cricket, when, to quote the *Canberra Times*, as a 'little-known Western Australian swing bowler', he took 5 for 7 in twenty-one deliveries against Victoria during the 1982-83 season. Ken would represent Western Australia on one hundred occasions over the course of eleven seasons. With a batting average of 27.33 and 261 wickets at 29.71 apiece, he made a valuable contribution to the cause. More recently, he has been awarded life membership of Western Australia Cricket Association.

For two seasons in the latter part of his playing career, he spent the Australian winter months with Somerset and his performances were broadly similar to those back home, with a first-class batting average of 27.22 and thirty-four wickets at 34.79. By then an accurate rather than a penetrative bowler, he reserved some of his most useful performances for List A games, where batsmen were obliged to take more risks against him. Summarising his time at Taunton, Ken says: 'I came to Somerset to round off my career in Australian first-class cricket. It was a privilege for me to be part of Somerset's cricket history and play on the best grounds against the best players in UK. I will always remember the Somerset supporters as something special; loyal, committed and great to play in front of.'

He returned to Australia in 1992 to join the Blackrock Angus stud his father had established in 1968. He was joined in the enterprise by his wife, Elizabeth, known as Liz, whom he had been married to in 1987. Liz would enjoy a career as a lawyer and remains a partner, at the time of writing, with Shaddicks, in the nearby town of Busselton.

Ken has learned his trade well, talking with infectious enthusiasm about his bulls and how he is forever continuing the search for the perfect example, looking, in his words, for 'a moderate birth weight, good growth and carcase in a docile package'. The sale each February of fifty bulls in the nearby town of Boyanup is an eagerly awaited event, attended by farmers from far and wide. As a result of the unrelenting efforts of Ken and his father before him, the company has built up a reputation for excellence, their prize bulls commanding eye-watering sums of money. Where his ancestor Alexander MacLeay had pored over his collection of insects, Ken now directs his efforts to rather more commanding specimens. Alexander left a lasting legacy and Ken and his father have done the same. The baton will be passed in time to the next generation of this distinguished family.

Ken MacLeay –
'I will always
remember the
Somerset supporters as
something special'
COURTESY OF
JOHN LEE

536
Andrew Richard Caddick
29 May 1991 v. West Indians, Taunton

According to Andy Caddick, a career as a professional cricketer was 'just about the last thing I had on my mind as a seventeen-year-old arriving in London'. He would, though, go on to enjoy a notable career as a successful opening bowler for his adoptive country. Born on 21 November 1968 in Christchurch, New Zealand, he was the son of Christopher and Audrey Caddick, who both hailed from the North of England. Audrey had emigrated to New Zealand in search of a new life shortly before her twenty-first birthday, her father having been a boiler-maker on Tyneside. Chris was raised in Melling, near Liverpool, where his father ran a business transporting goods via barges along the canals. With their enterprise devastated by the bombing during the Second World War and sent into decline by the increasing obsolescence of the canals, Chris, too, left for a new life in New Zealand, where he found work as a self-employed tiler and plasterer. Having met in a bakery in Christchurch, Chris and Audrey were married and had four children. Educated at Papanui High School, Christchurch, Andy – their third child – starred in his early years for the local Riccarton CC side as a batsman who could bowl. Then he grew to 6 feet 5 inches and developed into a quick bowler able to extract bounce from even the most placid of wickets. Some coaching from Dennis Lillee improved his technique but, perhaps because he came from the 'wrong side of the tracks', he was not given the opportunities he merited. A brother, Michael, was electrocuted at sixteen, while plastering. Rushed to hospital, he was soon pronounced dead. It was a defining moment for Andy who would leave New Zealand generally disgruntled with life and feeling the need for a fresh start.

He came to England hoping to work as a qualified plasterer and tiler – and would prove a useful addition to the dressing room when any aspect of DIY needed to be called upon by teammates. In his first year in London he wrote to Hampstead CC and Brondesbury CC and the former invited him along for a trial and snapped him up. He remained with them for three years, drawing enough attention to be invited to play for Middlesex Second XI on four occasions. And yet he slipped through Middlesex's fingers, just as he had slipped though those of New Zealand, whom he had represented at youth level.

As is the nature of these things, a number of people have subsequently claimed the credit for alerting Somerset to his potential, but Andy cites Hampstead's Roger

Andy Caddick – a quick bowler able to extract bounce from even the most placid of wickets

Oakley, who knew Somerset coach Jack Birkenshaw. Jack invited Andy for a trial in a friendly match against an Australian one-day side, where he 'got smashed all over the place on quite a flat wicket' but did enough to be invited to play for Somerset Second XI the following day at The Oval, where he took 8 for 46. Andy still recalls the events. 'I got more bounce than most bowlers there,' he says, 'and the ball swung, too.' Somerset moved quickly to secure his services, happy for him to play for Clevedon CC while he qualified by residence. During the 1991 season, he was selected for the two non-Championship matches – against the West Indies and Sri Lanka – and was voted Rapid Cricketline Second XI Cricket Player of the Year. In 1992 he was raring to go and soon announced himself with a return of 6 for 73 against Pakistan. A pattern began to emerge of regular devastating spells when he could tear through an opposing side. His seventy-eight five-wicket hauls in the first-class game are a testament to this, with perhaps the most striking example being his memorable 9 for 32 to claim an unlikely and wholly unexpected victory against Lancashire at Taunton in 1993. Having impressed in an England A tour of Australia, he was given his Test call-up in 1993. However, it was his misfortune to come up against an Australian side whose batsmen utterly dominated England and he was dropped ahead of the Fifth Test. It would not take long, though, for him to win back his place for the subsequent tour of the West Indies, where he came into his own as a Test bowler. It has often been said that he modelled his action on the New Zealand great, Richard Hadlee, but Andy clarifies that the similarities are coincidental. It was certainly the case that, when on song and in the right conditions, both men could be unplayable.

There then followed two frustrating seasons when he suffered from shoulder injury followed by shin splints, but Andy would return to his best both for Somerset and for England, where he formed an excellent opening bowling partnership with Yorkshire's Darren Gough. In many ways polar opposites, they got on well and complemented each other: Gough the extrovert, by turns aggressive or humorous as he explored ways to remove opposing batsmen, Caddick the introverted craftsman and quiet assassin, who stuck to his task, sometimes scowling when he felt the world was against him, but equally relatively undemonstrative when everything was going to plan. Sri Lanka's Arjuna Ranatunga summed the pair up by observing that: 'Caddick bowls. Gough competes.'

Many – including Andy, a man who speaks his mind bluntly – feel that, although he won a creditable sixty-two Test caps, he should have won more. It certainly came as a surprise to many that he was ignored after taking 105 first-class wickets during the 1998 season at 19.82 apiece. Part of the explanation for his not having gained more caps lies in the selectors' obsession with youth and a reluctance to select an older man when he had returned from injury in the latter part of his career. Perhaps they underestimated that a quick bowler with an easy, rhythmic approach can en-

Andy Caddick – he won sixty-two Test caps, but most observers thought he should have won more COURTESY OF SOMERSET COUNTY GAZETTE

joy and extended life as a player. Equally important might have been his manner. Andy was, and still is, straight-talking, not bothered by the more artful nuances of social interaction. His teammates talk of his straightforward, unflinchingly honest approach. Strangers often saw this as prickliness. Nasser Hussain and Duncan Fletcher are similar animals, which might explain why they related to Andy and rated him so highly. Teammate Peter Roebuck would write of Andy that 'he is not a sentimental man … and he can prickle like a thistle. He can seem chilly, too, almost hostile, for he has never learned the games of society. And so people [who do not know him] always think the worst of him. He does not get away with much. But there is no malice, merely cold air and no fire in the hearth.'

His last Test Match was in January 2003 at the SCG. It was quite some valedictory performance, given that he led England to victory by taking 7 for 94 in Australia's second innings. It was his last game of any significance before he was laid low for most of the 2003 season in England with a back injury. A lesser man might have called it a day but Andy would return to his brilliant best. During the 2007 season – when he was thirty-eight years old – he took seventy-five first-class wickets at 23.10 apiece, having played through the pain, before then having to spend 'five hours in the operating table on Christmas Eve', with 'all my muscles cut from my back and fusions done'. He continued contributing to the side until hanging up his boots at the end of the 2009 season. It had been a long and distinguished career, rewarded with a Benefit Year in 1999 and a Testimonial Year in 2009.

His career record puts him firmly in the pantheon of the Somerset greats. Over the course of 191 first-class games, he took 875 wickets for the county at 25.80 apiece and averaged 17.24 with the bat.

Married in 1995 to Sarah Louise Heard, he has a son and daughter, both born in Taunton. If domestic life was a source of happiness, then his business dealings have reflected his resilience following setbacks. In the early days he was employed during the winter months as a handyman at the County Ground. Later, with more money in his pocket, a troubled business venture led to a thumping loss, but Andy has subsequently enjoyed success in the commercial world. As with his cricket career, he has been able to thrive in a field where he derives great pleasure. Helicopters are a passion and, having qualified as a commercial pilot, he also buys and sells helicopters on behalf of clients. Andy has been quoted as saying that, 'It's amazing what doors open when you go to a meeting and people there might like cricket and enjoy talking about it.'

He is a regular visitor to the County Ground and there is a certain irony that a qualified plasterer and tiler, who was happy to spruce up the structures around the County Ground, should in time have a pavilion named after him – a constant reminder of what he gave to the county that remains his home. Stephen Brenkley has written of Andy Caddick that Somerset 'cherish him as families cherish eccentric aunts', an aside that merits one of Andy's gruff and laconic responses.

537
Adrianus Pelrus van Troost
28 June 1991 v. Surrey, Kennington Oval

Neil Burns, who kept wicket to Andre van Troost on a number of occasions, is better placed than most to assess him and is in no doubt that he was as pacey as any bowler he has ever seen. 'Rooster was very, very quick indeed,' he confirms. 'His bowling was very challenging to keep to because he got incredible bounce, especially at places like Taunton. Keeping to him could be both a nightmare and a thrill. He could cut the ball back into the right hander's body off the pitch, which made life deeply unpleasant for batsmen, even the very good ones. From my perspective, it was interesting to witness who had the stomach for the fight against him.' During a County Championship match at Bath in 1992, the West Indies and Middlesex opener, Desmond Haynes, a batsman who most certainly had the stomach for a fight, is convinced that the 6 foot 7 inch Dutchman's opening spell was the fastest he ever encountered and Hugh Morris, a gutsy and successful opening batsman for Glamorgan, vividly recalls negotiating a terrifying forty-minute spell of raw pace before close of play at Taunton one night. Neil Burns notes that, 'I had to stand so far back that time that I felt almost disconnected from the play.' Andre's Somerset teammate, Andy Cottam, writes

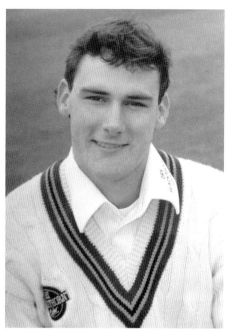

Andre van Troost – 'Rooster was very, very quick indeed' COURTESY OF JOHN LEE

that 'he was lightning quick' and that facing him in the nets 'was like being shot at'.

Born on 2 October 1972 in Schiedam in the Netherlands, Andre was the son of Aad van Troost, an engineer, and Anneke (née Oosterholt). The brothers, Andre and Luuk (who would also go on to play for the Netherlands), were raised in a cricket-loving family. Their maternal grandfather played club cricket for Excelsior CC and their mother, whom Andre describes as 'an amazing mum', oversaw teas and scoring. 'So we had no choice,' he jests. Educated at Spieringshoek College in Schiedam, he opted at the time not to further his studies but to pursue a cricketing career instead, having already been drafted into the Netherlands side while still in his mid-teens. Although he would be the second Dutchman to play first-class cricket for Somerset, he had arrived on the scene ahead of teammate, Roland Lefebvre, having been offered a contract after Peter Roebuck had encountered him in the Netherlands and invited him to the County Ground. When he arrived in England, he had only every played on hard pitches and had never worn spiked boots. He found his feet (in every sense) very quickly and, having terrorised local club cricketers while playing for Seaton in Devon, he was soon offered his chance to taste first-class cricket.

It would be fair to state that his exceptional speed was matched only by his waywardness. But at times, the combination of Caddick and van Troost was a pairing to strike fear into opponents. Incidents such as the fractured cheekbone suffered by Jimmy Adams when taken by surprise by the pace of a bouncer or the occasion when Rooster was withdrawn from the attack by umpire Barry Dudleston for intimidatory bowling, added to his fearsome reputation. He continued to play during the off-season, with spells in South Africa for Alma Marist CC and four first-class appearances for Griqualand West. He represented the Netherlands on thirty-four occasions, including ICC Trophy matches and winter tours. There were some, Andre included, who hoped that he might iron out any inconsistencies enough to be in contention for the England team, but, alas, it was not to be, in part as a result of recurring back problems that began to plague him. Over the course of sixty-seven first-class matches for Somerset, he would claim 140 wickets at 38.70 apiece, with four five-wicket hauls, and a batting average of 8.61, but only those who witnessed him on song will recall what the statistics can never tell: that he was one of those rare bowlers who could strike terror into opponents. Asked about his memories of life at the County Ground, he replies, 'I loved my time there.' Were there any negatives? 'Only the people who told me every day to bowl line and length: I just wanted to bowl as fast as possible. Why would I want to stop doing what I loved most, just because I was now getting paid for it?' he jokes.

After leaving Somerset in 1999, he made the decision to study as a mature student, having opted earlier in life to pursue his sporting ambitions. He had already begun in 1998 to embark on a

Andre van Troost – his exceptional speed was matched only by his waywardness
COURTESY OF BARRY PHILLIPS

BSc in Exercise Sciences and Marketing Management at the University of Gloucestershire in Cheltenham and, after completing his degree, he went on to obtain an MSc in Marketing Strategy at the University of Birmingham, which he completed in 2003. He was immediately taken on by Proctor and Gamble, who offered a role as a marketing manager in their Healthcare Department, his remit extending to UK and the Benelux region. Having arrived late into the world of business, he was making up for lost time and in September 2008 he was offered the role of Chief Executive Officer of the Netherlands Cricket Board. It seems strangely appropriate that within months, the former quick bowler had concluded that he missed the faster pace of life in the business world, and early in 2009 he joined Danone as a marketing manager overseeing Infant Nutrition. Promoted to the role of global marketing manager two years later, his career was clearly progressing seamlessly. In 2014 he left to join Lely, a Dutch company offering innovative solutions to the dairy industry, intended to make the world a better place for farmers and livestock alike. At the time of writing he is a vice president of the company, sitting on the board and with responsibility for Customer Care and Marketing. If, for all his unique talents, his dreams were never quite realised as bowler, the same could hardly be said of a business career that has gone from strength to strength.

After his marriage in 2002 to Rebecca (née Loveridge) ended in divorce, Andre has subsequently lived with his fiancée, Margo Ludolph, and their daughter. He enjoys games of club cricket for the Excelsior club where he launched his career. These days, it is hard to imagine that such a gentle giant was once a fearsome bowler capable of intimidatory bowling. If Neil Burns was best placed to venture an opinion on Andre van Troost the bowler, what does he make of the man? 'Rooster was generous, fair-minded and intelligent,' he confirms. 'Just an all-round brilliant person.' Which goes to show that even the good guys can sometimes make the meanest of bowlers and, yes, they can rise to the top in the hard-nosed world of business, too.

538
David Beal
16 July 1991 v. Sussex, Hove

Born on 17 July 1966 in Butleigh, David Beal was the son of Keith and Delia (née Young). The family had strong links with club cricket in Glastonbury. Notable among them was Keith, who gained a reputation as a useful cricketer over many years. David's uncle, Len, was a larger-than-life character famed in local circles for batting without gloves. 'His hands were enormous,' David reveals, 'and no one could find any gloves that fitted him.' He adds that Len put his hands to good use as a goalkeeper for Bath City, among other teams. 'Opposing centre forwards faced Uncle Len with a degree of dread,' David jokes. 'When they rose to meet crosses, he was as likely to take the man as the ball.'

Keith Beal was involved in the sheepskin business, working for many years for Morlands, a company founded on Quaker principles and with a long association with Somerset cricket as a sponsor, a host for occasional first-class fixtures and a breeding ground for cricketing talent. Sadly, the business was faced with insolvency in the mid-1980s, after having been in operation for over a century. As a result of the crisis, Keith led a consortium, setting up Fenland Sheepskins along with other former Morlands employees. David had worked for Morlands for seven months after leaving school, but then, for one year only, he worked for Clarks – another locally-based company with a strong Quaker tradition. Having subsequently joined his father's new business, David enjoyed the luxury of being granted leave to play for Somerset and – during the winters of 1987 and 1989 – for Wanneroo, in Perth.

Educated at Crispin School in Street, he had made his first appearance for Somerset Second XI in 1984 as a right-arm medium-pace bowler and had graduated to the first-class game in 1991, when he was offered a two-year contract by the county of his birth. In the event, he would make three Championship appearances in a season disrupted by a back injury, which ultimately brought his career to an end after only one season. He took a total of three wickets at 106.66 apiece and mustered one run in two innings. Thereafter he returned to club cricket with Glastonbury CC, enjoying what he describes as 'a brilliant year' in 1993, when sponsorship money enticed Joel Garner back to his old stamping ground. It was a time of healing for Joel, after the hurt of the termination of his Somerset contract, with David noting that, 'He was great, sharing his knowledge and his anecdotes with home and away teams alike.' It has been noted that some of Glastonbury CC's away fixtures took place on surprisingly damp wickets that took the sting out of Joel's missiles. The Glastonbury captain was quoted as observing wryly that there seemed to have been some surprising and very isolated rainfall during the summer months at certain grounds.

David Beal – 'a hardworking, knowledgeable, straight-talking and tough coach'

David was married in 1990 to Rebecca (née Knight), known as Becky, with whom he has two sons, Josh and Sam, and a daughter, Sophie. Both boys would prove to be talented club cricketers. Having been divorced, David was married in 2018 to Lucie (formerly Johnson).

Having left Somerset CCC, he returned to his father's company, Fenland, but started to pass on his cricketing expertise on a part-time basis from 1999, employed as an age group coach for the county, a role he retains at the time of writing. In 2005, he joined the full-time staff at Edgarley Hall (Millfield Prep), initially as groundsman-cum-coach, a role that, in his words, he 'thoroughly enjoyed'. He is now the Director of Cricket at Millfield Prep, part of a school with a long history of being a production line for first-class cricketers.

His former teammate, Julian Wyatt, describes David as 'a hardworking, knowledgeable, straight-talking and tough coach' and 'a genuine competitor', with a will to win. Colleagues also use the word 'passionate' when summarising his wholehearted approach to the role. With his work for the school and as a county age group coach, David Beal is ideally placed these days to channel that passion and to nurture young cricketers who may prove the stars of tomorrow.

539
Giles William White
10 August 1991 v. Sri Lanka, Taunton

Referred to by teammates as 'Chalky' White, Giles was born in Barnstaple, Devon, on 23 March 1972. Giles's mother, Christina (née Fisher), was an interior designer, and his father, John, a useful club cricketer who played for Exeter CC and later for nearby Thorverton CC, while working in the textiles industry, setting up factories over the years in locations ranging from Barbados to the West Country. Giles's passion for the game was ignited as a nine-year-old when John called his two sons into the house to watch the television coverage of Ian Botham's extraordinary pyrotechnics against Australia at Headingley in 1981. The innings that transformed the trajectory of the Ashes series arguably also set the course for Giles's life.

For a while he was educated at Exeter Cathedral School and was beginning to excel as a batsman, compiling a century on debut for the Devon Under-12 side. Having attended coaching sessions led by Peter Robinson at the County Ground, Giles befriended two Millfield School pupils – Jeremy Hallett (later of Somerset) and Robert Dawson (later of Gloucestershire) – with the result that Millfield were approached and Giles was granted a cricketing scholarship. He developed into a composed and patient batsman – qualities entirely in keeping with his personality. After leaving school, he completed a degree in Sports Management at Loughborough University.

Having made his debut against Sri Lanka in 1991, at the age of nineteen, he did not appear in any further first-class fixtures for Somerset. He had scored forty-two runs in his only innings and taken 1 for 30 with his leg-spin. Ever a modest man, Giles remained understated about his skills as a bowler, although others, notably Shane Warne, have been impressed.

There were subsequent appearances for the Combined Universities side and – during the summer vacations – for Somerset Second XI and Devon, for whom he had first turned out as a sixteen-year-old. Following his graduation, Giles was offered a contract by Hampshire, for whom he would play 126 first-class fixtures over the course of nine seasons. During that time he amassed eight first-class centuries, enjoying his most fruitful season in 1998, although the 2000 campaign was noteworthy for his having twice carried his bat – one of those innings being against Somerset, when he withstood a bowling attack that included a rampant Andy Caddick.

During the winters, he was employed as a pro and coach for a variety of clubs. After one season in Sydney, there were spells in Cape Town and then Perth. Giles regards those opportunities for young players to play and travel as a huge benefit for his generation and one, sadly, less likely to be explored in the modern game. Indeed, impressed by the

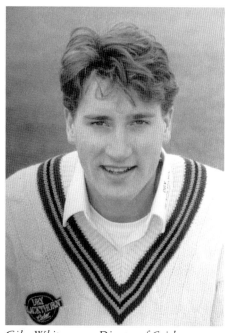

Giles White – now Director of Cricket at Hampshire

competitive nature of cricket in Australia, he had one eye, for a while, on a coaching career in Perth, once he had retired as a first-class player. In the event, those plans were not pursued.

Prior to his retirement he had worked in the marketing department of Hampshire CCC but, on hanging up his boots, he was offered employment as a part-time coach with the county he had served for the best part of a decade. Married in 1999 to Samantha (née Donald), who had also attended Millfield School, Giles had set up a property development company – Exbury Developments – with his wife. He would help in the running of that company alongside his coaching role, but was soon invited to take on a full-time role mentoring the Hampshire Second XI. His plans to emigrate to Perth were finally extinguished and his adoptive county, together with his burgeoning family – by then including three children – demanded his full attention. Impressed by his leadership skills, Hampshire promoted him to the role of Director of Cricket, a position he still holds at the time of writing.

Hampshire may now be his spiritual home, but Giles, a personable and popular character, retains his links with many of the former teammates at Somerset with whom he developed from schoolboy prodigy to first-class cricketer.

540
Mark Nicholas Lathwell
10 August 1991 v. Sri Lanka, Taunton

Mark Lathwell.

Dubbed 'Rowdy' by some teammates in ironic reference to his taciturn nature, particularly in the company of strangers, Mark Lathwell was possessed of extraordinary talent. Speak to anyone who played alongside him and the vast majority will inform you, without hesitation, that they have never encountered a player more gifted than this unassuming opener. Marcus Trescothick states that, 'I cannot overstate how brilliant Lathwell was.' Neil Burns, a man who has spent a lifetime in the game as player and coach, has written of Mark that he 'stands out for me as a young player touched by rare genius'.

Born in Bletchley, Buckinghamshire, on Boxing Day 1971, he was the second son of Derek and Valerie (née Bolton). It was Somerset's good fortune that, at the age of eight, Mark would move with his family to the Barnstaple area as a result of Derek's employment with Xomox (who manufactured hydraulic valves). Derek was himself a fine club cricketer and coach, involved over the course of many decades with Braunton CC in North Devon.

Educated at Braunton Comprehensive School, Mark managed initially to slip under the cricketing radar, despite his undoubted talent. A shy boy, he had always shunned publicity (and continues to do so) and, as with so many batsmen touched by genius, his play did not always conform to the norms as laid down in the coaching manuals. For a while, on leaving school, he worked as a bank clerk and there have no doubt been moments when he would happily have swapped his time in the spotlight for a life spent in his North Devon home embracing calm, certainty and complete anonymity.

His routine in those early years involved travelling from North Devon to Lord's for coaching each weekend. It entailed a nine-hour round trip, a reflection of his commitment to the game and the pleasure he derived from mastering the art of batting.

A place on the MCC School of Merit coaching course aided his progress, and he would spend a year on the Lord's ground staff. He impressed with a free-flowing 70 in his first competitive match for MCC Young Cricketers in 1990 and, having been promoted to opener in his second appearance for Somerset in the Second XI Championship, he scored 168 not out in a high-scoring game at Hove, ensuring that he became an established presence in the Somerset Second XI for the remainder of the season, also building on his burgeoning reputation with three appearances for England Under-19s.

Mark Lathwell – 'a young player touched by rare genius'

Having made his first-class debut against the touring Sri Lankans in 1991, he became a regular first team player the following season. It was not so much the runs amassed – although there were 1,176 of them at 36.75 – but the manner of his batting that caught the eye, with a rare ability to see the ball early, to play it late and to time it to perfection. Selection for the England A tour of Australia followed, and an innings of 175 against Tasmania had Ted Dexter salivating and opining that not since Colin Cowdrey had he seen cover drives so perfectly executed that they appeared to accelerate as they sped along the turf.

With a string of performances to delight crowds in 1993 as he hit a purple patch, the clamour for his selection by England became deafening, although Mark himself was not one to be overly concerned with what the newspapers might have to say, rarely bothering to read them. On 1 July 1993, the twenty-one-year old, heralded as the great hope for the future of English cricket, was awarded the first of two caps in the Trent Bridge Test. Suddenly he was in demand. Every request for his time and attention was a trial to be endured, every interview felt like a violation of his privacy. Entering an England dressing room full of strangers, with Somerset teammate Andy Caddick the only reassuring presence, was an ordeal perhaps more daunting than facing the Australian bowlers and their uncompromising sledging. To his credit, Mark did not wilt as some might have done. In his two Test appearances, he let his bat at least do the talking, where normally it sang. He was in many ways cut adrift without having had the chance to adjust to the elevated surroundings. But it came almost as a relief to walk away. The experience had been less a dreadful one and more a joyless one. Many would claim that his elevation came too early. His mother, Valerie, thought so, and she should know. But we are left to wonder whether Mark would ever have taken to a spell in the spotlight. Comparisons have inevitably been made with Harold Gimblett, who attended West Buckland School, a short drive from where Mark was raised and now lives. Both batted with freedom and fearless shot-making that defied convention. Both found fame a cross to be borne, a constriction. But whereas Harold brooded and harboured resentments, Mark has always been more inclined to live in the moment, never to express regrets. Free-spirited and joyous to behold when he held a bat in his hand, he found the other aspects of life as a professional cricketer a burden.

Although he was not selected for a third cap, despite having performed more than adequately, playing with a restraint not readily associated with his batting, he was by no means discarded, being invited to take part in the England A tour of South Africa. There was a sparkling century against Eastern Transvaal, but Mark found the experience oppressive: he was homesick, with reports asserting that he spent much of the tour 'dreaming of the darts nights he was missing in his local, back in Devon'. With his first child on the way, Mark was honest enough at a later stage to take himself out of the reckoning for future England A tours. His marriage to Lisa (née Bryan) and the upbringing of his two young sons – Jason and Sam – would prove a greater priority in his life than an England career.

He continued to contribute valuable runs for Somerset and remained a popular member of the team, yet some of the *joi de vivre* was waning. The good eye and quick hands were still there, but the fearlessness of youth, the courage to back his own talent and go for his shots, was seeping away. A new regime with an emphasis on fitness stripped even more spontaneity from proceedings. Runs around the block were becoming more important than runs in the middle, as David Gower had been heard to observe, wryly. It did not help that Mark, notable for his fondness for food, found it easy to put on weight. In his words: 'I've always liked food … lunches, teas, hotel breakfasts. I've got to start turning a few of them down.'

Dermot Reeve then arrived and while some thrived under his gruelling regime, Mark was not one of them. Marcus Trescothick would write that, 'Why Dermot felt

Mark Lathwell – every interview felt like a violation of his privacy
COURTESY OF IVAN PONTING

he had to try and change [Mark's] technique I'll never know, but attempting to persuade this utterly unconventional batsman to play in a more conventional fashion was the beginning of then end.'

A snapped anterior cruciate ligament in his right knee drew his 1999 season to a sudden, premature and painful close, but he would fight his way back. Having missed out on selection for the Cheltenham & Gloucester Trophy Final in 2001, he was left to wonder about his future in the game and made the decision to walk away the following December, shortly after his thirtieth birthday and with two years remaining on his contract. Chief Executive Peter Anderson encouraged Mark to reconsider and offered the captaincy of the Second XI. A Benefit Year was also surely on the cards but – given that the financial gains would have derived from the sort of social gatherings that Mark shrank from – this would have been no inducement. His batting average of 33.84 in 142 appearances fails to tell the whole story: it cannot capture the speed and ease with which the runs came or the delight they occasioned among spectators.

Mark took up a postman's round in Barnstaple while he sought coaching roles with local clubs and in local schools, also setting up an academy at a local prep school and an Under-13s indoor cricket league. In what Jon Henderson, writing in *The Guardian*, termed 'one of the most unlikely retreats into cricket's backwaters' he was persuaded after a break to turn out for Braunton CC, the club he had first appeared for as a boy and which his father and brother played for. His first steps were faltering as he adjusted to the slower pace of the ball and adapted his game, but he was soon into his stride. Appointed captain in 2003, he continued turning out for Braunton CC until 2010, when he called time on his playing days.

As a young man, he was asked about his hobbies and responded that they included cooking, eating and a good game of darts. Not much has changed. Among friends and family, cocooned from the spotlight, he is happy to live in the moment. He leaves it to others to fret about what might or might not have been. Somerset teammate Neil Burns sums up Mark thus:

> As a person, he was delightful company, very funny, sharp-minded and a team player. He chose his words carefully and never wasted any. I always felt there was a likeness to Steve Waugh in his personality. However, their respective careers, and lives, took very divergent paths. Steve overcame his natural shyness, and was forever challenging himself to explore new personal and professional frontiers. Mark backed off and chose the feeling of relief from having terminated his time in the spotlight. If I'd known back then what I've subsequently learned as a coach, I would gladly drop everything to take that uniquely talented young man under my wing and explore every possible way of ensuring that he'd never fallen out of love with cricket and failed to fulfil that astonishing potential.

541
Robert Julian Turner
10 August 1991 v. Sri Lanka, Taunton

The Turner brothers – Richard, Simon and Rob – all grew up starring for West-on-super-Mare CC, as did their father. Born in Malvern on 25 November 1967, Rob, the youngest son of Derek and Doris (née Watts), was raised in Weston-super-Mare, where his father was employed as Sales Director of an engineering company. Rob confesses that, 'I daydreamed of playing cricket whilst watching my predecessors battle it out during the festivals at Clarence Park.' One of those predecessors was his brother, Simon, seven years Rob's senior, who kept wicket for Somerset in six first-class matches as a stand-in for the injured Trevor Gard.

Unusually tall for a wicket-keeper, at well over six feet, Rob admits to having taken up the role in order to emulate Simon. In the event, he would do so with aplomb. Educated at Broadoak School, he was offered a place at Millfield School. It was at Millfield that his friend and fellow Somerset cricketer, Jonny Atkinson, coined the nickname 'Noddy', by which Rob became known by teammates. 'Apparently, I used to nod from side to side when I ran between the wickets,' Rob explains. 'It continued at Somerset because I would often nod off in the changing room while we were batting, especially after coming off the field when Mushy had bowled a lot of overs. The intense concentration keeping to him wiped me out!'

After leaving Millfield, Rob went up to Magdalene College, Cambridge, to study for a degree in Engineering. He was sponsored by Rolls Royce, who hoped at the time that he would become a full-time employee, although that was not to be. The allure of playing for his beloved county side would prove too great. While at Cambridge, Rob was a regular member of the Varsity team in each of the four seasons from 1988 to 1991 inclusive, being awarded his blue in 1990, before going on to captain the side in his final year. He also began to appear each winter for Claremont-Nedlands CC in Perth, where he doubled up as a cricket coach and Maths teacher at a local independent school. By that time he had become an accomplished wicket-keeper-batsman, although, back at the County Ground, he was faced with the immediate challenge that Neil Burns – another fine wicket-keeper and useful batsman – was in possession of the gloves. After his first-class debut against the Sri Lankan tourists, Rob would have to wait another year for his next appearance. The call to arms came on the morning of the Championship match against Glamorgan in July 1992, after an injury to Mark Lathwell created the opportunity, Rob playing as a specialist batsman.

Rob Turner – an outstanding wicket-keeper-batsman

Neither for the first nor the last time, the county was obliged to choose between two able keepers. Neil Burns did not yield up his post lightly, but he did so in 1992, when Somerset deemed Rob the number one choice, in large part based on a belief that he would contribute more runs than the man he was replacing. Rob insists that an important factor in his subsequent development, both as a keeper and a reader of spin, was his close bond with Somerset teammate Mushtaq Ahmed, whom he roomed with and spent many hours with in the nets.

The county's faith in the young wicket-keeper-batsman was rewarded with consistent performances over the years, though 1999 stands out as a particularly fruitful season, with Rob amassing 1,217 runs and effecting sixty-nine dismissals, achievements that made him statistically the most successful keeper that year and earned him a place on the England A tour of Bangladesh and New Zealand. He would also play a pivotal role in Somerset's march to the Cheltenham & Gloucester Trophy in 2001, making telling contributions with the bat from the first round until the last. Among a number of standout moments in the final was his removal of Shahid Afridi, the Leicestershire danger man – known with just cause as Boom Boom – on whom Leicestershire were relying to reach the total set them. In the fifth over, Afridi hit a steepling shot off Richard Johnson that look set to stay in the air for an eternity. The crowd became muted until eventually the ball found its way into the waiting gloves of Rob and there was a collective sigh of relief. The cheers followed. Memories were stirred of a Second XI fixture against Durham, a decade earlier, when, off the bowling of Andre van Troost, the ball was launched into the sky, to be spotted first by Roland Lefebvre, who shouted 'Noddy's'. Rob duly positioned himself while gravity began to work its magic. 'Still Noddy's', Roland shouted, as the breeze swirled. It landed a good six feet away from Rob's prostrate figure. The calamity was greeted with much laughter. Rob, too, had been able to see the funny side of things. An affable team man, he has – like anyone who knows their true worth – always been open to self-deprecation whilst being quietly confident. He would finally hang up his boots in 2005. In 211 matches first-class matches for Somerset, he had averaged 33.09 with the bat and effected 682 dismissals, joining a happy band of wicket-keepers able to claim in excess of 1,000 victims in all forms of the game – in his case including those appearances for Cambridge University.

He was married in 1999 to Lucy (née Mullins), who was among the first group of women to be elected a ladies playing member of the MCC. The couple have a son, Jamie, although they now separated. During the latter years of his first-class career, he had worked in the winter months as a stockbroker for Rowan Dartington, having been introduced to the world of finance by John Scott, who was a stalwart both of the company and of Weston-super-Mare CC. Although Rob enjoyed his time there, he made the decision to mentor the next generation as a Maths teacher and cricket coach, picking up where he had left off years earlier in Perth. He would remain a member of staff at Blundell's School in Tiverton for ten years before entering the state sector with Richard Huish College, who have forged close links with the Somerset cricket Academy. He is still there at the time of writing. Having daydreamt of playing for the county side he has supported since boyhood, he is now ideally placed to encourage the stars of tomorrow to fulfil their ambitions.

542
Iain Fletcher
28 August 1991 v. Hampshire, Southampton

[signature]

Born in Sawbridgeworth in Hertfordshire on 31 August 1971, Iain was the son of Roy Fletcher, who ran a black cab business, and Maureen (Née Smith). At the age of ten, he was offered a scholarship to study at Millfield School. 'I didn't have much idea what was happening, so I just went along with it,' he admits with a shrug. 'Being born on the last day of August meant I was always the youngest in my year and I was quite late to develop physically anyway, just a tubby little lad, but I was recommended by my primary school headmaster and Millfield must have seen some promise there.' Referred to by friends and teammates as 'Fletch', Iain was, and still is, an ebullient character, one of his teachers confirming that he was 'a happy-go-lucky kid' and noted as a beautiful striker of the ball – so much so that 'when Iain Fletcher and David Hemp [later of Glamorgan and Warwickshire] were at the crease together, everyone stopped what they were doing and watched, expecting some pyrotechnics'.

After leaving Millfield, he went on to study for a degree in Politics at Loughborough University, his course chosen on the basis that he enjoyed the cut and thrust of debate and opinion-sharing. Indeed, there is a recurring theme in Iain's life of pursuing the path of greatest interest and happily embracing change if events should take a turn for the worse.

He continued to progress as a cricketer at Loughborough and represented the Combined Universities, having by then established himself in the Somerset Second XI and Hertfordshire teams. Having been given his first-class debut in August 1991, just days before his twentieth birthday, he made an immediate impact with a half-century, although his progress was hampered by a subsequent ankle injury. In his second Championship game, he looked set fair for a maiden century against Middlesex at Bath, when he was struck on the hand by a delivery from Neil Williams that broke a bone on his right index finger and forced him to retire hurt. Thereafter, things did not work out quite as he had hoped and, between 1991 and 1994, he would make fourteen first-class appearances, with five half-centuries to his name and an average of 24.21.

Iain is full of praise for the support offered by the likes of Peter Robinson – 'an excellent man who really cared about his charges' – but admits that he encountered 'a decidedly blunt approach to man-management at the top'. He was not alone in feeling disenchanted at what some players regarded as a bullying culture. His observation in *The Cricketers' Who's Who* at that time is telling, with a reference to players being shouted down 'in a manner that belongs to the long gone repressive era and not the 1990s. Opinions aren't there to be correct, they are there to be aired.' Courageous words from a young pro. In Iain's case, he had the self-belief and strength of character to walk away. Straight, as it happened, into the testosterone-fuelled environment of life as a money broker with Harlow Butler UEDA. 'It wasn't for me,' he admits.

Iain Fletcher – 'everyone stopped what they were doing and watched, expecting some pyrotechnics'

'It was too dull and getting in at 6.15am every morning meant getting up at 5.00 am, sometimes after a night entertaining clients. Any camaraderie was false, too. One desk manager stubbed a cigarette into a drink and goaded his trainee to drink it. The lad did it to feel part of the group. But that's not strength: that's weakness. They then tried to get me to but I refused. I resigned after five months there.'

You have to admire his devil-may-care approach to life. He soon found himself work when he wrote to *Sporting Index* with a proposal that they give him £7,000 so that he could relate the vicissitudes of a year spent placing bets on sporting events. The end result was the entertaining *On Tilt: A Spreadbetter's Diary*, published in 2001. (For the uninitiated, the expression 'on tilt' refers to those moments when a gambler is no longer relying on cold logic in an attempt to recover losses.) Iain professes to being merely a hobbyist and not a career gambler. 'I enjoy the buzz. It's not unlike that feeling when a bouncer whistles past your nose: not for the faint-hearted.' Talking to him, it becomes evident that the art of batsmanship has parallels with gambling: preparing thoroughly, keeping a cool head, avoiding foolhardy risks or hubris and taking opportunities for runs when the odds favour you, knowing that you are possibly one misjudgement away from a setback. If you stumble, you dust yourself down and start over again.

He began writing regularly for *The Independent* and *The Independent on Sunday*, now both defunct, and *Scotland on Sunday*, for which he still writes. Iain was for a long while the go-to man when the papers wanted a report on some exhilarating stunt or other. His assignments ranged from a Formula One driving experience with Johnny Herbert to sky-diving, or to abseiling down Table Mountain in Cape Town. His enthusiasm remains undimmed as he recounts his exploits. 'The abseiling challenge involved having a heart monitor attached and I surprised them because my heart rate didn't rise as much as they'd expected. Maybe those years opening the batting had helped.' Whether he learned it at the crease or was born with it, he appears blessed with the *sangfroid* that stands any opening batsman or indeed any gambler in good stead. But not every assignment was accepted by this natural adventurer. 'I drew the line at tombstoning [diving off rocks] because I thought there were too many variables for me to be in control and I was relieved when the crocodile wrestling in Australia had to be cancelled because the guy who was organising it was diagnosed with cancer, which wasn't such good news for him.'

He has continued to write engaging and instructional items on gambling in the magazine *Inside Edge* and his latest book, *The Rough Guide to Poker*, was published in 2005. Since 2012, he has returned to the cricketing fold, becoming Director of Performance Cricket for the Hertfordshire side he represented for many years. His role involves overseeing the management of the Minor Counties team, women's cricket and the county age groups for boys and girls. Never married, Iain has settled in a village in Suffolk and retains his undiminished zest for life, something he shares in common with his two dogs – a Boxer and a German Shepherd. His faithful companions are always eager to follow his lead. As for Iain, he is prepared to go wherever life takes him, so long as the journey remains enjoyable. He is happy to take his chances.

1992

"Much of the verve came from the younger players, and two in particular, Mark Lathwell quickening pulses and run-rates, and Andy Caddick quickening the fall of top-order wickets."

Tony Lawrence (Western Daily Press)

Championship Position: 9 of 18

Durham were added to the list of first-class counties in a season when Somerset enjoyed mid-table respectability. Mark Lathwell was a revelation, bringing a breezy fearlessness to his time at the crease and exceeding 1,000 runs in his first full season. Richard Harden, Andy Hayhurst and Chris Tavaré also passed that landmark. The bowling was spearheaded by Andy Caddick, with seventy-one wickets, ably supported by the spin of Harvey Trump and the pace of Neil Mallender, who was elevated to the England side. Thumping victories in the last two matches of the season, with the Somerset batsmen compiling six centuries, left the faithful wondering if a corner had now been turned. A semi-final berth in the Benson & Hedges Cup and fifth place in the Refuge Assurance League, with nine games won, offered further grounds for optimism – although where Somerset are concerned, despair has been hope's constant bedfellow for much of the club's history.

After the astonishing success of Jimmy Cook's three-year tenure, it came as an anti-climax when South African Richard Snell failed to impose himself on the county game. Among the other new-joins, Nick Folland – formerly captain of Devon – brought experience and a level head and Keith Parsons would become an important member of the team, particularly effective as an all-rounder in one-day games.

543
Andrew Payne
25 April 1992 v. Gloucestershire, Taunton

Andy Payne was born on 20 October 1973 in Rawtenstall, Lancashire, the son of Brian, a supervisor in a manufacturing company, and Margaret (née Berry), a former Inland Revenue employee, now deceased. Brian has for many years been a pivotal figure at Rawenstall CC, having enjoyed spells as a player, captain, administrator and chairman. Andy recalls that 'I was taken to cricket in a pram and then was playing on the outfield by the time I was four, so there was never any hope for me, really!' Educated at Bacup and Rawtenstall Grammar School, he then went on to Accrington and Rossendale College. He was already making waves as an all-rounder, batting right-handed and bowling right-arm medium pace, and had been selected for Lancashire in age group cricket from Under-11 upwards. He was given his first taste of Lancashire League cricket at the age of fifteen with Rawtenstall CC. By 1991, at the age of seventeen, he became the youngest ever pro in the Ribblesdale League when invited to step into the breach by Whalley CC, following a long-term injury to their contracted professional. Andy would go on to play for Lancashire Second XI that season and for England Under-19s in 1991-92 and 1992-93, enjoying tours to Pakistan and India and a home series against the West Indies.

He took the opportunity to join Somerset in 1992, becoming coach Bob Cottam's first signing at the county, with Bob having previously encountered him while coach of the England Under-17s. After impressing during a friendly against the Netherlands, Andy made his first-class debut against Gloucestershire and proceeded to score an unbeaten half century, but was never able to stake his claim for First XI cricket on a regular basis. It cannot have helped his cause that he had arrived as a batsman who could bowl but found himself being deployed primarily as a bowler. During the winter of 1992-93, he had gained further experience at Villagers CC, in Pretoria. This would prove his only overseas engagement as a pro, although Andy confirms that he had such a wonderful experience with Villagers that he returned to South Africa for a holiday the following year – a twenty-first birthday present from his parents.

He was undoubtedly a livewire. In his autobiography, *Coming Back to Me*, Marcus Trescothick recounts that he shared a house with Jason Kerr, Paul Clifford (who made no first-class appearances) and Andy. Marcus's two most vivid memories of that time appear to have been the 'all pervasive smell of cat urine' and the antics of Andy, whom he describes as 'a menace' and 'a complete psycho whose most prized possession was the air rifle with which he spent most of his spare time shooting me'. Marcus notes that 'suddenly, out of nowhere, I'd take one in the side of the head and to this day I still carry a slight scar on my left cheek'. He concludes that 'it was like living with Lee Harvey Oswald' but that it was 'great fun'. 'Not strictly true,' Andy reveals. 'Yes, I did own an air rifle but it was my BB gun that I used to fire at Marcus. There were the fireworks, too. Marcus was watching TV once and I handed him a rocket I'd just lit. He casually took it from me without looking before realising what I'd done. I've never seen him move so fast.' He confesses that the club might have taken a dim view of things, had he inflicted any lasting damage on his housemate. 'Marcus was already a class act,' Andy notes. 'I remember seeing him take on Darren Gough, pulling him and cutting him with ease. He was clearly destined to go right to the top.'

Andy Payne – arrived as a batsman who could bowl, but found himself being deployed primarily as a bowler

There was certainly a good rapport between the group of young cricketers whom Neil Burns shepherded with great skill to the Second XI Championship in 1994. It came as a surprise to the players when seven of them, Andy included, were released at the end of the season. In the words of Second XI coach Peter Robinson, it was 'a harsh decision', but a reflection of the financial pressures and the need to form judgements about which players would make the grade at a more elevated level. Andy's view of events was that, 'It was politics but I think we were a young side who could have gone on and done really well for Somerset for the following ten years.' He stresses that he harbours no resentment or ill feeling about his early departure. Over the course of three seasons, he had made four first-class appearances, his impressive batting average of 62.00 bolstered by his unbeaten half century on debut. He took five wickets at 37.40 apiece.

Returning to Lancashire, he was welcomed back into the fold at Rawtenstall CC before being employed as the pro at Unsworth CC, then Baxendem CC and finally for four seasons at Flowery Field CC in the Saddleworth League before returning to Rawtenstall CC, where he spent seasons variously as an amateur or pro. His finest season was 2003 when (as an amateur) he accumulated more than 1,000 runs. He played his last game for his beloved home club in 2012, observing that each Monday morning his routine involved 'getting out painkillers for my back and I couldn't carry on like that'.

Andy has been twice married, on the first occasion in 2000 to Robyn Hewitson, a business development manager in the charitable housing sector and the mother of his son, Tom, who was born in 2002. He was married again in 2017 to Jane Crompton, an apprenticeship officer who liaises with colleges and companies to improve the employment opportunities for trainees. 'My wife goes by the name of Jane Crompton-Payne, for obvious reasons. Jane Payne doesn't set the right tone!' Andy observes.

When it comes to employment, his career as a professional cricketer has always taken precedence. As a young man, he had applied successfully to join the police service but that never materialised after the opportunity came to be paid to play the game he loves. A later plan to join the fire service was equally doomed. 'I managed to suffer a major knee injury shortly before the physical assessment, so that put the kibosh on that,' he reveals. He found work where he could each winter but for the last twelve years has been employed by the Together Housing Association, who manage 38,000 properties, the vast majority of them in Lancashire and Yorkshire. Initially, he worked on maintenance, but in more recent years has been a housing officer, overseeing the management of 650 properties. He also takes pleasure in watching the progress of his son, Tom, already establishing himself in club cricket.

By his own admission competitive to a fault as a sportsman – 'I even had to make sure I won at pool on honeymoon,' he admits – Andy is an easy-going, personable man. Having hung up his boots and put away his cricket gear, it is to be hoped that he has placed under lock and key the treasured weapons with which he once terrorised his erstwhile housemate, Marcus Trescothick.

544
Andrew Colin Cottam
7 May 1992 v. Sussex, Hove

When Somerset's former slow left-arm bowler Andy Cottam was asked by journalist Steve Jennings whether or not having a father as Director of Cricket at the county was an issue, his response – jocular but truthful – was that it was 'a hindrance'. Andy observes that his father's first signing was Mushtaq Ahmed, a cricketer of international class who inevitably claimed the spinner's berth.

Andy was born in Northampton on 14 July 1973, the son of Bob Cottam and his wife, Jackie (née Nice). Bob, a fast-medium bowler, was playing at the time for Northants, and had been awarded his fourth and final England cap earlier that year. Having enjoyed a successful first-class career with Hampshire and then Northants, Bob would take up a coaching position with Allhallows School on the Devon-Dorset border, with the family moving to nearby Seaton, when Andy was three. Bob would spend a period away coaching at Warwickshire, but returned to the West Country when offered the roles of bowling coach and Director of Cricket at Somerset.

Andy and his brothers, Mike and Dave, had worked their way up through the age groups in Devon while playing their club cricket for Seaton CC, and it

Andy Cottam – 'my career was over as a player and I was only twenty-two'

fell upon their mother, Jackie, to offer a taxi service for her cricket-loving offspring. Andy had taken late to spin bowling and recalls his first competitive game as a left-arm orthodox bowler. It was a game for Seaton Colts against Sidmouth Colts. The decision to reinvent himself as a slow bowler had paid dividends and he was soon elevated to the First XI. A year later he was playing for Devon under the captaincy of Nick Folland and by 1990, he was established in the Devon team and making regular appearances for Somerset Second XI.

A prolonged first-class career had appeared to beckon when he joined Somerset as a YTS (Youth Training Scheme) employee and was signed a year later as a full-time pro. Andy is happy to hand some of the credit to Peter Anderson, the club's Chief Executive and a man described by Peter Roebuck as 'a rather bossy ex-policeman'. Known affectionately as 'Panda', Peter was a leading light at Seaton CC and, having watched Andy's progress, was happy to stake his reputation on him. Things began reasonably brightly. In his second Championship appearance, against Gloucestershire, he found himself facing the West Indian paceman, Courtney Walsh. He recollects looking around after taking guard, and seeing their keeper, Jack Russell, standing approximately thirty metres back. Andy's first instinct was to think: 'This guy must be quick.' Shepherded by Neil Mallender at the other end, he secured his career-best score of thirty-one. It had felt like a rite of passage.

His season's haul of wickets in 1992 was only six in six first-class matches, but it was deemed a steady start. That year, he was selected for the England Under-19s against Sri Lanka and was named Somerset's Young Player of the Year. But then Mustaq Ahmed was announced as the club's overseas signing and, throughout 1993, Andy was only able to tread water. Somerset agreed that there was unlikely to be any opportunity to develop a first-class career at the County Ground. Granted permission to speak to five counties who had made enquiries, he vacillated between joining Essex, under the watchful eye of John Childs, or Northants, the county of his birth. Sentiment was perhaps given precedence, but, having played in pre-season fixtures, Andy failed to make it into the Northants First XI. Then came the news that Anil Kumble would be joining the Northants side, claiming the spinner's berth. History was repeating itself.

Andy made the call to play and coach in Australia. 'I had a great time and did well,' he confirms. 'I assumed my county cricket days were over when, out of the blue, Derbyshire offered me a last chance.' Derbyshire had been searching for a while for a left-arm orthodox spinner and hoped the fit would be a good one. Alas, things did not work out as club and player had hoped after Andy suffered a knee injury and his form and confidence evaporated. A parting of the ways was agreed.

'My career was over as a player and I was only twenty-two. I was devastated,' he admits. Heading back to Seaton, he began work for a local builder, Neil Miller, who formerly played for Seaton CC, although in the 1996 season Andy was invited back unexpectedly by his champion, Peter Anderson, for two cameo appearances. His first-class record for Somerset stands as eight matches played and nine wickets bagged at 58.66 apiece and a batting average of 6.44.

As a footnote, he left his mark in Somerset cricketing folklore, when he played in a Second XI match against Warwickshire Second XI in July 1997. Andy had been sent to hospital after his hand was broken while batting in the first innings and informed that he would be no longer required, given that Somerset had been set 612 to win. No one had counted on the genius of Marcus Trescothick. Andy was relaxing back in Seaton when he received a tap on the shoulder to say that a driver named 'Sticky' was waiting to rush him to the County Ground with the news that, 'Banger's on 250 not out and we're six wickets down. They may need you.' By the time Andy had arrived, changed, padded up and gingerly put a glove on his broken hand, the ninth wicket had fallen with only seventeen runs needed for an improbable victory. What followed was something of a blur. Andy did not face a ball as Marcus shielded him from the bowling before being run out for 322 with Somerset an agonising six runs behind Warwickshire.

Andy parted company with Somerset again at the end of the 1997 season and went on to play for Devon until 1999 during their successful period under the leadership of Peter Roebuck.

Thereafter, he left for Australia, where he enjoyed a career as a coach, with time at the WACA in Perth and a period at the National Spin Clinic, alongside, among others, Shane Warne. Married and with two children, he was subsequently divorced. In 2011, his book, *The Ultimate Guide for Young Cricketers and Coaches*, was published, distilling his know-how, gleaned from two decades in the game. Having subsequently worked for four years as a regional manager for the KI Group, a global company offering support services to the mining, oil and gas industries, he joined Skill Hire, a headhunting agency in the region, and became a cricketing consultant and once more a coach, as a director of ACE Coaching. He has recently agreed a two-year contract as National Coach to the Indonesian side. He may have spent much of his working life half a world away, but Andy admits that:

> *My heart is still with Somerset and I follow them avidly. When I do get back to Taunton to watch a game I just think it's the best place in the world. I love the County Ground more than Lord's, more than the WACA, more than anywhere else.*

545
Keith Alan Parsons
13 May 1992 v. Pakistan, Taunton

1 September 2001 is an auspicious date in the sporting calendar. It was the night that reality was suspended while the England football team played out of their skins in Berlin, registering a 5:1 win over Germany. For the thousands who flocked to Lord's for the final of the Cheltenham & Gloucester Trophy, it was the occasion, earlier that day, when Somerset landed their first silverware for eighteen seasons. And for two opposing players it was a day that they will never forget. Overcome by the occasion, Leicestershire's Scott Boswell found that he had lost the ability to function as a bowler and sprayed wide after wide. Even the most ardent of Somerset fans must surely have felt sympathy for the man and wanted the horror show to end. For Keith Parsons, it was the day he cemented his position in Somerset's cricketing folklore. Having steered his side to a commanding score of 271 with an unbeaten 60, including two lusty blows for six on the final two deliveries of the innings, he then turned the tables with two quick wickets when Leicestershire had looked well set at 105 for 1. Keith came away with his winner's medal and the Man of the Match award.

Born a twin on 2 May 1973 in Taunton, he was the son of Alan Parsons, a civil servant who worked for many years for British Telecom, and Lynne (née Clapper-

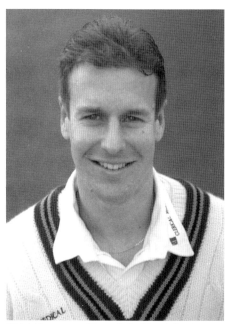

Keith Parsons – Man of the Match in the Cheltenham & Gloucester Trophy final of 2001

ton), who was employed at County Hall in Taunton. A useful cricketer, Alan captained the Civil Service XI and has been a leading light at the Taunton St Andrews cricket club. He also played for Somerset Second XI.

Keith and twin brother Kevin were already showing great promise as cricketers by the age of eleven, practising and competing with one another. Their development was overseen by their father, Alan, at Taunton St Andrews CC and by the coaches at Castle School and then Richard Huish College, both in Taunton. The twins played their part in helping Taunton St Andrews to win the Under-15 Club Championship and Richard Huish to secure the National Under-17 School Championship title and, having worked their way through the ranks both with Somerset and in representative games, they played together for England Under-19s. It has been noted that 'they both batted right-handed, loved soccer, rugby union and Viv Richards, passed 3 A-Levels and NCA coaching exams'. Keith would go on to use his skills as a player-coach over four seasons in New Zealand with Taita and Kapiti Old Boys, in the vicinity of Wellington, in North Island.

Somerset CCC have over the years fielded a handful of twins. Those who watched the Parsons brothers batting together confirm that scorers often relied on Keith's propensity for leg-side shots and Kevin's preference for off-drives as one of the few means of distinguishing them. The Rippon twins – Dudley and Sydney – had entertained Somerset supporters before and after the First World War, though their strange mannerisms had at times proved more engrossing than their dour approach to batsmanship. George Mirehouse, in 1884, had been the first twin to play for the county, although he and Tony Sutton, who appeared in 1948, were unlikely to be accompanied on the field by their twin sisters. Steve Waugh would come later, not accompanied by twin brother, Mark. In more recent times, the Overton twins – Craig and Jamie – have established themselves in the side. Kevin Parsons would be released by Somerset without having appeared in a first-class fixture, leaving Keith to fly the flag for the family while his brother carved a new career as an accountant.

With regard to his own development as a player, Keith praises Dermot Reeve for having inspired him, along with other members of the side, to adopt a tougher, winning mentality. He states that:

> *{Dermot} was someone who made the very best of his ability as a cricketer and he coached that way as well... He was brilliant for me and others as we started getting used to winning games. He taught us how to play smart cricket and that's what I took on board, to play sensible cricket to get us into a position to win games. Winning games can be about being brave enough to be there at the end and that's a characteristic I developed ... I liked to take responsibility to try and get us over the line with bat and ball.*

Keith did indeed gain a reputation for keeping a calm head and steering his team through the final overs of one-day games with the bat or being brought on as an accurate medium-pace bowler, adept at pinning back the opposition when they were threatening to cut loose.

A popular figure at the County Ground, he was referred to as 'The Housewives' Favourite' on account of a gentlemanly disposition and a clean-cut image marred only by a fondness for a regular (and invariably well-researched) flutter on the horses. He was also dubbed 'Orville' by the players at Taunton St Andrews – a reference to his 'ten-to-two' duck walk that never hampered his athleticism in the field. For all that he became regarded as a one-day specialist, he remained an important member of the first-class squad, appearing in 103 matches and averaging 28.62, with six centuries to his name and 106 wickets at 43.83 apiece. These and similar List A statistics do not tell the whole story of his preparedness to step up to the plate when a calm head was needed in trying circumstances. To the accolade 'Housewives' Favourite', we could add 'Unsung Hero'.

Keith parted company with Somerset in 2008, after seventeen seasons with the club. He went on to play for Cornwall and, having previously gained experience of captaincy when appearing for Somerset Second XI, was appointed captain of the Unicorns side, formed from the 'best of the rest' – university and Minor Counties players – to compete in the Clydesdale Bank forty-over competition. The team acted as a showcase for players who might otherwise have been overlooked by first-class counties. An example of a cricketer who benefited from the experience was Wes Durston, who, having earlier been released by Somerset, was offered a contract by Derbyshire as a result of his performances for Unicorns.

During the latter part of his playing career, Keith set up a corporate hospitality business. The venture was short-lived but it was at that time that he began to develop his skills as a public speaker and host. Married in 2002 to Sharon (née John), with whom he had two sons, both talented at sport, Keith has recently separated from his wife. Still based in Taunton, he is now employed at the Somerset County Sports store

Keith Parsons – gained a reputation for keeping a calm head and steering his team through the final overs of one-day games

at the County Ground, where he is the Corporate Sales Manager. He also coaches youngsters – as part of a joint project between the club and Richard Huish College – and works for the MCC Foundation, taking part in a scheme where promising players aged eleven to fifteen in the state school system in the vicinity of Taunton are invited to King's College for coaching sessions. Still as courteous and happy as ever to talk to fans, he remains a popular figure. As for his playing days, he observes that, 'It was something you looked forward to every day and look back on with fond memories.'

* * * * *

Kevin John Parsons

Kevin Parsons, twin brother of Keith, made no first-class appearances but three List A appearances for Somerset spread over the 1992 and 1993 seasons, and five for Somerset Cricket Board between 1992 and 2002, deployed as a right-handed batsman, with a highest score of 65. His right-arm medium-pace bowling was not called on in those fixtures.

His early experiences and career mirror Keith's (see above). Whereas Keith enjoyed a long and fruitful career with Somerset, Kevin was released by them at the end of the 1993 season. He continued to perform well in club cricket for Taunton St Andrews CC, with Keith observing in conversation with journalist Steve Jennings that Kevin 'was probably the best league cricketer in the region for a fair few years'. Keith is convinced that there was little to choose between them but that his twin brother's early departure was a matter of differing fortunes rather than any fundamental difference in ability or technique and adds that, 'Kev just moved on: he's been a massive support for me over the years and credit to him for getting on with it.' His career as an accountant has progressed seamlessly and Kevin now heads up the accountancy arm of Coopers Associates, major sponsors of Somerset cricket at the time of writing.

Kevin Parsons – 'probably the best league cricketer in the region for a fair few years'

546
Richard Peter Snell
20 May 1992 v. Essex, Taunton

Richard Snell has the distinction of claiming South Africa's first wicket after their return to the Test arena following twenty-two years in the wilderness. A sparsely attended match against the West Indies in Barbados, it was boycotted in large numbers, not in protest at the visitors but at the non-selection of local hero Anderson Cummins. An all-rounder who batted right-handed and bowled right-arm fast-medium, Richard took four wickets in each innings of a match won by the home side. Asked about his memories of that game, he responds that, 'I had Lara dropped at first slip for nought ... I think he went on to get quite a few [64 in the second innings]. And I think we were pretty inexperienced in Test cricket, so the fact that we basically had one bad session and lost the Test stands out.' It would prove the first of five Test appearances between 1992 and 1994, alongside forty-two One Day Internationals – a format well suited to his talents, with Richard being among the early examples of a pinch hitter, placed at the top of the batting order and given free rein to hit out. Prior to this, he had played for South Africa during the much-maligned Rebel Tour of 1990, led by Mike Gatting.

Born in Durban on 12 September 1968 (two years before the ICC ostracised South Africa), he was educated at Durban High School before attending Witwatersrand University, generally referred to as Wits University. While an undergraduate, he was drafted into the Transvaal side under the leadership of Clive Rice, by then a seasoned campaigner of international renown. Alongside Steven Jack, Richard formed one half of a youthful opening attack and lays the credit for his early development at Clive Rice's door, observing, 'What would take you three or four years to learn, you learned in six months because you had that experience standing next to you at mid-off.'

He was offered a one-year contract after having been recommended to Somerset by Transvaal teammate Jimmy Cook, whose astonishing feats for the county were still fresh in the memory. Although he proved popular with other team members and supporters – noted in some quarters for his boyish good looks – Richard never hit the heights as had been hoped. Essentially a pace bowler who could bat, wicket-keeper Neil Burns observes that, 'He used to make the ball wobble and dip horribly once it went past the bat, like no one else I have kept wicket to, so he presented a real challenge.' Neil also describes his former teammate as 'the most laid-back cricketer I've ever met', referring to Richard's approach to life rather than his dedication as a player.

Richard Snell – offered a one-year contract on the recommendation of fellow South African, Jimmy Cook

His efforts were enough to secure twenty-seven wickets for Somerset at 44.22 apiece in sixteen appearances. He averaged 27.25 with the bat.

He was just twenty-nine when he retired from the game to focus initially on a career as a physiotherapist, a role for which he had previously qualified. He then joined the family firm of Reno Industrial Africa, based in Midrand, between Johannesburg and Pretoria. The company provides heavy duty cleaning products and services of more or less every description.

These days, his is a voice still heard on occasions locally on broadcast media, happy to reflect on the game he once graced. There is a refreshing honesty and understated self-assurance about Richard's summary of his approach during his own playing days. 'I think that when you play, you should be supremely confident in your ability to perform,' he observes. 'You have good days and you have bad days, and I think as long as you feel that you played well, then it doesn't really worry you, about what people thought or the kind of press or that side of it.'

547
Nicholas Arthur Folland
18 August 1992 v. Worcestershire, Weston-super-Mare

[signature]

Nick Folland the headmaster might be a stickler for punctuality, but he was a late arrival to the first-class game at the ripe old age of twenty-nine years. He was already a player of some renown, having led Devon to the Holt Cup Trophy in 1991, their first major honour for fourteen years. Satisfied that Devon would be in safe hands under the captaincy of Peter Roebuck, whom he had persuaded to accept the challenge, Nick had taken the opposite direction of travel and decided to try his hand as a professional cricketer, while there was still time.

Born in Bristol on 17 September 1963 but brought up in Exmouth, he was the son of Geoffrey and Maureen (née Coles), both of whom worked in Social Services. From them, the son developed a sense that helping others trumps personal ambition. Nick's older brother, Neil, also played cricket for Devon and later for Bedfordshire (and also become a teacher). Educated at Exmouth School, Nick was a promising enough cricketer to have been selected for the Devon senior side at seventeen and to play for England Schools. He had been offered a trial with Gloucestershire as a sixteen-year-old, commuting up to Bristol and staying with his grandmother, but no contract was forthcoming and he subsequently left for Loughborough University, where he completed a degree in Sports Science & Recreation Management, before undertaking his PGCE, training to teach PE and Geography. Having originally considered a career in the probation service, his first job was in fact teaching 'troublesome deaf children' before he joined the staff at Blundell's School, in Tiverton. While teaching Geography A-Level and PE, he played on a regular basis for Devon, latterly as captain, appearing on occasions for Gloucestershire Second XI and for the Minor Counties XI. His appearances for the last of these included one match deemed first-class against India in 1990, when he impressed with scores of 26 and 82.

Peter Roebuck observed that 'as Folland built a formidable record, counties resumed knocking on his door. No longer was he a triallist, now he was wanted.' Asked at the time why he had decided to try his luck as a pro, Nick's response was that, 'It's only now that I've managed to sort out a deal where I can combine teaching with a first-class career. I would have been reluctant to give up my teaching career. I now feel far more at ease with myself as a player and certainly mentally far more positive and confident.'

An elegant left-handed batsman, he is described as 'fit, enthusiastic and a dasher', who looked immediately at home in the first-class game. Following a cameo appearance for Somerset in 1992, he enjoyed his first full season in 1993 and registered a century in each innings against Sussex at Taunton in July of that year. These would remain his only centuries in thirty-one first-class appearances, the bulk of them over two seasons. He came away with an average of 33.61. By the middle of the 1994 season, his curiosity or thirst for Championship cricket had been sated and he was ready for a return to full-time teaching. Nick had matured outside the narrow confines of professional sport and observes that, 'Perhaps I was too ingrained with an amateur mindset, having joined the first-class game and changing room at a later age than most.' Not for him the nomadic lifestyle and the four-day matches. But Nick learned from his experiences. He realised early in the adventure the step up in patience and concentration required, sometimes for many hours. In addition, he learned to eradicate error and how to bat with greater precision in decision-making. These lessons would be applied once he returned to a hugely successful Devon side and perhaps the crowning personal achievement in a distinguished career for them was his 249 not out against Oxfordshire at Torquay in 1999. Initially, he had played after his return under the leadership of Peter Roebuck, but then he enjoyed a reprise of his role as captain for two seasons at the turn of the millennium. There was plenty of mutual respect between the two men and Nick's loyalty was in evidence when he agreed to be a character witness in a court case in 2001 triggered by accusations of Peter's abuse of young house guests.

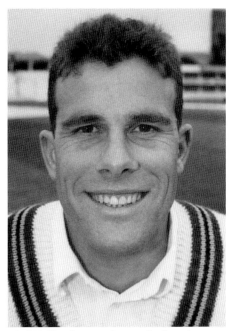

Nick Folland – came late to the first-class game and batted 'with an understated sense of purpose'

COURTESY OF SOMERSET COUNTY GAZETTE

He was married in 1992 to Dianne Lovering, and the couple would remain together for thirteen years. In 1994, Nick resumed his teaching role on a full-time basis at Blundell's, spending six years as a housemaster. In 2000, St Aubyn's Preparatory School, which had enjoyed a long association with Blundell's, was relocated to the latter's campus and, the following year, Nick took the reins of the new institution that, five years later, would become known as Blundell's Preparatory School.

In 2011, he left to take up the headship of St. John's on-the-Hill Prep School in Chepstow. After four years in Wales, he returned to the West Country when he was appointed Headmaster of Sherborne Prep School, where he remains at the time of writing. In 2005, he had met with Diane Franklin, an Australian Speech and Language Specialist, whom he had first met in her home country, when he was twenty-one. The two of them had reunited when she came over to live in England and worked with Nick at Blundell's Prep School. They were married in 2015 in Perth, Western Australia.

His summers are now spent in Desert Springs, Spain, enjoying the delights of his holiday home. In some senses, Nick has been, for much of his life, the metaphorical big fish in a small pool. A lot has been written of his elegant batting allied to his modesty, with one piece noting that he 'approaches the wicket with an understated sense of purpose'. The same phrase could equally well be applied to the way in which Nick has lived his life as a whole.

Nick Folland – 'fit, enthusiastic and a dasher'
COURTESY OF BARRY PHILLIPS

1993

"When I was offered the opportunity to play with Somerset,
I did not hesitate and grabbed it with both hands …
I absolutely loved my first year playing at Taunton and
proved to be very popular there."

Mushtaq Ahmed

Championship Position: 5 of 18

Aware of the adage that it is bowlers who win you first-class matches, Somerset turned to the Pakistani leg-spinner, Mushtaq Ahmed. He brought not only wickets – eighty-five of them – but also an ebullience that reminded everyone that cricket can be fun. Somewhat more taciturn was the figure of Chris Tavaré, captaining the side for the fourth season and leading them to fifth place in the Championship, with Richard Harden often asked to deputise as captain when Chris was absent. Richard also compiled three centuries and was the only player to top 1,000 runs.

Offering support to Mushtaq were Andy Caddick, who claimed fifty-seven wickets in his eleven appearances, and Graham Rose, now well into his stride as an entertaining and effective all-rounder.

Both Andy Caddick and Mark Lathwell were called up for Test duty, the latter on a wave of public and journalistic support. At the time of his call-up, Mark was in a minority in having misgivings about his elevation. More driven, Andy had no such doubts about his own selection.

Two of the debutants – Marcus Trescothick and Mushtaq Ahmed – would prove themselves cricketers of global standing. The third, Jason Kerr, would gain his wings in time as a coach, offering many years of valuable service to his adoptive county.

548
Jason Ian Douglas Kerr
8 May 1993 v. Australia, Taunton

Although a Lancastrian, Jason Kerr freely admits to his fond attachment to Somerset. 'I love this place,' he says of the County Ground in Taunton, adding that, 'I come to work every day with a smile on my face.'

Born in Bolton on 7 April 1974, he was the son of Len, who taught Maths and PE, and Janet (née Howard), who managed a retail outlet. Len was a useful club cricketer, a stalwart of Tonge CC in the Bolton League, and cricket ran in the family with Jason's younger brother, Andy, playing in the Second XI for both Somerset and Derbyshire. After attending Withins High School in the town of his birth, Jason went on to the Bolton Institute of Higher Education. Although his heart was already set on a career in first-class cricket, he took the precaution of undertaking a Business & Finance diploma and gained an initial coaching qualification, perhaps aware that, as a pace bowler, he was only ever likely to be one major injury away from terminating his career. By the time of the completion of his diploma, he had already appeared for Lancashire Second XI as a seventeen-year-old, but was offered a contract by Somerset. He had been invited for an England Under-17 trial where he was spotted by Somerset's then bowling coach, Bob Cottam, who persuaded him that he should make the move to the South West. After a net session in January 1992, he was signed immediately and joined Somerset that April.

Such was the continued progress of the young fast-medium right-arm bowler that he was selected for the England Under-19 tour of India in 1992-93. Slim and 6 feet 3 inches tall, he was possessed of a fine pace bowler's physique but was a competent batsman. Sadly, though, Jason was never able to command a regular place in the First XI. Over the course of nine seasons, from 1993 until 2001, he made fifty-eight first-class appearances, although he was more of a regular in limited-overs matches with ninety-six outings. He took 113 first-class wickets for Somerset at 40.33 apiece and among his highlights was a return of 7 for 23 against Leicestershire at Taunton in 1999, which included a devastating spell of swing bowling where he took 5 for 6 in 3.1 overs. Another moment of triumph was reaching the milestone of a hundred career wickets with a hat trick against the West Indies in 2000. As a batsman, he averaged 20.80 for the county.

During the winter months, he had enjoyed regular spells as a club pro in Australasia, employed at Gordon Districts in Sydney and later at Taita CC in Wellington, New Zealand, and at Subiaco Floreat CC in Perth, Australia. During his time in Perth, he shared a house in Cottesloe with Marcus Trescothick and Andre van Troost. The young troopers gave the beach full marks, but their accommodation left a lot to be desired. Writing in *Coming Back to Me*, Marcus, who was appearing for Melville CC, notes, dryly, that their house achieved the seemingly impossible feat of comparing unfavourably with his lodgings when he had first arrived at the County Ground, noting that, 'I was gazing up at the stars through the holes in my bedroom ceiling and any piece of food that wasn't nailed down was pinched by rats the size of bears.'

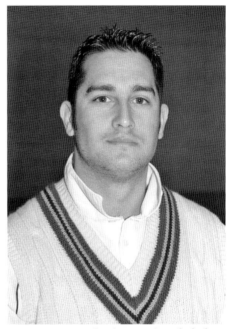

Jason Kerr – pace bowler turned coach, he has enjoyed a long association with Somerset cricket

Released at the end of the 2002 season, Jason joined Derbyshire, but his career there was cut short by a major shoulder injury. Matthew Reed notes that although Jason's bowling days were then over, he had the 'ability to hit cleanly and mightily' and attempted to reinvent himself as a specialist batsman. He was unable, though, to graduate from the Second XI. Calling it a day, Jason noted that, 'My body let me down one too many times.'

Falling back on the skills he had learned at college, he became an account manager for a company named Mortgage Fix in 2004, but this was short-lived and the attractions of cricket in general and the County Ground in particular proved too alluring. He was employed for a while by Bridgwater CC as a player and coach but was soon invited back into the fold by Brian Rose, who appointed him initially as a self-employed member of the Academy coaching team, before he was made a full-time employee and Second XI Coach. He would remain in post from 2005 until 2013, charged with helping young players to fulfil their potential and graduate to the first-class game. 2005 was also the year he became engaged to Donna Nelmes, a Lead Fire Fighter now working at the Fire Service Academy in Exeter. They had a daughter, Jasmine, but Jason observes that, at the time of writing, 'We haven't managed to get married yet, despite being engaged for thirteen years!' Fortunately, he has demonstrated rather more urgency in his planning and execution as a coach.

In 2013 he became the bowling specialist for the first team and was later made head coach. His impact on a young team – energised and at times brilliant in the field and with a clear strategy going into each game – is apparent for all to witness. At the time of writing, Jason has enjoyed a quarter of a century with Somerset and surely now knows the set-up as well as anyone. He describes the club he loves as being the closest a cricket county can come to a football club in terms of the passion it generates among its supporters. He remains delighted to play his part in helping to bring the best out of a new generation of talented players.

549
Marcus Edward Trescothick
13 May 1993 v. Lancashire, Taunton

Marcus Trescothick is a member of that exclusive band of Somerset-born players who have made their mark on the game well beyond the borders of the county, generating national and even international headlines. Jack White, Harold Gimblett and Jos Buttler also spring to mind. Yes, Marcus is technically Avon-born, but the formation of that ill-fated county in 1974 proved a twenty-two year aberration. Born in Keynsham on Christmas Day 1975, he was the son of Martyn and Linda (née Cox). Martyn, was a useful club cricketer who played for Somerset Second XI and turned down the opportunity of a contract with the county. Marcus describes his family as cricket-mad, although Linda's 'cricket-madness' extended in the main to making teas for Keynsham CC for thirty-five years and tolerating her husband's and son's obsession with the game. From the outset, it was clear that Marcus had talent. He is right-handed, but adopted a left-hander's grip as he stood in front of the television, reflecting (in mirror image) what he saw on screen. The only activity that appears to have deflected him from his destined course was the time spent as a competent goalkeeper in junior football.

Gloucestershire were the first to become aware of the young boy's extraordinary talents and drafted him into their Under-11 side, but they had cause to regret his century for them in only his second match. It was against Somerset Under-11s and

Marcus Trescothick – his talent was rarely in doubt, but perhaps no one could have predicted the longevity of his outstanding career

the county of his birth – and the one he supported – quickly put paid to any notions of his being poached. Educated at the Sir Bernard Lovell School, he was a big lad for his age and remains an imposing presence. Throughout his childhood and in the early years of adulthood, sausages had been his unerring protein of choice, earning him the moniker 'Banger'. His one-track diet must have helped to bulk him up. At every age group, he proved a forceful run-maker. In 1991, he amassed an astonishing 4,000 runs in all forms of the game and was deemed the outstanding player in youth cricket by *The Cricketer* magazine.

He broke into the first-class game at the age of seventeen. Former Somerset wicket-keeper Neil Burns observes that:

I saw Marcus Trescothick grow from a ten year-old run-making machine at school level ... His first-class debut sticks in the memory. It was a remarkable match between Somerset and Lancashire at Taunton, which ended in two days. Lancashire, chasing 88 to win in the fourth innings, were bowled out for 72, with Andy Caddick taking 9 for 32.

In such a low-scoring game, it was inevitable that his first appearance would prove inauspicious, but the Somerset hierarchy were already aware that here was an exceptional talent, likely in time to become an established Test player. On the other hand, perhaps no one could have predicted the longevity of his outstanding career.

His first full season in 1994 was a triumph, his selection for the England Under-19 side being the only thing that stood between him and becoming the youngest player to have scored 1,000 runs in the season for the county. There followed a lull as bowlers began to establish flaws in his technique. In Marcus's own words, 'My second season syndrome seemed to last longer than usual – about four seasons in total.' His dominance in age group cricket had allowed him to develop undetected flaws that would later be exposed in the first-class game before being ironed out. In particular, his tendency to try to hit every ball outside off stump left him vulnerable against top bowlers and Marcus would spend countless hours in the nets with Perth-based coach Peter Carlstein, learning the art of more judicious shot selection. At the same time, his ability to intimidate bowling attacks with his powerful stroke play would remain intact. Of less concern to his coaches was his famed lack of footwork, a conscious choice, allowing him to keep head and body still before executing his shots.

There had been some outstanding centuries, but he was still felt by some not to be fulfilling his considerable potential. If there were doubts, then they would not have been harboured by the fortunate few who saw him lead a run chase for the Second XI, having been set a seemingly impossible total of 612 by Warwickshire Second XI. When Marcus was finally run out for 322, Somerset had fallen just short of the target. It must rank as one of the most extraordinary innings in a losing cause. Here was undoubtedly an exceptionally good opening batsman. It was now a matter of time before he would impose himself at the top level.

There was further experience gained playing for two winters in Perth, during which time his work with his coach, Peter Carlstein, began to pay dividends. In particular, back on home soil, Marcus made runs in fine style against Glamorgan, while being watched by the recently appointed England coach, Duncan Fletcher. Duncan saw in Marcus a man who was capable of dominating opposing attacks for a number of years to come and felt that it was worth throwing a still up-and-coming player into the melting pot, even if it took time for him to adjust. When Nick Knight's finger was broken, the chance came and Marcus immediately established his credentials as an England batsman, with an assured innings of 79 in his maiden One Day International. If he was not already a household name, then he became one as a member of the Ashes-winning England team of 2005, playing his part in arguably the most compelling Test series since the Ashes contest of 1981. Marcus was given the freedom of his home town of Keynsham, made an honorary vice-president of Bristol City FC and, along with his England teammates, awarded an MBE. Could it get any better? It would in fact get much worse. Marcus has revealed the pain he suffered in his frank, award-winning autobiography *Coming Back to Me*, co-written with Peter Hayter, at the time the *Mail on Sunday*'s cricket correspondent. Homesickness had always been an issue but, during the 2006 tour of Pakistan and India, he was overcome with anxiety and unable to function. Marcus's courage in being prepared to share the torment he endured as he tried to conquer the condition has done much to open the lid on a problem that had for so long been ignored and misunderstood. Many a cricketer – and Somerset has had its share, including Harold Gimblett, at the time of writing the only man to have scored more runs for the county – has succumbed to depression and taken his own life. With a support structure, Marcus was able to address the problem, to take stock and bravely to walk away from international cricket. Despite his best efforts, he had to accept that involvement in future tours was untenable. He could leave with his head held high, with seventy-six Test appearances and 123 One Day International appearances to his name, averages of 43.79 and 37.37 respectively and a total of twenty-six centuries for his country.

Marcus Trescothick – Somerset is his lifeblood and Somerset needs him

England's loss was Somerset's gain, as he has been able to fight their cause for season after season. Captain of the side from 2010 until 2015, he has led them to within sniffing distance of the prize they covet above all others – the County Championship – most agonisingly in 2010, when they won widespread sympathy as Nottingham snatched the Championship in the dying seconds of the campaign and Somerset ended up as runners-up in all three domestic competitions. His contribution has been immense over more than a quarter of a century and, in his forties, he continues to defy the ageing process. There were nay-sayers ready to write him off in 2013 after he struggled for a while, following an ankle injury sustained at Trent Bridge, but he has come back fighting, also offering valuable advice, when it is requested, to younger members of the squad. At the time of writing, he has already amassed over 19,000 first-class runs for Somerset, with more than fifty centuries to his name. Added to this are approximately 10,000 runs in shorter forms of the game. He has been voted PCA Player of the Year on three occasions and was a *Wisden* Cricketer of the Year in 2005. But his career statistics, once they are set in stone, will fail to tell the story of his worth, of the confidence his presence at the crease gave to those around him, or the incisive contributions he made at first slip: not the most athletic of movers but a man with superb reflexes and a safe pair of hands. By his side, sharing his triumphs and his pain, has been his wife, Hayley (née Rowse). They were married in 2004 and have two daughters, Ellie and Millie.

Marcus surely has a long future at the club in whatever capacity. He is part of the furniture these days. Somerset is his lifeblood and Somerset needs him. Fame has brought him the odd lucrative deal. He has acted as a pundit for Sky and as a brand ambassador for the likes of Gray Nicholls and Herring shoes and he has used his profile for the wider good, not only in speaking up about stress-related illness but also as a patron of worthy causes. Latterly, he has acted as the Cricket Development coach at Taunton School and, more recently, he has been appointed a member of the ECB scouting network, spotting budding cricketing talent in the area and making recommendations as to how the promising youngsters can be helped to fulfil their potential.

Marcus is not going anywhere just yet. Most of us need an anchor in our lives. Perhaps elite sportsmen, exposed to stresses few can imagine, need one more than most. In his home county of Somerset and even more so in his wife, Hayley, and his two daughters, Marcus has security in any storm. He also has the support of the County Ground faithful, grateful for what he has given, and continues to give, to Somerset cricket.

550
Mushtaq Ahmed
13 May 1993 v. Lancashire, Taunton

In the sporting world, in contrast to most walks of life, it is possible – with talent, commitment and good fortune – for a man to rise from the very humblest of beginnings and achieve global fame. Mushtaq Ahmed was one such. One of ten children, two of whom died young, he was born on 28 June 1970 in the Sahiwal district of

Pakistan, where his father, Shamsudin, worked long hours in a cotton factory for a pittance, in order to provide for his family, all crowded in a three-roomed home. Although poor, they considered themselves better off than some, being in possession of three buffaloes in their back yard. Mushtaq's parents were determined that their children should benefit from an education in order to rise above their milieu, but Mushtaq had other ideas, spending every available moment bowling at a poplar tree, mimicking the action of Pakistani leg-spin bowler Abdul Qadir, whom he watched on a friend's television, having no mod cons in his own home. Indeed, far from being well-equipped, part of the house collapsed in a storm while Mushtaq was still a schoolboy and he was fortunate to have escaped unharmed. The term 'schoolboy' is used loosely, as young

Mushtaq Ahmed – rose from the very humblest of beginnings to achieve global fame

Mushy regularly played truant in order to practise his cricket alone. On one occasion, he was marched into school by his father to see his teacher and, in Mushtaq's words, 'They both beat me until one of the sticks actually broke on me.'

His breakthrough came when he played for his school against their wealthy rivals at the Comprehensive High School, who generally looked down on the rural poor. Having performed well, he was invited to join the school, with the inducement of a bicycle in order to make the daily four-mile journey. Communication was an issue at first, with Mushtaq having been brought up speaking Punjabi, which was neither spoken nor taught at the school, where the more 'refined' Urdu was the official language. Over the following years, he quickly progressed to first-class cricket with Multan CC in an environment where talent alone was not enough. A young man from a poor background needed champions. Offered a job with the United Bank, in order to give him financial security, he was released to play cricket whenever the need arose. In time, his father relented and accepted that it was impossible to curb Mushtaq's enthusiasm and that perhaps there were some positives to be had from it. Word was spreading and, at the age of seventeen, he was fast-tracked into the Pakistan one-day team, captained by Imran Khan, who would prove an inspiration with his belief in his young charge's ability.

There followed an Under-19 tour of Australia where once again the Punjabi speaker was obliged to learn a new language which left him at times bewildered as he struggled to extract meaning or to read the unfamiliar script. His exposure to McDonald's restaurants, for example, as he grappled with an alien concept, was harrowing at the time, but in hindsight a source of amusement. By 1992, he was an integral part of the Pakistani side who surprised observers by winning the World Cup. With the side all granted tracts of land as a reward for their efforts, they were also able to command astonishing fees to make guest appearances at any number of functions. Imran Khan called the team together and proposed that each of them should contribute fifty per cent of any fees to fund the building of a much-needed cancer hospital in the country. Unbeknown to Imran, most of the team, fuelled by greed, decided not to cooperate. Young Mushtaq's head was turned by the rebels, but the plan backfired when the country turned on them after news of what was seen as their treachery leaked out. Overnight, appearance requests dried up and Imran felt no longer able to lead the side.

Another culture shock was in store when Mushtaq was approached by Somerset. For all their faults, the county had always had a good eye for emerging talent and Mushy would not disappoint them. Collected from the airport by Graham Rose, he understood very little of what was being said but, on arrival at Taunton, was taken under the wing of a kindly Neil Mallender. 'Ghost' helped Mushy to undertake tasks such as shopping and later driving and taught him the basics of the language. Fortunately, Mushtaq was a quick learner. His wife, Uzma, whom he had recently married, joined him for a while, but found life in England difficult for a shy Muslim girl, unable to communicate with anyone.

Unbeknown to Somerset, Mushtaq had arrived still suffering from injury but played through the pain, enjoying a triumphant first season, with eighty-five first-class wickets. With admirable honesty, Mushtaq admits that, dazzled by the bright lights of Western civilisation, he began to lose focus but he underwent a reawakening in the winter of 1994-95 and came back stronger in 1995, with ninety-five wickets. At times during his spell at Somerset he undertook touring commitments with Pakistan, by whom he would be awarded fifty-two caps, but he remained with his adoptive county until 1998. Dermot Reeve had been appointed coach in the previous season and his spiky humour was a cause of friction between the two. Dermot's tendency to make jokes about his inability to understand what Mushtaq was saying were undermining, and Mushtaq had the courage to tell the club that he wished to leave immediately and to be released from his contract. Over the course of sixty-two first-class matches, he had taken 289 wickets at 26.32 apiece and had averaged 16.10 with the bat. If Somerset regretted the loss of their match-winning leg-spinner, that sense of regret would be compounded when he returned to the English game in 2003 with Sussex, where he was the key figure in their securing their first Championship, a feat repeated in 2006 and 2007. Sussex captain, Chris Adams, would state of Mushtaq at the time of his retirement from the county that, 'He leaves us as statistically, romantically and emotionally the best player ever to pull on a Sussex shirt.' Perhaps Chris was being swept along on a tide of emotion, given that Mushy had been the most important cog in their landing their three Championship titles. Perhaps he had chosen his words carefully in the sense that, technically, Ranji and C. B. Fry had pulled on plain white shirts rather than Sussex shirts. What is beyond doubt is that Somerset teammates and supporters would have been singing Mushtaq's praises had he been able to deliver three Championships for them. Indeed, one would have been enough to be going on with.

Mushtaq continues to grace the game with his ebullient presence. He was a commentator for a period with Sky, but the majority of his work since his playing days has been as a coach. For six years from 2008, he was England's spin-bowling coach and takes some credit for Graeme Swann's development under his tutelage. He also enjoyed a brief spell as Surrey's bowling coach and, in 2014, was appointed to a similar position with the Pakistan side. Since 2016, he has been Head Coach of the Pakistan National Cricket Academy. He remains committed to his family, including his wife, Uzma, and their three children, and to the faith he neglected briefly when undreamed of riches and the temptations of an alien culture fell into the country boy's lap.

Mushtaq Ahmed – a brilliant exponent of wrist spin and an ebullient team member

1994

"At Bath, supporters sat back and wallowed in the
precocious talents of Trescothick and Lathwell, who
took Surrey's attack apart with all the exuberance of youth."

Richard Latham

Championship Position: 11 of 18

A ndy Hayhurst took over the captaincy surrounded by much optimism, but by
the end of May – a disastrous month for the skipper and his team – every one
of the first eight matches against county opposition in all competitions had ended
in straight defeat. Andy and the team coach, Bob Cottam, shared a few home truths
with the underperforming unit and these appeared to provoke a positive response. It
must have been the mother of all team talks. Suddenly, the serial losers had become
unbeatable. But the progress was illusory. The problem was a lack of strength in
depth. When the key players performed, all was well. When they were unavailable or
off colour, defeat came too readily.

Andy Hayhurst, Mark Lathwell and Richard Harden all topped 1,000 runs.
Marcus Trescothick would surely have done so, too, had he not been called away to
captain the England Under-19 side. The principal wicket-takers – Andy Caddick and
Mushtaq Ahmed – were unavailable for much of a season of undulating fortunes for
their county. Among the debutants, Piran Holloway would contribute most to the
cause, although Simon Ecclestone would be tipped by many as a future captain, before
his career was cut short by recurring injury problems.

In his final season at Somerset, Neil Burns, summoned all his know-how to
lead the Second XI to the Rapid Cricketline title, having been toppled from the
wicket-keeping top slot by the arrival of Cambridge blue, Rob Turner.

551
Vincent Paul Clarke
28 April 1994 v. Gloucestershire, Bristol

Vau Clarke

Vince Clarke was born in Liverpool on 11 November 1971, the son of Vincent (known as Vinnie) and Sandra (née Sutherland) who emigrated to Australia, bringing Vince up in Perth. After attending Craigie Primary School and Sacred Heart College, a Roman Catholic School in the Perth suburb of Sorrento, Vince went on to study for a diploma in Social Training at Perth TAFE [Technical & Further Education] College. He had by then developed into a useful leg-break bowler, included in the Western Australia development squads from Under-14 through to Under-19 levels as an all-rounder, capable of both leg-break and seam bowling. At 6 feet 3 inches, he was able to use his height to good advantage and from 1990 began to play for a number of seasons for Wanneroo CC. In 1991, he played indoor cricket for the Western Australia side who emerged as winners in a national tournament. His skills also stretched to softball (a version of baseball), where he starred as a pitcher for his home state.

Vince returned to the country of his birth in 1993 when he joined Bridgwater CC as their pro and was given a number of opportunities with Somerset Second XI. As a result of his efforts, he was offered a one-year contract for the 1994 season. In the event he played a pivotal role in the march of the Second XI under the leadership of Neil Burns to the Rapid Cricketline Championship title. Vince was the leading wicket-taker, bowling either his leg-breaks or seam as conditions dictated. He was only selected for two games with the First XI, coming away with a batting average of 11.50 and one wicket for a total of 105 runs. Writing in the *Somerset Year Book*, Richard Latham asserted that Vince, along with other newcomers, had 'found the move into first-class cricket a mighty leap'. He was released at the end of the 1994 season.

Returning to Australia, he was taken on by Hamersley Carine CC before coming back to England after joining Leicestershire, whom he would stay with for two seasons before, yet again, being released as he struggled to establish a regular first team place. Back in Perth, he joined Nollamara Turf CC for four seasons as a pro and was becoming a well-established figure in Grade cricket, having also gained coaching qualifications at the WACA. In England, Derbyshire agreed to take Vince on for the 1997 season and here he registered his highest first-class score with an innings of 99. It has been noted wryly that Vince had been caught behind one short of his maiden century while going for his shots, having taken note that, with nine wickets down and Devon Malcolm (the archetypal No. 11) as his partner, decisive action had been called for. He would remain with Derbyshire for three seasons, although in the last of these he made no first-

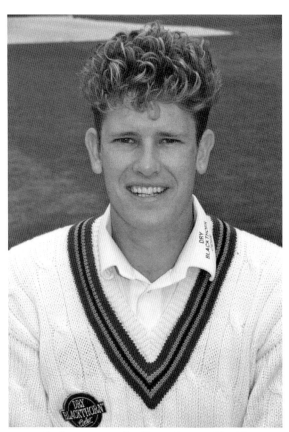

class appearances. Matthew Reed has written of Vince's 'medium paced dobbers which he used, on occasion, to very good effect, as they could wobble alarmingly, as well as being hard to get after'. The same writer has also praised what he describes as 'a masterclass in cool headed composure' when Vince bowled the final over in the 1998 semi-final of the NatWest Trophy, ensuring that Leicestershire fell three runs short of the required total. He was not asked to bowl in the final, which opponents Lancashire won at a canter.

Married to Natasha in 1998, he returned home for good the following year, playing for a number of years for Wanneroo CC again and garnering praise from the Western Australian Cricket Association for his work as a groundsman. Nor were

Vince Clarke – a versatile all-rounder, capable of leg-spin or seam bowling

his green fingers deployed only in preparing wickets. Vince had set up a Gardening and Landscaping business in Perth and, as his work commitment increased, he was obliged to leave Wanneroo CC at the end of the 2006-07 season, with his head held high as the club's leading wicket-taker for the season, just as he had been during Somerset Second XI's march to the Rapid Cricketline title in 1994. He remains in Perth, likely these days to be laying turf rather than extracting turn or movement from it.

552
Paul James Bird
19 May 1994 v. Warwickshire, Taunton

[signature]

Paul Bird suffered a debilitating injury, just when his first-class cricketing career was about to take flight. Statistics can sometimes lie and a return of no wickets taken and 166 runs conceded makes grim reading, but does not convey the true picture. His debut against Warwickshire was noted as the game where Brain Lara was pilloried for taking a call on his mobile phone while fielding in the slips but later redeemed himself with a century in the second innings. Paul takes up the story. 'I was pretty pleased with my bowling in the first innings. I should have had a couple of wickets, when I found the edge of the bat, but in the second, the umpires only kept the game alive because the crowd had come to see Brian Lara bat. The conditions were terrible. The ball was so wet it was like a bar of soap. You could hardly grip it, let alone bowl with it.' Paul gained his revenge in the one-day game against Warwickshire when he bowled Lara in a match that was broadcast live on BBC2.

He played five limited-overs games in 1994 and his other scalps included the then England captain, Mike Atherton. Paul continues, 'I was very pleased with the way things went in the one-day games as I was pretty miserly – only conceding around four runs per over in my five games.' Throughout that 1994 season he had been an integral part of the Second XI's success with thirty-nine wickets.

At the end of the 1994 season, Paul was offered a new two-year contract on the basis of his performances and was informed that he would enjoy a prolonged run in the First XI in 1995. Sadly, he broke down during a pre-season net with a serious shoulder injury. Having been taken to hospital for an exploratory operation, he awoke to be told by the doctor that his career was over. A rotator cuff muscle had been severely damaged and his shoulder would never again be able to bear the strains of bowling on a regular basis. It was the end of a dream for the twenty-three-year-old local boy.

Born in Bristol on 7 May 1971, Paul was the only child of Elizabeth (née Spikes) and Garry, who enjoyed a long career in the tobacco industry. While attending Backwell Comprehensive School, Paul came up through the Somerset age groups but, having begun studying for his A-Levels, was denied time off to play for the Somerset Second XI on a regular basis. He therefore made the decision to leave school and join Lloyds Bank in Bristol, having been given assurances that he would be released to play cricket. At 6 feet 3 inches and a genuinely quick bowler who relied on out-swing combined with a straighter delivery that nipped back off the seam, Paul was by now attracting wider interest with his performances for Optimists CC and was approached

Paul Bird – a promising career was ended prematurely by a serious shoulder injury

by Gloucestershire, who included him in their Under-19 side for two seasons. It was Optimists CC teammate Jeremy Tavaré (brother of Somerset captain, Chris) who informed Somerset that they were in danger of losing out on securing the services of a promising opening bowler. Two winters at the First XI pre-season training at Taunton followed, before Paul was invited to spend time in club cricket in Australia as part of an exchange scheme that had earlier seen future Australian legend Shane Warne come to Bristol. Somerset had now seen enough to make a decision and offered a contract in 1994.

Paul suffered his heart-breaking and career-ending injury ahead of the 1995 season and he was obliged to seek employment outside cricket. Following in the footsteps of his father, Garry, he would spend the next nineteen years of his working life with Imperial Tobacco in various sales and marketing roles. Married in 1999 to Victoria (née Handley), whom he met while she was studying at UWE in Bristol for a degree in Physiotherapy, he would continue to enjoy his club cricket for the likes of Optimists CC, Chippenham CC and Claverham CC. As Paul relates, 'I've had to rest the shoulder between each weekend match and, while it's still often painful to bowl, it certainly helps being married to a physiotherapist!' Their daughter, Alice, is already showing great promise as a cricketer and has represented Somerset at a junior level.

In 2015, Paul purchased a specialist tobacconist's shop from his father. Originally opening its doors in 1930, the retail outlet was one of 250 in Bristol at the time, but is now the last one standing in the city, with customers coming from far and wide. Garry had bought the enterprise after his retirement from Imperial, but felt it was time to sell on to the next generation. Paul now talks with as much knowledge and enthusiasm about cigars or pipes and pipe tobacco as he does about cricket, extolling the various virtues of a Robusto or a Churchill cigar or comparing the merits of a Peterson versus a Parker pipe. To enter the premises of Birds of Baldwin Street, Bristol, is to be transported to another world. To sit back and enjoy a hand-rolled Cuban cigar and reminisce about cricket is a rare treat. Paul Bird's dreams of a first-class career were ended abruptly and cruelly by irreparable damage to his shoulder, but things have turned out well for him.

553
Matthew Dimond
2 June 1994 v. Hampshire, Taunton

Matt Dimond was born in Taunton on 24 September 1975, the son of Roger and Gill (née Horwood). Roger worked as an electrician for the South Western Electricity Board (SWEB) and Gill as a theatre sister at Musgrove Park Hospital in Taunton. Educated at Castle School and Richard Huish College, Matt was selected to play for the England Under-17 side and was introduced to the Somerset Second XI in 1993. Still an eighteen-year-old schoolboy when he was given his first-class debut, he remembers the match at the County Ground with great clarity. In a rain-affected game, a highlight was bagging his first wicket, when he caught and bowled Winston Benjamin. If his first appearance provided quiet satisfaction, then his second generated more excitement. A right-arm bowler of distinctly lively pace, Matt came close to completing a heady hat trick when he had David Byass caught behind by Rob Turner before trapping Bradley Parker LBW for a golden duck. On the following delivery, Michael Vaughan was run out by a direct hit from Mushtaq Ahmed. No hat trick, then, but a few column inches in the newspapers. Matt went on to claim what would prove a career best 4 for 73 in the innings. His future was looking bright.

A successful season with the Somerset Second XI (who won the Rapid Cricketline Championship title that year) was followed by a tour of the West Indies as part of an England Under-19 side captained by Somerset teammate, Marcus Trescothick. Sharing the new ball with Matt on a number of occasions was a young Andrew Flintoff, who in his autobiography *Being Freddie*, in light-hearted vein, lays the blame for his later back problems at the door of the two Somerset players. Freddie writes of the match in Guyana that, 'I had just finished my spell and was wandering towards mid-off as Matthew Dimond ... prepared to start his over. He went back to his mark then just blacked out, so I had to carry on bowling.' Freddie then writes of his later injury woes, 'I blame Marcus Trescothick, our captain in the West Indies, for bowling me into the ground.' The records indeed bear witness to the fact that he bowled rather more overs than his teammates.

Whereas the subsequent careers of Marcus and Freddie blossomed, Matt's stalled, initially because he was laid low by what turned out to be chickenpox, contracted in the Caribbean and then, to add to his woes, he suffered a stress fracture of the back immediately after his recovery from that setback. Thereafter, he never progressed as hoped. Over the course of four seasons, he would make only five first-class appearances, averaging 17.75 with the bat and taking six wickets at 52.66 apiece, be-

Matt Dimond – 'the experience of first-class cricket was a really positive one and the fulfilment of a boyhood dream'
COURTESY OF JOHN LEE

fore his release at the end of the 1997 season. He continued to appear regularly for Somerset Second XI and subsequently for Somerset Cricket Board until the 2002 season, including appearances in the NatWest Trophy. He has subsequently enjoyed success with local club sides Taunton St Andrews CC, Bishops Lydeard CC and finally Staplegrove CC, where he joined forces with another former Somerset pace bowler, Ian Bishop, the pair of them wreaking occasional havoc against local batsmen.

In his early years as a cricketer, Matt worked in the off-season for Shell as a general assistant and then as a sales rep. He has subsequently enjoyed a career in information technology in the health-care sector. For four years, he helped GP practices across the West Country to embed systems, testing software and training staff. Latterly he has taken on responsibility for implementing improvements to information systems for Welsh Assembly Primary Care, project managing and overseeing the delivery of training.

Married in 1999 to Rachel (née Berryman), a legal executive, Matt was later divorced and was married again in 2012 to Sarah (formerly Pelling), an IT consultant. He has two sons – Nathan and Leighton – and two daughters – Lucy and Ruby.

These days, he has finally accepted that his body is no longer able to put up with the rigours of turning out for Staplegrove CC week in and week out and has hung up his boots. Asked about his time at the County Ground, Matt responds that, 'I've fond memories of being in the Somerset side and of my tour to the Caribbean, too, with a number of future Test players.' Does he regret that he never pressed on after promising beginnings? 'I've no regrets at all,' he says. 'The experience of first-class cricket was a really positive one and the fulfilment of a boyhood dream, but I've certainly never missed the limelight or the intensity, the weight of expectation and the pressure to perform that comes with the territory.'

554
Bradleigh Thomas Peter Donelan
9 June 1994 v. Yorkshire, Bradford

B.T. Donel

Brad Donelan was born in Park Royal, Middlesex, on 3 January 1968, the son of Terry and Patricia (née Smith). When asked to describe his father's occupation, Brad is unable to encapsulate it in one word. 'Entertainer, compere, comedian and so on,' he replies. 'He made a name for himself appearing on Hughie Green's *Opportunity Knocks*, doing a stand-up routine and spent the following years doing the clubs until my cricket career took off and he started coming along to watch me, instead.'

Brad was educated at Finchley Catholic High School, where he first took up cricket in a serious way as a thirteen-year-old, but, by the time he had reached school-leaving age, he had developed strongly enough to be invited out to Australia to play for Fairfield CC in Melbourne. He was fortunate enough to have relatives who believed in his ability and an uncle paid for his flight, so that he could spend a season there. Brad also worked a night shift in Sainsbury's to fund this trip and to buy his first car.

'After that, I struggled for a while to land a contract,' Brad reflects. He was then invited to join the Lord's ground staff, where he remained for two-and-a-half years. He went back to Melbourne, this time to play for Northcote CC in the winter of 1987-88. The experience of an Australian summer compared well with his time in the Sainsbury's freezers. In the words of his father, never one to spare any blushes, Brad 'left as a spotty boy and came back a man'. 6 feet 2 inches tall, he had developed into a useful right-arm off-spin bowler and right-handed batsman. Having developed a taste by now for cricket in the Antipodes, he returned the following year to play for Otago B and Southland CC, enjoying some success, in particular with the bat. On coming back to England, he was offered a contract by Sussex and began to establish himself in the Second XI. He would make his first-class debut, the first of fifty-two such matches for the county over five seasons, in July 1989. Continuing to further his cricketing education, he was invited at the recommendation of Jeremy Lloyds to coach in Western Province in the winter of 1990-91. Brad describes it as an exhilarating and memorable time. Nelson Mandela had been released from captivity, there was joy and optimism in the air and the unbridled enthusiasm among the underprivileged youngsters he coached left a lasting impression. Coaching schoolboys and helping them to fulfil their potential would thenceforth become his mission. The man who had once, in his own words, spent time 'in the wilderness' in his youth was determined to give a helping hand where he could.

Released by Sussex at the end of the 1993 season, he came away with a batting av-

Brad Donelan – his zest for the game remains undiminished and his energy considerable

erage of 25.11 and 105 wickets at 43.50 apiece. With his sights set on a career in coaching, he opted to complete an HND in Leisure and Recreational Management at Loughborough College, to add to his coaching badges. This would be a busy time for Brad, who combined his studies with the role of First XI coach for the Men's and Women's sides at Loughborough University, whilst also acting as the cricket professional at Uppingham School, a venerable institution not far from Loughborough, which was just as well, given that Brad had a final year of studies to complete. 'I managed to juggle morning lectures, my work for the school and evening nets at Loughborough for that year,' Brad confirms, 'though I had to rely on fellow students to take notes for me for the afternoon lectures.' Both the Loughborough University teams he coached would become British Universities Champions two years in succession. He also began playing for Warwickshire Second XI, having been invited to do so by their coach, Bob Woolmer, with the promise of possible further first-class cricket. In the match against Somerset Second XI, he had performed well with a tidy eleven overs in which he took 2 for 26 and Peter Robinson duly approached Brad with the offer of a short-term contract for the remainder of the 1994 season. In the event, his first-class career with Somerset would amount to one match in which he scored no runs and took one wicket for a combined 59 runs.

After graduating, he took up a full-time position as the Commercial Manager at Uppingham School and he would remain there until 2003, appearing on a number of occasions for Cambridgeshire in Minor Counties matches. In the interim he was married in 1999 to Amanda (née Slater), now a primary school headmistress, with whom he has two sons, the elder of them, Harry, already demonstrating the skills – as a left-arm orthodox spin bowler and capable batsman – that may lead him to follow in the paternal footsteps.

Between 2005 and 2010, he took up another post as Commercial Manager and Cricket Professional at Birkenhead School in Wirral. In this role, he has helped to generate income by maximising use of the school facilities and has overseen training of the staff to optimise coaching for every age group.

Cheshire has since remained home for Brad and his family and in 2010 he set up his own Action Kids Courses business, offering the chance for young children to develop their skills in an enjoyable environment. He also supports local primary schools to plan and improve the provision of their Physical Education curriculum. Latterly he has set up the Wirral and Cheshire Cricket Academies and acts as a scout for Lancashire CCC.

His zest for the game remains undiminished and his energy considerable. Blessed with the ability to teach and develop his young charges in an engaging way, he has certainly found his niche. Those dark nights filling freezers and wondering if he had a future in the game are distant but not forgotten. Opportunity once knocked for his father and has subsequently been grasped by Brad, too, when his chances arose.

555
Simon Charles Ecclestone
4 August 1994 v. Durham, Taunton

Somerset had to move decisively to secure the services of Simon Ecclestone. They saw in him not only a forceful batsman capable of drawing the crowds and taking games away from opponents, but also a future captain. They had not counted on his dodgy knees putting paid to all their plans and his.

Born on 16 July 1971 in Great Dunmow, a market town in Essex, he was the son of Jonathan and Pippa (née Herring). His brother, Giles, was also a talented cricketer who would play for Cambridgeshire and Essex Second XI. Educated at Bryanston School, Simon won the Cricket Society Wetherell Award, having been deemed the leading all-rounder in schools cricket in 1989. Having come up through the Essex age groups, he would go on to Durham University, where he captained the cricket team and completed a degree in Social Sciences, before enjoying a year as a postgraduate at Keble College, Oxford, where he was awarded a blue in 1994.

Somerset coach Bob Cottam beat a path to Simon's door during the 1994 season, offering him a three-year contract and the longer-term prospect of the captaincy. In 1995, he would only appear in seven first-class matches but made his mark with a batting average of 47.20. Blighted by knee injuries and obliged to stop bowling, he continued to make sporadic appearances, but still managed to compile some ex-

Simon Ecclestone – a forceful batsman capable of drawing the crowds and taking games away from opponents

COURTESY OF SOMERSET COUNTY GAZETTE

hilarating innings. Following centuries in three different limited-overs formats, he struck the first of his three first-class centuries in 1997, an eighty-nine-ball innings of 133 against his alma mater, Oxford University. In thirty-six first-class matches for Somerset, he averaged 36.09 with the bat and took eleven wickets at 40.00 apiece. During the winters, he had played cricket in successive seasons in Australia and South Africa.

6 feet 3 inches tall and a powerfully built left-handed batsman, he was a crowd-pleaser who loved nothing more than putting opposing bowlers to the sword. Historians of the game in Somerset would have reason to compare him to the legendary Herbie Hewett, a similarly punishing left-hander capable of intimidating a bowling attack. Some had perhaps harboured dreams that Simon might similarly have led the team to exceed all expectation, just as 'The Colonel' had done back in 1892 before he had marched off to a career as a barrister – flounced off in high dudgeon , some said – when the Committee had failed to step into line. There was no flouncing when Simon's time at the County Ground came to an end. Just those dodgy knees. 'It was basically a wear and tear injury,' Simon explained at the time. 'I had torn the cartilage a couple of times in the past and gave up bowling [in 1996] because I kept aggravating the injury ... I felt confident about the knee during the 1997 season and that had given me a new lease of life. It was totally out of the blue when I had to give up. Running and twisting was the problem for me and there were two occasions during [my] last season when the injury flared up.' A popular team member, he was given a fine send-off when his teammates arranged a farewell dinner at Canterbury, after the end-of-season fixture with Kent. Journalist Mark Easterbrook would write that, 'In a season of disappointments, there was no greater setback to Somerset ambitions last summer than the retirement through injury of vice-captain, Simon Ecclestone.'

During one off-season, he had helped his cousin, James Ecclestone, to set up quality confectioners Casemir Chocolates (now known as the Grown Up Chocolate Company, supplying their products to proud beacons of excellence such as The Dorchester Hotel and Virgin Atlantic, as well as to outlets of more dubious repute, viz. The Playboy Club and the Houses of Parliament). But on leaving Somerset, Simon was offered employment with the PCA (Professional Cricketers' Association). His brief was to introduce a more robust system for dispensing legal and financial advice to players, helping them to pursue employment or businesses of their own once their cricketing days were over. A further string to his business bow would be the company he set up in 2002 – So Sport Ltd – supplying sport-themed leather goods to premium retailers or as corporate gifts. In the meantime, he had impressed the PCA with his dynamism and was made a director in 1999, the overseeing of the commercial interests of the organisation coming within his ambit. He was also charged with introducing the cricnet website. Grasping the democratic nature of the internet earlier than some, Simon arranged for complimentary laptops to be placed in every county dressing room, with players invited to submit match reports, unleashing the journalist within.

In 2001 he was married to Eliza (née Norman), with whom he has two daughters, Sasha and Rose, and a son, Max. In 2004, he left the PCA for a change of career, becoming a teacher at The Skinners' School in Tunbridge Wells. Here he taught English and Philosophy & Ethics, also coaching the Rugby First XV and Cricket First XI. He would leave the teaching profession in 2012 to return to the PCA as the Personal Development Manager for the South and South East, mentoring players at Middlesex, Kent and Essex. He undertook the work on a part-time basis for two years before handing the reins to David Townsend, brother of former Somerset batsman, Gareth.

Simon was thereafter able to work full-time alongside his wife, Eliza, in the management of their farm and estate near Sevenoaks. He observes that, 'I've always enjoyed forestry and manage over five hundred acres of woodland.' He is also involved in several biomass heating projects and he and his wife have developed a number of commercial and corporate events, using the woods and estate grounds. Added to this he has undertaken what he modestly describes as 'a fair bit of property development'.

Simon has spoken about his premature exit from the first-class game. There is a refreshing honesty about his appraisal that 'I was only just getting going in the game and there was an exciting future ahead of me. I've always tended to be over-optimistic but … I was hoping to achieve quite a bit more … maybe getting into the England one-day squad and maybe captaining Somerset.' He still cherishes the happy memories, though. For a while he rekindled his playing career at club level with Saffron Walden CC and then with Reigate Priory CC, where he joined forces with former university friends and fellow county cricketers James Bovill and Gregor Macmillan, helping the side to win the Surrey Championship repeatedly between 2005 and 2010. Simon was described at the time as 'one of the most exciting batsmen in club cricket'.

'They were a very enjoyable few years,' he says, 'until it took me until Wednesday to walk again after a Saturday match and I had to give up: not a good handicap with a chainsaw in your hands.'

At the time of his retirement from the game the knees might have gone, but his propensity for smiting the ball had remained intact until the last. Latterly, he has started growing cricket bat willow trees on his land, in the hope that they can one day be crafted into bats capable, in the right hands, of punishing bowlers the way he once did.

556
Piran Christopher Laity Holloway
18 August 1994 v. Essex, Weston-super-Mare

Piran Holloway was born on 1 October 1970 in Helston, Cornwall, the son of Chris and Mary (née Laity). Chris was an engineering draughtsman, later going on to become a successful commercial artist, still based in Cornwall. Mary, who worked initially for the County Council, became a headmistress. For those unfamiliar with but interested in the derivation of their son's unusual Christian name, St Piran is said to have become a Fifth Century Cornish hermit after he had allegedly been washed up in Cornwall (a straightforward arrival rarely being the preferred option for early saints). His first acolytes are said to have been 'a badger, a fox and a bear'. The Cornish folk were clearly a harder nut to crack, but St Piran apparently won them over by the miracle of rediscovering the art of smelting tin and becoming the patron saint of tin miners, once prevalent in the area. His flag – a white cross on a black background – is a familiar sight in the region, having been adopted as the flag of Cornwall (or Kernow).

Equipped for life with Christian names derived from his paternal and maternal side and from the ancient history of the county of his birth, Piran was educated at Millfield School for five years before going to Taunton School to study for his A-Levels – in Economics, History and Biology. He would then complete a degree in Sports Science at Loughborough University between the years 1990 and 1994. Although educated in Somerset, he continued to represent Cornwall at youth level, and was selected for the English Schools Under-15s as a left-handed wicket-keeper-batsman. Bob Cottam, working at the time as the National Cricket Association's regional coach for the South West, was an enthusiastic champion during Piran's form-

Piran Holloway – an accomplished wicket-keeper-batsman, born in Cornwall

ative years. Indeed, it was Bob – who had gone on to become Warwickshire's Director of Coaching – who persuaded Piran to try his luck in the first instance with the Midlands county. Here he made his first-class debut in 1988 as a seventeen-year-old, fresh out of the sixth form at Taunton School. Piran has observed that his elevation came so speedily and unexpectedly that, although he was still 'shy, almost introverted' when he arrived at Edgbaston, he was not overawed. 'I hadn't been taken for trials or anything,' he says. 'It was just Bob taking a punt on me ... I didn't really know what was expected of me and so I made mistakes, as you do.' He would go on to play for the England Under-19 team in 1989 and 1990, establishing a burgeoning reputation as a fine wicket-keeper and a sound technician with a bat in hand, described by journalist Paul Bolton as 'a quiet but determined batsman with a hidden confidence'. His maiden first-class century came in 1990. He would play in fourteen first-class fixtures for Warwickshire but, finding a regular place elusive, opted to follow his mentor Bob Cottam down to Taunton.

Piran himself cites the subsequent arrival of former Warwickshire captain, Dermot Reeve, as a turning point. 'Dermot came with a lot of fresh ideas,' he observes. 'It was an enjoyable environment to play cricket in and I prospered.' Encouraged to express himself at the crease, Piran enjoyed a run of form in the late 1990s and scored more freely in limited-overs cricket, but thereafter he found himself spending time in the Second XI. He reacted positively to the new circumstances, good pro that he was, recognising the need to take responsibility when surrounded by less experienced players. This in turn kindled an appetite for coaching, with Piran describing himself as 'a caring coach' whose preferred modus operandi was to 'build a relationship with each player'. After gaining his Level Three coaching badge, he set up his own company in 1997, working with local schools. Having enjoyed winters in Perth playing in grade cricket and coaching, Piran had also been employed in the city teaching leadership skills to businessmen. On parting company with Somerset, he opted to carve out a life for himself in Perth, taking out Australian citizenship. He had made 114 first-class appearances for the county, with a batting average of 31.14, including eight centuries and – more unusually for a wicket-keeper batsman – bowling statistics of no wickets at a cost of 69 runs. He had effected fifty-five dismissals (all caught and none of them stumped).

Having arrived in Perth in 2003 intending to enjoy a career in coaching (and hoping at some point to return to England), he took on additional work selling real estate for APG Homes. He clearly took to the role, remaining with them until 2014, when he left to take up the position of Sales Manager with the Summit Homes Group, also based in Perth. He stayed with them for nearly two years, before taking up senior positions – latterly that of General Manager – with Express Two Storey Living, another Perth-based company specialising in high quality homes that can be constructed rapidly and affordably.

His saintly namesake had (allegedly) been washed up on the shores of Cornwall, but Piran has travelled the globe and made Western Australia his home. The once-shy Cornish lad is now an able and confident spokesman for his company, fortunate enough to indulge during his spare time in his favoured hobby of surfing, beloved of many a resident of, or visitor to, the county of his birth, though there is rather more in the way of sunshine and less in the way of rain in Perth.

1995

"Without his [injured] strike bowlers, Hayhurst had to lean even more heavily on the willing Mushtaq. The little leg-spinner toiled away, often on unhelpful wickets, yet remained eager to grab the ball at every opportunity."

Richard Latham

Championship Position: 9 of 18

Peter Bowler, a batsman, and Jeremy Batty, a bowler, had both arrived, though Bowler the batsman would have a more lasting influence on the club's fortunes, taking over in due course as captain. His impact was immediate, too, with a total of 1,619 runs, including six centuries, in his first season with Somerset. There was valuable support from Richard Harden, whose 1,429 runs included five centuries. Piran Holloway enjoyed a number of productive innings, too. Although Mark Lathwell amassed 1,000 runs, the joyful abandon was less in evidence. Marcus Trescothick suffered a poor season, with technical faults needing to be ironed out if he was to fulfil his rich potential. Had the sky-high hopes for the Lathwell-Trescothick opening partnership been over-egged?

Mushtaq Ahmed gave the lie to the old joke about Somerset that 'they toil not, neither do they spin'*. He was the pick of the bowlers, completing a gruelling 952 overs and taking ninety-five wickets. Needing only five more in the final match of the season to reach the milestone of a hundred, he was struck down by a virus and unable to play. With Andy Caddick only available for six first-class matches and Andre van Troost for seven, it was left to Harvey Trump (developing his skills as he learned from Mushtaq) and Graham Rose to offer support.

There was a flurry of excitement as the team hit a rich vein of form in June and a further raising of hopes and heart rates as Somerset advanced to the semi-finals of the Benson & Hedges Cup, but consistency once again proved elusive.

* For those unfamiliar with the Authorised Version of *The Bible*, the text runs: 'Consider the lilies of the field, how they grow; they toil not, neither do they spin.'

557
Peter Duncan Bowler
27 April 1995 v. Glamorgan, Taunton

Known to teammates as 'Tom', following a quip from coach Bob Cottam that he had won 'Tom Bowler' in a raffle, Peter had come to Somerset in 1995 already a seasoned campaigner and successful run-maker. He was born on 30 July 1963 in Plymouth, Devon, his father, Peter, at the time a member of the Australian Navy and his mother, Etta (née MacGregor), a Scot. Brought up in Australia, he would adopt the hard-edged desire to win instilled in their sportsmen. Educated at Scots College in Sydney and Daramalan College in Canberra, he impressed with his batting exploits as a youngster and made his debut in Grade cricket at fourteen before going on to represent Australia Under-19s, whom he then captained the following season. Opting for a more challenging environment, he then enjoyed spells with Manly CC and Northern Districts CC before trying his luck in England with Leicestershire, with whom he graduated to the first-class cricket arena in 1986. Here he made a dream start, scoring a century on debut. He returned to Australia, enduring a brief and unsuccessful spell with Tasmania before joining Derbyshire in 1988 and once again scoring a century on debut, heralding the first of ten English summers in which he would exceed 1,000 runs. Batting in a correct, uncomplicated way, he accumulated runs consistently, becoming the first man to reach 2,000 runs in the 1992 season. He continued to impress, his wicket never yielded lightly, unruffled when the ball passed the bat, going through his routine, later described by Somerset Chief Executive Peter Anderson as 'elbows out, tapping down an imagined divot, a dismissive look at the bowler and back to the crease'.

While with Derbyshire, he gained a taste of life on the other side of the tracks when he worked for a while on BBC Local Radio reporting, among other matters, on the fortunes of Derby County, during the winter. Writer and broadcaster Pat Murphy would describe Peter as 'one of the most articulate and interesting talkers ... in the English game'. Another BBC employee clearly impressed by the part-timer was Joanne (née Hunt), whom he was married to in 1992 and with whom he has three children - Robert, Rebekah and Matthew.

Peter parted company with Derbyshire in 1994 as he sought a fresh start. Somerset had recruited a fine asset, able to add ballast to their batting. During the 1996 season, he was the obvious candidate to stand in when Andy Hayhurst was relieved of the captaincy, following the Lancastrian's loss of form. Over the following two seasons in which he was official club captain, Peter was beset with back problems that hindered his performance to such a degree that he was obliged to undergo an operation in the winter of 1998-99. Having handed over the captaincy to Jamie Cox, he bounced back at the age of thirty-five with his desire to win and hunger for runs as strong as it had ever been. He continued in the same vein until leaving on a high at the end of the 2004 season having amassed 1,000 runs for the tenth time and averaged a fraction under fifty that year. He remained a gritty competitor to the last, reprimanded by the ECB after an altercation with Shane Warne, a man not noted for his emollience, who was also penalised for his conduct. At the time of his departure, by then forty-one, Peter was the oldest man playing county

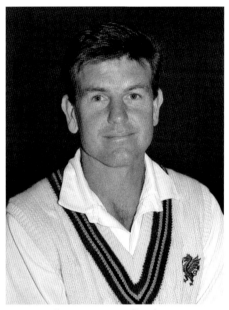

Peter Bowler – an outstanding batsman, consistently among the runs over a long and distinguished career

cricket. With 160 first-class matches for Somerset, his batting average was 41.38 and his occasional off-spin yielded fourteen wickets at 38.57 apiece.

Preparing for life after the death of his playing career, he had completed a degree in Law at Nottingham Trent University, fitted it around his cricketing commitments, and then went on to undertake a Legal Practice Course at the same institution. He began work as a solicitor with Clarke Willmott, a company with a long association with Somerset cricket, before joining Foot Anstey, a law firm with a strong presence across the West Country. In 2007 his career took on a new trajectory when he founded Grenfell Ltd, a company involved in the development and selling of real estate, since dissolved. Having then gained his Chartered Insurance Institute qualification, he founded Ambro Finance Ltd, based near Taunton. The West Country might only fleetingly have been his home as a child, but he has set down roots there in adulthood.

Peter also offers his services as an engaging after-dinner speaker, recalling his encounters as a first-class cricketer with self-effacing humour. His observation concerning his low-risk approach to batsmanship serves as an example of this. In Peter's words, 'I was the greatest generator of income for clubs, greater than Flintoff, Botham and the rest. Whenever I went out to bat, the stands emptied and bars and restaurants were filled to capacity.'

Over the course of his career, he had garnered respect across the county circuit and had performed consistently for nearly two decades, amassing almost 20,000 first-class runs and forty-five centuries and demonstrating his ability as a limited-overs player, appearing in five Lord's finals, twice as a winner. The absence of an England cap, particularly when he hit his purple patch at Derbyshire in 1992, remains a mystery. Here was one of the unsung heroes of the game. Draw up a template of the ideal professional cricketer, the man for all seasons, and you have described Peter Bowler to a tee.

558
Jeremy David Batty
1 June 1995 v. Yorkshire, Taunton

A likeable Yorkshireman, known to friends and teammates as Jez, Jeremy Batty was born on 15 May 1971 in Bradford, the son of David and Rosemary (Née Evans). His father coached at the Yorkshire Academy and played cricket for many years in the Bradford League. David and Rosemary owned a sports shop named D & R Sports. Sited in Bradford, it was run in the main by Jeremy's mother. An aptitude for the game ran in the family, with Jeremy's younger brother, Gareth – a combative cricketer and never one to shy away from a confrontation – enjoying a successful career with Yorkshire, Worcestershire, Surrey (whom he captained) and England. Jeremy recalls with a wry smile that, with a seven-year age gap between the siblings, he graciously allowed his younger brother to win whenever they played the game together in those early days. Educated at Bingley Grammar School, he then went on to take a BTEC course in Leisure Studies at Horsforth College. A right-arm off-spinner, he was taken on by Yorkshire and would endear himself to locals when he made his first-class debut as an eighteen-year-old against fierce rivals, Lancashire. His impact was immediate. A return of 3 for 75 in the first innings was followed by 5 for 118 in the second. The future looked bright for the teenager, more so when he was selected in 1990 to play for England Under-19s against their Australian counterparts. He would prove a useful member of the side at Yorkshire, making sixty-four first-class appearances and taking 140 wickets for his native county. He had also enjoyed a number of winters between 1989-90 and 1994-95 as a pro in Zimbabwe and then South Africa.

Having been released by Yorkshire, he was offered a contract by Somerset ahead of the 1995 season, having previously impressed Somerset's Bob Cottam in claiming two five-wicket hauls in Yorkshire Second XI's away fixture against Somerset

Second XI (at North Perrott) in 1994. In his first year at the County Ground, he was given only four first-class outings but was by some considerable distance the most successful wicket-taker for the Second XI. Jeremy admits to frustration at having few opportunities for Championship cricket in his first season, but in 1996, with Mushtaq Ahmed unavailable, he was selected on a more regular basis. His wickets proved too expensive for the club's taste, though. Released at the end of his second season with Somerset, he had appeared in twenty first-class fixtures for them, taking thirty-nine wickets at 55.25 apiece and averaging 17.84 with the bat.

He had been married in 1996 to Liz (née Lawrence), a graphic designer, now sadly deceased. Having left Somerset, he was offered employment by Royal and Sun Alliance, with whom he enjoyed a four-year stint offering healthcare insur-

Jeremy Batty – his first-class career began in a blaze of glory, when he took five Lancashire wickets for Yorkshire as an eighteen-year-old
COURTESY OF JOHN LEE

ance to clients. His employers were happy for him to share his services while he plied his trade as a cricketing pro. Signed by Middleton CC in the Central Lancashire League, Jeremy remained with them for two seasons before being taken on by a variety of clubs in the Bradford League. He has subsequently continued to play club cricket wherever his work has taken him and has the distinction of having played for three Minor Counties – Cheshire, Shropshire and Buckinghamshire. For a while, he branched out into events management, but in 2010 he returned to the field of private healthcare cover, as a consultant with Independent Healthcare Solutions. His next moves were to the role of business development manager with Consilium Employee Benefits and then with Chase Templeton. At the time of writing, he is employed by Chartwell Healthcare Ltd, based in Oxfordshire with his second wife, Sabina (formerly Malik), a successful businesswoman, with whom he has three sons, one of them from Sabina's previous marriage.

Looking back at his two years with Somerset, Jeremy recalls: 'They were enjoyable times. I thought the atmosphere was great – a lovely club and friendly support staff everywhere.' Kind words from a personable man.

1996

"I want you to go into the dressing-room and tell Hayhurst
he's dropped, bring in Marcus Trescothick in his place and
ask Peter Bowler to take over the captaincy ... Sod the press.
I'm Chairman of the Cricket Committee. It's my decision.
I'll take full responsibility."

Brain Rose to Peter Anderson (quoted in Coming Back to Me*)*

Championship Position: 11 of 18

Ensconced once more, now as Chairman of the Cricket Committee, Brian Rose
moved with brutal decisiveness to strip an out-of-form Andy Hayhurst of the
captaincy (handing it to Peter Bowler) and put his faith in the young Marcus Trescothick, whom he felt represented the future of Somerset cricket. Marcus notched up
a score of 178. Fortune had favoured the bold. It was a sad and ignominious end to
Andy Hayhurst's reign as skipper.

With Mushtaq away on international duty, the county called on the services of
Australian all-rounder, Shane Lee. His quick bowling was useful (with forty first-
class wickets and twenty-five in the AXA Equity & Law League) but his batting was
a revelation, with 1,300 first-class runs and five centuries. Peter Bowler, sure and
steady as ever, and Mark Lathwell, showing flashes of his former brilliance, were also
among the runs. The bulk of the wickets fell to the pace attack of Andy Caddick and
Graham Rose.

A middling position in the County Championship did little to excite supporters,
but fifth equal in the Sunday League was creditable. It should be noted in defence of
the outgoing captain, Andy Hayhurst, that he topped both the batting and bowling
averages in that format. He had reasons to feel hard done by.

Among the debutants were Shane Lee (see above) and Kevin Shine. Shane shone,
while Kevin would make useful contributions as a quick bowler and later as a coach.

559
Shane Lee
2 May 1996 v. Surrey, Taunton

[signature]

His younger brother, Brett, enjoyed global fame as one of the fastest bowlers of his generation, his image familiar to many, even among the non-cricketing community, when he lowered his head in despair after failing by two runs to guide Australia to victory during the 2005 Ashes series, Andrew Flintoff offering words of comfort to a respected foe. Shane, like his brother, was capable with bat and ball in his hand. More strongly built and less pacey than Brett, he nevertheless proved a useful all-rounder who appeared in forty-five One Day Internationals for Australia.

Born in Wollongong, New South Wales, on 8 August 1973, Shane was the son of Robert (Bob) and Helen Lee. Bob was a qualified metallurgist employed at the BHP steel works. Educated at Oak Flats Senior High School, Shane would go on to study for a degree in Psychology & Marketing at Wollongong University. Selected for the Australian Under-19 side, he was offered a full-time scholarship at the Australian Cricket Academy, but declined it, opting instead to attend on a part-time basis and to complete his degree concurrently. Having broken into the New South Wales team in the 1993-94 season, he was a member of the team who won the Sheffield Shield Final at a canter, against Tasmania, although his contribution – no wickets and a duck – was not his finest. By 1995, he had been elevated to the national limited-overs team and he was therefore an established all-rounder by the time he joined Somerset for a season in 1996, as a short-term replacement for Mushtaq Ahmed. Heavily-built and a powerful hitter, whereas his bowling had met expectations, his batting far exceeded Somerset's hopes. Over the course of seventeen first-class appearances he would score 1,300 runs at an average of 61.90, with five centuries to his name, his 167 not out at Bath having been a particular treat for spectators. He also took forty-eight wickets at 25.93 apiece

Shane had developed a taste for cricket in England and the following year he was offered a contract with Enfield CC, in Lancashire League cricket. There were press reports – incorrect as it happened – of an off-the-field fracas, which puckered into the odd headline before it blew over. Shane pointed out with his usual Aussie directness that, 'I play the game hard, I have a beer and I'll have a chat to anyone after the game – that's how Australians play the game of cricket.'

He would enjoy one last brief hurrah in England with Worcestershire in 2002,

Shane Lee – his batting far exceeded Somerset's hopes COURTESY OF JOHN LEE

before, at the age of twenty-nine, his career was cut short by knee injuries. Shane and brother Brett had formed a rock band named *Six & Out* in 2000. There were five members in total, their name derived from the old playground rule designed to discourage sixes. The group were all New South Wales players and, listening to their output, this was perhaps a more important criterion than musicality. In settling for a career in cricket rather than the music industry, they had all chosen well. Shane's career as a businessman has been, on the whole, more successful, though not entirely free of mishap.

In 1998, he had set up a company named Sporting Frontiers, coordinating events and in-ground signage on behalf of clients. In 2000, he became co-founder of the Insite Organisation, a marketing and communications agency with wider ambitions than his first foray into the marketing arena. The company covered everything from media buying to public relations and event management. Shane continued to develop the business until it was sold in 2010. During that period, he had cause to regret a different investment decision. Having been introduced in 2003 to a property developer named Kovelan Bangaru, Shane and fellow cricketers (and band members) Michael Bevan and Brett were persuaded to invest sizeable sums of money in a company named Streetwise Administration. Streetwise they were not, as the company soon headed towards administration while Kovelan Bangaru enjoyed a lavish lifestyle at his investors' expense. They were forced to go to court in an attempt to retrieve the money.

Latterly, he has enjoyed spells as a Senior Business Development Manager with Sportingbet Australia and as a Director of the Marylebone Capital Corporation (MCC), an investment vehicle with a particular focus on India. At the time of writing, he is a commercial director with Isentia, a company focussed on providing insights for companies through their data analysis.

Asked the secret of success in life, Shane's response is, 'Believe in yourself, work hard and enjoy the moment.' An Aussie through and through, then.

560
Kevin James Shine
2 May 1996 v. Surrey, Taunton

[signature]

Born on 22 February 1969 in Bracknell, Berkshire, Kevin Shine was the son of Joe and Clair (née Sheehan). Educated at Maiden Erlegh Comprehensive School in Reading, he demonstrated from a young age more interest in the art and science of bowling than he did in the traditional curriculum, opting to leave school at sixteen and follow his dream of becoming a first-class cricketer. Establishing his reputation as a pace bowler with Reading CC, he was given a trial by Derbyshire Second XI in 1985 but it was Hampshire who offered him a contract the following year. For two seasons he appeared for their Second XI whilst also playing for Berkshire, before, in 1989, he was granted his debut against Middlesex at Lord's, performing creditably and having the satisfaction of bowling Mike Gatting. He remained with Hampshire until the end of the 1993 season, playing fifty-four first-class matches for them and enjoying the occasional devastating spell, most notably his 8 for 47 against Lancashire in 1992. He then joined Middlesex, where his time was short-lived and dogged by a serious injury, Kevin noting wryly that he was told that his services were no longer required four days before an operation to remove a bone spur 'the size of an acorn' from his left ankle. He had played through the pain during the latter part of the season but perhaps wondered if his sacrifice had been worth it. Some remodelling of his action was required but Somerset, needing to strengthen their pace attack, snapped him up. He would play for them in thirty-three first-class matches and take ninety-four wickets at 33.01 apiece, his best spell again coming against Lancashire, this time at Taunton in 1997. Never anything other than a tail-ender, he mustered an average of 9.00 with the bat.

Having left Somerset in 1998 – in his words 'forced to retire at the age of twenty-nine through injury' – he was married later that year to Bethan (née Edwards). Earlier in his career, Kevin had jointly written a weekly column for the *Reading Chronicle* with footballer Jason Harris and had also been employed during the winter breaks by Orico Systems, a computer software and engineering company. His ambition remained to become a successful coach and, as well as a spell as Director of Coaching for the Berkshire Indoor Cricket Centre (combined with playing once more for the county of his birth), he also worked as a weight-training instructor and then leisure centre manager for Neal Training, a company headed by John Neal, who retains links with the cricketing fraternity and has long been a proponent of a holistic approach to

fitness and coaching, incorporating an understanding of physiology and diet, allied to technique. It is an approach shared by Kevin, who describes John as his 'great friend and mentor'. Having honed his craft, Kevin returned to the fold at Somerset in December 2000, taking up the position of Head Coach. His planning was precise and the regime strict, with routines mapped out to the minute and no stone left unturned. At the end of the 2004 season, the club announced that he had been given the newly-created post of Director of Development, although that appointment proved short-lived when – to the surprise of many and ahead of some well-known names – he was offered the job of bowling coach to the England squad.

Kevin Shine – a quick bowler who has turned successfully to coaching

His meticulous approach had trumped the celebrity status of other candidates. In a reprise of his changing circumstances at Somerset, he was then, after two years, replaced by Allan Donald and offered a role overseeing the development of up-and-coming fast bowlers at the National Cricket Performance Centre at Loughborough. Working closely with Loughborough University, Kevin and the team have been at the forefront of utilising technology to understand the biomechanics of bowling, seeking to find ways of maximising a bowler's speed while reducing stress on the body and the risk of the sort of injuries that had cursed his own career and that of many of his contemporaries. Fast bowling will always place unnatural strains on the body, but as Kevin works with academics and technicians to improve matters, he ruminates sometimes on his own career as a self-coached paceman, blessed with the physique and athleticism needed to be effective and on occasions proving unplayable, but blighted too often by injury.

561
Ian Emlyn Bishop
3 July 1996 v. Pakistan, Taunton

Ian Bishop was born in Taunton on 26 August 1977, the son of Brian, an accountant who worked in the area for a variety of companies, including Debenhams, and who was married to Jane (née Pooke), a dental nurse. Educated at Castle School in Taunton, Ian represented Somerset at Under-14 level but thereafter went under the radar. Having gone on to the Somerset College of Art & Technology (SCAT), he studied Leisure and Tourism together with Physical Education. 'I had a notion that I wanted to get involved in sport, one way or another, but I was happy playing club cricket for Staplegrove at that stage,' Ian confirms. 'I'd not had any coaching. I suppose people would have described me as having raw talent. It was actually my college tutor who got in touch with Peter Robinson and told him he had a young quick bowler he and Bob Cottam should look at.' Ian was duly taken on for the summer before being then offered a one-year contract for the following season. The future looked promising, but after a change of regime, the tide turned. Determined to take up his role as the alpha male at the County Ground, Dermot Reeve's first words to Ian were a curt, 'Get a haircut.' Not even a greeting. Nor was there any attempt to help Ian to develop his bowling technique. 'I think it's fair to say he made his mind up without knowing much about me,' Ian says. 'He didn't even bother to find out that I'd been the leading wicket-taker for the Second XI in 1996.' Selected for a handful of Second XI matches during the 1997 season, Ian was called into the office in July of that year and told he was being released. He had appeared in one first-class match and come away with no wickets for 29 runs in his seven overs and two runs with the bat in each of his two innings.

His desire to play first-class cricket had not been crushed, though, as he dusted himself down and tried to establish himself once more. Initially playing for Staplegrove CC on Saturdays and as a pro for Sidmouth CC in Devon each Sunday, he became a member of the successful Devon side led by Peter Roebuck. 'Roeby was tremendous,' Ian says. 'He really encouraged me and helped me.' Ian then had a second opportunity at first-class level after a chance meeting that led to a trial with Surrey in the Second XI. A contract followed in 1999, with Ian also appearing for a strong Sunbury CC side at club level. That winter, he enjoyed a one-season contract with Wanneroo CC in Perth, Australia. 'The coaching at Surrey was more focussed than it had been at Somerset,' Ian confirms, 'with Alan Butcher helping me to iron

Ian Bishop – would knock at the door of the First XI, without ever quite establishing a regular place

out a few things with my delivery.' For two seasons, Ian would knock at the door of the First XI, without ever quite establishing a regular place.

Subsequently offered the chance to join Sussex, he would decline, although he now says that, 'With hindsight, I should have gone there.' Instead, he returned to Devon as a pro at Bovey Tracey CC, continuing to be selected for Devon. There then followed a spell with West Bromwich Dartmouth CC in the Midlands, a second spell at Bovey Tracey CC and then Callington CC in Cornwall. By then somewhat of a cricketing rover, he enjoyed spells as the pro at Budleigh Salterton CC in Devon and Bridgwater CC in Somerset.

Having been married in 2004 to Jennifer (née Derrick), a medical rep, he has four children, including twins. Ready to settle down and enjoy bringing up his family, he returned once more to his roots and played for Staplegrove CC, no longer a pro, but deriving great pleasure from coaching young players, including his own children. He hopes to pursue more coaching opportunities in the future.

Ian has worked briefly for Devondale Electrical and for a more prolonged period in sales for Howdens Joinery, an Ilminster-based kitchen fitting company. Latterly, he has embraced further changes. Recently divorced, he has at the time of writing commenced a new role as a showroom manager for Total Plumbing, a business with outlets across the West Country offering plumbing products to the trade and the public alike.

Asked – admittedly on a bright, sunny day – whether or not he misses the first-class game, notwithstanding the trials and tribulations he had to endure, Ian replies: 'Definitely on a beautiful day like this. It's hard to beat playing in the County Championship and I've always been a bit of a restless sort when it comes to cricket, preferring to play rather than watch.' There are compensations with life in Taunton. A new job, his family, helping to develop the young players at Staplegrove and the regular starring roles as he rips through opposing teams, still generating a fair bit of zip and movement, even in his forties.

1997

"Success is never final, failure is never fatal
and courage is all that matters."

Dermot Reeve

Championship Position: 12 of 18

Dermot Reeve was appointed to oversee coaching and instil a winning mentality into the squad. His uncompromising focus on fitness, diet and an intense sense of purpose was welcomed by some but not all. Despite Dermot's best efforts, the team appeared to tread water. Maybe they were treading water more frantically than had previously been the case. Writing in the *Somerset Year Book*, Richard Latham would concede that: 'Perhaps we expected a magic wand from Reeve.'

Only Rob Turner exceeded 1,000 runs, but Simon Ecclestone was not far off that mark in his thirteen appearances. The loss through a broken finger of Richard Harden, the rock around whom (or which) many a Somerset innings was built, was a blow. Graham Rose was the stand-out performer, averaging over fifty with the bat and topping the bowling averages. He took sixty-three wickets, while Andy Caddick (despite his limited appearances), Kevin Shine and Mushtaq Ahmed (also unavailable for some fixtures) all claimed fifty or more victims.

Among the new arrivals were Mike Burns and Steffan Jones, both of whom would play their hearts out for the county. Luke Sutton, too, would enjoy a successful first-class career, although the presence of Rob Turner, who filled the wicket-keeper-batsman role with distinction, would mean that he would feel obliged to leave the county of his birth and fulfil his early promise elsewhere. A cameo appearance by Stuart MacGill, a world class leg-break bowler, forms no more than a footnote in the annals of Somerset cricketing history.

562
Michael Burns
23 April 1997 v. Surrey, Kennington Oval

Mike Burns has always been comfortable with the notion of hard graft. Born on 6 February 1969 in Barrow-in-Furness, he was educated at Walney Comprehensive and Barrow College of Further Education, serving an apprenticeship in the dockyards as a fitter with the Vickers shipbuilding company. His route to first-class cricket would combine serendipity – being in the right place at the right time – with gritty application. A tough competitor, he was also a rugby league player, good enough to be offered trials with Barrow RLFC and Carlisle RLFC.

He cut his cricketing teeth as a wicket-keeper and forceful middle-order batsman with local side Vickerstown CC and would be invited to play for Cumberland. He is described by one of his club teammates from that time as 'a great character in the dressing room with a great sense of humour'. It is an epithet that would ring true throughout his career. Mike was offered a trial with Glamorgan Second XI in 1990, but it failed to lead to a contract. He plied his trade instead with Netherfield CC in Kendal, having been recommended to them by a former Vickerstown teammate. In one particular match, after the loss of their pro – Rod Tucker, who later became an Elite Panel umpire – Netherfield CC called on the services of Dermot Reeve, by then with Warwickshire. He and Mike guided the side to victory with an unbroken stand in which they both registered half-centuries. Recognising in Mike a will to win and the determination to extract every ounce of potential that was true of his own approach, Dermot immediately recommended that Mike be invited to Edgbaston. His trial proved a success and Bob Cottam, Warwickshire's coach at that time, offered a contract. Mike would remain with Warwickshire until 1996, deployed as the back-up wicket-keeper-batsman to Keith Piper, standing in on those occasions when Keith was injured.

During the winters, he plied his trade as a club pro in South Africa, Zimbabwe and New Zealand. He remained connected to his Cumbrian roots, working when he could for the family grocery business back home, run by his mother and his stepfather, Stan. He was married in Barrow in 1994 to Carolyn (née Gooster), with whom he has a daughter and son. Carolyn was the organiser of Dermot Reeve's Benefit Year at Warwickshire.

Hungry for regular first-team cricket, he responded with alacrity when Dermot

Mike Burns – a down-to-earth, unaffected and wholehearted cricketer, who served Somerset well

suggested a move to the South West, after having been made Director of Cricket at Somerset. Seeing in Mike a trusted lieutenant who would be good for team morale but recognising that Rob Turner was an automatic choice for the wicket-keeping berth, Dermot persuaded his protégé to reinvent himself as a specialist middle-order batsman and medium-paced seam bowler, with a natural away-swing from right-handers. He became an important member of the side and cites the arrival of Jamie Cox as an important part of his continued development. Informed by the Tasmanian that he was seen as an integral part of any success, Mike responded by taking on a greater weight of responsibility. Throughout his career, his tendency for self-effacement had led him to underestimate his worth. In conversation with journalist Steve Jennings, Mike would later confess that: 'In a way, I was a better player than I thought I was. I was just happy to be there but never thought I could make a difference…It took me a while to realise I was there on merit. I wish I'd had more belief.'

He would be made vice-captain under Jamie Cox (who encouraged Mike to enjoy a winter as a pro with Lindisfarne CC in Tasmania). Thereafter, he was appointed captain for two years until the arrival of Graeme Smith in 2005. It was a daunting step up from dressing room joker to leader, but despite some setbacks (in part explained by an extensive squad injury list) he grew into the role and was awarded a Benefit Year in 2005, though that season – to his surprise and disappointment – was his last. Over the course of 134 first-class appearances for Somerset he would score more than 7,000 runs at an average 34.69, including eight centuries, his highest score being 221 at Bath. His sixty-eight wickets came at 42.11 apiece and he also made occasional cameo appearances behind the stumps.

He had been an active member of the club in the winters, too, helping out with the construction and painting and decorating of the Sir Ian Botham stand and involved in an administrative capacity in the office (before he handed the reins to Ian Blackwell). Mike Burns has always been prepared to roll up his sleeves and get on with any job. On retiring as a first-class player, he has continued to live in Somerset and played for four years for Taunton St Andrews CC while also appearing for his native Cumberland, before throwing in his lot with Cornwall. He worked for a period selling outdoor equipment and sportswear for North Gear and Bradbury, but admits that times were tough financially while he trained for his true chosen vocation – that of umpiring. As with his playing career, he set out with humble beginnings, attending an umpiring course at Weston-super-Mare, run by the Somerset Cricket Board. He joined the Reserve List in 2012, although in his maiden first-class fixture as umpire, when he stood with Jeremy Lloyds, Somerset hosted Cardiff University and his services were rarely called on as Nick Compton and James Hildreth piled on a combined total in excess of 500 runs. He was finally promoted to the First-Class Umpires List in December 2016. His future now looks assured. The boy from Barrow has done well for himself.

Down to earth, unaffected and wholehearted, here is someone, in the words of writer David Foot, with a 'sense of perspective', the writer adding that, 'when morale was low, he told [teammates], in effect, that they were lucky to be in employment'. Every side should have such a man to keep his colleagues grounded during times of success, or motivated when the going gets tough.

563
Steven Herzberg
23 April 1997 v. Surrey, Kennington Oval

Born on 1967 in Carshalton, Surrey, Steve Herzberg was the second son of Louis and Brenda (née Shaw). When Steve was nine years old, the family emigrated to Australia where Louis took up a post as a hospital consultant and a university lecturer in Neurology. Steve attended the Hollywood Senior High School in Perth before going on to Curtin University, also based in the city that by then he called home. Here he gained a degree in Business, specialising in Marketing, which has subsequently stood him in good stead. A business career would have to wait, though, while he tried his hand at first-class cricket for a number of seasons. In Australia he would play grade cricket for a number of teams, with spells in Perth, North Hobart and Sydney, before he was appointed captain of Subiaco-Floreat CC in his home city in 1995-96. He had played Sheffield Shield cricket both for Western Australia and Tasmania.

A tall right-arm bowler at 6 feet 4 inches and a competent batsman, he was, in the words of writer David Foot, 'a lofty off-spinner who relied on bounce rather than turn'. Never quite able, throughout his career, to command a long run in any County Championship side, his initial spell in England was with Worcestershire where he remained for three seasons from 1990 until 1992, without ever making a first-class appearance but becoming a useful member of the Second XI. His next spell in England was not until 1995, when he spent one season with Kent, appearing in only a handful of Championship fixtures. He returned to the country of his birth in 1997 for one season with Somerset and once again endured the frustration of never holding down a regular first team place. His debut was somewhat of a triumph, when he scored 56 with the bat and accounted for both Surrey openers when brought on, his 2 for 25 including a wicket on his first delivery, although Steve is the first to admit he was fortunate, having served up a gentle full toss that was patted back tamely to him by Darren Bicknell. Over the course of the season, he would take ten wickets at 28.10 apiece and in eight innings (including three not outs) registered an impressive batting average of 41.40.

Steve Herzberg is that rare beast, a Jewish first-class cricketer. He played for an Australian XI at the Maccabiah Games – modelled on the Olympics and open to Jewish athletes from around the globe – in 1989 and 1993, captaining the team in the latter and leading them to the Gold Medal. He would go on to coach in Israel for two years after his departure from Somerset and coached the Israeli national side at

Steve Herzberg – 'a lofty off-spinner who relied on bounce rather than turn'
COURTESY OF JOHN LEE

the ICC Trophy in 1997. In 2008, at the age of forty-one, he played for an Israeli side against India, the team having been brought together to celebrate the sixtieth anniversary of the founding of the state of Israel.

Steve's first significant involvement in the world of business had been in sales, as a Territory Manager for Cadbury Schweppes between 1994 and 1996. Following his period as a cricket coach, he ventured back into the business world once more, combining the knowledge gleaned from his degree with hands-on coaching experience in bringing the best out of his charges. In 2005 he set up a consultancy, NRG Solutions, alongside his wife and mother of his three children, Michaela, who had spent her working life in marketing in one guise or another. As Managing Director of Sydney-based NRG, Steve has worked as a consultant for a number of significant companies across Australasia and Thailand, mentoring them in presentation skills, sales training and leadership development. He has latterly taken on the additional role of Director of Business Development at Blake eLearning, a company whose goal is to improve literacy through innovative and engaging solutions.

If his first-class career never quite gained traction as he had hoped, the same could hardly be said of his successful business career.

564
Richard William Sladdin
28 June 1997 v. Oxford University, Taunton

Richard Sladdin was born in Halifax on 8 January 1969. His father, Raymond, was married to Elsie (née Swinbank) and Richard was one of three siblings. Educated at Sowerby Bridge High School, he began training to become an accountant before

opting instead for a life as a professional cricketer. As a youngster, he had
played for the now-defunct Mytholmroyd Methodists CC, alongside his elder
brother, Nigel, who would years later, in
2004, endure the calamity of witnessing the club's pavilion being reduced
to ashes during his tenure as Chairman.
A reinvented Mytholmroyd CC side
rose like a phoenix and the team were
delighted to welcome Richard back into
the fold in 2015. Sadly, his reputation
was about to go the way of the old 'Mytholmroyd Meths' pavilion.

A left-arm orthodox spin bowler,
he was selected at eighteen and again
the following year to play for the English Cricket Schools Association and
was subsequently given an airing with
Leicestershire Second XI before being
offered professional terms by Derbyshire, for whom he made his first-class

*Richard Sladdin – a left-arm orthodox spin
bowler who claimed six wickets in his only
first-class appearance for Somerset*
COURTESY OF JOHN LEE

debut in 1991. One of a group of highly-regarded newcomers to the side, he drew
praise from his captain, Kim Barnett, who had been impressed from the outset. Chris
Adams, writing in his autobiography *Grizzly*, recounts that Richard 'arrived on trial
from Yorkshire and bowled Kim out twice in an old, much-used net that was turning
square. That made Kim's mind up. Sladdin was taken on.' In the event, his progress
was hampered by the county's preference for seam-friendly wickets that blunted his
effectiveness. He had the misfortune to encounter Graeme Hick on a benign track in
1993 and returned the dismal figures of 1 for 203, the runs having been plundered at
an average of five per over. If this was a blow to his self-confidence, then his 0 for 190
the following season against Durham gave the remnants of his belief in his powers a
further mauling. At the time of writing, it remains the worst recorded return for a
Derbyshire bowler. In mitigation, the strip is described in one source as resembling
'a motorway rather than a cricket wicket'. Derbyshire and Richard bade farewell to
one another at the end of the 1994 season and it seemed that a career in league cricket beckoned. He had by then gained additional experience in the winter months
engaged as a pro and coach for a season in New Zealand and subsequently at Mitchell's Plain CC in Cape Town.

Unexpectedly, he received the call from Somerset in 1997. His former Derbyshire teammate, Peter Bowler, was by then ensconced as Somerset's captain and was no doubt hoping that Richard would fulfil some of that early promise. As it transpired, he played on three occasions for the Second XI and in only one first-class fixture, against Oxford University. With a creditable return of 5 for 60 in the second innings, he came away with six wickets for Somerset at 17.50 apiece. He did not bat in the match.

Thereafter, he played for a while for Sowerby Bridge CC (in the Halifax League) and was associated with their Cricket Asylum coaching school. When he received his Level Two coaching certificate he found that his appetite for the game had been rekindled and, when Walsden CC were too cash-strapped to re-engage their Sri Lankan professional, Ranil Dhammika (a first-class cricketer in his home country) they turned to a more affordable left-arm spinner. Richard rewarded their faith with fifty wickets in his inaugural season of 2013 at 13.70 apiece and played his part in their securing the Central Lancashire Premier League title. After agreeing to appear the following season as an amateur, he then returned to Mytholmroyd CC for the 2015 season.

His subsequent fall from grace was a crushing humiliation. Lured by a vigilante group into a sting where he was expecting to meet with a teenage girl, he found he had been duped. The events were posted on the internet, leaving an indelible stain. The image of Richard, cornered and frightened, suggests naivety rather than a history of predation. Certainly, when his one-year sentence was handed down at Bolton Crown Court, it was noted that he had readily owned up to his guilt and had shown contrition. He has paid the price for his mistake. He is fortunate to have had the help and support of his father and brother, both of whom have suffered in the backlash, with vigilantes causing extensive damage to their property.

Earlier in his life, Richard had managed to pick himself up when it had become apparent that his days as a professional cricketer were over. Once more, he has a life to rebuild.

565
Benjamin James Trott
28 June 1997 v. Oxford University, Taunton

Ben Trott was born in Wellington, Somerset, on 14 March 1975, the son of Alan Robert and Jane Elizabeth (née Buttle). Educated at Court Fields Community School in his home town, he went on to study for his A-Levels at Richard Huish College in Taunton, before completing a BEd degree course in Physical Education and IT at the University College of St Mark & St John in Plymouth (now Plymouth Marjon University). His teacher training included experience as a primary school teacher. Having already appeared on a number of occasions for Somerset Second XI, he was still an undergraduate in his third year of studies when he was handed his first-class debut. It would be one of three appearances at that level during his short stay at the County Ground. A tall, right-arm fast bowler able to use his height of 6 feet 5 inches, he took seven wickets at 26.28 apiece while averaging a less impressive 1.00 with the bat.

During this time, he spent one winter after his graduation in 1998-99 at Claremont-Nedlands CC, in the leafy suburbs of Perth, but with opportunities limited at Somerset, he joined Kent in

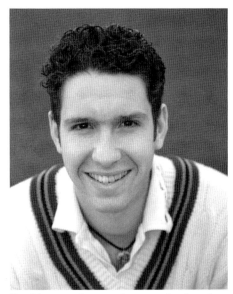

Ben Trott – a Somerset-born pace bowler who went on to enjoy greater success with Kent

2000. As well as being on the playing staff, he was given the opportunity to test his metal as a fledgling educator with responsibility for youth coaching. Having bedded down in his first season, he put in his most memorable performances in 2001. In his maiden Cheltenham & Gloucester game for Kent, against Cumberland, he won the Man of the Match Award for his 5 for 18, and in the Championship match against Essex at Tunbridge Wells, he turned in the remarkable figures of 6 for 13, following a haul of 5 for 65 in the first innings. He cites the highlight of that memorable year, though, as Kent's winning the Norwich Union League on the last game of the season. He was released at the end of the 2004 season, having made thirty-one first-class appearances for them and having taken eighty-one wickets.

Thereafter, he combined his educational and cricketing experience in the employ of Kent County Council while based at Kent CCC. Given the title of Study Centre Manager, his brief was to oversee the establishment of a facility to enhance numeracy and literacy through sport. After two years, he moved on and set up his own coaching business – BT Sports – offering coaching to individuals and schools and organising fun days for children, encouraging them to take up cricket or improve their prowess. After a year, he was offered a role as Operations Manager at the University of Kent, in Canterbury, in charge of their sport and all other aspects of physical activity and recreation. Ben remained with the University of Kent for a decade before setting up his own concern again, naming his company BT Contracts.

Married to Ella (formerly Brocklebank), Ben has been active in recent years in raising funds for Pilgrims Hospices for the terminally ill and their families in East Kent. As well as acting as master of ceremonies over the years at fundraising events, he has joined Ella in raising money via a number of gruelling cycling and running events, all in a fine cause. A very good bowler and a good man, Ben is an inspirational coach who has found his niche in life.

566
Nicholas Ross Boulton
19 July 1997 v. Pakistan A, Taunton

Nick Boulton was born in Johannesburg, South Africa, the son of Michael and Pauline, who had both emigrated there from England. Pauline was a primary school teacher and Michael a tailor who trained and worked in Savile Row, running a shop in partnership there, before opting to start his own tailoring business in Johannesburg. Educated at The Ridge School, a private prep school in his home city, Nick had already been selected for Transvaal Under-14s as a left-handed batsman and occasional right arm bowler when he was sent to England to complete his education at King's College in Taunton. Here, he continued his development as a cricketer, overseen by former Somerset cricketer, Dennis Breakwell. He was chosen at national level in a number of schoolboy representative matches and, having made his debut for Somerset Second XI as a sixteen-year-old, was still a sixth-former at King's College and described as 'a prolific schoolboy batsman' when selected for what would prove his only first-class match for the county in 1997. Nick came away with scores of one and fourteen and was not asked to bowl. He would continue to appear for the Second XI until his release in 1999. For a number of winters, he would return home to Johannesburg to play for Old Edwardians CC, coached by Somerset legend Jimmy Cook and captained by Richard Snell. Also beginning to establish themselves in the side were future stars Graeme Smith and Stephen Cook.

After his release by Somerset, Nick appeared both for Devon and Worcestershire, before being offered a contract by the latter in the middle of the 2000 season. His contract was renewed in 2001 but for one season only, with opportunities to appear in the First XI proving limited. An articulate man with a fine mind, Nick had chosen to try his luck as a cricketer rather than going to university and admits to occasional moments of introspection when he wonders how his life might have turned out had he opted for a degree. In the event, whereas his career as a first-class cricketer never took flight, he has succeeded in other fields.

It was time for him to forsake his original dream and follow another. His overriding passion has always been conservation and he worked for three years as a senior game ranger at Londolozi Game Reserve, a privately-run enterprise in the Kruger National Park. In 2005, he was married to Tara (née Sinclair), who was born and bred in the UK. With thoughts of a future family – the couple now have three children – Nick saw the need to pursue a more lucrative career and took the opportunity to go into partnership running a recruitment business, Client Services Ltd, based in London. The company specialises in matching employees and employers in the technology sector and continues to thrive, with Nick now the joint owner, he and his colleague having bought out their third partner in 2011.

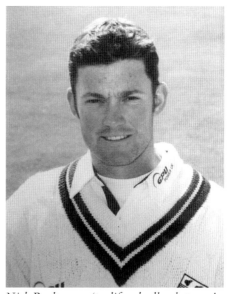

Nick Boulton – a 'prolific schoolboy batsman' who played in only one first-class match for Somerset COURTESY OF JOHN LEE

Since 2015, he has also been a partner in Jellyfish Meetups, which he set up with a colleague, Craig Mullen, creating a thriving community of like-minded individuals – entrepreneurs, enthusiasts and business leaders – wishing to share the latest ideas and developments in technology. The organisation works closely with Code Club, providing volunteers to coach children across the country in how to master code and develop their computer literacy.

Nick has remained committed to making the world a better place, whether helping kids to become the technology experts of the future or highlighting the plight of endangered species. Each year he takes his family back home on safari in his native South Africa. His indulgence is fly fishing, a pastime he has enjoyed since he was a young man. He is joined on most of his fishing jaunts by a fellow-enthusiast, his brother, Jonathan, who still resides in South Africa and has enjoyed a long career in club cricket in the Natal District. Nick and his wife and children are dual citizens of the UK and South Africa. Asked whether he considers himself South African or English these days, he responds, 'I refer to England as 'home' but, if I'm honest, I'm a bit of a contrarian. Put me in a roomful of English friends and I'll probably root for South Africa, just to wind them up!' Get him on to the subject of conservation, though, and his views are firmly held and his passion unwavering.

567
Luke David Sutton
19 July 1997 v. Pakistan A, Taunton

Born in Keynsham on 4 October 1976, Luke Sutton was the son of David and Molly (née Fedigan). Educated at Millfield School, he is described by one former teacher there as 'a lovely lad, an excellent pupil, no trouble at all, apart from the occasion when, from memory, the army had to be called in and an area sealed off because of a package left hidden under the stairs, which turned out to be his Physics project'. Luke was already attracting more welcome attention as a schoolboy, captaining England Under-15s in 1992 (with Liam Botham among his teammates) and winning the Jack Hobbs Award for Cricketer of the Year in his age group, later going on to win the Gray Nicholls Award for English Schools Cricketer of the Year in 1995. A fine wicket-keeper-batsman, a successful career as a first-class cricketer was predicted well beyond the boundaries of Somerset. He took a degree in Economics at Durham University and continued to progress, appearing for the British Universities side in the Benson & Hedges Cup.

A twenty-year-old undergraduate at the time of his first-class debut for Somerset, Luke acquitted himself well with a total of five catches behind the stumps. There followed an appearance against Sri Lanka with four more catches to his credit, but his Championship debut the following summer at Grace Road, Leicester, would prove altogether more fraught. Luke recalls that he 'hardly ate a crumb at breakfast: I was a wreck.' The day before he had cadged a lift to the team hotel with Graham Rose and assumed that Graham would be taking him to the ground. Watching the other players leave one by one, the greenhorn was reticent about speaking up. He relates that, 'I watched and waited in reception until I realised everyone had gone. I had to take decisive action.' There was much hilarity in the dressing room when he arrived in a black cab, still as nervous as a kitten. Recovery time was limited. The match was an unmitigated disaster for Somerset and for Luke. 50 for 8 at lunch, the side were bowled out for 76, Luke contributing a duck. He recites with a smile the ensuing press report: 'Sutton shouldered arms to a ball that can only be described as straight, being that it clattered into middle stump.' Somerset proceeded to lose by an innings and 85 runs inside two days. Mercifully, things would get better, although this would prove his final first-class appearance for the county, leaving him a batting average over three matches of 13.66, with ten catches held. His game had developed further, with winters spent as a pro in Sydney and then in Port Elizabeth, South Africa, and later Perth, Australia. Somerset were reluctant to release him, but, with Rob Turner firmly in possession of the wicket-keeping berth, they accepted the inevitable at the end of the 1999 season.

Luke moved to Derbyshire, where for a while he had to play second fiddle to their wicket-keeper, Karl Krikken, and was selected initially as a batsman. Good enough to score eleven first-class centuries and to carry his bat on one occasion, he also came to be regarded as an excellent technician behind the stumps. While things went from good to better on the pitch, Luke suffered tragedy in his personal life when his partner, Nia

Luke Sutton – a talented wicket-keeper-batsman: born in Somerset but obliged to leave in order to taste regular first-class cricket, he thrived at Derbyshire

Walters, was killed in a road accident in September 2004. Luke revealed that he had already purchased an engagement ring and was about to propose. He has spoken with great candour about his struggles with depression, triggered by the event, and his gratitude that he has been helped through his personal crises by an understanding employer and by the love of another good woman, Jude (née Hughes), whom he was married to in 2006, and with whom he would have twin daughters, Albie and Amelie. Derbyshire had agreed with a heavy heart to let their club captain leave them in 2005 in order to start his career afresh, despite his importance to the side and his strong bond with the club. Their compassion and understanding is laudable.

Arriving at Lancashire as a replacement for Warren Hegg, Luke confesses to feeling very much an outsider, being the only new-join in the dressing room. He describes his first taste of life at Old Trafford as 'like the first day at school', but if there was any reluctance among the supporters to embrace an outsider, it evaporated when he scored an unbeaten 151 against Yorkshire in his first season. A county cap was a formality thereafter and, when it was awarded, the next season, Luke followed up the brief ceremony with a golden duck, jesting that, 'I almost thought I should be handing it back.' After five seasons at Lancashire, he was welcomed back to the fold at Derbyshire in 2011 and was asked once more to captain the side. At the end of the season, he announced his retirement as a player, citing the mounting pressures of managing all aspects of his life. As ever-present as the pressure to perform was the increasing list of injuries he suffered, most of them regarded as occupational hazards for a wicket-keeper. When he lists the three knee operations, the multiple breaks to little fingers and to both thumbs, together with regular dislocations of digits, the trials and tribulations borne by professional sportsmen come into sharp focus. There are, of course, compensations aplenty. Luke had not many years earlier described being a cricketer as 'a fantastic life … I love the lifestyle so much'.

By the time his playing days ended, he had established a burgeoning business, running sports camps for kids, which he has subsequently expanded. With a bright, enquiring mind and an eye on his career beyond the game, he has always had his fingers (broken or otherwise) in more than one pie. He collaborated with his elder brother, Noel, in setting up a charity, raising money for research into CAH, a condition suffered by a nephew, Freddie. Among the money-raising efforts they planned was the Three Peaks Challenge, involving climbing Ben Nevis, Scafell and Snowdon within a twenty-four hour period. The gesture is typical of Luke, with one reporter observing that, 'Everyone one agrees he is a lovely man. Lovely but adroit as well.'

As for his main business venture, he had set up Activate (originally launched in 2005 with his friend Toby Mitchell, whose background lay in football coaching). The company now runs approximately 300 sports courses for young people each year. In addition, Luke has added a further string to his bow, incorporating the managing of finances and schedules for elite sportsmen, his most notable client being Jimmy Anderson. Latterly, Luke has invested in a further venture, Breathesport, an app allowing fans to interact with a number of top sporting names in a live setting, focussed around key events where opinions, ideas and anecdotes can all be shared.

Luke deserves plaudits not merely for his ability as a first-class cricketer and leader on the field, but as a man of courage who has overcome the sort of adversity and mental health issues that might have broken a lesser man. He has also had the courage to speak up about his depression in the hope that it will help others. 'It's extremely embarrassing to admit to a weakness,' he observes, adding that, 'I'm proud to have found the strength of character to seek treatment.' He is not alone. Coincidentally, another of Keynsham's finest, Marcus Trescothick, has been on a similar journey.

568
Philip Steffan Jones
19 July 1997 v. Pakistan A, Taunton

Born in Llanelli, Carmarthenshire, on 9 February 1974, Steffan is the son of Lyndon Jones, who played rugby for Llanelli RFC and Swansea RFC and Second XI cricket for Glamorgan, and was married to Ann (née Cole). Growing up as a talented all-round sportsman in the Principality, there was always the likelihood that Steffan's love of cricket would be matched by a passion for rugby union. These days, he is involved in the coaching of schoolboy cricket and rugby and, in the latter case, he agitates for innovative ideas, arguing, for example, for the 'bio banding' pioneered in New Zealand. The theory is that planning the progress of boys or girls at similar stages of physical development makes more sense than streaming by age. At present the well-built early developers are able to steamroller their way through matches and are rarely obliged to learn more nuanced approaches, such as mastering the side-step. Steffan's gripe is that, 'The game [of rugby] is American Football without the pads or helmets. It's just about joining the dots in terms of the pattern you're playing and picking beasts.' Somewhat of a 'beast' himself, he should know. He stands 6 feet 2 inches tall and weighed in at fourteen stone of solid muscle during his prime. He remains supremely fit in his forties.

After selection for the Welsh Schoolboys rugby side, he graduated to the senior game and enjoyed a brief but successful career in rugby union, playing as a powerfully-built full-back or wing three-quarter for Swansea, Bristol (who loaned him for a while to Exeter) and Moseley. Steffan would on occasions strike fear or horror into his rugby coaches when occasionally flouting the rules and relying on intuition. Moseley's then coach, John White, is said to have made it clear to his charge that he would never again play for Moseley after, instead of kicking for touch in the dying seconds of a match against Orrell, he decided instead in a moment of bravado to 'take on the phalanx of advancing Orrell attackers, was caught in possession, penalised for not releasing and Orrell kicked the penalty to snatch victory'. At that point, a career devoted to cricket appeared the sensible option. It is worth observing that Steffan remains independently minded, and unprepared to accept received wisdom without scrutiny.

After his schooling in Llanelli and Neath, and some village cricket opening the bowling along with future Glamorgan and England bowler Simon Jones, he com-

Steffan Jones – a nomadic cricketing career that embraced a remarkable six stints at first-class counties over twelve seasons

pleted a degree in Physical Education & Sport Science at Loughborough University, before securing a PGCE qualification at Homerton College, Cambridge University, in 1997. He was awarded his blue and starred in the Varsity match with nine wickets in a drawn game. Prior to this, he had been a member of the Academy at Glamorgan CCC, appearing regularly for the Colts and Second XI. He would also make one-day appearances for Wales (later taking part in a victory over England in 2002 that was met with great rejoicing in the Valleys). It was Somerset rather than Glamorgan who offered him professional terms in 1997, by which time he was playing his rugby at Exeter RFC. The initial approach had come unexpectedly, when he was engaged in teacher training at a school in Essex, the headmaster informing him that Dermot Reeve was on the line, inviting him to come for a trial for Somerset Second XI against Kent Second XI at Ashford. The year marked the start of a nomadic cricketing career that embraced a remarkable six stints at first-class counties over twelve seasons. After Cambridge University, two of those stays would be with Somerset, with spells at Northamptonshire and Derbyshire sandwiched between them, and a swansong with two List A appearances for Kent, during a one-month loan from Somerset.

As for his time at the County Ground, his disappointment at being asked to stand down for the returning Graham Rose for the 1999 NatWest Trophy Final was ameliorated when he was part of the team who triumphed at Lord's two years later. A right-arm pace bowler and a capable attacking batsman, who gave heart and soul, he enjoyed his best season for the club in 2001, with a haul of fifty-nine first-class wickets, and his hours spent in the gym helped him to achieve his target of a verified 90 mph delivery during the Lord's final.

The initial parting of the ways in 2003 was triggered by a desire to play regular first-class cricket at a time when there was a pool of fast bowlers at the County Ground and Steffan's role was becoming limited to that of a one-day player. Welcomed back into the fold in 2007 under the captaincy of Justin Langer, he would play his part in Somerset's winning of the Second Division championship.

He would play for Somerset in a combined total of eighty-four first-class games, averaging 19.76 with the bat (including two centuries) and claiming 224 wickets at 36.79 apiece. Having tasted cricket far and wide, he feels a real affinity for Somerset cricket in particular, citing, as a huge part of that, the passion of the supporters – in bountiful evidence at the Cheltenham & Gloucester Final of 2001, whether measured by attendance or decibels generated. His links with the county were further strengthened by his marriage in 2002 to Alexandra (née Kimmins) in Taunton.

This most peripatetic of cricket careers took another turn when Steffan renewed his acquaintanceship with Derbyshire and was granted a contract that combined one-day appearances with a coaching role. Although Derbyshire planned to retain him, he was offered the opportunity to return to the county of Somerset as the Head of Cricket and Elite performance at Wellington School, while playing his club cricket at that time for Bridgwater CC. He was given additional responsibility for Wellington School's rugby side. He was also invited by Somerset to work with the county's Under-13s and acts as a bowling scout as the search for up-and-coming talent continues.

In concert with his work with the school's pupils, Steffan offers his services more widely as a strength and conditioning expert, specialising as a bowling coach. Always conscious of the need for fitness during his own playing career – to the point that some of his teammates accused him playfully of being a fitness fetishist – Steffan's focus remains on 'building the athlete first'. Like any innovative thinker, he is prepared to modify his views and suggests his single-minded focus on gym work during his own playing days was limiting, that all-round athleticism is an important pillar and that ironing out issues with a bowler's run-up and action is paramount in improving performance and longevity. He believes that a naturally talented individual is only able to thrive in the upper reaches of any sport if his approach to his physical condition has been optimised. 'Give me a fine bowling prospect for eight weeks and I'll hand you back a faster and fitter bowler,' he asserts. He currently has two ventures on top of his work with Wellington School – Cricket Strength and Pacelab. Recently, he has spent time with Hobart Hurricanes, where he worked with Test bowlers Shaun Tait and Stuart Broad, garnering praise from them for the improvements he helped to bring about.

Steffan continues to be an effective coach, whether of international stars or of budding young cricketers. With regard to the county he now regards as home, he still plays his important part in a wider attempt by schools in the region to 'up their game' and develop the stars of the future.

569
Stuart Charles Glyndwr MacGill
19 July 1997 v. Pakistan A, Taunton

Stuart MacGill has always been a man apart, a contradictory and sometimes confrontational character, noted as much for his love of literature as he was for his volatility. He might share his initials with the famous Sydney Cricket Ground, but his father, Terry, and grandfather, Charlie, had both represented Western Australia, their headquarters in Perth being the best part of a 2,500 mile drive from Sydney. Born on 25 February 1971 in the Perth suburb of Mount Lawley, Stuart was the son of Terry and Jenny, both schoolteachers in the city. Stuart's paternal grandfather would remain an influential figure in his life. 'He was a macho bloke,' the grandson recalls, 'and after he retired he went on cruises around the Mediterranean and other places and filled my head with tales of Greek myths and Roman gods.' It was clear from the outset that Stuart was unlikely to conform to any stereotype of a typical first-class cricketer.

Educated at Christ Church Grammar School in Perth, he was offered a scholarship with the Commonwealth Bank Australian Cricket Academy in 1990, managed by former international Rod Marsh. He broke through into the first-class game with Western Australia in 1993 and thus began the career of a man described as having 'the best strike rate and the worst luck of any modern spin bowler'. His ill fortune was to have been a contemporary of Shane Warne, who took the leg-spinner's berth for Australia, allowing only limited opportunities for his understudy – opportunities that would generally be taken with devastating effect.

His development was steady at first and, struggling to make his mark at Western Australia, he would take a year out of the game before transferring his allegiance to New South Wales in 1996-97. In that intervening period, he earned his crust by selling music video compilations to pubs. It was only after experiencing English conditions in 1997 that he would enjoy his breakthrough season in Australia. That year in England had involved a season as overseas pro for a strong Heathcoat CC side, based at Knightshayes, near Tiverton, a stately pile now owned by the National Trust. During his time there, Stuart was selected for a Devon team led by Peter Roebuck and also for Somerset Second XI. Debarred as an unregistered overseas player from County Championship fixtures, his one first-class appearance for Somerset came against the touring Pakistan A team. He took four wickets at 30.75 apiece and made scores of

Stuart MacGill – a man apart, who ploughed his own furrow COURTESY OF JOHN LEE

seven and twenty-five. Had Somerset not already had fellow leg-spinner Mushtaq Ahmed on their books, they may well have negotiated a contract, but it was not to be. Returning to New South Wales, he took a hatful of wickets in Sheffield Shield matches and made his Test debut. He would be obliged to wait in the wings while Shane Warne weaved his magic, taking his opportunities when they arose, such as the time he stepped into the breach during Warne's infamous drugs ban for twelve months in 2003-04. He would in fact take 208 Test wickets in just forty-four matches, but, as with the larger-than-life Shane Warne, Stuart was often only a hair's breadth away from controversy. Sometimes he was undoubtedly in the wrong. Witness the time, which he regretted hugely, when he slapped his club captain's face for turning up without his favoured Kookaburra balls. But on other occasions, it could be argued that he had right on his side. He refused to take part in a tour of Zimbabwe on moral grounds and was unshrinking in his condemnation of Cricket Australia's endorsement of Kentucky Fried Chicken. In his words, 'I don't think you can have any of us advertising junk food … It's just wrong in so many ways.'

Stuart would later credit his clear moral compass to his Church of England upbringing and his subsequent rejection of religious belief. His view, expressed to a *Sun Herald* reporter, was that having been brought up an Anglican and being an atheist, he needed to replace his former beliefs with a robust moral code. Admitting that he struggled on a number of occasions to control his temper, particularly in the heat of the sporting battle, he nevertheless claimed it as some sort of triumph that he had not repeated his misdemeanour of striking a teammate.

With his continued success in Australia, he was inevitably invited back to England and spent three seasons from 2002 until 2004 with Nottinghamshire. His playing career came to an abrupt end in May 2008 when he announced, after the Second Test of Australia's tour of the West Indies, that he was leaving the game as a result of nerve and muscle problems that made it impossible to continue bowling. Decisive to the last, there was no going back. He had always been single-minded – a man apart, who ploughed his own furrow and rarely consulted others – usually reading a book in the dressing room, rather than bothering with how his teammates were progressing.

Married in 1989 to Rachel Friend, who had starred in the television series, *Neighbours*, he would have two children. On retiring from the game, it was always unlikely that this most unconventional of men would be pigeonholed into just one career. Perhaps he has a low boredom threshold, as evidenced by an unfinished course in Industrial Relations at the University of Western Australia or his half-completed Wine & Beverage diploma. But he managed to find regular and enjoyable employment. He worked as a commentator for SBS for the 2009 Ashes series and as a radio co-host and a member of 'The Grill Team' on Triple M Sydney. From 2012, he has been deploying his love of, and expertise in, fine wine to contribute to the lifestyle website, Live 4. Latterly, he has made further contributions to international cricket, albeit for the old enemy, coaching the England Lions in 2017 and asked by England to oversee the development of Mason Crane at the nets in the SCG. The results have been spectacular, with Mason's bowling for the club side Gordon CC sufficiently fruitful to result in a call-up to the New South Wales Sheffield Shield side – the first overseas player to have been so honoured since Imran Khan.

Inevitably, though, controversy has dogged him as often as triumphs have come along. For two-and-a-half years, Stuart was in a legal dispute with Cricket Australia over the non-receipt of injury payments, with an out-of-court settlement finally being reached in July 2017. Having agreed a divorce with his former wife, Rachel, in 2013, he subsequently became engaged in 2016 to Julie Singleton, although the relationship soured when Julie successfully took out an Apprehended Domestic Violence Order, banning her erstwhile fiancé from coming near her. That infamous Stuart MacGill temper had allegedly boiled over once more.

Complex and non-conformist? Undoubtedly. Flawed? Yes, and unable at times to adhere to the standards he tried to set himself. Volatile but bookish, he remains a man who ploughs his own unique furrow. And the career statistics tell that he was most certainly a brilliant exponent of the art of leg-spin who could have done great things for Somerset, though that was not to be.

1998

"No praise can be too high for Caddick, whose capacity
to bowl long spells and dart the ball all over the place off
the seam was acknowledged by teammates, coach,
opponents, spectators and the media. Everyone,
in fact, except the England selectors!"

Richard Latham

Championship Position: 9 of 18

Andy Caddick was the stand-out performer, with 105 wickets at an average of
19.82. The pity of it was that he had little support. The batting rarely rose above
the mediocre and was more often than not woeful, with not a single player muster-
ing a thousand runs. Among the other bowlers, Graham Rose took fifty-two wickets
and newcomer Matt Bulbeck thirty-two in only eight appearances. Sadly, Mushtaq
Ahmed, was struggling with injury problems and concerns about his wife's difficult
confinement back in Pakistan. He was released on compassionate grounds after six
ineffectual appearances, his departure representing a sad loss for Somerset.

In a cold, wet and generally miserable season, ninth place in the Championship
did nothing to warm the spirits and the limited-overs campaigns were even more
forgettable.

The debutants included Matt Bulbeck, whose hugely promising career would be
cut cruelly short by injury, and Adrian Pierson, whose largely injury-free career was
in its autumn. Greg Kennis would later play a more significant part in the county's
fortunes as a coach and the existing incumbent in that role, Dermot Reeve, would
enjoy a handful of outings in limited-overs cricket. If the club officers had responded positively to Peter Roebuck's pleas that Dermot should be plucked from relative
obscurity in Hong Kong and offered a contract by Somerset back in 1983, he could
have done so much more for the county as a player.

570
Adrian Roger Kirshaw Pierson
17 April 1998 v. Yorkshire, Leeds

Quite literally a high-flier in his post-cricketing career, with innumerable air miles under his belt, Adrian Pierson was also much-travelled while enjoying a peripatetic playing career, representing four different first-class counties and one Minor County side. A long-limbed, right-arm off-break bowler, 6 feet 4 inches tall, he came later than many to the first-class game.

Born in Enfield on 21 July 1963, he was the son of Patrick Blake Kirshaw Pierson and Patricia Margaret (née Heard). After attending Kent College, an independent school in Canterbury, he was offered a place studying for a degree in Aeronautical Engineering at Hatfield Polytechnic (originally set up in concert with the de Havilland Aircraft Company as an institution to train apprentices and now evolved into the University of Hertfordshire). His formal studies were supplemented by his work as an engineer on light aircraft at the Elstree Aerodrome. Adrian already had an affinity for the subject matter, his great uncle, Reginald Kirshaw Pierson, known as Rex, having been chief designer of the Vickers Vimy plane. Famously, it was the first plane to be flown non-stop across the Atlantic Ocean – by Alcock and Brown in 1919 – and subsequently the first to complete the trip from the UK to South Africa and to Australia. For all that an interest in aeronautics ran deep, Adrian successfully begged his father to support his decision to forsake a degree and join the Lord's ground staff in 1984. Taken on by Warwickshire and given his chance in the First XI in 1985, his initial County Championship scalp was a while coming, but it was the prized one of Viv Richards. Any elation was short-lived as Ian Botham proceeded to open his shoulders and score 138 not out in 65 deliveries, including twelve sixes.

Adrian gained further experience as a player and coach in the winter of 1985-86 at Walmer CC in Port Elizabeth, South Africa, but then missed a large portion of the 1986 English season owing to a back injury. He was further in the wars in 1990, requiring shoulder surgery in Zimbabwe, while he was playing for Manicaland CC. Despite these setbacks, he would remain with Warwickshire until the end of the 1991 season before joining Cambridgeshire for one season. Always possessed of a strong work ethic, Adrian was by then plying his trade, when not playing cricket, for a Design Consultancy, Tobasgo, who produced sports magazines, programmes and the like. In 1990 he had been married to Helen Marjella (née Ross), with whom he would have a daughter and son.

In 1993, he joined Leicestershire. If his time at Edgbaston had seen his career taking off, the budding pilot reached full cruising height at Leicester. In his second season there, he recorded his career-best figures of 8 for 42 against his former club, Warwickshire, and he was given the sort of prolonged bowling spells that are meat and drink to a spin bowler, taking 235 first-class wickets for his new county over the course of five seasons, including a triumphant year in 1996, when Leicestershire won the County Championship.

The next destination was the County Ground at Taunton, where former Warwickshire teammate, Dermot Reeve, was in residence. Arriving there in 1998 already by now a seasoned veteran, Adrian would stay with Somerset for three seasons. Over the course of thirty-two

Adrian Pierson – took 363 first-class wickets over the course of sixteen seasons, including three years at Somerset in the autumn of his career

first-class appearances, he would claim forty-one wickets at 47.41 apiece and surprise some observers with his batting that yielded an average of 21.00, including an unbeaten century against Sussex at Hove in 1998. He left to join Derbyshire, initially as a player and assistant coach and then, from 2003 and to the surprise of some, as first team coach.

Off-season, he had continued to work in event management and as a marketing account handler. This man of many talents was in addition a fine golfer, winning golfing tournaments for the cricketing fraternity, but he was also progressing as a pilot, having built towards his commercial pilot's licence and subsequently enjoying an alternative career as a flying instructor. At this point he had hoped to combine coaching young cricketers – helping them to get their careers off the ground – with mentoring those who wished literally to take wing. Sadly, not everyone at Derbyshire proved supportive, with Dominic Cork in particular publicly criticising Adrian's methods. Believing that he was being undermined by 'interfering committee members', Adrian found his position untenable and he and Derbyshire parted company in 2003.

Thereafter, he redirected his focus to the industry he had first become involved with as a trainee engineer at Elstree Aerodrome. He has been a commercial pilot for a number of years and remains one, at the time of writing. He has stayed actively engaged in club cricket as a coach, player and (as recently as 2016) captain at Houghton-on-the-Hill CC in Leicestershire. Few of his passengers can know that the safe hands into which they are putting their trust have spun their way to 363 first-class wickets over the course of a sixteen-season journey.

571
Matthew Paul Leonard Bulbeck
21 May 1998 v. Surrey, Taunton

Whom the gods wish to destroy they first call promising. So wrote Cyril Connolly in *Enemies of Promise*, published back in 1938. It was Matt Bulbeck's cruel fate to have been blessed with extraordinary gifts as a left-arm swing bowler, at times unplayable, but to have been dogged by injuries that cut short what many were predicting would be a career at the highest level of the game.

Born in Taunton on 8 November 1979, he was the son of Paul, who would later become head of security at the County Ground, and Carolyn (née Franklin). Educated at Taunton School and Richard Huish College, he showed early promise, graduating in club cricket from Bishop's Hull CC to Taunton St Andrews CC and training at the Somerset Cricket Academy while completing his A-Levels. In September 1997, he spent time at the Madras Pace Foundation, set up in the city now known as Chennai, to help young quick bowlers from around the globe to hone their skills. Here he was coached by Dennis Lillee and Jeff Thomson. Expectations were by now high for the 6 feet 3 inch fast-medium left-armer, who was also a competent batsman, and he was invited to join the England Under-19 side against Pakistan Under-19s in 1998, when he opened the bowling with Somerset's Jamie Grove (at the time with Essex). A tour of New Zealand followed early in 1999, with a series against Australia Under-19s later that year.

At the County Ground, after graduating to the Second XI as a seventeen-year-old, he continued to impress. Former club Chief Executive Peter Anderson would recall in conversation with journalist Steve Jennings that 'I signed Matt Bulbeck after Peter Bowler came out of the nets and said "Chief – this lad Bulbeck is swinging the ball both ways in the Indoor Nets. If he can swing it indoors, he can swing it anywhere."' Matt would subsequently become the first graduate of Somerset's new Academy to play for the senior side.

Granted his first-class debut in 1998, he was quick out of the starting blocks, with three wickets in each innings and two undefeated knocks. Six more wickets in his second match and another decent innings that had his batting average reading a heady 80.00 meant that hopes among the supporters were rising that here was a major talent. If 1998 was a season of great promise, then 1999 was a year of consolidation, with fifty-one wickets. Bowling coach Kevin Shine would describe Matt as a 'potential England bowler'. Asked in *The Cricketers' Who's Who* to name the young player to watch, his teammates all appeared to be convinced that Matt was that person. Then came the first cruel blow, when he was out of the game for fourteen months with a stress fracture of the spine that necessitated a major operation. Bravely and determinedly, he fought back to full fitness, taking fifty-eight first-class wickets

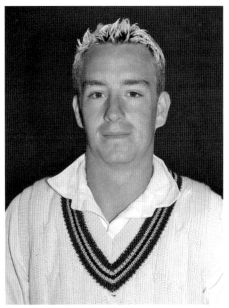

Matthew Bulbeck – a hugely promising left-arm swing bowler whose career was cut short by injury

in sixteen matches during the 2002 season. 'My rhythm got better and better that year,' Matt would observe in conversation with journalist Mark Easterbrook, adding that he 'felt great in the last game of the season against Lancashire'. He was taken on that winter by Applecross CC in Perth as their pro. He then suffered a second major setback, when he was rendered unable to bowl by a further unrelated back injury. It occurred during a friendly with Sussex, when Matt was forced to withdraw after four overs and drove off to hospital to seek the advice of a specialist. The problem was diagnosed as an inflammation of the facet joints in his spine and two vertebrae that, in his words 'were falling apart'. Matt relates that, 'The pain could be excruciating: it was like being punched in the kidneys every time I tried to bowl.' He was unable to play a single match during the 2003 season and, having been set a deadline of the start of April 2004 to prove his fitness, he was unable to meet it and parted company with Somerset. He had been advised that painkillers might have allowed him to play for a couple more years, but, in the long run, the extra exertion could have affected even his walking. He was not prepared to take that risk. In forty-seven first-class appearances for Somerset, he had averaged 21.60 with the bat and taken 152 wickets at 30.36 apiece.

How does a young man whose vertebrae and his dreams are both shattered pick himself up? In his own words, 'When I first left Somerset in 2003, I spent the best part of a year coaching on a self-employed basis, but that wasn't really for me. I applied for a job working for Somerset Activity and Sports Partnership, which I got and I now teach PE full-time in primary schools around the county.'

Married in 2005 to Helen (née Baker), Matt has remained rooted in the West Country. After four years as a pro at Torquay CC, where he focussed on his batting, he then joined Taunton CC as their pro in 2008, later settling for village cricket with North Curry CC. Matt has always had a natural talent for sports of most kinds. He was a decent goalkeeper in his youth and a very good golfer (often to be seen teeing off with Ian Blackwell while they both played for Somerset). It was unlikely that he would walk away from the world of sport. More surprising is his enthusiasm for bell-ringing, a skill he mastered with his usual ease and which he now teaches. Asked how he feels about the highs and lows he has experienced, Matt has stated that, 'Giving up cricket was hard for me to take, but I had to move on.'

572
Gregor John Kennis
14 August 1998 v. Northamptonshire, Taunton

Greg Kennis is unusual in being a Japanese-born first-class cricketer, although he had arrived in England by the time of his first birthday. His father, Michael, married to Sally, worked for Lloyd's Register of Shipping and played for a number of years for the company cricket team, also working as a qualified coach. Greg was born in Yokohama on 9 March 1974 and grew up in Surrey. Educated at Tiffin Boys School, he was fortunate enough to live in East Molesey with a cricket academy, run by Neil Stewart (brother of Alec and son of Micky), at the bottom of the road. Having attended the academy as a pupil, he would return there after leaving school to help with coaching duties during the winter months, having also appeared for Surrey through the age groups.

After a year on the MCC ground staff, he was offered a contract with Surrey in 1994. A top order right-handed batsman, he demonstrated his prowess with an innings of 258 for Surrey Second XI against Leicestershire Second XI at Kibworth in 1995 and was duly acknowledged as the Second XI Batsman of the Season. He failed, however, to make the grade in first-class cricket and appeared for the First XI on only six occasions before opting to join Somerset in 1998. Once again, Greg was unable to command a regular first team slot and was released after just one season. However, he was recalled on a summer contract in 1999, after a major injury to Mark Lathwell.

In six first-class appearances, he would score 298 runs at an average of 24.66, with 175 of those runs coming in the first innings of his final first-class game, against New Zealand, in 1999. Although recalled again the following year, he was out of the game for six weeks with disc trouble in his lower back and, to add to his woes, suffered a broken hand. He retired early at the age of twenty-six, enabling him, for a while at least, to spend more time pursuing his other great interest, horse racing, where he took delight in touring the racecourses of England.

Having already been awarded his coaching certificate, and having gained further experience over five winters as a player and coach in Perth, Australia, with Claremont-Nedlands CC and then Marist Newman Old Boys CC, he concluded that his future lay in coaching. Taking advantage of the contacts he had built up over those five seasons, he set up an academy of his own in Perth, giving young English cricketers the opportunity to play abroad in more clement conditions. Among his charges was a young Moeen Ali. In the winter of 2005-06, he met up with former teammate, Jason Kerr, who had just taken over leadership of the Somerset Academy and was there to observe the latest crop of young hopefuls. Impressed by what he saw, Jason invited Greg to join him as Assistant Academy Coach, specialising in batting.

'I jumped at the opportunity,' Greg confirms. 'That then grew to becoming involved with the Under-17s, which led to me taking on a larger part-time role with the Somerset Cricket Board. That saw me heading up the winter age group training programme.'

New opportunities came his way with a

Greg Kennis – 'the really exciting thing for me is to be able to be a member of a team of people who are trying to write history at Somerset'

351

speed and frequency that he might once have hoped for during his playing career. After subsequently taking over the running of the Emerging Player programme, he was appointed full-time Head Coach for the Somerset Cricket Board. Latterly, he has been made Assistant Coach in charge of the Second XI. Put more simply, every young player who has come through the ranks has at some point come under his influence.

How does it feel to be part of the team? 'I'm loving every minute of it,' he declared in a recent interview. 'It's a very tight-knit group, but there is the opportunity to challenge and question what is going on as well. The really exciting thing for me is to be able to be a member of a team of people who are trying to write history at Somerset. That's what's driving everybody forward.'

If the young guns can show the composure he did when notching up his 175 against New Zealand, then he will have played his part, though he will be rooting for them to be given more than his paltry six starts.

*   *   *   *   *

Dermot Alexander Reeve

Making six List A appearances for Somerset in 1998 was Dermot Reeve, who had been appointed Senior Coach in 1997 and would remain in that role for four seasons. Born on 2 April 1963 in Kowloon, Hong Kong, his parents, Alexander James and Monica (née Regan), were both teachers, with Monica also a well-respected scorer. Educated at King George V School in Kowloon, Dermot was offered a place as a member of the Lord's ground staff. While still undergoing that apprenticeship, he played for Hong Kong in the 1982 ICC tournament. On the basis of what he saw, Peter Roebuck urged Somerset to sign Dermot, but they declined to do so. Instead, he tried his luck with Sussex, joining them in 1983. Over six seasons he was deployed primarily as a bowler, and, frustrated by the lack of opportunity with the bat, threw his lot in with Warwickshire. Things worked out rather well for both parties. Made captain in 1993, he led the county the following year to a treble, winning every honour barring the NatWest Trophy, where they lost in the final. Two more trophies followed in 1995, rounded off with an OBE in 1996 for his services to cricket. An innovator – he was a pioneer, for example, of the reverse sweep – and full of positive energy, he squeezed the very last drop of talent out of himself and his teammates. He played in three Tests and twenty-nine One Day Internationals.

Having retired from first-class cricket because of an arthritic hip, he was offered the role of Senior Coach at Somerset by Peter Anderson. The brief was straightforward: 'Do whatever you and Bob Woolmer [as coach] were doing at Warwickshire.' He immediately insisted on a more gruelling fitness regime and attempted to instil the positivity that had been his trademark at Edgbaston. His methods were embraced by many, but not by everyone, and one or two players have spoken of being cast aside. He made useful contributions during his six appearances for Somerset, although his best days as a player were clearly behind him.

After leaving Somerset, he enjoyed a high profile as a host and pundit on Channel 4, but was relieved of his post after the revelation that he had developed a cocaine habit, with Dermot admitting to having taken the drug while working. He also owned up to having used marijuana during his playing career, although only during the off-season. He has talked with candour about the way in which his addiction to cocaine came to dominate his life and came close to destroying him.

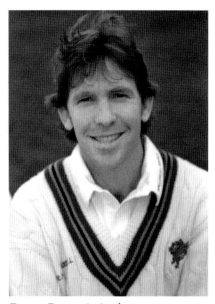

Dermot Reeve – insisted on a more gruelling fitness regime and attempted to instil the positivity that had been his trademark at Edgbaston

At one point happily ensconced in a fabulous waterside home in Clontarf, Australia, his life fell apart as he struggled with addiction and he relied on coaching work where he could find it. A two-year spell as coach with Central Districts in New Zealand was marred by further controversy, when he was accused of selling fake Don Bradman autographs on eBay. More poignantly, he was obliged at a later date to put his leather-bound presentation copy of *Wisden*, given to him as a Player of the Year in 1996, to raise much-needed cash.

Twice married and twice divorced – to Julie and then Fiona, the founder and CEO of Elliona, a Sydney-based nailcare brand – and the father of four children, Dermot has known good times and bad. He is building his life afresh and free of drugs. A spell as Assistant Coach at Pune Warriors in the Indian Premier League was followed by his appointment as coach with Subiaco Floreat CC, a Perth-based team with long-standing links to Somerset, who have provided them with a regular flow of pros. Rediscovering his Midas touch, Dermot has led them to recent honours.

'I left myself in a predicament,' he admits, 'but you know, I believe I'll be OK and keep working and keep coaching and be able to look after myself.' He gives every impression that his boundless energy and positivity will see him through.

1999

"It had looked something of a gamble to make
Tasmanian newcomer Jamie Cox the captain ... [but]
he was, perhaps, the principal reason that Somerset
rose from ninth to fourth position in the Championship
table. He brought another dimension to the top-order
batting in the limited-overs matches, too."

David Foot

Championship Position: 4 of 18

The new captain, Jamie Cox, carried on where he had left off in his native Tasmania, scoring copious amounts of runs and heading up the county's batting averages. It was a fine season, too, for Rob Turner, who was the only other man to exceed a thousand runs. Rob was the leading Englishman in the national averages and the most successful wicket-keeper, too, with sixty-nine dismissals. Andy Caddick, once again recalled to the England attack, still managed to take seventy-one first-class wickets for Somerset in thirteen appearances. Matt Bulbeck impressed, too, with fifty-one victims. A commendable fourth place ensured that Somerset would be playing in the top tier in 2000, when the County Championship would be split into two divisions.

The Sunday League had already been divided into two groups of nine, and Somerset, in the Second Division, gained immediate promotion by securing the runner-up slot, after winning thirteen of their sixteen matches. They also reached the final of the NatWest Trophy, losing to Gloucestershire at Lord's. There were many reasons to believe that the club had turned a corner.

Among the debutants, Jamie Cox transformed the fortunes of the side and Paul Jarvis briefly brought the benefit of his experience in the twilight of a successful career.

573
Jamie Cox
15 April 1999 v. Cambridge University, Cambridge

Speaking in 2014, Jamie Cox observed that, 'To come and have the opportunity to mould a young group is very exciting.' He was talking about his appointment to the role of General Manager with the St Kilda Aussie Rules Football Club, although the observation could equally have applied to his arrival at Taunton, fifteen years earlier. Somerset have always been obliged to look well beyond the county and national boundaries in order to strengthen the side. The club's ability to recruit men not yet household names in England who have gone on to prove their worth has been outstanding. Up-and-coming players such as Greg Chappell and Viv Richards went on to become giants of the game. Others, such as Jimmy Cook, were already legends in their own back yard but unknown over here. Jamie Cox falls into the latter category. He was an inspired choice with a proven track record as an opening batsman in Sheffield Shield cricket and leadership qualities that set him apart.

Born on 15 October 1969 in Burnie, a Tasmanian city, he was the son of David and Kaye Cox. David was a fine all-round sportsman, starring for Wynyard both at cricket and Aussie Rules Football. He was a member of the Wynyard team involved in arguably the local footballing scene's most bizarre Tasmanian State Grand Final, when – in 1967 – the Wynyard crowd, disagreeing with the referee's decision, surged onto the pitch and removed the goal posts, thus denying North Hobart a scoring opportunity. It was deemed a 'no game'. The two-year-old Jamie would have been unaware of the shenanigans, but he would go on to inherit his father's ability as a cricketer and footballer. Educated at Wynyard High School (where he became the all-time record run-maker in Australian schools cricket), he then went on to Deakin University in Victoria, where he took a Bachelor of Business degree. Sufficiently talented an Aussie Rules footballer to have been offered a contract with Essendon around the time of his eighteenth birthday, he was faced with a choice between a career in football or cricket. He chose the latter, based in the part on the fact that he had already broken into the first-class game with Tasmania. He would enjoy a long and fruitful opening partnership with fellow alumnus of Wynyard CC, Dene Hills. Both averaging approximately forty, they would amass nearly 20,000 runs for Tasmania between them in a combined total of 280 appearances but – to the surprise of many observers – neither of them received a single Test call-up.

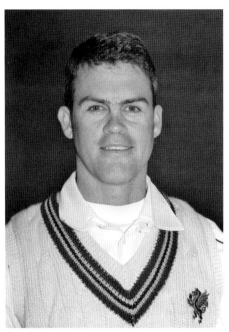

Jamie Cox – a proven track record as an opening batsman in Sheffield Shield cricket and leadership qualities that set him apart

Somerset saw in Jamie a man of talent, experience, intelligence and tenacity that made him a perfect fit to captain a side in need of a leader. He was joined on his journey to England by his wife, Helen (née Carver), so that his adoptive county would become somewhat of a second home. What he lacked in knowledge of English conditions, he made up for in a singular lack of arrogance that meant he listened to wise counsel. His impact as a batsman was immediate, too, with large centuries chalked up in his first two innings for the county. In that first season, he would go on to amass 1,617 runs at an average of 57.75.

He led Somerset to three Lord's finals, including the Cheltenham & Gloucester Trophy, won in 2001. His bond with the county was further strengthened with the birth of his son, Lachlan William Joseph, in Somerset. Jamie remained for six seasons, coming back on the last of these as cover for Ricky Ponting, whom he had persuaded to join the county, albeit briefly (and very successfully). Over the course of ninety-one first-class games for Somerset, he averaged 47.43, with seventeen centuries (of a combined total of fifty-one in all first-class games). There were six centuries in limited-overs matches, too. Vic Marks would comment that, 'His simple, pure style of batting was a delight to behold. Few players have pummelled the off-side boundaries at Taunton with such elegance.'

After leaving Somerset at the end of the 2004 season, he played for Tasmania for a couple more seasons before retiring. He sits in the pantheon of their all-time greats, with a record number of appearances and nearly 12,000 runs for them. He had also assured his place in Tasmanian folklore with his unbeaten century against Western Australia in 1997-98 that made him the first player to have carried his bat in a Sheffield Shield Final.

For a while, Jamie was involved in journalism, having already tried his hand with his 'Postcards' newspaper column, and he was employed as an analyst and commentator with ABC. Then in 2006 he replaced Allan Border on the Australian Board of

Selectors, a role he would retain for five years. He was also an administrator at the Australian Institute of Sport for two years, a member of the team charged with optimising the performance of the Australian contingent at the Beijing Olympic Games. Then, from 2008, he was High Performance Manager at the South Australian Cricket Association, a post he held until May 2014, a year that would prove a personal nightmare. First, he was at the centre of a Big Bash League storm over alleged contractual breaches when approaches were said to have been made to three players – Kieron Pollard, Brad Hodge and Jono Dean – during the embargo period. Such off-the-record discussions were reputedly commonplace and many felt that (to quote one source) South Australia were 'a casualty of flawed BBL rules'. The South Australian Cricket Association incurred a fine of A\$50,000. The regulations were subsequently changed, but not before Jamie had taken the only course he felt open to him and resigned. The shocking death of the side's opening batsman, Phil Hughes, felled the following November by a lethal bouncer against New South Wales, set the seal on a miserable year for everyone associated with the side.

Jamie needed a complete break from the past, and in January 2015, he took up a post as General Manager of the St Kilda Aussie Rules Football Club based in Melbourne, Victoria. The role involves overseeing coaching and the medical support teams. 'I was ready for a change,' he has said, adding that, 'I'm no novice at the game, but I'm coming here to manage the football experts and to get the best outcome from this group.'

He still has fond memories of his time in England, revealing that 'Helen and I often talk about how lucky we were to spend six years in Somerset. We loved every minute of it …They were amazing days in Taunton. It was just terrific and I can't say enough good things about it.' Those positive sentiments are matched by the feelings of the Somerset faithful, grateful to the Tasmanian who came over, scored plenty of runs and lifted the Cheltenham & Gloucester Trophy at Lord's in 2001.

Jamie Cox – a perfect fit to captain a side in need of a leader

574
Paul William Jarvis
15 April 1999 v. Cambridge University, Cambridge

By the time he arrived at the County Ground, Paul Jarvis was a seasoned campaigner. Already into his thirties and a former England player, his days as a main strike bowler might have been behind him, but he brought with him a wealth of experience, invaluable when imparting advice to the younger players or making occasional appearances as a useful back-up.

Born in Redcar on 29 June 1965, he was the son of David and Marjorie Steele, but after Marjorie's subsequent marriage to Malcolm Jarvis, Paul grew up regarding Malcolm as his father. Both David and Malcolm were fine cricketers, with Malcolm playing league cricket for twenty-five years. Paul's brother, Andrew, would play for England Under-15s and be offered trials with Northamptonshire and Derbyshire.

Paul began making waves with the local Marske CC side, enjoying his initial outing as a nine-year-old in the Under-13s side and later going on to play an important role in the unprecedented success of the junior teams. The Under-13s would win the Lord's Taverners Trophy and the following year the Under-15s would be losing finalists. Educated at Bydales School (now Outwood Academy Bydales), he left school to work for a brief while as a trainee groundsman, reporting to former Nottinghamshire, Derbyshire and Somerset batsman, Maurice Hill. But Marske CC were always unlikely to hang on to the services of the speedster for long, given his extra yard of pace, delivered from a relatively slight and lithe frame. He was soon snapped up by Yorkshire, becoming at the time, at the age of sixteen years and seventy-five days, the county's youngest ever debutant. He began to tick off other records, too, becoming the youngest player to complete a hat trick in the John Player Special League, then laying claim to the same record in the County Championship. He also gained valuable experience abroad with spells in Sydney and Cape Town. By the 1987 season, he was putting together a compelling case for Test selection, with eighty-one first-class wickets and a return of 4 for 43 in the Benson & Hedges Cup Final at Lord's. It would be Paul's misfortune to be drafted into the England side at a time when they were pitted against strong opposition, often on slow tracks, ill-suited to his brand of fast, skidding deliveries. He also began to be plagued by the sort of regular injuries (in particular back problems) that are too often an occupational hazard for fast bowlers. Married in 1988 to Wendy Jayne (née Tester), with whom he would have a son and daughter, his decision to sign up for the Rebel Tour to South Africa in

1990 was met with opprobrium in some quarters, but the twenty-four year old had to consider the alternatives. A promise of approximately £80,000 after tax and a five-year ban from official Tests had to be weighed against an uncertain future as an England player, in which he was just one injury away from losing his place in the side. As Paul would explain, the decision to decline was a lot easier for players who didn't have 'a wife, a child and a mortgage' to consider. The tour was fraught with problems, not helped by the pronouncements of captain Mike Gatting, whose abilities as a cricketer were equalled by a singular lack of diplomacy, and a seemingly gargantuan appetite for controversy to match his famed liking for pies. Having dismissed the demonstration that greeted the new arrivals as 'a few people dancing and singing', he and his team were met with a hostile reception at every turn. At one Greek restaurant in Pretoria, the staff walked out, refusing to

Paul Jarvis – his days as a main strike bowler might have been behind him, but he brought with him a wealth of experience

serve the team. Mike Gatting took control of the situation, heading for the kitchen while Paul and others were roped in to waiting duties. A planned second tour was cancelled, although Paul's newfound expertise was deployed working for South Africa Travel in York during the 1992-3 off-season.

He regained his place in the England side in 1993, when the ban on the 'Rebels' was lifted after three years, but he continued to be plagued by injuries. He made nine Test appearances in total, rather less, in the view of many, than his talents merited. Leaving Yorkshire in 1993, he would spend five seasons with Sussex, also enjoying five winters in Wellington, New Zealand, with Onslow CC.

His move to Somerset came in 1999 and he remained for two seasons, appearing in nine first-class fixtures and taking twenty-six wickets at 29.23 while averaging 8.22 with the bat. His appearances in limited-overs games totalled thirty-three, with some telling contributions. After calling time on his first-class career in 2000, he had been playing and coaching in South Wales when an emergency call came from Somerset, asking him to stand in for two List A games as a result of a veritable plague of injuries to the quick bowlers, with Graham Rose, Andy Caddick, Richard Johnson, Peter Trego and Joe Tucker all indisposed.

With an eye to his future, Paul had embarked on a Sports Science degree and then gone on to coach for a variety of clubs. His coaching would take him to Lansdown CC in Bath, Swindon CC and the Suffolk Minor Counties team, which would in turn lead to a spell as Director of Cricket at Framlingham College. He would go on to coach the England Women's fast bowlers. Not one to be tied down to a one-track career, Paul also spent time working for an IT company in Hemel Hempstead. Latterly, he has been involved in property maintenance, happy to roll up his sleeves and engage in painting, decorating and refurbishing, including at two properties in Ipswich that were owned by his second wife, Caroline. She shares his dynamism and appetite for business, initially having enjoyed a career in the transport industry before later offering her services as an interim manager and running a consultancy business in the Railway sector. Their combined talents have come together in two related enterprises. Sherston Rare Breeds was begun in November 2010, when Paul and Caroline bought a number of pigs. After an initial purchase of three Gloucester Old Spots, others followed, including a select band of Mangalitsas, Large Blacks and Tamworths. There were ducks, guinea fowl, chickens and sheep, too. Paul has described his role as a general handyman. Rather than uprooting the stumps of opposing batsmen, he has taken to hammering in fence posts and the like, happy to leave the administration and paperwork to his wife.

In 2014 they opened an additional enterprise, having converted The Angel, a former pub in Sherston. Its final days as a public house had been inglorious when, in the 1990s, after centuries quenching the thirst of the locals, it had become notorious for its sex shows. It now offers food and drink to an altogether more savoury clientele as well as smart bed and breakfast rooms.

Paul is a man with his finger in a number of pies (some of them, presumably, quite literally his rare breed pork pies). No one could accuse him of sitting back and taking life easily after his retirement as a player. Nor has he been forgotten back where his career began in Teesside. He may now be ensconced in the Wiltshire countryside, but in 2017 he was inducted into the North Yorkshire & South Durham Hall of Fame, where the boy who had started out as a nine-year-old making his first competitive appearance and developed into a devastating speedster, is still remembered fondly and celebrated as a local legend.

575
Ian Jones
2 June 1999 v. Durham, Chester-le-Street

Ian Jones was born on 11 March 1977 in Edmonton, London, the son of Ronald Jones, a prison officer known as Ronnie, and Dianne (née Gill), a nurse. At the time of Ian's birth, Ronnie was training at Pentonville Prison, but Ian was brought up in his parents' home county of Durham from the age of three. He was educated at Fyndoune Community College in Sacriston, and completed a City & Guilds Diploma in Engineering. By then he was already making waves as a right-arm pace bowler and competent batsman, 6 feet 4 inches tall, well-built and powerful. Having worked his way through the Durham age groups, he became the first recruit to the newly established Durham Academy. A regular in the Durham Second XI throughout the 1995 and 1996 seasons, he suffered a stress fracture in his lower back early in 1997, putting him out of action for more than a year. He never made any first-class or List A appearances for the county.

Ian was and remains a modest and affable character, never one to push himself forward, but he was persuaded by teammate John Morris to write to Derbyshire, Somerset and Sussex. Somerset came back, ahead of the 1999 season, with the most attractive offer. Appropriately enough, he was invited to make his first-class debut against his former county. In a drawn game, he claimed one wicket, but his batting surprised some observers, with scores of 18 not out and 35 (after he had been promoted to nightwatchman in the second innings). There was a second major setback when he suffered serious injury to his left ankle after a freak accident when he trod on a cricket ball during practice and tore three ligaments. As a result, he endured two sessions of surgery and missed the whole of the 2000 campaign. Having fought his way back to fitness, he would play in only three first-class matches for Somerset, coming away with six wickets at 56.83 apiece and averaging 26.00 with the bat. Arguably his most telling contribution had come in the Norwich Union match against Surrey at The Oval. The Somerset folklore has it that he was summoned from the stands as an emergency replacement. He was in fact in London, helping his good friend Ian Blackwell to celebrate his (Blackie's) birthday. 'I was recovering from the night before,' Ian confesses, 'when I received a call telling me that Noddy [Rob Turner] and Richard Johnson were ill and could I be there on stand-by.' In a match limited to ten overs per side, he registered an impressive 3 for 14 – all of his victims bowled – in his two overs. Jamie Cox and Ian Blackwell, none the worse for wear, then knocked off the

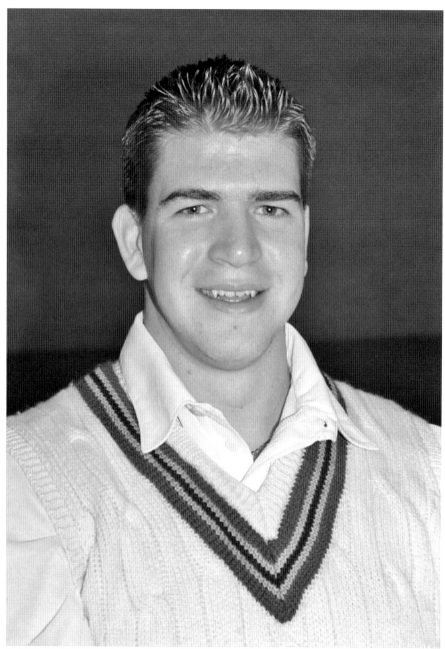

Ian Jones – a fast-bowling career cut short by serious injuries

runs with overs aplenty to spare.

Having parted company with Somerset, Ian tried his luck with Middlesex, after being offered a trial season in 2002. He acquitted himself well in his only first-class fixture but soon decided on a future outside cricket. Beginning as an operative with Roadtechs, he embarked on a career in the repair and maintenance of roads and other aspects of the transport infrastructure. After two years, he left to join Ennis Prismo in a similar role before joining DBi Services initially as a contract supervisor and later as the manager of the Northern region. In 2017, he returned to Roadtechs (whose headquarters are in Sheffield) as their Regional Business Manager for the North.

Married to Clare (formerly McCaw), Ian has two stepchildren, Rosie and Jack, and a daughter, Katie. He has continued to enjoy club cricket, initially for Chester-le-Street CC and latterly for Sacriston CC, turning out for the local club where he honed his skills as a boy. In addition, since 1999, he has enjoyed boxing as a means of keeping fit. As a member of the Ultra White Collar Boxing organisation, Ian has been able to raise sponsorship money for cancer research. 'It's a triple benefit,' he observes. 'I enjoy it, it raises money for a great cause and its helps me lose weight!'

Somerset might be a long haul these days for a man happily ensconced with his family in Durham, but Ian speaks fondly of his time at Taunton. 'A really welcoming place,' he says. 'It still feels like a home from home.'

576
Zakaria Saqib Mahmood
25 June 1999 v. New Zealand, Taunton

Zak Mahmood describes himself as 'a dreamer'. He is a man with a restless urge to be a catalyst for change, whether involving himself in charitable work close to home or establishing his latest bold business ideas on the world stage. Born in Kettering on 24 August 1977, Zak was the son of Raja Rashad Mahmood, married to Azra (née Khanam). Rashad had emigrated from Pakistan in the 1960s and worked as a mechanic, before being employed as a data processor. With Zak and five other children to provide for, Azra was obliged to toil in what her son describes as 'a sweat shop in Silvertown in the borough of Newham'. Educated at Hartley Primary School, Langdon Comprehensive and Havering College in Essex, Zak confesses to having struggled with his schooling, with reading particularly problematical and exam results disappointing, until his dyslexia was diagnosed by a lecturer – David Hannigan – and he was given the support he needed before going on to complete a degree in Computer

Zak Mahmood – his dreams of a career in first-class cricket turned into a nightmare in a debut clouded by concussion

Science at King's College, University of London. 'It was challenging but worthwhile,' he observes. 'My life changed once I realised how I absorbed and processed information.' As is often the case, dyslexia has proved a blessing for a man who approaches creative challenges unfettered by convention.

He enjoyed success at club cricket as an all-rounder in London, for Ilford CC and Southgate CC and in Pakistan for Gul CC in Rawalpindi as a sixteen-year-old schoolboy and then for three seasons from 1997 until 1999 with P & T Gymkhana CC in Lahore. His achievements with both bat and ball were at times outstanding. Having played for Essex Second XI in 1997 and 1998, he was invited for a trial match with Somerset Second XI in 1998 at a time when the club were searching for a match-winning leg-break bowler. 'I remember arriving at the match and seeing a totally green pitch and thinking: "How will I perform on that surface alongside a five-man seam attack?"' Zak observes. 'Luckily, I bowled well and was able to apply pressure on the Hampshire players, allowing the seamers to attack at the other end.'

Having been offered a contract for the 1999 season, his appearances were limited to three matches for the Second XI (in which he claimed four wickets) and one first-class appearance. Having suffered a blow to the back of his head from a bouncer from Kevin Shine whilst preparing for the match, the resultant concussion went unnoticed by the medical staff for many days and led to a mediocre performance. Zak acknowledges that he was in no fit state to play. 'I had pins and needles in my legs and wasn't in control of things,' he admits. But he refuses to lay the blame at the door of the coaching staff. 'These days, there's a greater understanding of the effects of concussion,' he notes. 'Back then, you were expected to play through it.' Bowling against New Zealand, he took no wickets, conceding forty-three runs in his three overs. In a strange match in which twenty-four no-balls were called out, Zak was adjudged to have transgressed on six occasions. His seven not out in the first innings was followed up with a duck in the second. Regrettably, his time at Somerset was then blighted from the beginning of July, when a serious injury to his right hand forced him to call time on his aspirations as a first-class cricketer and he opted to pursue a business career.

For five years, from 2000 until 2005, he worked as a management consultant with Deloitte Consulting. While with them, he was married in 2002 to Annie, with whom he would have four children. After leaving Deloitte, he spent three years in a similar role with Capgemini Ernst and Young Consulting in the UK. There followed a further two years with T-Mobile, where he enjoyed a senior role overseeing major transformation programmes. Zak studied concurrently for an Executive MBA at Cass Business School in London.

By then, he was ready to branch out on his own and set up Sinclair Adamson & Co Ltd, whose stated aim was to give a boost to international students, helping budding entrepreneurs to hone ideas and providing them with venture capital. A change in government policy, restricting the opportunities for international students, forced a rethink. 'I still harbour ambitions to open a business school for entrepreneurs one day,' says Zak – a man brimming with ideas and one who refuses to be defeatist when things go awry. Forced by circumstances to chart his career anew, his goal for his latest concept – INTCAS – is to create a global community where students and educators can be more readily matched, using the very latest technology. The idea was sparked by the difficulties a cousin had encountered in attempting to further his education in the UK. The enterprise has attracted negative publicity in some quarters as it aims to clean up an industry blighted by unscrupulous operators who are misleading families and education institutions. It was clear that by enabling honest families aspiring to educate their child abroad in a fair, transparent and compliant way, his solution would disrupt the status quo. In 2017, he became the subject of a deeply upsetting online hate campaign, orchestrated by anonymous sources bent on stopping him in his tracks. He affirms that the question marks about him and his business are without foundation.

Zak is in the throes of expanding the enterprise into multiple jurisdictions across the world, forming relationships with major education bodies and governments, and is now working with investment banks to secure sufficient funds to enable INTCAS to become a truly worldwide concern. He is restless in his pursuit of his goals and expansive in his ideas. He is also firmly of the view that every lesson in life, good or bad, and every experience, whether his dyslexia, or his triumphs and setbacks as a professional cricketer or as a businessman, have shaped his journey towards becoming a global entrepreneur. Zak, who styles himself 'Chief Dreamer', insists that he has 'lots of ideas but not all the answers' and that it is his aim 'to connect the world through education and make it a better place'. These are laudable aims for a man who recalls his own early struggles and the opportunities he was given to make the most of his talents.

2000

"Perhaps the most lasting memories of 2000 for
Somerset fans will be those provided in the Test arena
by Caddick, who again proved himself a world class
bowler, and Trescothick, whose maturity, poise, power
and skill made him England's Cricketer of the Year."

Richard Latham

Championship Position in Division One: 5 of 9

This was a season of significant changes. The introduction of two divisions in the County Championship meant that interest was maintained until the death. Somerset steered clear of the drop, achieving fifth place. Another innovation was that of central contracts for England players. This meant that Andy Caddick and Marcus Trescothick were rarely available to fight Somerset's corner. Andy was already a Test bowler of stature. Marcus repaid the faith of the selectors in full and would be named Professional Cricketers' Association Player of the 2000 Season. A bright future looked assured for a player who – the odd setback notwithstanding – had long promised greatness.

The evergreen Peter Bowler was the only man to top 1,000 runs for the county, although Jamie Cox came close. Steffan Jones was the leading wicket-taker with forty scalps, although Andy Caddick, with twenty-five wickets at 11.76 in his three appearances, represented the greatest threat to opposing batsmen. Without the two England players in their ranks for much of the season, the team too often failed to press home any advantage and win matches. In their Sunday League matches, they started off at a canter, winning their first four matches, but then ran out of steam and stumbled over the finishing line, clinging onto their First Division status by a narrow margin.

Among the debutants, Ian Blackwell and Peter Trego would prove the buccaneering, devil-may-care all-rounders beloved of Somerset supporters.

577
Ian David Blackwell
7 April 2000 v. Oxford Universities, Taunton

[signature]

There is irony in the fact that the twenty-year-old Ian Blackwell, standing well over six feet tall and weighing in at somewhere between sixteen and seventeen stone, should have worked for a while as a private investigator, a role requiring a gift for invisibility. But here was a man not given to conformity and one not averse to stealing the show with his pyrotechnics at the crease. Here was a player who emptied the bar whenever he walked to the crease. Blackie – as he was known by teammates – smote the ball hard, high and far in the best Somerset cricketing tradition.

Born in Chesterfield, Derbyshire, on 10 June 1978, he was the son of John and Marilyn (née Bennett). Educated at Manor School and Brookfield Community School in the town of his birth, he was encouraged from the outset in his cricketing endeavours by a father who was a useful club cricketer and would later play for Derbyshire Over-50s. Ian appeared for the county at all age groups, having made his first appearance for them as an eight-year-old. He was also a good enough footballer to represent Sheffield Wednesday Young Owls. Unsurprisingly for such a clean striker of the ball, he also developed into a fine golfer.

By the time of his first-class debut for his native county as an eighteen-year-old, Ian's mighty exploits were already the stuff of local legend. In one innings – an unbeaten double-century – such was the power of his hitting that he was responsible for the loss of seven balls in a match at Bolsover. 182 of his runs had come in boundaries. It was a sign of things to come. He confesses that on his debut he was 'completely terrified and in awe', praising former England player Phil DeFreitas for taking him under his wing and proffering helpful advice.

During the winters in the early part of his career, Ian played for Delacombe Park CC in Frankston, one of the less genteel suburbs of Melbourne. But then, back at Derbyshire, there was a falling out with Dominic Cork, an abrasive character and catalyst for a number of abrupt departures from the county. Frustrated at having been made to bat as a tail-ender and only asked to bowl infrequently, Ian wanted out. He found his natural home at the County Ground, even working over the winter in the club office, enjoying an administrative role he inherited from Mike Burns in 2001. He made invaluable contributions for his adoptive county as a left-arm orthodox spin bowler but more spectacularly as a powerful middle-order batsman, capable of tearing any attack apart on his day. By the 2001 season, he was fully into his stride as a batsman and his wickets were considered a bonus. Typically from thereon in he would average in

Ian Blackwell – smote the ball hard, high and far in the best Somerset cricketing tradition

the order of fifty with the bat, but it was the manner in which the runs were stacked up that caught the eye. Those who witnessed him in full flight need no reminders, but the facts are there for all to see. In 2001, batting at No 7, he scored a century in each innings against Northamptonshire. In 2003, he scored a 134-ball double century. Derbyshire were the county on the receiving end, on that occasion. And it was Derbyshire who suffered again when he plundered a sixty-seven-ball century in 2005, securing the Walter Lawrence Award for the season's fastest hundred.

Offered the chance to captain the side on a temporary basis after the departure of Graeme Smith, during the 2005 campaign, he was appointed club captain for 2006, but was obliged to step aside when a shoulder injury meant that he was unavailable for a number of months. At the end of the 2008 season, he was ready for a fresh start. His first-class batting average for Somerset across 120 appearances stood at 45.17 (including twenty-one centuries). His 210 wickets had come at 40.90 apiece. Durham came knocking and Ian's impact was immediate. His 949 runs at 45.19 and forty-seven wickets at 22.63 apiece were an essential ingredient in Durham's march to the County Championship and enough to secure him their Player of the Season Award. The following year, he did not shirk when, at Chester-le-Street, Somerset were obliged to throw caution to the wind on a worn track as they chased an unlikely victory in order to secure their first County Championship title. Ian, in his guise as a bowler of spin, was the smiling, joking assassin, as his former teammates' hearts were broken. In 2010, he was signed by Central Districts in New Zealand, to play in their T20 fixtures.

In 2012, he was loaned by Durham to Warwickshire when Jeetan Patel was called up by New Zealand and, as a result, he gained another Championship winner's medal. His appearance for them in the forty-over Clydesdale Bank Final at Lord's – a tied match which Warwickshire lost as a result of taking fewer wickets – was his final appearance. There had been an undercurrent of injury during much of the latter half of his career, with repeated shoulder problems, three operations and ultimately a diagnosis of arthritis in his left shoulder. 'I knew after that Lord's final I was done,' Ian says. 'My body had taken a battering and the surgeon recommended I stop.'

His efforts had been rewarded with one Test appearance for England (against India in Nagpur), his fellow debutants, Alastair Cook and Monty Panesar, going on to enjoy more prolonged Test careers. More suited to the one-day than the five-day game, he won thirty-four ODI caps for his country, all bar two of them outside England. For sheer consistency over the first decade of the new millennium, he was pre-eminent among his country's all-rounders and the manner of his run-gathering was exhilarating.

During his career, he had enjoyed spells of commentary for Sky and BBC Radio Somerset, but he turned immediately upon retiring to umpiring and was added to the Reserve List in 2014, standing in first-class fixtures the following year and graduating to Championship fixtures in 2016. 'As a player, you always had confidence in umpires who used to play,' he observes. Asked about his ambitions, in a case of rare circumspection on Blackie's part, he replies that, 'I'll go as far as I can, taking each game as it comes.'

He was married in 2006 to Elizabeth Rachel (formerly Tarr), known as Beth, with whom he would have a son. Ian's achievements at county level – Cheltenham & Gloucester and T20 Trophies and Division Two Winner at Somerset and County Championships at Durham and Warwickshire – would be the envy of many. He was somewhat of a one-off, capable of doing things many others on the county circuit could only dream of accomplishing. Throughout his playing career, he remained true to himself, backing his own judgement, his strength and technique, and playing his cricket in a wholehearted and entertaining way. 'Cricket's an amazing game, played by differing characters with varying builds,' he says. 'You can't have eleven mannequins going out on to the cricket field. If you did, it would be a very sad state of affairs.' Indeed it would.

578
Peter David Trego
7 April 2000 v. Oxford Universities, Taunton

Pete Trego bestrides the generations as a cricketer. In one sense, he is, to parody Gilbert and Sullivan, the very model of a modern first-class cricketer, able to bat, bowl and field with equal proficiency, but also well-versed in the ways of social media, and the possessor over the years of frequent new looks and innumerable tattoos. And yet, he is in touch with supporters, who share his love for the game – 'one of us', as the saying goes, at a time when interactions between elite sportsmen and their paying public are becoming sanitised. Cricket has undoubtedly changed in recent years. Pete Trego has not. He is still the ebullient, open-hearted young man he always was.

Born in Weston-super-Mare on 12 June 1981, he is the son of Paul Trego, a taxi driver at the time and later a financial adviser, and Carolyn (née Marquiss), known as Carol, who runs a vintage furnishing shop in the town. He enjoyed a happy childhood, alongside his brother, Sam. Their variants on the game of cricket included serving tennis balls to each other at short range, a set-up inspired by the West Indian pace attack. Pete observes that, 'those games always had a painful outcome', but stood them in good stead. 'Sam and I are the best of friends, these days,' he adds.

For a while, Pete showed little or no interest in his schooling. Sport was his only love. He recalls his mother, Carol, being informed by the local Primary School that her son was not engaged in the project he had been set. When she enquired as to the subject matter, she was informed that it was 'flowers'. 'Try monsters,' she informed them. 'You might have more success.' It worked. Mothers, of course, normally know best.

He attended Wyvern Comprehensive School in Weston-super-Mare and was always likely to follow his brother, Sam, in trying his luck as a professional cricketer (although, in the event, Sam made no First XI appearances). Having played in age group cricket at county and national level, including for the England Under-19

Peter Trego – in an early incarnation, looking fresh-faced and about to embark on a long a successful career

side, Pete made his first-class debut in 2000, but was struggling to establish himself in the side. It was Steve Waugh who suggested to him that he had the talent to succeed but would only do so with regular first-class games. In 2003, he moved to Kent, although that experience proved disappointing, with Pete feeling neither welcomed nor part of the county's long-term plans. There followed a brief spell in Minor Counties cricket with Herefordshire, before Middlesex offered him terms in 2005. It was the combined persuasive powers of Ian Blackwell and Brian Rose that led to his return to the fold at the County Ground. Having watched Pete playing for Middlesex against Glamorgan in Cardiff, Brian met his fellow Westonian after the game and informed him: 'I think it's time for you to come home, Pete.' Thereafter he would become for many years an integral part of Somerset's success. A medium-pace bowler and hard-hitting batsman, he has played in 200 first-class matches for Somerset, averaging 33.62, with fourteen centuries and fifty half-centuries to his name. In addition, he has taken 349 wickets for the county at 36.62. In 2007 he was voted the leading all-rounder in English first-class cricket by the Cricket Society. Over the years, his batting has come increasingly to the fore as his bowling pace has inevitably slowed, but it is a tribute to his fitness that, at the age of thirty-seven, he has been offered a white-ball contract for the 2019 season. Among his many memorable moments, the Championship win at Taunton against Yorkshire in 2009 (when his

Peter Trego – still the ebullient, open-hearted young man he always was

murderous knock of 103 not out in fifty-four deliveries, including nine sixes, helped Somerset to chase down a winning target of 476 with overs to spare) ranks high. His own choice, though, would be the Champions League T20 match in Hyderabad in 2011 against Kolkata Knight Riders. With Somerset missing their big guns, he stepped up to the plate and hammered a composed seventy runs that set up an unexpected victory and carried his team through to the final stages of what would prove an exhilarating and lucrative adventure for the overwhelming underdogs. His services have been called upon elsewhere in the world in T20 cricket, but, sadly, and unfairly in the eyes of many, he has been overlooked for England honours in the short form of the game, having to be satisfied with appearances for the England Lions. There have certainly never been any question marks over his big match temperament. Julian Wyatt, who coached Pete for a while, states that, 'He definitely had the character to survive at the highest level.'

When not plying his trade in warmer climes during the off-season, Pete has enjoyed a number of unexpected jobs from lifeguard to trainee financial advisor and from builder to menswear salesman, the last of these appropriate for a man noted as a snappy dresser. In recent years, he has worked for the construction company DriBuild on an occasional consultancy basis and latterly has been employed in the commercial department at Somerset CCC, as he prepares for life after his playing days. He also writes for *The Cricketer* magazine, his personal experience of the radical changes in the game giving him a perspective on events well worth listening to.

Married in 2000 to Claire (née Bromley), he has three children – Amelia, Davis and Dexter. Asked about those tattoos he has had etched on him, he confesses that most of them tell no particular story. 'I'm my own worst enemy,' he confesses, with his usual candour. 'I've just had them done when I'm bored, but the only special ones are the stick figure self-portraits on my left forearm, copies of the pictures of me that my children did, when they were young.'

Pete has certainly embraced the modern age and is active on social media. He has grown used to the good and the bad, but admits to one heart-warming tale of redemption. Having been trolled by a young lad who left personal details, Pete contacted the perpetrator's mother to offer supportive advice. This led to a meeting, the presentation of a signed shirt, a handshake and a letter of apology. It was a positive outcome in an arena often blighted by negativity and vitriol. One small victory for good old-fashioned humanity.

One of Somerset's evergreens, he continues to play his part in brightening the days of the cricket-watching public. They love their hard-hitting all-rounders in Taunton. Pete Trego returns that love. 'It's a real pleasure to get up in the morning and come here,' he says, adding that, 'My ambitions lie here with Somerset and I want to finish my career with some silverware.' Somerset supporters will hope that his wish comes true.

579
Jamie Oliver Grove
11 May 2000 v. Leicestershire, Leicester

It takes courage to step into the spotlight. In sport, as in art (in its many guises) or politics, anyone brave enough or committed enough to bare themselves to public scrutiny is as likely to be ridiculed as lionised. It is so much easier to stand on the sidelines and judge. The internet is awash with critics of no discernible talent, happy to express opinions devoid of fact or nuance. Jamie Grove discovered just how brutal things can be in the public domain when he was sent death threats and all manner of violence was threatened upon his then girlfriend after he had conceded twenty runs in an over, including three wides and three no-balls, (which effectively lost his side the match) while playing for Leicestershire in the T20 semi-final of 2003. 'I know I completely screwed up. There were 20,000 people telling me that,' he admits. That one over and its aftermath would herald the end of a career that had begun with great hopes.

Born on 3 July 1979 in Bury St Edmunds, he was the son of Chris and Patricia (née Studholme). Chris was a talented all-round sportsman who played semi-professional football for Dagenham FC and captained the Sudbury cricket team, with whom Jamie would cut his teeth as a bowler. The son gained his first experience of senior cricket as a seven-year-old when drafted into the Sudbury CC Third XI, making his debut for the First XI as an eleven-year-old. He was offered no favours, though, observing that, 'I got bounced first ball, without a helmet.' Perhaps that was the moment when Jamie concluded that life might be more fun as a fast bowler. He would state years

Jamie Grove – his main asset as a bowler was his sheer pace

later how much he relished the gladiatorial challenge, observing that, 'I loved having a brand new ball in my hand, looking down the wicket and seeing a world class player at the other end.'

Educated at St James Middle School (which has since closed its doors) and County Upper School, both in Bury St Edmunds, Jamie subsequently went on to complete a BTEC in Mechanical Engineering. Having been brought up in the state system in a Minor County, his progress to first-class cricket was doubly hard and required parental encouragement and resilience on his part. Jamie recalls with a wry smile an experience where, 'I got five wickets and fifty runs for Suffolk in an Under-15 game and then got dropped: they brought in a nice little public schoolboy for the next game.' But, blessed as he was with the ability to bowl exceptionally fast, news of his ability spread beyond the county boundary and he was offered a contract by Essex when he reached the age of sixteen. The first season might rightly be termed a disaster. Immediately on his arrival, Jamie was instructed by the bowling coach, Geoff Arnold, to move from the sideways action he had always deployed to a more front-on delivery. He was obliged to build up his technique from scratch and then suffered a torn cartilage in his left knee that put him out of action for the remainder of the season. He was still regarded as a fine prospect and was invited to play for England Under-17s in two matches against Scotland, although he describes the second of these as a 'shocking game' that he feared had put paid to his chances. In the event, he was selected for England Under-19s for the World Cup in South Africa. Here he was overseen by former Lancashire player, John Abrahams. John observes that Jamie's main asset was his 'sheer pace', but, in a clue as to why a promising career never quite took off, adds that 'he was a confidence player: if things were going well he was good, but it only took a little thing not to go well and he would focus on that.'

Having returned to Essex ahead of the 1998 season, he enjoyed his first Championship outings. It is a measure of the relative isolation of players brought up through the Minor Counties system that, in Jamie's own words, 'Until I did my first twelfth man duties at Essex, I had never seen a game of first-class cricket.'

By the end of the 1999 season, struggling to hold down a regular first team place and having been bedevilled by shin splints and a fracture, he was released by Essex. Fortunately, he knew he would be welcomed by Somerset. At an earlier Second XI fixture at North Perrott, in Somerset, he had impressed with a six-wicket haul in the second innings and eight wickets in the match. Kevin Shine had stood beside him as he fielded at square leg and offered a contract there and then, should he leave Essex. Jamie describes the move to Taunton as 'the best decision I ever made' and talks not just about the more holistic approach to training (including diet) than he was accustomed to, but also the meticulous planning on the part of coach Kevin Shine. In conversation with David Tossell, author of *Following On*, Jamie recalls happy times at Taunton. 'I lived 200 metres from the ground. I used to walk across the river to go to work and get a paper on the way. Even at Championship games you would get a few thousand people and at the one-day matches the atmosphere was unbelievable.'

His debut for Somerset proved a triumph with a return of 5 for 90 against Leicestershire, but he failed to hold down a regular first-team place. Over the course of two seasons before his release in 2001, he took twenty-seven first-class wickets at 45.25 apiece and averaged 10.75 with the bat.

If joining Somerset was the best thing that had happened to him, then, by his own admission, leaving them was his biggest regret. Although he had been a regular in List A games, it was Championship cricket that he derived most pleasure from and when approached by Jack Birkenshaw (by then Leicestershire's coach) with the promise that he would become their opening bowler in Championship games, a move appeared an enticing prospect. Somerset agreed to release Jamie, despite there being one year left on his contract. It proved a mistake on his part. Jack Birkenshaw was replaced and in the ensuing chaos, Jamie's career stalled. Then came his nightmare appearance in the T20 semi-final on Finals Day at Trent Bridge. Recovering from injury, lacking match practice and not fully fit, he had a torrid time. The abuse he suffered on social media – including on the club website – was intolerable. He had intended to alert the police after the threats extended to his then girlfriend, Virginia, later his wife, but was dissuaded from doing so by the club. Furthermore, Leicestershire's stand against the abuse was at best equivocal. A parting of the ways was inevitable and although other offers came his way, Jamie left the first-class game in 2003.

He would carve out a new career, falling back on his knowledge of engineering, employed in sales in the air compressor and spray gun sectors. Initially an area sales manager with Airchannel Ltd, he has in recent years enjoyed in the role of sales director of Chelmer Pneumatics & Compressors Ltd. After returning to club cricket with Sudbury CC, with whom his cricketing odyssey had begun, he now plays for Exning CC in Suffolk – well away from the spotlight and all the good and bad that comes with fame.

580
Joseph Peter Tucker
23 August 2000 v. West Indians, Taunton

Recalling his first-class debut for Somerset, Joe Tucker observes that, 'I was quite nervous at the start, but once I'd got my first ball out of the way, it was like any other game.' He had scored fourteen runs before enjoying a memorable moment when he claimed the scalp of Brian Lara – for a while the most prized wicket in world cricket – with only his second delivery. It was a more-than-useful contribution to an unexpected victory against the tourists, for which the club won £11,000 from the sponsors, Vodafone. Perhaps not quite 'any other game', then. Sadly, though, this would prove to be Joe's only wicket in a foreshortened first-class career.

Born in Bath on 14 September 1979, he was the son of Geoff Tucker, a lorry driver, and Chris (née Thomas), a nurse. Awarded a sports scholarship to Colston's School, an independent school in Bristol, he continued his studies at Richard Huish College while a member of Somerset's Cricket Academy. A right-arm pace bowler and a competent right-handed batsman (capable of big scores in club cricket), he worked his way through the Somerset age groups and was selected for his Second XI debut at the age of fifteen. Having attended the Dennis Lillee Coaching School in Madras (Chennai), Joe hoped to kick on and establish a regular first team place. He continued to demonstrate his ability while a member of the England Under-19 touring side in New Zealand in early 1999, claiming ten wickets in three appearances. Perhaps his most striking contribution was his stand with Somerset teammate, Matt Bulbeck, in the Second Test in Wellington. The pair came together – both of them requiring runners because of injuries they had picked up – with England reeling on 149 for 6 and facing defeat, but held out manfully until stumps. A draw was declared with the England Under-19s on 191 for 6 at the close. It had been a patient rearguard action.

There was a major setback to Joe's aspirations when he began to suffer increasing back problems, brought on by the wear and tear over the years and exacerbated during the England Under-19 tour. On his return to the County Ground, a stress fracture of the lower back was diagnosed. He needed immediate surgery and missed the entire 1999 season and thirteen weeks at the start of the following campaign. The return to full fitness was slow and gruelling, but his cause was helped by the Somerset squad's acknowledged exercise fanatic, Steffan Jones. The two of them set themselves challenging targets, competing on matters such as body fat and bowling speed. Indeed, as a result of their fitness regime, Joe came back bowling faster than he had prior to the injury. In a pre-season friendly against Orange Free State, the opposing openers remarked that he had sent down the fastest spell of bowling they had encountered. He was at that stage regularly sending down deliveries in excess of 90 mph and hopes were high. He was selected for another first-class match, this one against Lancashire, early in the 2001 season, but he became beset by further back problems and a second major operation was required. At the time of his release by Somerset, at the end of the 2003 campaign, he had played in only two first-class matches, taking one wicket at a total cost of 129 runs and averaging 19.00 with the bat.

He tried his luck with trial matches for four counties – Gloucestershire, Leicestershire, Derbyshire and Worcestershire – all of them aware of the raw pace he could generate, but, in Joe's words, 'My body wasn't allowing

Joe Tucker – his effectiveness as a pace bowler was blunted by injury

me to bowl as fast as I wanted to.' He would settle in time for club cricket, returning for a while to the Purnell CC team where he had started out as a boy. For two seasons he would captain the side, but he has subsequently hung up his boots, now that he has a family to think about. Married in 2008 to Joanna (née Say), he has three daughters.

Joe confesses to having been a fearless thrill seeker in his time and has long been passionate about motocross (involving a 450 cc motorbike and considerable opportunities for injury). His cousin, Martyn Tucker, was a semi-professional rider, whereas Joe has competed as an amateur, in the British Schoolboy Championship and subsequently in the Phoenix National Championship. Obliged to give up motocross for a while within the terms of his contract with Somerset, he returned to the sport once his first-class career was behind him. These days, he gets his kicks via downhill mountain bike riding.

As for his business career, he coached for a while but his heart was never quite in it. After a period working in a flower market, he joined his brother-in-law's construction firm. Having learnt the ropes, he has branched out and is the owner of Tucker & Co. South West Ltd, based in Radstock, a company he set up in 2010, involved in the erection of steel-framed buildings. His projects have included the overhaul of the North Parade cricket ground in Bath, as well as a number of projects at the County Ground.

Things never quite worked out with Somerset as Joe had hoped, following his setbacks with injury, but, to quote David Foot, writing in *Sixty Summers*, 'Who could possibly blame him for basking in the fact that on his debut he had Brian Lara out second ball, hooking to fine-leg?' As it happens, Joe is not the sort to dwell on any past glories, fleeting or otherwise. He is much more likely – if not working on his latest building project or spending time with his family – to be enjoying the adrenalin rush of sky diving or some such, or careering downhill at speed on his mountain bike.

*   *   *   *   *

In the thirty years leading up to the new millennium, Somerset cricket had changed markedly, as had the game in general. The first new arrival in 1971 – Brian Close – had been a tough competitor of the old school, regarding all but the most essential protective gear as an insult to manhood, and reluctant to accept that limited-overs cricket had any worth. Three decades on, the debutants coming through the ranks had not only been born after Brian's retirement, but were inhabitants of what would soon become a wholly different world, where social media would be all-pervasive, razzmatazz and commercialism would be rife, and players would require a level of fitness and all-round skills their forebears would have only dreamed of in their worst nightmares. The County Ground had changed, too. No longer were the players required to endure facilities the Victorian poor might have balked at. The place had been spruced up, although it had retained much of its charm and intimacy.

Somerset entered the new millennium frustrated that they had been unable to secure any further silverware, following their brief flirtation with winning ways in the late 1970s and early 1980s. For the bulk of their 125-year history, they had been, at best, the happy-go-lucky entertainers and, at worst, the whipping boys. How glorious it had felt to be a Somerset supporter for a few heady years. How sad that steps were not taken to ensure that the good times would last forever. After the infamous civil war, supporters perhaps wondered if success would ever come their way again, but they need not have worried unduly. A day-trip to Lord's for the Cheltenham & Gloucester Trophy Final lay just around the corner. Better still, a local boy, born and bred in Taunton, would guide his side to victory, ending the Somerset innings with a couple of lusty sixes, of course, because that had always been the way they went about things down in the West Country outpost.

At the time of writing, the set-up is now more sharply focussed on success than it has ever been, and the support still passionate. Surely some day, and hopefully soon, the county will secure their first Championship and there will be dancing in the streets of Taunton and broad smiles in the more refined environs of Bath. That will be some party. It might even stir the bones of the likes of Herbie Hewett – Somerset's first captain in the era of the County Championship and arguably still their finest – entombed in Norton Fitzwarren. Or it might rouse the remains of the late, great Sam Woods, lying in his grave just a lustily-struck six away from the County Ground, and never one to miss a good knees-up. It will surely happen. And when it does, it will have been well worth the wait.

ADDENDA

113
Eustace Tickell Hill

The player shown in error on Page 189 of *Somerset Cricketers 1882-1914* is a young O. M. Samson (Player 125). Included here is an image of Captain E. T. Hill in the uniform of the 19th Hussars, kindly provided by his granddaughter, Theodora Lee-Smith.

Married to Florence Muriel (née Bowen), known as Muriel and an accomplished concert pianist, Eustace brought up his young family at Winterbourne Park in Gloucestershire, where Muriel's piano recitals were a highlight of the social calendar. In 1913, they moved for a while to The Gronda, an imposing house four miles from Chepstow with a wonderful view of the Bristol Channel.

Further details of Eustace's life are included in *Somerset Cricketers 1882-1914*.

*   *   *   *   *

128
Alfred Edward Bailey

Richard Miller, a leading light in Scottish cricketing history, has established that Alfred Bailey was born on 13 March 1871, his birth registered with the surname Evans, which he shared with his mother, Eliza. Although Eliza Evans is listed as the wife of 'John Evans' (a presumed error) a mere month later in the 1871 census, there is no record of an official father on Alfred's birth certificate. It is difficult to ascertain whether the census entry was a case of obfuscation – perhaps because John and Eliza were common-law husband and wife – or whether it results from an error of transcription. Alfred was one of four children: Frederick John (b. 1869 and known variously as Fred or John), Alfred, Rhoda (b. 1878) and Emily Sedona (b. 1880). The latter two births were registered with the surname of their father, John Bailey, a bricklayer, and with Eliza (formerly Evans) as their mother. In the case of Emily, her father is noted as being deceased, having died earlier in the year. Details of any marriage certificate have proved elusive.

Alfred clearly rose from the most humble of beginnings and his career as a first-class cricketer remains a tribute to his talent and tenacity. As for his own family, Alfred had two sons – John and Robert – following his marriage to Elizabeth (née

Three cricketers who played for Somerset prior to the First World War.

Top Left: *Eustace Hill – shown here in the uniform of the 19th Hussars, he guested in two first-class matches for Somerset in the late 1890s* COURTESY OF THEODORA LEE-SMITH

Top Right: *Alfred Bailey – a hardworking pro, whose origins remained a mystery, until the diligent research of Richard Miller shed new light*

Bottom Left: *Richard Selwyn-Payne – whose one appearance came in 1906*

Hunter), who hailed from Irvine in North Ayrshire. John Bailey inherited Alfred's sporting prowess and was on the books at Charlton Athletic FC. Robert, described as an excellent cricketer, footballer and runner, would become a police constable in Kent but died of pneumonia in 1940, at the age of thirty-six.

* * * * *

175
Richard Bethune Fripp Selwyn-Payne

It was noted in *Somerset Cricketers 1882-1914* that the image of Richard Selwyn-Payne, taken from Eddie Lawrence's *Players, Photographs & Statistics*, had no provenance attached to it. The image now shown, taken from a team photograph of the Burnham on Sea Hockey XI of 1910-11 is confirmed as a true image of a player who appeared on only one occasion for Somerset, in 1906.

* * * * *

Two signatures were omitted in error from Somerset Cricketers 1919-1939 and are included here for completeness.

262
Guy Fife Earle

318
John Russell Watson

* * * * *

The following updates apply to *Somerset Cricketers 1946-1970*:

THOMAS EASTWOOD DICKINSON (Player 417) made his debut at Weston-super-Mare and not Taunton, as previously stated. It should also be noted that Tom died in Nottingham on 25 June 2018 following a struggle with Alzheimer's disease. He was eighty-seven.

PETER JAMES EELE (Player 419) died of a heart attack at home in Wellington on 24 January 2019. He was eighty-three.

MERVYN JOHN KITCHEN (listed as Player 429) in fact made his first-class debut on 28 May 1960 versus Middlesex at Lord's (and not against Cambridge University on 29 June 1960, as previously stated). Mervyn's correct Player No. is 428.

FREDERICK JOHN HERTING should therefore have been listed as Player 429 (and not 428, as previously stated).

GEOFFREY CLAYTON (Player 443) died on 19 September 2018 at the age of eighty, having spent the latter years of his life living in sheltered housing in Delph, near Oldham.

Index of Somerset Cricketers 1971-2000

Order of debut appearance in first-class matches shown in brackets.
Four (unnumbered) players appeared only in List A matches.
Page reference for each player's biography is also given.